Current
CONTROVERSIES

Gasoline

Other Books in the Current Controversies Series

Gasoline

Debra A. Miller, Book Editor

GREENHAVEN PRESS
A part of Gale, Cengage Learning

GALE
CENGAGE Learning·

Detroit • New York • San Francisco • New Haven, Conn • Waterville, Maine • London

GALE
CENGAGE Learning·

Elizabeth Des Chenes, *Director, Publishing Solutions*

© 2012 Greenhaven Press, a part of Gale, Cengage Learning

Gale and Greenhaven Press are registered trademarks used herein under license.

For more information, contact:
Greenhaven Press
27500 Drake Rd.
Farmington Hills, MI 48331-3535
Or you can visit our Internet site at gale.cengage.com

Articles in Greenhaven Press anthologies are often edited for length to meet page requirements. In addition, original titles of these works are changed to clearly present the main thesis and to explicitly indicate the author's opinion. Every effort is made to ensure that Greenhaven Press accurately reflects the original intent of the authors. Every effort has been made to trace the owners of copyrighted material.

Cover image copyright © Konstantin Sutyagin/Shutterstock.com.

LIBRARY OF CONGRESS CATALOGING-IN-PUBLICATION DATA

Gasoline / Debra A. Miller, book editor.
  p. cm. -- (Current controversies)
  Includes bibliographical references and index.
  ISBN 978-0-7377-6227-3 (hardcover) -- ISBN 978-0-7377-6228-0 (pbk.)
  1. Gasoline--Prices--United States. 2. Gasoline industry--United States. 3. Energy consumption--United States. 4. Energy policy--United States. I. Miller, Debra A.
  HD9579.G5U5428 2012
  338.4'3665538270973--dc23

                                                         2012004708

Printed in the United States of America
 1 2 3 4 5   16 15 14 13 12

FD194

Contents

Chapter 1: How Does Oil and Gasoline Dependence Affect the US and the World?

Gasoline-powered cars and trucks are major producers of carbon dioxide and other greenhouse gases that cause global warming. Although transportation is responsible for nearly one-third of the carbon emissions into the atmosphere, little is being done to reduce these emissions because of the world's dependence on petroleum fuels to operate its vehicles.

America's dependence on foreign oil supplies causes American drivers economic pain in the form of skyrocketing gas prices. In 2010, US drivers in almost every state spent more of their income on gasoline than they did in 2009.

Approximately 39 percent of the money spent by the United States on foreign oil imports goes to countries that are hostile to America. The US appetite for oil funds terrorist organizations and drives up the price of oil worldwide, providing resources to people who want to do us harm.

Chapter 2: Are Rising Gasoline Prices a Serious Problem?

Foreword

By definition, controversies are "discussions of questions in which opposing opinions clash" (*Webster's Twentieth Century Dictionary Unabridged*). Few would deny that controversies are a pervasive part of the human condition and exist on virtually every level of human enterprise. Controversies transpire between individuals and among groups, within nations and between nations. Controversies supply the grist necessary for progress by providing challenges and challengers to the status quo. They also create atmospheres where strife and warfare can flourish. A world without controversies would be a peaceful world; but it also would be, by and large, static and prosaic.

The Series' Purpose

The purpose of the *Current Controversies* series is to explore many of the social, political, and economic controversies dominating the national and international scenes today. Titles selected for inclusion in the series are highly focused and specific. For example, from the larger category of criminal justice, *Current Controversies* deals with specific topics such as police brutality, gun control, white collar crime, and others. The debates in *Current Controversies* also are presented in a useful, timeless fashion. Articles and book excerpts included in each title are selected if they contribute valuable, long-range ideas to the overall debate. And wherever possible, current information is enhanced with historical documents and other relevant materials. Thus, while individual titles are current in focus, every effort is made to ensure that they will not become quickly outdated. Books in the *Current Controversies* series will remain important resources for librarians, teachers, and students for many years.

In addition to keeping the titles focused and specific, great care is taken in the editorial format of each book in the series. Book introductions and chapter prefaces are offered to provide background material for readers. Chapters are organized around several key questions that are answered with diverse opinions representing all points on the political spectrum. Materials in each chapter include opinions in which authors clearly disagree as well as alternative opinions in which authors may agree on a broader issue but disagree on the possible solutions. In this way, the content of each volume in *Current Controversies* mirrors the mosaic of opinions encountered in society. Readers will quickly realize that there are many viable answers to these complex issues. By questioning each author's conclusions, students and casual readers can begin to develop the critical thinking skills so important to evaluating opinionated material.

Current Controversies is also ideal for controlled research. Each anthology in the series is composed of primary sources taken from a wide gamut of informational categories including periodicals, newspapers, books, US and foreign government documents, and the publications of private and public organizations. Readers will find factual support for reports, debates, and research papers covering all areas of important issues. In addition, an annotated table of contents, an index, a book and periodical bibliography, and a list of organizations to contact are included in each book to expedite further research.

Perhaps more than ever before in history, people are confronted with diverse and contradictory information. During the Persian Gulf War, for example, the public was not only treated to minute-to-minute coverage of the war, it was also inundated with critiques of the coverage and countless analyses of the factors motivating US involvement. Being able to sort through the plethora of opinions accompanying today's major issues, and to draw one's own conclusions, can be a complicated and frustrating struggle. It is the editors' hope that *Current Controversies* will help readers with this struggle.

Introduction

> "Although Americans are now dependent on gasoline to fuel their cars, trucks, and other transportation vehicles, gasoline was not even marketed as a transportation fuel until the late nineteenth century, when the automobile and the internal combustion engine were invented."

Gasoline is a widely used fuel made from petroleum—a so-called fossil fuel that comes from crude oil, a mix of hydrogen and carbon naturally created from the remains of plants and animals that lived millions of years ago. According to the US Energy Information Administration (EIA), each forty-two–gallon barrel of crude oil is refined into about nineteen gallons of gasoline and the rest is used to make various other products, including kerosene, diesel fuel, heating oil, and jet fuel. Today, gasoline is the main transportation fuel in the United States; EIA says it accounts for about 66 percent of all the energy used for transportation in the United States and 47 percent of all US petroleum consumption. In 2010, Americans used 378 million gallons of gasoline each day, or about one gallon per day for every man, woman, and child in the country, and much of this gasoline comes from oil that is imported from foreign countries. Although Americans are now dependent on gasoline to fuel their cars, trucks, and other transportation vehicles, gasoline was not even marketed as a transportation fuel until the late nineteenth century, when the automobile and the internal combustion engine were invented.

In fact, crude oil itself did not exist as an energy source until 1859, when Edwin Drake dug the world's first oil well in the small town of Titusville, Pennsylvania. Drake's goal was to distill the petroleum to create kerosene for lighting homes and businesses. Finding an inexpensive type of lamp oil was an exciting prospect because at that time most people used either simple candles or whale oil for lighting, and overfishing of whales had led to a decline in the whale population and a dramatic increase in whale oil prices. Drake's discovery was the impetus for a massive oil rush that attracted speculators from around the country in search of what was called Black Gold. Later, much larger deposits of oil were discovered in Texas, and a new industry—the refining of oil for kerosene fuel for use in lamps—was created.

During these early decades of the age of oil, gasoline was viewed simply as a useless by-product, while kerosene was considered the main product. Gasoline was either discarded or sold in relatively insignificant quantities for such purposes as a treatment for lice, a way to remove stains from clothing, or as a fuel for portable stoves or lanterns. All of that changed with the advent of the automobile in the late nineteenth century. In the early 1900s, American entrepreneur Henry Ford founded an automobile company to produce vehicles with internal combustion engines that could run on gasoline. Ford's Model T car, the first mass-produced automobile, was launched in 1908. The Model T gave Americans an affordable vehicle to replace horse-drawn carriages, and it made the internal-combustion engine the standard for all future automobile manufacturers. Other forms of gas-powered transportation soon followed, including trucks, airplanes, and boats. This was the beginning of America's century-long love affair with the automobile, as well as the start of the nation's dependence on gasoline as a transportation fuel.

Largely because the United States first discovered the value of oil deposits, it dominated world oil and gas production throughout the early twentieth century. In the early days, US fields produced more than 70 percent of world oil production, and five large American oil companies eventually developed oil interests both in the United States and around the globe, including Mexico, Venezuela, and the Middle East. At the beginning of World War II (1939–45), US companies produced not only all of the oil used in America but also nearly 40 percent of oil found outside the United States and the Soviet Union. Over the years, however, US oil production declined. A prediction made in 1956 by Shell geophysicist M. King Hubbert—that US petroleum production would peak between the late 1960s and early 1970s and then begin a rapid decline—ultimately came true. The Middle East now holds the world's largest deposits of oil, although oil fields have also been discovered in many other countries.

Today, the United States is capable of producing only about 37 percent of its petroleum needs, forcing the country to rely on oil and gas imported from other nations. America now imports oil from Canada, Saudi Arabia, Mexico, Venezuela, Nigeria, Colombia, Iraq, Angola, Russia, Algeria, Brazil, Kuwait, Ecuador, Congo, and Norway. It also imports finished gasoline from countries such as the United Kingdom, the US Virgin Islands, France, Canada, the Netherlands, Norway, Germany, Russia, Italy, and Middle East nations. The US dependence on foreign sources for oil and gas is increasingly seen by many experts as a problem, for several reasons. Commentators argue, for example, that it makes the nation vulnerable to countries that are unstable or hostile to US interests and requires that it spend large sums of money on military operations to keep this oil flowing. In addition, foreign oil dependence forces the United States to compete with developing countries such as India and China, which are rapidly increasing their oil usage and are expected to create even more explosive demand in the future. And scientists note that dependence on any fossil fuel also contributes to air pollution and global carbon emissions that are causing the world climate to change in potentially catastrophic ways. Some of these factors have already led to higher US gasoline prices at the pump, which most analysts predict will rise even higher in future years.

Many experts have urged US policymakers to take steps to transition the US economy away from oil toward other types of more abundant, less polluting energy sources, such as natural gas, electricity, or renewable energy. So far, however, no viable substitute has yet been developed. The authors of the viewpoints included in *Current Controversies: Gasoline* discuss the issues surrounding the US dependence on gasoline, including the impact of this dependence, whether rising gas prices are a serious problem, whether public transportation is a viable idea, and how the United States might eventually wean itself away from fossil fuels.

CHAPTER 1

How Does Oil and Gasoline Dependence Affect the US and the World?

Chapter Preface

High gasoline prices in recent years have raised concerns regarding America's reliance on imported oil, but this is not the first time that the United States has been faced with energy issues. Energy, in fact, has been at the top of the domestic policy agenda several times since 1970, the year that experts say the United States reached its peak level of oil production. Although it is hard to imagine a time when the nation was energy self-sufficient—producing enough oil to provide for all of its needs—this actually was the case in the 1950s and early 1960s. As the country began to rely more and more on imported oil, US policymakers became increasingly worried that this could leave the country vulnerable to price increases and supply disruptions that it could not control. These worries came true and reached a crisis stage a couple of times in the 1970s, when Middle Eastern oil-producing countries sharply reduced oil exports to the United States.

The first energy crisis occurred in the early 1970s, when Richard Nixon was president of the United States. Worried about the growing US reliance on foreign oil, President Nixon initially resisted the elimination of quotas that restricted the amount of oil that could be imported from foreign countries and encouraged domestic oil producers to explore for new oil reserves. US consumption of oil, however, continued to grow, forcing Nixon to abandon the quotas in 1973 because US oil producers could not keep up with demand. The president's worst fears were realized, however, in October of that same year when members of the Organization of Arab Petroleum Exporting Countries (OAPEC)—Kuwait, Saudi Arabia, and Libya—joined with Egypt and Syria to announce an oil embargo against the United States. The embargo action was taken in response to a US decision to provide supplies to the Israeli military during the 1973 Arab-Israeli War (also called the Yom

Kippur War). The embargo halted oil shipments to the United States from OAPEC countries, and OAPEC threatened to do the same to other countries if they also supported Israel in the conflict.

The 1973 oil embargo had an immediate and devastating effect on the US economy and American lifestyles. Gas prices more than tripled almost overnight and lines at gas stations stretched for blocks. President Nixon completely banned the sale of gasoline on Sundays, extended Daylight Savings Time, and instituted a system of voluntary rationing that called on homeowners to turn down their thermostats and businesses to cut their work hours. Many schools and factories in the Northeast temporarily closed in the winter of 1973 as a cold snap hit amid the oil shortages. Meanwhile, the stock market dropped a whopping 45 percent over the next two years, as a severe recession hit the United States and the rest of the western world. The embargo was finally lifted on March 18, 1974, after negotiations of a peace deal between Israel and Syria appeared to be moving forward. However, the damage caused by the embargo continued to ripple through the US economy. Unemployment rates soared; the US inflation rate hit double digits; and the value of the US dollar sank throughout the 1970s.

The Arab oil embargo demonstrated in the most dramatic fashion possible the dangers of relying on imported oil. In response, President Nixon urged Congress to pass legislation to authorize a trans-Alaska oil pipeline to bring oil from a newly discovered oilfield in Prudhoe Bay, Alaska, to the southern United States. The Alaskan pipeline was built and in 1977 began bringing an extra 2 million barrels per day of domestically produced oil to the American market. A political scandal called Watergate focused America's attention away from the energy crisis and resulted in the resignation of President Nixon in August 1974, but later in the decade, President Jimmy Carter proposed a number of additional actions designed to reduce the nation's vulnerability to imported oil. In 1977, President Carter proposed a new energy policy, calling it the moral equivalent of war. His plan emphasized conservation, taxes to encourage people to switch to smaller cars, and a transition away from natural gas and oil to coal, nuclear power, and solar energy. He also urged the creation of a federal Department of Energy. Carter even installed solar panels on the White House as a symbolic gesture to show the nation's new commitment to becoming energy independent. Some of Carter's proposals passed the Congress, and a new Department of Energy was created, but energy companies and the American public resisted any sort of scheme for aggressively taxing gasoline and other fossil fuels. Nevertheless, domestic production increased, Americans began driving smaller cars, and US imports of foreign oil during this period were reduced.

Another oil shock occurred late in President Carter's term, caused by the 1979 Iranian revolution. Radical Islamic fundamentalists overthrew the pro-American Shah (that is, king) of Iran and installed the Ayatollah Khomeni as leader. The turmoil of the protests and revolution disrupted Iran's production and export of oil, and caused oil and gas prices in the United States to once again rise sharply. Even after the new Iranian regime settled into power, Iran's oil exports never again reached their prior levels. President Carter responded by deregulating oil prices, allowing domestic production to increase, and decreasing imports, but this did not contain prices. Once again, US drivers waited in long lines to buy gas at inflated prices and Americans worried about another recession. Unable to offer an easy solution to the crisis, President Carter was voted out of office, and Americans elected Republican Ronald Reagan to the presidency in 1980. Fortunately for President Reagan, oil exporters in places such as Mexico, Nigeria, Venezuela, and the USSR (now Russia) expanded their production, and world oil prices entered a period of decline after 1980—a period that lasted for almost two decades. As a result, Americans quickly forgot about the problem of imported oil, and President Reagan had the solar panels on the White House removed—an act that demonstrated policymakers' abandonment of energy as a top national priority.

In recent years, however, energy has once again moved onto the national agenda. This time, rising prices are linked more to rising world demand rather than to reductions of exports by oil producers. Emerging economies such as China and India are rapidly consuming more and more oil as their economies grow, even as US energy demand continues to increase as well. Oil-producing countries are struggling to increase exports to meet this demand, but this situation makes the world vulnerable to even small oil supply disruptions. The political uprisings in the Middle East in 2011, called the Arab Spring, have caused some disruptions—in Libya, for example—raising fears about the future of world oil supplies. The authors of the viewpoints in this chapter address this issue of how oil and gasoline dependence affects the United States and the rest of the world.

Gasoline Usage by the Transportation Sector Is a Major Driver of Global Warming

Deborah Gordon

Deborah Gordon is an author, energy policy consultant, and a senior associate in the Energy and Climate Program at the Carnegie Endowment for International Peace, a nonprofit organization dedicated to advancing cooperation between nations and promoting active international engagement by the United States.

The Earth's rapidly warming temperatures over the past several decades cannot be explained by natural processes alone. The science is conclusive: both man-made and natural factors contribute to climate change. Human activities—fossil-fuel combustion in transportation and other sectors, urbanization, and deforestation—are increasing the amount of heat-trapping gases in the atmosphere. These record levels of greenhouse gases are shifting the Earth's climate equilibrium.

The Role of Transportation

Climate impacts differ by sector. On-road transportation has the greatest negative effect on climate, especially in the short term. This is primarily because of two factors unique to on-road transportation: (1) nearly exclusive use of petroleum fuels, the combustion of which results in high levels of the principal warming gases (carbon dioxide, ozone, and black carbon); and (2) minimal emissions of sulfates, aerosols, and

Deborah Gordon, "Summary," *Carnegie Papers: The Role of Transportation in Driving Climate Disruption*, Energy and Climate Program, Carnegie Endowment for International Peace, Number 117, December 2010, pp. 1–2. carnegieendowment.org. Copyright © 2010 by Carnegie Endowment for International Peace. All rights reserved. Reproduced by permission.

organic carbon from on-road transportation sources to counterbalance warming with cooling effects. Scientists find that cutting on-road transportation climate and air-pollutant emissions would be unambiguously good for the climate (and public health) in the near term.

Transportation is responsible for nearly one of every three tons of greenhouse gas emissions but represents less than one of every twelve tons of projected emission reductions.

Transportation's role in climate change is especially problematic, given the dependence on oil that characterizes this sector today. There are too few immediate mobility and fuel options in the United States beyond oil-fueled cars and trucks.

U.S. and international policy makers have yet to tackle transportation-climate challenges. In its fourth assessment report, the Intergovernmental Panel on Climate Change (IPCC) [a United Nations organization created to study and report on climate change] found that the global transportation sector was responsible for the most rapid growth in direct greenhouse gas emissions, a 120 percent increase between 1970 and 2004. To further complicate matters, the IPCC projects that, without policy intervention, the rapidly growing global transportation sector has little motivation to change the way it operates, because consumer choices are trumping best practices.

Transportation Solutions Needed

Herein lies a fundamental mismatch between the climate problem and solutions: transportation is responsible for nearly one of every three tons of greenhouse gas emissions but represents less than one of every twelve tons of projected emission reductions. Clearly this sector is a major contributor to climate change; therefore, it should be the focus of new policies to mitigate warming. Government must lead this effort as the market alone cannot precipitate the transition away from cars and oil, which dominate this sector.

Policy makers need to remember four essential findings and recommendations when developing new strategies for ensuring that the United States maintains its leadership position in the global economy:

1. On-road transportation is an immediate high-priority target in the short term for reducing greenhouse gas emissions and mitigating climate change in the United States and around the globe.

2. The transportation sector is responsible for high levels of long-lived carbon dioxide (CO_2) and ozone precursor emissions that will warm the climate for generations to come.

3. The United States (and other nations) must transition quickly to near-zero greenhouse gas (GHG) emission cars and trucks, largely through low-carbon electrification for plug-in vehicles.

4. America's transportation culture must adapt to rely less on fossil fuels through technological innovation, rational pricing, and sound investments that expand low-carbon mobility choices and fundamentally shift travel behavior.

Oil Dependence Makes US Drivers Vulnerable to Rising Gas Prices

Deron Lovaas and Justin Horner

Deron Lovaas is the Federal Transportation Policy Director for the Natural Resources Defense Council (NRDC), an environmental group. Justin Horner is a policy analyst for the NRDC.

Unrest in the Middle East continues to raise concerns about our dependence on foreign oil at the same time that Americans have been suffering from the skyrocketing cost of gasoline.

To curb America's perilous oil addiction, we need effective government policies that will increase the availability and use of efficient vehicles and clean fuels, as well as promote smart growth and public transit.

This report updates the 2007, 2008, 2009, and 2010 research by the Natural Resources Defense Council (NRDC) [an environmental advocacy group] identifying the states whose citizens feel the greatest economic pain from gasoline prices and those states that are doing the most to break their addiction to oil.

Like the previous editions, this report again ranks U.S. states in two critical areas related to our nation's continuing addiction to oil. First, it calculates gasoline price vulnerability—the percentage of personal income spent on gasoline by the average driver in each state. Second, it ranks states based on their adoption of solutions to reduce their oil depen-

Deron Lovaas and Justin Horner, "Executive Summary," *Fighting Oil Addiction: Ranking States' Gasoline Price Vulnerability and Solutions for Change*, Natural Resources Defense Council, 2011, pp. 1–3. www.nrdc.org. Copyright © 2011 by Natural Resources Defense Council. All rights reserved. Reproduced by permission of the Natural Resources Defense Council.

dence—measures they are taking to lessen their vulnerability and to bolster America's security. The data yield some clear conclusions:

- Oil dependence affects all states, but some states' drivers are hit harder economically than others. Drivers in almost every state in 2010 spent a higher percentage of their income on gasoline than they did in 2009, and drivers in the most vulnerable states spent more than twice as large a percentage of their income on gasoline as drivers in the least vulnerable states.

- Drivers are being hit even harder right now than they were in 2010.

- While some states are pioneering solutions and many are taking some action, many states are still taking few (if any) of the steps listed in this report to reduce their oil dependence.

Drivers in every state but two were spending a larger percentage of their income on gasoline [in 2011] than in 2008—and often a good deal more.

Gasoline Price Vulnerability

NRDC's vulnerability ranking is based on the average percentage of income that states' drivers spend on gasoline. The differences are significant. In 2010, average drivers in the least vulnerable state—which for the fifth year in a row is Connecticut—spent less than 3 percent of their income on gasoline. Average drivers in the most vulnerable state—which for the fifth year in a row is Mississippi—spent more than twice as large a percentage (more than 7 percent) of their income on gasoline.

Gasoline price vulnerability generally increased from 2006 through 2008. There was a striking reversal of that trend in

2009, due largely to much lower gas prices, with drivers in every state spending a lower percentage of their income on gasoline than in 2008 (and with drivers in all but five states spending a lower percentage than in 2006). The original trend then reasserted itself, with drivers in all but four states more vulnerable in 2010 than in 2009, though not quite as vulnerable as before the 2009 blip; drivers in 45 of the 50 states were still spending a lower percentage of their income on gasoline in 2010 than in 2008.

The huge increases in gasoline prices in the first few months of 2011 have more than closed the rest of that gap. In fact, as of this April [2011], drivers in every state but two were spending a larger percentage of their income on gasoline than in 2008—and often a good deal more. In Mississippi, for instance, average drivers in April spent more than 11 percent of their income on gasoline (compared with more than 9 percent in 2008 and more than 7 percent at the end of 2010).

As the economy slowly recovers, drivers clearly remain quite vulnerable—and citizens in the high-ranking states are feeling the pinch more.

State Action on Oil Dependence: The Best and the Worst

Although some states are adopting strong measures to reduce their oil dependence, too many others are still taking little or no action.

The solutions rankings in this report are based on the range of key actions that states can take to reduce oil dependence, with particular focus on policies that can have substantial impact and can be replicated by other states.

NRDC research shows that the 10 states doing the *most* to wean themselves from oil are:

1. California

2. Oregon

3. Massachusetts

4. New York

5. New Jersey

6. Maryland

7. Connecticut

8. Rhode Island

9. Washington

10. Vermont

In contrast, the 10 states doing the *least* to reduce their oil dependence are:

1. Nebraska

2. North Dakota

3. Alaska

4. Iowa

5. Arkansas

6. South Dakota

7. Indiana

8. Missouri

9. Wyoming

10. Ohio

The failure of these 10 states—and many others—to take meaningful action to reduce oil dependence exacerbates the national security, environmental, and economic harms associated with our current transportation habits. These and other states need to be drivers of change.

The Benefits of Reducing Oil Dependence

Especially with the struggling economy, persistently high unemployment, and high gasoline and diesel prices, reducing oil dependence can yield significant benefits. These can include lowering the economic vulnerability that many residents face and creating new income from the sale of low-carbon fuels and efficient vehicles. As the recent unrest in the Middle East makes very clear, decreasing oil consumption also enhances America's national security by reducing dependence on sources of oil that are politically unstable or controlled by unfriendly national governments. In addition, reduced oil consumption decreases both air pollution and the carbon pollution that causes global climate change.

State Policies for Reducing Oil Dependence

Although the [Barack] Obama administration has taken some strong actions on energy and climate policy, states continue to be critical players in creating less oil-intensive transportation habits. State strategies include:

- *Clean and efficient vehicles.* Vehicles that cut global warming pollution reduce oil consumption considerably. Fourteen states, led by California, have adopted effective clean car rules. Twenty-two states have requirements for the efficiency of the state government fleet.

- *Clean fuels.* Three states have or are developing a low-carbon fuel standard (LCFS), seeking to reduce the greenhouse gas (GHG) intensity of motor vehicle fuel, and several states have signed a memorandum of understanding to explore a regional LCFS in the Northeast and Mid-Atlantic. The future of clean transportation energy, however, may be electrification. Twenty-six states have an incentive to spur greater deployment and use of plug-in hybrid and fully electric vehicles.

- *Transportation system efficiency.* An area where states can play a particularly large role in reducing oil dependence is promoting transportation system efficiency— i.e., integrating land use and transportation policies and designing them to reduce vehicle-miles traveled and promote alternatives to driving. Three states have codified or are implementing targets for reducing vehicle-miles traveled. Eight states have adopted telecommuting policies to encourage companies to enable their employees to opt out of driving. Seventeen states are taking action to encourage cars already on the road to use less gasoline by placing restrictions on idling. Sixteen states have adopted smart-growth/growth management policies to curb sprawl and reduce the associated traffic. Public investment can also be a critical strategy for states seeking to reduce oil dependence, and in 2010, New York, Massachusetts, and New Jersey led the way in prioritizing the funding of public transit through the allocation of state funds.

States that adopt cutting-edge plans to reduce oil dependence help make the nation more secure, protect drivers' wallets, and enhance global environmental health. These states' policies can serve as examples for the many states that have thus far taken little or no such action—and lead the way for national policies as well.

Federal Recommendations for Reducing Gasoline Price Vulnerability

The Obama Administration must enact effective energy and transportation policies that complement and support the actions of leading states. The Administration has made progress, but there is more to do, including:

- Raising the bar for new light-duty vehicle and heavy-duty vehicle fuel economy and carbon dioxide pollution standards, aiming for the equivalent of 62 miles per gallon by 2025 for light-duty vehicles; and

- Overhauling the federal transportation program, with prioritization and investment for maintenance and repair of our decaying infrastructure, a national oil-savings objective, more investment in public transportation, and a new infrastructure bank for new projects.

The US Dependence on Foreign Oil Funds America's Enemies

Jonathan Powers

Jonathan Powers is a US Army veteran and chief operating officer of the Truman National Security Project, a national security leadership institute that recruits, trains, and positions progressives to lead on national security issues.

The U.S. sends approximately one billion dollars a day overseas to import oil. While this figure is staggering by itself, the dangerous implications of our addiction are even more pronounced when analyzing where our money goes—and whom it helps to support.

Examine what the true costs of our oil addiction meant during the year 2008:

- *One Billion Dollars a Day Spent on Foreign Oil*: In 2008, the United States imported 4.7 billion barrels of crude oil to meet our consumption needs. The average price per barrel of imported oil for 2008 was $92.61. This works out to $1.19 billion per day for the year.

- *Our Annual Oil Debt Is Greater than Our Trade Deficit with China*: Our petroleum imports created a $386 billion U.S. trade deficit in 2008, versus a $266 billion deficit with China. This national debt is a drain on our economy and an anchor on our economic growth.

- *We Overwhelmingly Rely on Oil Imports. . .*: In 2008, we consumed 7.1 billion barrels of oil in the United States, meaning that the 4.7 billion barrels of crude oil we imported was 66% of our overall oil usage. About one out of every six dollars spent on imports by the U.S. is spent on oil, representing 16% of all U.S. import expenditures in 2008. According to calculations from the Center for American Progress, U.S. spending to import foreign oil amounted to 2.3% of our overall GDP [gross domestic product] in 2008.

- *. . . to the Detriment of National Security*: Vice Admiral Dennis McGinn, retired Deputy Chief of Naval Warfare Requirements and Programs, captured the national security dangers of our addiction to oil in 2009 testimony before the U.S. Senate Environment and Public Works Committee: "In 2008, we sent $386 billion overseas to pay for oil—much of it going to nations that wish us harm. This is an unprecedented and unsustainable transfer of wealth to other nations. It puts us in the untenable position of funding both sides of the conflict and directly undermines our fight against terror."

A comprehensive energy strategy . . . is vital to our national security, to the safety of our men and women in uniform, and to the fight against terrorism.

Our oil addiction drives up prices worldwide, pouring funds into the coffers of foreign regimes that hold anti-American sentiments, harbor terrorists, and otherwise threaten America's national security. As the Council on Foreign Relations wrote, "major energy consumers—notably the United States, but other countries as well—are finding that their growing dependence on imported energy increases their strategic vulnerability and constrains their ability to pursue a broad range of foreign policy and national security objectives."

The one billion dollars a day that Americans send overseas on oil floods a global oil market that enriches hostile governments, funds terrorist organizations, and props up repressive regimes. Former CIA [Central Intelligence Agency] Director Jim Woolsey explains it this way:

> "Except for our own Civil War, this [the war on terror] is the only war that we have fought where we are paying for both sides. We pay Saudi Arabia $160 billion for its oil, and $3 or $4 billion of that goes to the Wahhabis, who teach children to hate. We are paying for these terrorists with our SUVs." . . .

A comprehensive energy strategy—one that cuts our addiction to fossil fuels, boosts clean energy technology, and moves our nation dramatically towards greater energy independence—is vital to our national security, to the safety of our men and women in uniform, and to the fight against terrorism.

A Dangerous and Unstable Addiction

While the U.S. imports 66% of our oil, that figure includes both friendly nations such as Canada and Mexico, as well as a litany of countries whose regimes are either unstable, unfriendly, or both.

In 2008, the U.S. imported about 4 million barrels of oil a day from countries labeled "dangerous or unstable" by the State Department. Using the $386 billion total cost as cited by Vice Admiral McGinn, this means that about 39% of our oil import costs were from "dangerous or unstable" nations.

Nearly one-fifth of the oil consumed by the U.S. in 2008 (18%) was imported from countries of the Middle East and Venezuela. This total represents over one-fourth of our overall imported oil (28%) in 2008. While Venezuela is not on the State Department's "dangerous or unstable" list, it has maintained a distinctly anti-American foreign and energy policy under President Hugo Chavez. Venezuela was one of the top five oil exporters to the United States, and we imported 435 million barrels of oil from it in 2008.

Buying from Friendly Countries—or Even from the United States—Doesn't Help

The price of oil is set globally. That means that even when we buy oil from friendly countries, we drive up demand, inflating prices that enrich unfriendly countries. For instance, despite U.S. laws against purchasing oil from Iran, the global demand for oil—aided by U.S. consumption habits—helps to drive up the global price of oil and line the pockets of the Iranian regime. Oil wealth funded about 60% of the Iranian national budget in 2008. *The Economist* calculated that, in his first term, Iranian President Mahmoud Ahmadinejad benefited from "a windfall of $250 billion in oil sales." The United States currently consumes approximately one-fourth of the world's oil, inadvertently bolstering Iran's bottom line, despite the laws on the books.

Depending on oil to produce the energy that runs our nation makes America vulnerable, while simultaneously providing enormous resources to those who would do us harm.

All oil demand hurts our national security—regardless of whether the oil is produced here at home or bought overseas. Whether oil is directly purchased from nations on the State Department's "Dangerous or Unstable" list, or is bought from West Texas, U.S. demand increases global oil prices that fund our enemies.

According to testimony from Truman National Security Project Chief Operating Officer Jonathan Powers, every $5 increase in the global price of crude oil represents:

- An additional $7.9 billion for Iran and President Ahmadinejad;

- An additional $4.7 billion for Venezuela and President Chavez; and,

- An additional $18 billion for Russia and Prime Minister Vladimir Putin.

Unfortunately, even if we buy oil from a friendly country like Mexico, problem countries in the Middle East can hold us hostage by forcing up global oil prices—as Middle Eastern countries in OPEC [Organization of Petroleum Exporting Countries] have done time and time again. Buying from friendly or domestic sources does not solve our problem, because the countries with the greatest reserves—notably, Saudi Arabia—are such major producers that they set the global supply. Even if we drilled in every untapped well in America, we simply do not have enough oil from friendly countries and under the earth at home to offset OPEC's power. By staying addicted to oil, regardless of where we purchase it, we give OPEC countries the power to cripple our economy and bring America to its knees. . . .

A Better Alternative

Depending on oil to produce the energy that runs our nation makes America vulnerable, while simultaneously providing enormous resources to those who would do us harm. It is time for us to take control of our energy future, cut our dependence on oil, and defund terrorist threats with comprehensive energy legislation.

National security, military, and intelligence experts have spoken out about the need for a comprehensive strategy that takes on the destabilizing effects of fossil fuel dependence and global climate change.

"Without bold action now to significantly reduce our dependence on fossil fuels, our national security will be at greater risk," testified Vice Admiral Dennis McGinn, before a U.S. Senate panel. "Fierce global competition and conflict over dwindling supplies of fossil fuel will be a major part of the future strategic landscape."

"Moving toward clean, independent, domestic energy choices lessens that danger and significantly helps us confront the serious challenge of global climate change. Because these issues are so closely linked, solutions to one affect the other. Technologies and practices that improve energy sources and efficiency also reduce carbon intensity and carbon emissions, and, most critically, increase our national security."

A panel of 11 former generals and admirals echoed Vice Admiral McGinn's testimony in a report entitled *National Security and the Threat of Climate Change*, stating, "Climate change, national security, and energy dependence are a related set of global challenges . . . dependence on foreign oil leaves us more vulnerable to hostile regimes and terrorists, and clean domestic energy alternatives help us confront the serious challenge of global climate change."

Marine General James Mattis put it more succinctly when he was asked at a Brookings [Institution] meeting in 2007 about the most important area of research for aiding the men and women under his command: "Unleash us from the tether of fuel."

America's military leaders are not waiting to take action on the threats posed by our dependence on fossil fuels. The Defense Department considers climate change such a strategic threat that it is part of the military's long term planning. The CIA has opened a center to track the threat of climate change. The Army, Navy, Air Force and the Marines have all committed to reducing their carbon pollution.

For example, in October 2009 the Navy launched the *USS Makin Island*, a first-of-its-kind hybrid powered amphibious assault vehicle that emits less carbon and saved the Navy $2 million in fuel costs during its maiden voyage alone. The Marine Corps has even created a model Forward Operating Base (FOB) in Quantico, VA, which will allow the Marines to test a hybrid power station that is set to be deployed in Afghanistan by mid-2010.

Just as the military is innovating its own energy habits, America as a nation must do the same, with a comprehensive approach to clean energy and climate change that will have a measurable impact on these threats.

The need is immediate. "We have less than ten years to change our fossil fuel dependency course in significant ways," testified Vice Admiral McGinn. "Our nation's security depends on the swift, serious, and thoughtful response to the interlinked challenges of energy security and climate change."

High Oil Prices Threaten the World Economy

The Economist

The Economist is a weekly newspaper that provides insight and opinion on international news, politics, business, finance, science, and technology.

The price of oil has had an unnerving ability to blow up the world economy, and the Middle East has often provided the spark. The Arab oil embargo of 1973, the Iranian revolution in 1978–79 and Saddam Hussein's invasion of Kuwait in 1990 are all painful reminders of how the region's combustible mix of geopolitics and geology can wreak havoc. With protests cascading across Arabia, is the world in for another oil shock?

There are good reasons to worry. The Middle East and north Africa produce more than one-third of the world's oil. Libya's turmoil shows that a revolution can quickly disrupt oil supply. Even while [Libyan leader] Muammar Gaddafi hangs on with delusional determination and Western countries debate whether to enforce a no-fly zone, Libya's oil output has halved [in 2011], as foreign workers flee and the country fragments. The spread of unrest across the region threatens wider disruption.

The markets' reaction has been surprisingly modest. The price of Brent crude [a major trading classification of oil] jumped 15% as Libya's violence flared up, reaching $120 a barrel on February 24th. But the promise of more production from Saudi Arabia pushed the price down again. It was $116 on March 2nd—20% higher than the beginning of the year, but well below the peaks of 2008. Most economists are sanguine: global growth might slow by a few tenths of a percentage point, they reckon, but not enough to jeopardise the rich world's recovery.

That glosses over two big risks. First, a serious supply disruption, or even the fear of it, could send the oil price soaring. Second, dearer [meaning costlier] oil could fuel inflation—and that might prompt a monetary clampdown that throttles the recovery. A lot will depend on the skill of central bankers.

Even without a disruption to supply, prices are under pressure from a second source: the gradual dwindling of spare capacity.

Of Stocks, Saudis, and Stability

So far, the shocks to supply have been tiny. Libya's turmoil has reduced global oil output by a mere 1%. In 1973 the figure was around 7.5%. Today's oil market also has plenty of buffers. Governments have stockpiles, which they didn't in 1973. Commercial oil stocks are more ample than they were when prices peaked in 2008. Saudi Arabia, the central bank of the oil market, technically has enough spare capacity to replace Libya, Algeria and a clutch of other small producers. And the Saudis have made clear that they are willing to pump.

Yet more disruption cannot be ruled out. The oil industry is extremely complex: getting the right sort of oil to the right place at the right time is crucial. And then there is Saudi Arabia itself. The kingdom has many of the characteristics that have fuelled unrest elsewhere, including an army of disillusioned youths. Despite spending $36 billion so far buying off dissent, a repressive regime faces demands for reform. A whiff of instability would spread panic in the oil market.

Even without a disruption to supply, prices are under pressure from a second source: the gradual dwindling of spare capacity. With the world economy growing strongly, oil demand is far outpacing increases in readily available supply. So any jitters from the Middle East will accelerate and exaggerate a price rise that was already on the way.

What effect would that have? It is some comfort that the world economy is less vulnerable to damage from higher oil prices than it was in the 1970s. Global output is less oil-intensive. Inflation is lower and wages are much less likely to follow energy-induced price rises, so central banks need not respond as forcefully. But less vulnerable does not mean immune.

Dearer oil still implies a transfer from oil consumers to oil producers, and since the latter tend to save more it spells a drop in global demand. A rule of thumb is that a 10% increase in the price of oil will cut a quarter of a percentage point off global growth. With the world economy currently growing at 4.5%, that suggests the oil price would need to leap, probably above its 2008 peak of almost $150 a barrel, to fell the recovery. But even a smaller increase would sap growth and raise inflation.

Shocked into Action

In the United States the Federal Reserve will face a relatively easy choice. America's economy is needlessly vulnerable, thanks to its addiction to oil (and light taxation of it). Yet inflation is extremely low and the economy has plenty of slack. This gives its central bank the latitude to ignore a sudden jump in the oil price. In Europe, where fuel is taxed more heavily, the immediate effect of dearer oil is smaller. But Europe's central bankers are already more worried about rising prices: hence the fear that they could take pre-emptive action too far, and push Europe's still-fragile economies back into recession.

By contrast, the biggest risk in the emerging world is inaction. Dearer oil will stoke inflation, especially through higher food prices—and food still accounts for a large part of people's spending in countries like China, Brazil and India. True, central banks have been raising interest rates, but they have tended to be tardy. Monetary conditions are still too loose, and inflation expectations have risen.

Unfortunately, too many governments in emerging markets have tried to quell inflation and reduce popular anger by subsidising the prices of both food and fuel. Not only does this dull consumers' sensitivity to rising prices, it could be expensive for the governments concerned. It will stretch India's optimistic new budget. But the biggest danger lies in the Middle East itself, where subsidies of food and fuel are omnipresent and where politicians are increasing them to quell unrest. Fuel importers, such as Egypt, face a vicious, bankrupting, spiral of higher oil prices and ever bigger subsidies. The answer is to ditch such subsidies and aim help at the poorest, but no Arab ruler is likely to propose such reforms right now.

At its worst, the danger is circular, with dearer oil and political uncertainty feeding each other. Even if that is avoided, the short-term prospects for the world economy are shakier than many realise. But there could be a silver lining: the rest of the world could at long last deal with its vulnerability to oil and the Middle East. The to-do list is well-known, from investing in the infrastructure for electric vehicles to pricing carbon. The 1970s oil shocks transformed the world economy. Perhaps a 2011 oil shock will do the same—at less cost.

The World Energy Threat Has Only Worsened in 2011

Michael T. Klare

Michael T. Klare is a professor of peace and world security studies at Hampshire College in Massachusetts and the author of several books on energy topics.

Here's the good news about energy: thanks to rising oil prices and deteriorating economic conditions worldwide, the International Energy Agency (IEA) reports that global oil demand will not grow this year [2011] as much as once assumed, which may provide some temporary price relief at the gas pump. In its May *Oil Market Report*, the IEA reduced its 2011 estimate for global oil consumption by 190,000 barrels per day, pegging it at 89.2 million barrels daily. As a result, retail prices may not reach the stratospheric levels predicted earlier this year, though they will undoubtedly remain higher than at any time since the peak months of 2008, just before the global economic meltdown. Keep in mind that this is the *good* news.

As for the bad news: the world faces an array of intractable energy problems that, if anything, have only worsened in recent weeks. These problems are multiplying on either side of energy's key geological divide: *below ground*, once-abundant reserves of easy-to-get "conventional" oil, natural gas, and coal are drying up; *above ground*, human miscalculation and geopolitics are limiting the production and availability of specific energy supplies. With troubles mounting in both arenas, our energy prospects are only growing dimmer.

Here's one simple fact without which our deepening energy crisis makes no sense: the world economy is structured in such a way that standing still in energy production is not an option. In order to satisfy the staggering needs of older industrial powers like the United States along with the voracious thirst of rising powers like China, global energy must grow substantially every year. According to the projections of the U.S. Department of Energy (DoE), world energy output, based on 2007 levels, must rise 29% to 640 quadrillion British thermal units by 2025 to meet anticipated demand. Even if usage grows somewhat more slowly than projected, any failure to satisfy the world's requirements produces a perception of scarcity, which also means rising fuel prices. These are precisely the conditions we see today and should expect for the indefinite future.

It is against this backdrop that three crucial developments of 2011 are changing the way we are likely to live on this planet for the foreseeable future.

Tough-Oil Rebels

The first and still most momentous of the year's energy shocks was the series of events precipitated by the Tunisian and Egyptian rebellions and the ensuing "Arab Spring" in the greater Middle East. Neither Tunisia nor Egypt was, in fact, a major oil producer, but the political shockwaves these insurrections unleashed has spread to other countries in the region that are, including Libya, Oman, and Saudi Arabia. At this point, the Saudi and Omani leaderships appear to be keeping a tight lid on protests, but Libyan production, normally averaging approximately 1.7 million barrels per day, has fallen to near zero.

When it comes to the future availability of oil, it is impossible to overstate the importance of this spring's events in the Middle East, which continue to thoroughly rattle the energy markets. According to all projections of global petroleum output, Saudi Arabia and the other Persian Gulf states are slated to supply an ever-increasing share of the world's total oil supply as production in key regions elsewhere declines. Achieving this production increase is essential, but it will not happen unless the rulers of those countries invest colossal sums in the development of new petroleum reserves—especially the heavy, "tough oil" variety that requires far more costly infrastructure than existing "easy oil" deposits.

In a front-page story entitled "Facing Up to the End of 'Easy Oil,'" the *Wall Street Journal* noted that any hope of meeting future world oil requirements rests on a Saudi willingness to sink hundreds of billions of dollars into their remaining heavy-oil deposits. But right now, faced with a ballooning population and the prospects of an Egyptian-style youth revolt, the Saudi leadership seems intent on using its staggering wealth on employment-generating public-works programs and vast arrays of weaponry, not new tough-oil facilities; the same is largely true of the other monarchical oil states of the Persian Gulf.

The world can accommodate a prolonged loss of Libyan oil. Saudi Arabia and a few other producers possess sufficient excess capacity to make up the difference. Should Saudi Arabia ever explode, however, all bets are off.

Whether such efforts will prove effective is unknown. If a youthful Saudi population faced with promises of jobs and money, as well as the fierce repression of dissidence, has seemed less confrontational than their Tunisian, Egyptian, and Syrian counterparts, that doesn't mean that the status quo will remain forever. "Saudi Arabia is a time bomb," commented Jaafar Al Taie, managing director of Manaar Energy Consulting (which advises foreign oil firms operating in the region). "I don't think that what the King is doing now is sufficient to prevent an uprising," he added, even though the Saudi royals had just announced a $36-billion plan to raise the minimum wage, increase unemployment benefits, and build affordable housing.

[The 2011 earthquake in Japan] has forced Japan to increase its imports of oil, coal, and natural gas, adding to the pressure on global supplies.

At present, the world can accommodate a prolonged loss of Libyan oil. Saudi Arabia and a few other producers possess sufficient excess capacity to make up the difference. Should Saudi Arabia ever explode, however, all bets are off. "If something happens in Saudi Arabia, [oil] will go to $200 to $300 [per barrel]," said Sheikh Zaki Yamani, the kingdom's former oil minister, on April 5th. "I don't expect this for the time being, but who would have expected Tunisia?"

Nuclear Power on the Downward Slope

In terms of the energy markets, the second major development of 2011 occurred on March 11th when an unexpectedly powerful earthquake and tsunami struck Japan. As a start, nature's two-fisted attack damaged or destroyed a significant proportion of northern Japan's energy infrastructure, including refineries, port facilities, pipelines, power plants, and transmission lines. In addition, of course, it devastated four nuclear plants at Fukushima, resulting, according to the U.S. Department of Energy, in the permanent loss of 6,800 megawatts of electric generating capacity.

This, in turn, has forced Japan to increase its imports of oil, coal, and natural gas, adding to the pressure on global supplies. With Fukushima and other nuclear plants off line, industry analysts calculate that Japanese oil imports could rise by as much as 238,000 barrels per day, and imports of natural gas by 1.2 billion cubic feet per day.

This is one major short-term effect of the tsunami. What about the longer-term effects? The Japanese government now claims it is scrapping plans to build as many as 14 new nuclear reactors over the next two decades. On May 10th, Prime Minister Naoto Kan announced that the government would have to "start from scratch" in devising a new energy policy for the country. Though he speaks of replacing the cancelled reactors with renewable energy systems like wind and solar, the sad reality is that a significant part of any future energy expansion will inevitably come from more imported oil, coal, and LNG [liquified natural gas].

The disaster at Fukushima—and ensuing revelations of design flaws and maintenance failures at the plant—has had a domino effect, causing energy officials in other countries to cancel plans to build new nuclear plants or extend the life of existing ones. The first to do so was Germany: on March 14th, Chancellor Angela Merkel closed two older plants and suspended plans to extend the life of 15 others.

On May 30th, her government made the suspension permanent. In the wake of mass antinuclear rallies and an election setback, she promised to shut all existing nuclear plants by 2022, which, experts believe, will result in an increase in fossil-fuel use.

China also acted swiftly, announcing on March 16th that it would stop awarding permits for the construction of new reactors pending a review of safety procedures, though it did not rule out such investments altogether. Other countries, including India and the United States, similarly undertook reviews of reactor safety procedures, putting ambitious nuclear plans at risk. Then, on May 25th, the Swiss government announced that it would abandon plans to build three new nuclear power plants, phase out nuclear power, and close the last of its plants by 2034, joining the list of countries that appear to have abandoned nuclear power for good.

How Drought Strangles Energy

The third major energy development of 2011, less obviously energy-connected than the other two, has been a series of persistent, often record, droughts gripping many areas of the planet. Typically, the most immediate and dramatic effect of prolonged drought is a reduction in grain production, leading to ever-higher food prices and ever more social turmoil.

Intense drought over the past year in Australia, China, Russia, and parts of the Middle East, South America, the United States, and most recently northern Europe has contributed to the current record-breaking price of food—and this, in turn, has been a key factor in the political unrest now sweeping North Africa, East Africa, and the Middle East. But drought has an energy effect as well. It can reduce the flow of major river systems, leading to a decline in the output of hydroelectric power plants, as is now happening in several drought-stricken regions.

By far the greatest threat to electricity generation exists in China, which is suffering from one of its worst droughts ever. Rainfall levels from January to April in the drainage basin of the Yangtze, China's longest and most economically important river, have been 40% lower than the average of the past 50 years, according to *China Daily*. This has resulted in a significant decline in hydropower and severe electricity shortages throughout much of central China.

The Chinese are burning more coal to generate electricity, but domestic mines no longer satisfy the country's needs and so China has become a major coal importer. Rising demand combined with inadequate supply has led to a spike in coal prices, and with no comparable spurt in electricity rates (set by the government), many Chinese utilities are rationing power rather than buy more expensive coal and operate at a loss. In response, industries are upping their reliance on diesel-powered backup generators, which in turn increases China's demand for imported oil, putting yet more pressure on global fuel prices.

Wrecking the Planet

So now we enter June with continuing unrest in the Middle East, a grim outlook for nuclear power, and a severe electricity shortage in China (and possibly elsewhere). What else do we see on the global energy horizon?

Despite the IEA's forecast of diminished future oil consumption, global energy demand continues to outpace increases in supply. From all indications, this imbalance will persist.

Take oil. A growing number of energy analysts now agree that the era of "easy oil" has ended and that the world must increasingly rely on hard-to-get "tough oil." It is widely assumed, moreover, that the planet harbors a lot of this stuff—deep underground, far offshore, in problematic geological formations like Canada's tar sands, and in the melting Arctic. However, extracting and processing tough oil will prove ever more costly and involve great human, and even greater environmental, risk. Think: BP's *Deepwater Horizon* disaster of April 2010 in the Gulf of Mexico.

Such is the world's thirst for oil that a growing amount of this stuff will nonetheless be extracted, even if not, in all likelihood, at a pace and on a scale necessary to replace the disappearance of yesterday's and today's easy oil. Along with continued instability in the Middle East, this tough-oil landscape seems to underlie expectations that the price of oil will only rise in the coming years. In a poll of global energy company executives conducted this April by the KPMG Global Energy Institute, 64% of those surveyed predicted that crude oil prices will cross the $120 per barrel barrier before the end of 2011. Approximately one-third of them predicted that the price would go even higher, with 17% believing it would reach $131–$140 per barrel; 9%, $141–$150 per barrel; and 6%, above the $150 mark.

The price of coal, too, has soared in recent months, thanks to mounting worldwide demand as supplies of energy from nuclear power and hydroelectricity have contracted. Many countries have launched significant efforts to spur the development of renewable energy, but these are not advancing fast enough or on a large enough scale to replace older technologies quickly. The only bright spot, experts say, is the growing extraction of natural gas from shale rock in the United States through the use of hydraulic fracturing ("hydro-fracking").

Proponents of shale gas claim it can provide a large share of America's energy needs in the years ahead, while actually reducing harm to the environment when compared to coal and oil (as gas emits less carbon dioxide per unit of energy released); however, an expanding chorus of opponents are warning of the threat to municipal water supplies posed by the use of toxic chemicals in the fracking process. These warnings have proven convincing enough to lead lawmakers in a growing number of states to begin placing restrictions on the practice, throwing into doubt the future contribution of shale gas to the nation's energy supply. Also, on May 12th, the French National Assembly (the powerful lower house of parliament) voted 287 to 146 to ban hydro-fracking in France, becoming the first nation to do so.

The environmental problems of shale gas are hardly unique. The fact is that all of the strategies now being considered to extend the life-spans of oil, coal, and natural gas involve severe economic and environmental risks and costs—as, of course, does the very use of fossil fuels of any sort at a moment when the first IEA numbers for 2010 indicate that it was an unexpectedly record-breaking year for humanity when it came to dumping greenhouse gases into the atmosphere.

With the easily accessible mammoth oil fields of Texas, Venezuela, and the Middle East either used up or soon to be significantly depleted, the future of oil rests on third-rate stuff like tar sands, shale oil, and extra-heavy crude that require a lot of energy to extract, processes that emit added greenhouse gases, and as with those tar sands, tend to play havoc with the environment.

Recurring shortages, rising prices, and mounting discontent are likely to be the thematic drumbeat of the globe's energy future.

Shale gas is typical. Though plentiful, it can only be pried loose from underground shale formations through the use of explosives and highly pressurized water mixed with toxic chemicals. In addition, to obtain the necessary quantities of shale oil, many tens of thousands of wells will have to be sunk across the American landscape, any of one of which could prove to be an environmental disaster.

Likewise, the future of coal will rest on increasingly invasive and hazardous techniques, such as the explosive removal of mountaintops and the dispersal of excess rock and toxic wastes in the valleys below. Any increase in the use of coal will also enhance climate change, since coal emits more carbon dioxide than do oil and natural gas.

Here's the bottom line: Any expectations that ever-increasing supplies of energy will meet demand in the coming years are destined to be disappointed. Instead, recurring shortages, rising prices, and mounting discontent are likely to be the thematic drumbeat of the globe's energy future.

If we don't abandon a belief that unrestricted growth is our inalienable birthright and embrace the genuine promise of renewable energy (with the necessary effort and investment that would make such a commitment meaningful), the future is likely to prove grim indeed. Then, the history of energy, as taught in some late twenty-first-century university, will be labeled: How to Wreck the Planet 101.

CHAPTER 2

Are Rising Gasoline Prices a Serious Problem?

Chapter Overview

Toni Johnson

Toni Johnson is a senior staff writer for the Council on Foreign Relations, an independent, nonpartisan membership organization, think tank, and publisher.

Although considerable attention has been given to the role of market speculation in recent price volatility, many energy experts say demand is rising and oil supplies are increasingly constrained, which puts upward pressure on oil and, consequently, gas prices. Political unrest in the Middle East, a recovering global economy, and revived demand in the emerging markets have all contributed to rising oil prices. U.S. gas prices in the spring of 2011 were more than $4 in some places and heading toward the record highs of 2008, when gas rose to nearly $5 per gallon. The U.S. Energy Information Administration (EIA) estimates that in 2011, gas prices will cost the average consumer at least $825 more than in 2010. The U.S. debate over protecting consumers against high gasoline prices has largely focused on increasing domestic supplies or finding ways to reduce consumer demand, but there is also concern about balancing these against environmental and economic issues.

Components of Gasoline Price

The EIA, an arm of the U.S. Department of Energy, breaks the price of retail gasoline into four components: the cost of crude oil; the cost of refining and fuel-blending; federal and state taxes; and distribution and marketing expenses.

- *Crude oil*: This is the raw material used to make commercial-grade gasoline, known in much of the world as petrol. The cost of crude oil accounts for the largest percentage of what U.S. consumers pay for gas at the pump. On average, about 51 percent of every dollar spent on retail gasoline went to crude suppliers in much of the last decade, according to the EIA. In 2008, when gas and oil prices were at their highest, crude represented an average of 75 percent of U.S. gas prices and currently hovers at around 70 percent, according to April 2011 analysis from oil industry advocate the American Petroleum Institute (API). "You cannot decouple gas prices from crude prices," says one API analyst. "If you want to help the consumer at the pump, you have to make sure crude prices don't rise too much." According to the EIA, a $1 change in crude prices corresponds roughly to a 5-cent change in wholesale gasoline prices.

- *Refining*: The process of turning crude oil into products for consumer use accounts for about 7 percent of the retail price of gasoline, on national average. In the United States, refining requirements in different regions can affect gas prices. California, for instance, has the highest air quality rules, including stricter requirements for ethanol fuel-blending and sulfur content. Thus, gas prices in the West Coast region, dependent on California refineries, are significantly higher than the national average. Refining capacity can also have a price effect, as was the case in 2005 when Hurricane Katrina knocked out 20 percent of refining capacity in the Gulf region, which caused gas prices to increase.

- *Taxes*: The percentage of every dollar spent on gasoline that goes to federal or state governments has decreased in recent years. According to the EIA, taxes currently account for about 14 percent of the retail price Americans pay for gas, though this number is a national average and percentages vary significantly from state to state. The national average, including a federal tax of 18.5 cents per gallon, is 49.5 cents, but some states' gas taxes go as high as nearly 70 cents.

- *Distribution and marketing:* The combined prices of purchasing and transporting gasoline from refineries to gas stations (often via intermediary distribution points) and the costs of operating the stations account for about 10 percent of the retail price of gasoline, according to EIA data.

Oil Supply and Demand

While U.S. consumption has fallen slightly in the last five years, China, the world's second largest consumer of oil, and countries such as India and Brazil are seeing a marked increase in oil demand. Some experts say these emerging markets have played a major role in the volatility in crude prices, which in the last few years have fluctuated widely, going as high as $145 per barrel in mid-2008 before dropping to $30 and then rising again to above $100 in 2011. "As long as the emerging economies, especially the big ones, keep growing, the demand for oil will keep growing," said CFR's [Council on Foreign Relations] Michael Spence in March 2011. "So, the kind of situation we saw before the crisis in 2006 through 2008, when there was a big spike in commodity prices, could return."

Demand also has outpaced new oil investment, leading to a tightening of global production capacity. For the last few decades, Saudi Arabia, the only country with notable spare production, has attempted to act as a price buffer by raising or lowering its production in response to the market, but in recent years the country has had less room to act. Smaller margins of spare production capacity mean any potential disruptions in the oil supply have a marked effect. In 2011, the supply of oil in the Middle East became a significant concern and caused oil prices to increase as countries in the region including Libya, one of the world's top twenty oil producers, became embroiled in an ongoing pro-democracy movement. In the short term, the uprising known as the Arab Spring has instilled a new sense of insecurity in oil markets. In the longer term, what happens in the Middle East could have serious implications for oil supplies.

"If future oil demand has any hope of being met, significant investment must take place to develop Middle East and North African oil reserves," writes Paul Stevens, a senior fellow at Britain's Chatham House, noting that political uncertainty could reduce interest future investment by international oil companies. "This could mean that an impending oil supply crunch, with crucial implications for oil price levels, could come sooner rather than later."

Oil executives claim they are just as much at the mercy of market forces as consumers.

Some experts say that high oil prices are here to stay. "The age of cheap oil is over, though policy action could bring lower international prices than would otherwise be the case," International Energy Agency head Fatih Birol said in March 2011. However, CFR Adjunct Senior Fellow Atul Arya cautions against predicting permanently higher oil prices. "We can't say with confidence that prices will stay high," he says, noting that historically, prices have bottomed out with new production coming online and the softening of demand due to high oil prices and other economic factors.

Factoring in Ethanol

The EIA expects ethanol-blended fuel, currently 10 percent per volume in a gallon of gasoline (E10), to account for nearly

10 percent of U.S. consumption in 2011. A 2008 Energy Department study estimated that, on average, ethanol-blending saved the U.S. consumer anywhere from 20 cents per gallon to as much as 35 cents per gallon that year. A more recent ethanol industry report argues that in 2011, gas prices have been at least 12 cents lower than expected, thanks to the fuel additive.

But effects on prices, especially going forward, remain a topic of political debate. Some critics of corn-based ethanol, such as the environmental group Natural Resources Defense Council, argue that the 45 cent per gallon federal tax credit for blending masks the true price effect, and that the Renewable Fuel Standard, which mandates an increasing use of ethanol-blending—from nine billion gallons in 2008 to 36 billion gallons by 2022—is enough to incentivize production. Corn, a major ethanol feedstock, is also subject to commodities market fluctuations and production problems that could increase ethanol prices. Thanks to low global corn stocks, ethanol prices are at a two-year high, though still lower per gallon than crude. Still, others argue that because of its heavy reliance on corn, ethanol is in competition with food, driving up food prices, especially for the world's hungriest.

Policies to Ease Gas Prices

U.S. policymakers have implemented a number of initiatives to either increase U.S. production of oil or lower consumption, but many of these take years to have an effect and thus have had limited impact on consumers in the short term. And though lawmakers in the last decade have brought oil companies to task for high prices, oil executives claim they are just as much at the mercy of market forces as consumers.

"No one person, organization, or industry can 'set' the price for crude oil," Marvin E. Odum, head of Shell Oil Company, told the Senate Finance Committee on May 12, 2011. "Stated simply, oil is a global commodity. And oil companies are price takers, not price *makers*." Some analysts note that though gross oil industry profits seem large, the industry's profit margin (which takes in the cost of oil production) ranks 114 out of 215 industries—making on average a little over 6.5 cents for every dollar.

Still, the [Barack] Obama administration and Democrats in Congress already have renewed attempts to end $4 billion in annual oil company subsidies, but it is unclear whether it will affect prices. On May 14, [2011] President Obama also announced new plans to aid new domestic drilling, including leasing new parts of the Gulf of Mexico and Alaska, and encouraging drilling on unused energy leases on land and offshore.

Increasing domestic drilling, proponents say, will reduce U.S. dependence on foreign oil as well as encourage lower oil prices by increasing supply. Shale oil advocates estimate production using hydraulic fracking (inserting liquids into a well to push out trapped oil) could yield as much as two million barrels a day by 2015—more than what is currently produced offshore in the Gulf of Mexico. Similarly, there is intense interest in boosting conventional offshore and deepwater production—which some argue could yield an additional two million barrels in the next five years.

Many experts contend that reducing consumption through demand-reduction policies is the biggest buffer against high gas prices.

However, such endeavors face challenges. Some projects will require oil prices to stay high to justify new investment and will take years to bring up to scale. And environmental issues such as water use and quality concerns, as well as greenhouse gas intensity, could slow development or raise costs through environmental compliance. For example, shale gas production—which also uses fracking—is under fire for water pollution concerns, and U.S. offshore production and leasing has slowed after the Obama administration imposed new environmental regulations following the four-month Deepwater oil spill [in the Gulf of Mexico] in 2010.

Other analysts say the United States does not hold enough oil to make a significant impact. "In 2009, the U.S. produced about 7 percent of what was produced in the entire world, so increasing the oil production in the U.S. is not going to make much of a difference in world markets and world prices," EIA analyst Phyllis Martin told the *Huffington Post*.

Instead, many experts contend that reducing consumption through demand-reduction policies is the biggest buffer against high gas prices. Overall, CFR's Arya says that what should be communicated to consumers by policymakers is that the world is already "thinking about what's next" when it comes to dealing with oil dependence.

The United States is already implementing new corporate average fuel economy standards, and consumers have moved toward purchasing more fuel-efficient cars. [A recent] *Scientific American* article explores demand-reduction policies, including increased use of biofuels and alternative-fueled vehicles, and attaching new crude oil or gas taxes.

Unlike API, which favors reducing current gas taxes to help the U.S. consumer, some experts see a massive increase in gas taxes—in effect raising prices even further—as the simplest way to deter consumption. The United States pays the lowest fuel tax and thus lower fuel prices than any other industrialized nation and less than some emerging-market countries, such as China.

Increases in Gas Prices Act as a Drag on the Economy

Dante Chinni

Dante Chinni is a journalist and the director of Patchwork Nation, a project of the Jefferson Institute, an independent research and education organization that studies politics, socio-economics, and culture.

Are the hopes for an economic recovery disappearing into our gas tanks? On Thursday [April 28, 2011] the Commerce Department reported economic growth had slowed to an annual rate of 1.8 percent. It had been projected to be as high as 4 percent.

There are many influences on that dip—from trade imbalances to reduced government spending—but it's hard to ignore the influence of gas prices. The numbers are dramatic. A Patchwork Nation analysis of data from GasBuddy, finds prices are up over a dollar-a-gallon compared to last year in some places—and, as is usually the case, pain has not been spread evenly.

To be clear no one has been spared a hit at the pump, but some types of counties—like the sparsely populated Mormon Outposts in the Mountain West—have seen much smaller bumps than others. And as one might expect, the big city Industrial Metropolis counties, not only have the highest prices overall, sitting just shy of $4 a gallon, they also have seen the biggest increase. A gallon of gas is more than a dollar more than it was in April 2010.

How does that translate into economic pain exactly? Directly and indirectly. A recent analysis from Deutsche Bank finds that every penny increase in average gas prices at the pump in the United States equals $1.4 billion siphoned out of the US economy.

But a lot of the real pain depends on where you live, what stage of the "recovery" your community is experiencing and your driving habits.

The Differences

The increase in gas prices has swamped the country, sparing no one. The bumps in most of our 12 county types are pretty uniform—between 92 cents and $1.01. The Mormon Outposts overall have managed well, with an increase of only 55 cents a gallon from last year. . . .

But there are some differences in what gas actually costs today because there are differences in what those communities usually pay. So, on average, gas in less-wealthy Minority Central counties is 20 cents-a-gallon cheaper than it is in the Monied Burbs. And the people who live in and around the nation's biggest cities—the Industrial Metropolis counties— pay the most of all.

Understanding the pain, however, is not that simple, because in the end what you pay for gas is only a part (sometimes a small part) of your actual gas bill and of rising prices. Among other things, taxes play a role, as well as the formula blends required in your area.

There are also bigger questions about what kind of car you drive and how long your commute is. No one likes $4-a-gallon gas, but it helps if you only have to fill up every other week, or even live car-less, as you might be more likely to do in a dense urban area.

And, of course, there is how much disposable income you have. Are you diverting money into your gas tank that was supposed to be going to your family vacation to London or that was supposed to be going to your grocery bill? That makes a difference in what the gas price hike means.

Where It Hurts . . . and for How Long

Look at the higher prices in the small town Service Worker Centers and the African-American heavy Minority Central counties, where gas prices are up 94 cents-a-gallon and 93 cents-a-gallon respectively in the last year.

[The] increase in gas prices . . . is going to eat away at the thing the U.S. economy needs to get going again— consumer spending.

In both those county types, the unemployment rate is still over 10 percent. People there . . . , on average, were hit hard by the recession as we have noted in other reporting and are still in pretty bad straits. When they have to basically pay an extra dollar for every gallon of gas the headwinds for them get stronger. The pain in those places is felt directly and pushes any recovery talk off.

Add in the fact that they are more rural locales, places where driving tends to be more necessary, and you compound the problem. Kip Ward, who lives in Lincoln City, Ore., a Service Worker Center that Patchwork Nation visits, figures his daily commute, home and back, at 400–500 miles a week.

The Monied Burbs have bounced back some from the recession, but increase in gas prices there is going to eat away at the thing the U.S. economy needs to get going again—consumer spending. Most of the people who live in these counties aren't poor, but pulling an extra $50 a week away from them will make an impact. That's money that can't be spent at local coffee shops and restaurants.

And, yes, higher gas prices will take a toll on family vacations in the Monied Burbs, many of which are taken in tourist hubs like, Lincoln City and other Service Worker Centers.

Tractor Country counties, rural and not especially wealthy, rely on fuel not only for driving, but also for farming equipment. They would seem to be especially hard hit, but the agricultural economy in them shielded them from most of the great recession and rising food costs actually have helped them.

"At $7 a bushel for corn, they better not complain about anything," joked Dennis Walstra, Mayor of Sioux Center, Iowa, a Tractor Country community we visit. That was a few weeks back. Corn is now at $7.60 a bushel.

2012 Approaches

There is no sign as yet that the gas price increase is over. In fact, further political instability in the Middle East, could push it higher still—closer to $5 or more.

And, while it is early, all of this could end up being a big part of the coming presidential race. Much of your economic reality is perception. Whatever the national headlines say about the stock market or the job market, it's what you see and feel outside your door that makes the real impact.

The potential for a prolonged, painful recovery can't be welcome news at the White House. Even if gas prices have returned to earth by then, the impacts on the economy and the recovery will likely linger. The 2012 political field has not yet taken shape, but the economic landscape may be starting to and so far it is not pretty.

Rising Gas Prices Transfer Wealth from Poorer Americans to the Rich

Dan Froomkin

Dan Froomkin is senior Washington correspondent for The Huffington Post, *a web-based American newspaper and blog.*

The next time you're gritting your teeth as you fill your tank with $4 gas, here's something to consider: Your pain is their gain.

The last of the Big Five oil companies announced first-quarter earnings Friday, so the totals are in. Between the five of them, ExxonMobil, BP, Shell, Chevron, and ConocoPhillips made $34 billion in profits in the first three months of 2011—up 42 percent from a year ago.

That's about $110 for every man, woman, and child in the United States—in just three months.

Exxon alone cleared a cool $10.7 billion profit from January through March, up 69 percent from 2010. That's $82,175 a minute.

Enriching the Rich

Why the staggering increase in earnings? Precisely because you're paying $4 a gallon for gas.

Gas prices shoot up when oil prices shoot up, and when oil prices shoot up for reasons that have nothing to do with how much it costs to bring it out of the ground, it's a windfall for the folks who produce it.

The average cost to produce a barrel of oil, including exploration, development, extraction and taxes, is about $30, according to a U.S. Energy Information Administration survey. The going rate to buy one is about $113.

Why is the price so high? Part of it is increased demand and geopolitical worries. But no less an authority on the matter than Goldman Sachs acknowledged earlier this month [April 2011] that speculation is at least partially responsible, driving oil prices up faster and higher than supply and demand could possibly explain.

That means the people who are betting on oil prices are actually making the price of oil go up.

And while the pain is widely felt—consider all the Wal-Mart shoppers who are agonizing over how to make it to the end of the month—the benefits are not being widely shared.

The industry's powerful Washington mouthpiece, the American Petroleum Institute, argues that the staggering earnings simply reflect oil and gas companies' tremendous contributions to the economy, and that their stock prices are shoring up the nation's pension funds.

Every visit to the gas pump reflects a transfer of money from the many to the few—and in most cases, from the not-so-rich to the super-rich.

Adam Sieminski, chief energy economist for Deutsche Bank, thinks the numbers get too much attention. "The overall profit numbers look really big because they're really big companies that move a lot of product around," he says. "To say that they're enormous profits only works if you're talking about the total number. They're not enormous profits if you compare them across other companies and other industries."

Siemenski even accentuates the positive. "Yes, when gas goes up, everybody squeaks, because it's uncomfortable," he says. But high oil prices mean, among other things, that "it becomes more attractive to do alternative energy. . . . The worst thing that ever happened to wind and solar power companies was when oil prices collapsed in 2008 and early 2009," he says. Furthermore, when gas gets pricey, "people who made a decision to get a Prius instead of a Hummer get a payback, and from a societal standpoint, that's probably good."

And yet, the fact of the matter is that every visit to the gas pump reflects a transfer of money from the many to the few—and in most cases, from the not-so-rich to the super-rich.

Enriching Shareholders

By and large, the oil companies' profits are not finding their way back into the communities from which they came; are not being used to create more jobs; and are not being invested in new equipment and exploration.

Some of that money is going back out the door in the form of larger dividends to stockholders. But in the case of two of the big five in particular—Exxon and ConocoPhillips—more than half of their total profits are being used to buy back their own stock.

Fully $5.7 billion of Exxon's haul went to buy back its own stock—and the company announced that it expects to buy back yet another $5 billion's worth in the second quarter of the year. Conoco earned $3 billion in the first three months of 2011—and spent $1.6 billion of that to buy back 21 million of its own shares.

Buying back stock is not an uncommon tactic among publicly held companies, particularly when they experience a sudden and possibly temporary uptick in revenue. Buybacks are almost guaranteed to send stock prices up, by boosting earnings per outstanding share, increasing the demand for the stock and sending a signal that the company thinks its stock is undervalued.

But from the viewpoint of a company's CEO, other top brass and its board of directors, stock buybacks have all sorts of particular advantages, as well.

Top executives, after all, often get significant stock options. If stock prices don't go up, such options are worthless. By contrast, the higher the stock price goes, the more valuable the option. (Exxon's stock is up 32 percent from six months ago.)

Buying back shares benefits existing shareholders, no one else. And more than anyone else, it benefits existing management.

Companies that buy back their stock can either retire it or simply keep it themselves, under the control of the board of directors, to reissue later or award as bonuses.

Dividends, by contrast, are not nearly as good a deal for company executives. For one thing, they are taxed as income. An increase in the stock price is not taxed as income; it's not taxed at all until the stock is sold—and only then at the capital gains tax rate, which is limited to 15 percent. (Fifteen percent would be a lot for the median American family, which pays less than 5 percent of its income in federal taxes. But it's a huge break to those paying income tax at the highest marginal rate of 35 percent.)

"Buying back shares benefits existing shareholders, no one else. And more than anyone else, it benefits existing management," says Henry Banta, an energy industry analyst and partner in the Washington D.C. law firm of Lobel, Novins & Lamont.

"They're basically enriching themselves," says Daniel J. Weiss, a senior fellow at the Center for American Progress. "With this windfall, they enrich the board of directors, senior managers, and shareholders."

And in 2007, when Exxon was using $30 billion a year from the previous oil-price bubble to buy back its shares, *Bloomberg* columnist David Pauly wrote: "In most cases, stock buybacks are suspect. . . . Managements should ignore investors' call to repurchase their shares and invest money in ways that will increase profit, not just earnings per share."

Most Shareholders Already Are Rich

As for the dividends paid by Exxon and the other oil giants, there may be a lot of shareholders, total—including a lot of pension funds and mutual funds—but the vast majority of shares are held by a very small elite.

Edward N. Wolff, an economics professor at New York University, studies wealth distribution. His latest study includes data through 2007. When it comes to total equity in stocks, Wolff says, "it's still very concentrated in the hands of the rich."

"Less than half of households owned stock as of 2007," he says. "Probably less now" because of the financial crisis, he suspects: "Probably more like 45 percent, maybe less." That includes 401ks, mutual funds and the like.

"Even that really overstates things because a lot of the people who do own stock own very small amounts," Wolff says. As of 2007, the percentage of households that owned $5,000 or more of stock was 35 percent; only 22 percent owned $25,000 or more.

Who's got the rest? The wealthiest 1 percent of households has 38 percent, Wolff found; the wealthiest 5 percent has 69 percent; the wealthiest 10 percent has 81 percent.

The bottom 60 percent of households owns 2.5 percent of the total stock. Not so very much.

Hoarding Profits

There's another thing the big oil companies are doing with their profits: they're hoarding them. If precedent holds, as soon as oil prices started shooting up again, a lot of that money started going into the bank for safekeeping—and adding yet more to the $1 trillion or so in corporate cash lying fallow and slowing the recovery.

And as it happens, a not insubstantial chunk of last quarter's profits were a direct gift—from the taxpayers. Somewhere between $4 billion and $9 billion of the industry's annual profits comes from federal subsidies.

President Barack Obama has proposed repealing $4 billion a year in subsidies; the American Petroleum Institute says the proposal would actually cost the industry about $90 billion over the next decade.

Response to Obama's proposal was lackluster at first, from both sides of the aisle.

But Democrats, afraid of being thrown out of the White House by an angry, gas-impoverished voting public, are suddenly seeing the fight to repeal those subsidies as a winning political issue.

Although the repeal would neither increase nor decrease the price of gas, it would take a bite out of Big Oil. And pushing for the repeal will almost inevitably highlight the modern Republican Party's nearly lockstep allegiance to the thriving oil and gas interests—something that, in a period of high gas prices and even higher profits, couldn't be good for them.

But yet another thing the industry does with all its cash is buy influence in Washington.

For instance, Exxon, during the same quarter it made nearly $11 billion, spent just a tiny fraction of that on lobbying. But that was still a whopping $3 million.

High Gas Prices Are Causing Many Americans Financial Hardship

Lydia Saad

Lydia Saad is a senior editor at Gallup, a public opinion survey firm.

The slight majority of Americans, 53%, say they have responded to today's steep gas prices by making major changes in their personal lives, while 46% say they have not. Sizable proportions of adults of all major income levels have made such changes, including 68% of low-income Americans, 54% of middle-income Americans, and 44% of upper-income Americans. . . .

Although employed Americans are more likely to report driving an above-average amount—and are thus greater consumers of gasoline—they are less likely than non-employed Americans to have made major lifestyle changes to deal with rising gas prices, 49% vs. 58%. This likely reflects the higher average income of employed Americans, but may also indicate they have less flexibility in their lives to cut back on driving.

These findings come from a *USA Today*/Gallup poll conducted May 12–15 [2011], in which 67% of Americans say the recent high gas prices have caused them financial hardship, including 21% who say they have caused them severe hardship. This is among the highest levels of reported hardship Gallup has seen on this measure since 2000, and is similar to the 71% found when average gas prices nationwide topped $4 per gallon in 2008 and the 72% when they first exceeded $3 per gallon in 2005. . . .

Americans Driving Less, Steering Toward Cars That Are More Fuel Efficient

Among the 53% of Americans who report having made major changes in their lives to deal with gas prices, the most common strategy, mentioned by a third of them, is simply driving less. Additionally, 16% specifically report they are cutting back on vacation travel, 15% are being more careful in planning errands and other local trips, and 15% have either purchased a more fuel-efficient vehicle or are looking into it. Smaller segments are doing less "leisure driving," carpooling, using public transportation, walking more, biking more, and driving more slowly.

While equal percentages of men and women say they are driving less in response to changes in gas prices, men are nearly twice as likely as women to say they have purchased or plan to purchase a more fuel-efficient car.

Rather than driving less, 12% of those making major changes due to gas prices say they are cutting back on groceries, clothes, and other expenses to absorb the higher gas costs. . . .

Low-income Americans who have made major lifestyle changes due to high gas prices primarily report significant hardships, including driving less and cutting back on household expenses. By contrast, those in middle- and upper-income households are relatively more likely to report driving less for vacations and errands.

Additionally, while equal percentages of men and women say they are driving less in response to changes in gas prices, men are nearly twice as likely as women to say they have purchased or plan to purchase a more fuel-efficient car, 20% vs. 11%. Women, on the other hand, are twice as likely (16% vs. 8%) to say they have cut back on other household expenses.

The responses of adults who have made changes to deal with high gas prices vary by age, with those 55 and older much more likely than younger adults to say they have been more careful about running errands but less likely to say they are using a more fuel-efficient car.

Bottom Line

Average gas prices in the United States have increased by nearly $1 a gallon since January [2011], with half of that increase occurring since March. This increase has clearly caught Americans' attention, with 67% saying it has caused them financial hardship. Additionally, the slight majority of Americans report that they have made real changes in their lives to deal with high fuel costs. Driving less is the obvious, and most common, response, whether that be driving less in general, cutting back on vacation travel, or consolidating errands. Additionally, some Americans, particularly those under 55, have switched to a more fuel-efficient car, while others, particularly lower-income Americans, have cut back on other household and living expenses to be able to put gas in their tanks.

Compared with Other Industrialized Countries, US Gas Is Cheap

Sarah Terry-Cobo

Sarah Terry-Cobo, formerly a reporter and research assistant on the Center for Investigative Reporting's Carbon Watch series, is a freelance reporter specializing in science and environmental policy issues.

What's the true price of gasoline? . . . California has some of the dirtiest air in the nation. Consequently, it has some of the strictest rules for gasoline, meaning it burns cleaner than it does in many other states. But cleaner fuels are more expensive.

Clean air requirements, combined with supply and refining constraints, make the price of California gas consistently among the highest in the nation. Turmoil in the Middle East is another factor that pushes up the global price of crude oil. Even though the average price for a gallon of regular unleaded gas in California fluctuates around $4, some experts argue that $4 a gallon is much less than the real cost.

Compared with other industrialized countries, the U.S. has it cheap. *The Economist* notes that American consumers pay about half of what Europeans pay, which is up to about $8.50 per gallon (or $2.25 per liter). The media website Good has a nifty chart showing the disparity in prices across the Atlantic, and PBS' *NewsHour* explains the effect Middle East turmoil has on the retail price of gas. While politicians on both sides of the aisle bicker about why gas is expensive, Sen. Jeff Bingaman, (D-N.M.), is one who explains the real reasons, and as David Roberts notes, he is lonely in doing so.

The Cost of Clean Air

Even though reducing toxic chemicals in gasoline might make it more expensive, the EPA [Environmental Protection Agency] argues that clean air provides long-term cost benefits. A recent study of the Clean Air Act showed "the public health and environmental benefits . . . exceed their costs by a margin of four to one."

From 1990 to 2010, these regulations have prevented "23,000 Americans from dying prematurely, [and] averted over 1,700,000 incidences of asthma attacks and aggravation of chronic asthma." In the same two decades, it also prevented more than 4.1 million lost workdays due to pollution-related illnesses.

California is among the leaders in the U.S. in implementing clean-air regulations to limit pollution from carbon dioxide and other greenhouse gases. Its ambitious Global Warming Solutions Act aims to reduce greenhouse-gas pollution to 1990 levels by the year 2020—goals similar to the United Nations' Kyoto Protocol. And the state's Air Resources Board will introduce the nation's second pollution-trading system, known as cap-and-trade, for greenhouse gases on Jan. 1, 2012. Under that system, if a company does not meet its pollution limits, it can buy a carbon offset, a promise to reduce pollution elsewhere.

But the market isn't the only method the board is using to reduce air pollution and greenhouse gases. In fact, the board estimates only one-fifth of the reductions will come from cap-and-trade. The other four-fifths will come from increased energy-efficiency standards, improved recycling and composting programs, the highest standard for fuel efficiency in cars, and the state's low-carbon fuel standard.

The cost of clean air programs may be high, but so is the cost of pollution. A 2008 study commissioned by CSU [California State University] Fullerton's Institute for Economic and Environmental Studies notes that the cost of air pollution for the greater Los Angeles region adds up to more than $1,250 per person per year.

For the Central Valley, where one-third of the nation's produce originates, the cost is more than $1,600 per person per year. These costs include treatment for respiratory illnesses like asthma, which are disproportionately borne by children younger than 5, the elderly, and minority populations. Other costs include lost workdays, missed school days, and premature deaths.

But health effects are just some of the financial impacts of burning fossil fuels—gasoline and diesel fuel, in particular. Harmful air pollution can affect food and fiber crops. The U.S. Global Change Research Program noted in a 2009 report on climate change that greenhouse gases can reduce crop yields for "soybeans, wheat, oats, green beans, peppers, and some types of cotton."

Although $4 a gallon may seem expensive, there are many social and environmental costs that Americans don't pay for at the pump.

And the cost of oil spills? Some early estimates put the price of cleaning up the massive spill in the Gulf of Mexico at up to $20 billion. Every year, states spend more than $600 million to clean up leaking underground gasoline storage tanks.

In the last three decades, businesses, states, and the EPA have cleaned up 401,874 leaking underground gasoline storage tanks, with an estimated 93,123 more sites awaiting cleanup, according to an EPA representative. In 2010, the agency set aside $66.2 million in a fund for states to use for cleanup activities. The agency spends about $2 million to $3 million each year for cleanup on tribal land.

Although $4 a gallon may seem expensive, there are many social and environmental costs that Americans don't pay for at the pump. While these costs are hidden, the cost to society is high.

This story was produced by the Center for Investigative Reporting, the nation's oldest independent, nonprofit investigative news center in the United States. More at cironline.org.

High Gas Prices Might Shock the Nation into Cutting Its Dependence on Oil

Myles Spicer

Myles Spicer is an author, writer, and blogger who frequently blogs for Daily Kos, *a progressive online news site and weblog with political analysis on US current events.*

Recently, there has been a blizzard of editorials about the need for conservation of oil and gas. While I heartily agree with this position, I fear the American public is merely tilting at windmills. Why? Because all these sermons about energy conservation lack both urgency and reality. And that is dangerously unacceptable.

There is absolutely nothing new in what you are going to read here—and that is exactly why it is so interesting.

There is no gas "crisis" that has suddenly appeared. There are no "surprises" to $4/gallon gas. Everything—everything—that has precipitated this rise in price has been known for at least decades. So why is there so much shock and discussion?

Consider these facts:

- First and foremost, oil is a finite product! It was never if we were going to run out of oil . . . it was always when. The real problem is that no one ever seems to address that issue, as long as oil remains cheap. Gutless leaders avoided telling us that; the oil companies and automakers stonewall it; and consequently, Americans just don't get it! And of course now [in January 2008], the leadership of our country is in the hands of two former oil company executives—both of whom lead us to believe we can "drill our way" out of this situation. That may be good for their compatriots in the oil industry, but it is no solution to this problem. In fact, it is counter-productive in a variety of ways.

- The major portion of world oil production has always been in the hands of despotic, uncaring, unreliable countries. Nothing new here.

- Americans have enjoyed the very lowest gas prices (and gas taxes) for decades; and we have known that forever.

- The oil companies are cleaning up in this apparently "new" crisis . . . and cleaning our pockets as well. We know that, too. Exxon made $15 billion of net profit in the past . . . 6 month[s] alone. . . . Surprised? You shouldn't be—it's easily discovered from many financial sources. If, as [former] President [George W.] Bush says, we are in a "war", then I have always believed profiteering during a war bordered on immoral, if not illegal.

- Natural disasters, such as [Hurricane] Katrina, are common, almost annual occurrences around the world, which periodically impede oil production. This is not new.

- The Energy Bill earlier passed by the Republican Congress had strong incentives for more drilling . . . and meager incentives for alternate energy, and limited emphasis on conservation. Again, crafted with the direction of the Bush team, it provided significant additional handouts to the oil companies, which is exactly what we do not need. The bill was widely reported—no surprises here either. The only possible surprise, to me, is the lack of outrage.

- Mass transit in our country is decades behind in development. The busses have a reputation for low class travel; the trains are woefully behind Europe and Asia; and local mass transit is far behind as well. But we know that.

The Need for $10/Gallon Gasoline

So, if we know all this; and if it is not new; and if it will eventually have grave consequences, then why is nothing being done? And, why would I propose $10/gallon gasoline? Well, the second question answers the first. We just do not get it!

Incremental raises just pinch, but do not really hurt. The oil cartel is very clever about this—they keep price points high enough to gobble up unconscionable amounts of money, but low enough so we are not incented to seek alternatives. We continue to buy our SUVs, we burn fossil fuels like there is no tomorrow, and we complain. Under this system, no leader has emerged to tell us the Emperor has no clothes. Alternate energy sources continue to lag. And there is no really effective solution in sight. Worse yet, there is absolutely no urgency to this very critical and imminent issue. If you think $100/barrel oil is expensive now, consider what the last barrel removed from the earth will be worth. In fact, that barrel will likely end up in the Smithsonian as a relic of a past civilization. Hopefully there will be some sort of transit available to go see it!

The only real solution [to oil dependency] is a shock so enormous and devastating that it will . . . wake us up to the reality of the situation.

Regarding alternate energy sources, I have for years examined the stock in a variety of Hydrogen, wind power and other alternate energy companies. I like to track these efforts. Without exception, these firms are small, under funded, losing money (few if any are profitable), and very much on the fringe of our economy. Plus, there is little coordination among them to synergize their efforts. Take Hydrogen for example. Yes, we can produce Hydrogen-powered vehicles, but the mass production for fuel, distribution, storage and other requirements to make it a viable fuel are decades away. The race to find a replacement for oil-based fuels, as well as the abundance of that resource, may already be lost.

The only real solution [to oil dependency] is a shock so enormous and devastating that it will . . . wake us up to the reality of the situation.

And when will that be? I am not an oil expert, all we DO know is that there is only so much of it on earth . . . we are burning it by the billions of barrels each year . . . less is being discovered and all is harder to get . . . the emerging nations are coming online to exacerbate consumption . . . the world's population is growing quickly . . . and it will run out. In 15 years? In 30 years? Even 40 years? What does it matter? At best it is a generation or two. Curiously, Saudi Arabia, which supplies 1/8 of the world's production is quite secretive and unclear about its true remaining reserves. And more drilling only prolongs the demise of fossil fuels, and keeps us asleep. That is the real danger of drilling in the Alaskan Wildlife Preserve [Arctic National Wildlife Preserve]—it is not a solution. In my mind, the only real solution is a shock so enormous and devastating that it will once and for all wake us up to the reality of the situation. At $10/gallon, that would get someone's attention.

Maybe we could get a leader who tells us the truth of the situation, creates a national (or even international) full court press on alternate energy sources, and levies an excess profits tax on the oil companies. Especially one not wedded to the oil industry.

Maybe we can finally get people off the roads and onto a clean, fast, widely scaled mass transit system that will be built in years, not decades. Maybe Americans will discover the pleasures of travel in speedy, beautiful trains with first class service and downtown to downtown service. Maybe, for regional travel, busses will become cleaner and more attractive; and terminals will be located in desirable parts of towns.

But, none of this will happen with small incremental raises in the cost of gas; and there is the added problem that these small increases hurt the poor more than any others—especially the working poor who must travel to jobs. At $10/gallon, the outrage of the average worker would be so great and disasterous, action would be demanded—not just complaining. So, maybe rather than slowly bleeding to death, we might be better "getting it on" and get our wake up call sooner than later.

So, what will it take? $10/gallon gasoline would surely do it. But there is one other solution that is even better. . . . That is $3/gallon gas . . . and the hope that America finally wakes up, elects some gutsy leadership, and does all that is needed NOW to assure our continuing prosperity. Hello . . . is anyone listening?

There Are Many Benefits to Higher Gas Prices

KNS Financial

KNS Financial, a personal financial advice company, was founded by New Jersey economist Khaleef Crumbley. Crumbley, using his company name, has written numerous articles for Redeeming Riche$, a financial blog and website.

In the last few months [early 2011] we have seen a sharp increase in the price of oil. This has caused many to search for ways to save money on gas—from driving less to finding cheaper gas! However, higher energy prices are not a universally negative situation, and there are some who actually welcome the increase due to the many benefits of higher gas prices. . . .

Changes in Consumer Behavior

Most of us simply drive along to and from work, church, grocery stores, events, friends' homes, and anywhere else that we feel like going. It isn't until gas prices begin to skyrocket that we began to consider our actions. As with pretty much every other good or service, higher prices leads to lower demand.

Whenever we see a rapid surge in gas prices, we tend to see a lot more people carpooling (even posting ads on Craigslist); the sale of fuel-efficient vehicles rise, and people even consider public transportation. Some even begin to wonder if their car is a luxury or necessity!

Employers even start to offer telecommuting (working from home) as a perk to many employees—or as a way to show employee appreciation.

Also, when more of our income is devoted to gas and energy costs, we tend to cut back on more frivolous activities. This sudden burst of financial responsibility can definitely be seen as one of the benefits of higher gas prices!

New Technology Seems More Affordable

There are alternative sources of energy available to us today. However, they typically are more expensive to produce and access than oil. This means that when oil/gas prices are cheap, no one gives a second thought to these other sources of energy. However, once oil prices begin to soar, it becomes much easier for proponents of alternative energy sources (and their respective industries) to be taken seriously.

This goes for alternative energy sources, such as solar power for houses and corporate buildings, wind and hydro-electric power for small communities, and even electric hybrid vehicles. Also, we must consider research and development of alternative fuel sources—such as ethanol from sugar cane or corn—as another benefit of higher gas prices.

This doesn't even take into consideration all of the oil that is used to make various plastics, medicine, clothing, and fertilizer! When the price of oil rises, research into alternative inputs for the manufacturing of these items increases along with it!

Certain Industries Will Take Off

Many industries hate seeing higher oil prices, as it makes their cost of doing business that much higher. It gets more expensive to make certain materials, ship intermediate and finished goods, travel to meetings, and many other aspects of business. Workers begin to demand more money in order to offset their own increased cost of living as well.

However, there are some industries that thrive when oil prices shoot up! With more expensive oil, you will have an increased interest in surveying, drilling and extracting, transporting, and refining the costly energy source!

Not only will these companies and their suppliers see good times, but higher prices should mean a lot more jobs are created within these sectors as well! Another group that benefits from higher gas prices are the shareholders in these various companies.

Higher Tax Revenue

In thinking of the benefits of higher gas prices, we can't forget our dear old uncle Sam. Every time a gallon of gas is sold, a portion of that price goes to our government in the form of taxes. The more that is collected in the form of gasoline tax, the less tax help is needed from other areas!

CHAPTER 3

Is Public Transportation an Answer to Rising Gasoline Prices?

Chapter Preface

One of the most controversial public transportation issues in the United States is whether it makes sense to build high-speed rail systems similar to those in other countries, such as France, Spain, Germany, and China. Although several states have rejected such proposals, California voters in 2008 passed a proposition authorizing $9.95 billion in general obligation bonds to finance a high-speed rail system. The California system, as planned, would eventually link all major California cities, including San Diego, Los Angeles, San Jose, Fresno, San Francisco, and Sacramento—eight hundred miles of track with a total of twenty-four different stations. If built, high-speed trains will travel on this system at about 220 miles per hour, allowing passengers to travel between major metropolitan regions of Los Angeles and San Francisco in under three hours, and all the way from San Diego to Sacramento in a little more than three-and-a-half hours. The costs of building such a system, however, are huge, especially at a time when the nation is focused on budget cuts and the national debt. This and other criticisms may ultimately doom the California high-speed rail project before it ever gets started.

According to its proponents, high-speed rail has a number of advantages and benefits, not the least of which is that it would be an important, high-tech infrastructure upgrade for America, allowing Americans to take pride in the nation's ability to still think big. In addition, the California High-Speed Rail Authority (CHSRA), an agency created to develop and shepherd the project through to completion, says high-speed rail would produce real economic, environmental, and community benefits. Perhaps most importantly, the project would create many new jobs, not only to build the rail system but also to staff and maintain it. Also, cities served by the high-speed train system are expected to see expansive economic development around the new rail stations, as local transportation is connected to the rail terminals and restaurants and other businesses are created to service rail passengers. And California businesses are expected to benefit generally from quicker transportation of people and goods, and relief of congestion on nearby freeways. In addition, supporters claim that high-speed rail will turn a profit, unlike slower train systems that are notorious for slow and poor service. The environment will benefit, meanwhile, because trains will run on electric power that will increasingly be obtained from renewable energy sources such as wind and solar, reducing air pollution and smog. And these fast trains use only a fraction of the energy used by planes or cars, so that will reduce gasoline usage as well as greenhouse gas emissions.

High-speed rail detractors, on the other hand, generally emphasize the high cost of building such elaborate rail systems. One group critical of the California plan, Californians Advocating Responsible Rail Design, has estimated that the total cost of the California high-speed rail project will be $65 billion, and others have speculated that this could rise to $100 billion with inflation over the years it will take to build. In fact, original cost estimates have already proven to be low. The initial San Francisco-to-Anaheim segment was initially estimated by the CHSRA to cost between $35.7 and $42.6 billion, but a more recent estimate was $63 billion.

Much of this money will have to come from federal funds, with the rest supplied by the state. However, the US Congress is in a budget-cutting mood, especially with regard to public transit monies, so the prospects of cuts in federal funding loom. In September 2011, for example, the House of Representatives' Appropriation Subcommittee on Transportation, Housing and Urban Development reduced President Barack Obama's fiscal 2012 request for $8 billion for rail systems to $7 billion, cutting funds for California's project and funding only Amtrak and some smaller rail programs. This legislation still must be approved by the Appropriations Committee, and both the full House and the Senate, but it threatens to halt California's high-speed rail dream. CHSRA can use about $6.3 billion in earlier federal grants and monies from an initial bond offering that state taxpayers approved in 2008, but these sources would pay for only a part of the initial rail segment. California Governor Jerry Brown has decided to review the entire project before agreeing to issue additional state bonds, and some commentators suggest that the state must secure private funding to make the project possible.

Yet the potential for private funding depends on just how profitable high-speed rail might be once it is built. According to supporters, the one US high-speed rail system currently in place—Amtrak's Acela Express service linking Washington, DC, with Boston—is profitable, even though Amtrak as a whole is not. But most of the other high-speed rail systems in the world, such as those in Europe, are government-subsidized. According to some estimates, Germany's system is one of the most expensive, requiring annual subsidies of $11.6 billion over ten years ending in 2006. Some commentators say it may be possible to cover operating costs from rider fees, but probably not capital costs such as maintenance and replacement parts.

Other obstacles facing California's high-speed rail development are the objections from property owners who will live close to planned rail routes. Already, angry citizens from the communities of Atherton, Palo Alto, and Menlo Park have begun protesting the project, after realizing that it could mean constructing elevated train tracks through the middle of town—construction that Palo Alto residents have said would divide the city like a Berlin wall. Opposition has only increased as planning for the project has continued. Because of this opposition, and because the $6.3 billion in federal funds must be spent before 2012, the state has decided it must start the project in the Central Valley, rather than in the more populated San Francisco corridor—a decision that could result in a railroad to nowhere if the rest of the rail line is never built.

High-speed rail is the most ambitious type of public transportation project being considered, but many public transportation advocates would rather see government funds spent on maintaining and upgrading existing means of public transit, such as buses and subways. Viewpoints in this chapter examine whether various types of mass transit might offer alternatives to cars in this age of rising gas prices.

Rising Gas Prices in 2011 Caused Drivers to Turn to Public Transportation

Sean Barry

Sean Barry is a campaign associate for Transportation for America, a coalition of housing, business, environmental, public health, transportation, equitable development, and other organizations dedicated to improving America's transportation system.

The higher gas prices become, the more likely people are to start looking for alternatives. And the shift has already begun.

Demand for mass transit is surging everywhere—from Nashville, Tennessee to Eau Claire, Wisconsin; Terre Haute, Indiana to Pasadena, California. Virginia Governor Bob McDonnell is encouraging his constituents to bike, walk or carpool at least once every two weeks. And, residents in Peoria and central Illinois started coordinating ridesharing schedules online.

In that same vein, the *Las Cruces Sun-News*, one of the largest newspapers in New Mexico, encouraged readers to consider new options in an editorial this week [April 2011] opining:

> The economic decision to choose public transportation over one's personal vehicle could turn into a positive for all concerned.

> People who've never tried it may actually like it. And if a bus is going where they're going? Yes, they'll be more likely

to continue using that mode of transportation. It beats paying almost $4 a gallon for gasoline, especially when the personal vehicle gets about 15 miles per almost $4.

Last time gas prices topped $4 and demand for [public] transit surged, . . . some of the biggest increases in demand came in areas less associated with transit, like the Southwest.

Rising Demand for Public Transportation

Gas prices at or above $4 a gallon generate the need for 670 million additional passenger trips on transit systems, resulting in more than 10.8 billion trips per year, according to the American Public Transportation Association.

Bicycling has become a popular alternative, with new riders benefiting from recent investment in bike facilities and programs. Mirroring the increased demand for transit in 2008, biking increased 15 percent nationwide and 23 percent in the 31 largest bike-friendly cities that year, with a similar uptick occurring today, according to Peopleforbikes.org.

Last time gas prices topped $4 and demand for transit surged, cities with well-established public transit systems like New York and Boston saw increases in transit usage of 5 percent of more, while some of the biggest increases in demand came in areas less associated with transit, like the Southwest. But these are many of the same communities that lack the capacity for a large surge in ridership.

Often lost in the discussion is the fact that many people are stuck without realistic alternatives to pain at the pump: streets too dangerous to walk or bike, destinations too far away, no available transit service, no easy options.

Most of the talk in Washington has focused on the supply side of the gas prices equation—speculation, domestic drilling and the like. But a real-world shift in demand is happening right before our eyes. With the nation's comprehensive surface transportation bill overdue for renewal, this ought to lend greater urgency to the need for robust investment in an array of options to ensure no one gets stranded or left behind.

Record Mass Transit Ridership Could Result If Gas Prices Rise Higher

PR Newswire

PR Newswire is a global provider of news and information distribution services for public relations professionals and other communicators.

A study released today [March 2011] by the American Public Transportation Association (APTA) predicts that as gasoline prices continue increasing, Americans will turn to public transportation in record numbers. APTA is calling on Congress to address this impending demand by providing a greater long-term investment in public transportation.

Public Transit Ridership Increases

The analysis reveals if regular gas prices reach $4 a gallon across the nation, as many experts have forecasted, an additional 670 million passenger trips could be expected, resulting in more than 10.8 billion trips per year. If pump prices jump to $5 a gallon, the report predicts an additional 1.5 billion passenger trips can be expected, resulting in more than 11.6 billion trips per year. And if prices were to soar to $6 a gallon, expectations go as high as an additional 2.7 billion passenger trips, resulting in more than 12.9 billion trips per year.

"The volatility of the price at the pump is another wake up call for our nation to address the increasing demand for public transportation services," said APTA President William Millar. "We must make significant, long-term investments in public transportation or we will leave our fellow Americans with limited travel options, or in many cases stranded without travel options. Public transit is the quickest way for people to beat high gas prices if it is available."

The [Barack] Obama Administration's transportation authorization blueprint and proposal . . . increases public transit investment by 128 percent over the next six years.

Many of the public transit systems across the country are already seeing large ridership increases, some reaching double digits in the month of February as compared to the previous year. For instance; the South Florida Regional Transportation Authority in Pompano Beach, FL increased by 10.6 percent; Southeastern Pennsylvania Transportation Authority of Philadelphia, PA increased by 10 percent; and the Capitol Corridor Joint Powers Authority of Oakland, CA increased by 14 percent.

"We saw this same story in 2008 and several times before where high gas prices caught our country without adequate travel options," said Millar. "However, this time we can write a happy ending and make sure investment is made to expand public transportation so that more Americans have a choice in how they travel."

Public Transit Investments Needed

APTA supports the [Barack] Obama Administration's transportation authorization blueprint and proposal which increases public transit investment by 128 percent over the next six years. This type of investment would help close the gap for the 46 percent of Americans who do not have access to public transportation. . . .

The projected estimates use the 2010 APTA Public Transportation Ridership Report as a baseline. The ridership is then increased by the reported elasticity multiplied by the projected price change to show ridership growth at a given increase above the average price for regular gasoline as reported in the last 2010 report by the Energy Information Administration of the U.S. Department of Energy.

The United States Must Invest in Public Transportation

Christian Science Monitor

The Christian Science Monitor *provides national and international news both online and through its weekly news magazine.*

High gas prices are prying record numbers of Americans from their cars and onto buses, subways, and commuter trains. That has many pluses: It eases pocketbook expenses, road congestion, and pollution. But it's also straining providers of mass transit—a signal for needed change.

In Washington DC, the Metro subway and bus system is so stretched at peak hours that officials say the government and other large employers may have to mandate staggered work schedules if gas goes over $5 a gallon—once unimaginable.

In San Francisco and the Bay Area, seats near the doors of some BART trains have been removed to create more standing room for a surge in commuters. Meanwhile, about 20 percent of the nation's public bus operators have had to reduce service because of the high cost of diesel fuel, according to the American Public Transport Association (APTA).

Expanding Mass Transit—A Difficult Task

Mass-transit ridership that's at its highest in 50 years presents an opportunity to beef up outdated systems in many areas of the country. But it's not going to be easy.

For starters, the same price pinch that's squeezing drivers is being felt by transit operators. They must pay more for fuel and their revenue sources are declining as the economy slows.

Christian Science Monitor, "For Mass Transit, Mass Investment: With Record Ridership and Fuel Prices, Subways, Trains, and Buses Are Strapped," June 16, 2008. Copyright © 2008 by Christian Science Publishing Society. All rights reserved. Reproduced by permission from the *Christian Science Monitor*, www.csmonitor.com.

More people may be exchanging traffic for tokens, but in some cases, fares cover as little as 20 percent of operating expenses. Mass transit depends greatly on local, state, and federal money—from sales taxes, for instance, which are slowing with the economy, and from gas taxes, which have not kept up with inflation.

Only 20 percent of Americans live near public transport.

As a result, public transit operators are increasing fares and delaying projects and improvements—just what the country doesn't need at a time of increased demand. APTA estimates that $45 billion to $60 billion annually is what's needed to invest in America's aging public buses, rail transit, and facilities. Yet current capital spending is only about $13 billion a year.

Public officials may wonder whether the demand is here to stay. During the 1970s oil crises, when folks lined up for gas, public ridership increased—but then dropped again. Only 5 percent of Americans now commute to work using public transport.

America's passion for automobiles—for the independence and comfort they provide—runs deep, and carmakers want to keep it that way with more fuel-efficient models. At the same time, only 20 percent of Americans live near public transport.

It's one thing to take temporary measures such as extending hours, adding more train cars, and bringing back bus-only lanes. It's quite another to expand train station parking areas and construct subway or light rail lines.

But those who hesitate should consider this: The days of $1.50-a-gallon gas are long gone, while traffic congestion is growing. Over the next 50 years, the US population is expected to increase by 150 million people. An ongoing trend back to urban areas shows at least some people are tired of the expense and time of exurban living.

Look to Seattle for an example of needed foresight. It's nearly finished with its 1996 expansion to its commuter rail network, and just in time. Last year [2007], ridership shot up 28 percent—the highest rate in the country.

Rejecting High-Speed Rail Systems Is a Mistake Given Rising Gas Prices

Rob Kerth

Rob Kerth is a policy analyst with the Frontier Group, a public policy organization that works for a cleaner environment and a fairer and more democratic society.

Last Friday [March 4, 2011], Florida Gov. Rick Scott officially drove the nail in the coffin of the proposed high-speed rail line from Tampa to Orlando. The decision to reject $2.4 billion in federal funds for the line was, according to Scott, all about the money—specifically, the desire to protect Floridians from what he believed would be inevitable cost overruns and operating subsidies for the train.

Just how big those overruns would be, or whether they would exist at all, is a point of some contention. Scott relied on the ideologically driven Reason Institute's estimate of a potential $3 billion cost overrun in rejecting the high-speed rail line. His claim that the train would require ongoing taxpayer support once it began running, meanwhile, conflicts with an independent study released Wednesday by the Florida Department of Transportation which concluded that, far from needing a subsidy, the Tampa-to-Orlando line would have produced operating surpluses as large as $29 million per year within a decade.

But for the sake of argument, let's assume that Scott is right and Floridians do end up on the hook for $3 billion in the process of building a state-of-the-art high-speed rail system. What does that really mean?

One way to understand it is to consider that Floridians drive more than 190 billion miles every year—an average of roughly 10,500 miles per person. That amount of driving requires roughly 8.5 billion gallons of gasoline. That means that every time gas prices rise 35 cents, Floridians pay out an extra $3 billion annually for gas—the same as the high-end estimate Governor Scott gave for cost overruns from the rail project.

By failing to invest in transportation alternatives like high-speed rail, we are consigning Americans to further dependence on fossil fuels.

As it turns out, last week gas prices rose by 19 cents—the second largest 1-week increase since 1990. And since Valentine's Day, gas prices have increased by more than 40 cents. In other words, if gas prices remain at their current levels, Floridians will face a $3 billion hit to their pocketbooks this year—only instead of that money going toward the construction of clean, cutting-edge transportation that creates jobs and boosts the Florida economy, it will instead find its way into the pockets of multinational oil companies and the coffers of countries from Saudi Arabia to Venezuela.

Shortsighted Decisions

Rick Scott isn't the only governor making shortsighted decisions about high-speed rail. When Wisconsin's Governor Scott Walker rejected funding for high-speed rail in his state, he cited the expected $8 million annual operating subsidy as the reason for his cancellation. Wisconsinites drove 58 billion miles in 2009, consuming about 2.5 billion gallons of gas in the process. That means that over the course of a year, Wisconsinites pay out an extra $8 million dollars if the price of gas rises 0.3 cents.

At times of fiscal distress, its fully appropriate for public officials to be careful about the expenditure of public funds.

But it is important to remember that inaction is a form of action, and that by failing to invest in transportation alternatives like high-speed rail, we are consigning Americans to further dependence on fossil fuels—and further exposure to oil price spikes like the ones this winter.

High-speed rail makes sense. By refusing to invest in it when they have the chance, Governors Scott and Walker are keeping their states at the mercy of gas prices. If the governors really want to look out for the financial best interests of their constituents, it's time to stop making penny-wise, pound-foolish choices, and make the critical investments that will pay off for their states over the long term.

Increases in Public Transportation Use Are Shortlived

Owen McShane

Owen McShane is director of the Centre for Resource Management Studies, an organization established to educate the public about planning issues and promote quality planning projects in New Zealand.

Since the oil spike in the early seventies, enthusiasts for public transport have predicted that high prices for petrol would trigger a public transport revolution as people finally broke their "addiction" to the motor car and changed their travel mode to buses and trains.

Since then, price bubbles have increased public transport use, and lowered car miles traveled. But these changes have proved to be short-lived. More drive more.

Yet standard theory says that people respond to prices. Surely people should respond to increased petrol prices by changing their mode of travel. But why hasn't it happened in the past? More importantly, will it magically happen in the future?

Many Responses to Higher Gas Prices

The answer is that most drivers do respond to increased oil prices but they have many choices as to how to respond. You may switch to public transport provided it takes you where you want to go at a reasonable price. The problem is that part of the "reasonable price" includes the price of the increased time it takes to get to the final destination. Also, surveys reveal that when people climb into their car at the end of the day they feel they have actually arrived at "home." Bus and train travel significantly defers their arrival in their own private space.

So, given time, people change their behaviour in many ways, so as to maintain the comfort, convenience, and overall efficiency of the car. For example:

1. They may decide to buy a smaller or more fuel-efficient car.

2. They may relocate either their home or their job to reduce travel costs and times—provided the land market is flexible.

3. If the local land-market is inflexible they may move to another town, or another country.

4. They may modify all their travel behaviour by better trip planning, commuter car-pooling (with prioritized parking) and general ride and task sharing.

5. They may choose to telecommute, car-pool, park-share, and ride-share.

People know how they want to live and they value their personal mobility.

Fuel costs are only a small component of total motoring costs. Cars today are lasting longer, are more reliable, are cheaper to run, and are kept in use longer. When oil was cheaper total costs of motoring were higher. That's one reason why we are driving more.

Sudden spikes in petrol prices do affect the transportation modal split, but these spikes carry less significance than media reports would suggest, and tend to be of much shorter duration than the advocates of transportation revolution predict. People know how they want to live and they value their personal mobility.

No Time for Massive Investments in Public Transit

This is not a trivial issue because [local government] councils ... are demanding that government funds massive investments in public transport because of the current oil spike, the upward blip in public transport use, and of course "Peak Oil."

The Peak Oil pessimists seem to believe no alternative to the petrol driven car exists. They also seem to ignore the increasing evidence of vast oil and gas reserves being discovered from everywhere, the eastern Mediterranean to the shores off Brazil and the American Great Plains.

A host of emerging technologies will more than compensate for any increase in the price of oil-based fuels—even for vehicles that continue to run on fossil fuels. Think of the hybrid car topping up the batteries from solar panels in the roof. Robot cars and electronically convoyed trucks hugely increase lane capacity. There are so many it would need another column to list them. The pessimists complain that it will take far too long to ring such changes in the vehicle fleet. In the next breath they talk about reshaping the urban-form, mainly by the densification of our major cities. Short of another Luftwaffe arriving on the scene, such urban renewal is hardly likely to happen overnight. Technology churns faster than cities. Try buying a Gestetner, a Telex machine, a slide rule, or a film for your camera.

Urban economist, Anthony Downs, writing in "Still Stuck in Traffic?" reminds us:

> "... trying to decrease traffic congestion by raising residential densities is like trying to improve the position of a painting hung too high on the living room wall by jacking up the ceiling instead of moving the painting."

Yet [governments] throughout the affluent world, seem determined to raise the ceilings—with no regard for costs.

The Need for More Roads

One of the arguments used against building more roads—and especially against more motorways—is that as soon as they are built they become congested again because of "induced demand." Such "induced demand" is surely the natural expression of suppressed demand. It seems unlikely that motorists will mindlessly drive between different destinations for no other reason than they can.

This is the time to invest in an enhanced roading network while making incremental investments in flexible public transport.

However, let us accept for a moment that "induced demand" is real, and suggests that improving the road network is a fruitless exercise. Advocates of expensive rail networks claim they will reduce congestion on the roads and improve the lot of private vehicle users as a consequence.

But surely, if the construction of an expensive rail network does reduce congestion on the roads then induced demand will rapidly restore the status quo. Maybe the theory is sound after all. It would explain why no retrofitted rail networks have anywhere resulted in reduced congestion.

This is the time to invest in an enhanced roading network while making incremental investments in flexible public transport. Roads can be shared by buses, trucks, vans, cars, taxis, shuttle-buses, motor-cycles and cyclists—unless compulsive regulators say they are for buses only. Railway lines can be used only by trains and if we build them in the wrong place they soon run empty. The Romans built roads and we still use them.

In a techno-novel published in 1992, [author] Michael Crichton pauses in his narrative to explain what an email is. That's not long ago.

The one certainty is that the internet/computer world will have the same impact on transport as it has already had on communications. Transport deals with bits while communication deals with bytes.

The end result will be a similar blurring of the line between public and private transport that has already happened between public and private communication. The outcomes are beyond our imagination.

We should get used to it, and realise that making cities more expensive and harder to get around in does not make them more liveable.

Recession Hits Transit Budgets Despite Rising Need

Bob Salsberg

Bob Salsberg is a reporter for The Associated Press, *a US-based global news agency.*

Boston—On a chilly evening last February, a commuter train bound for Worcester, Mass., broke down outside Boston, transforming passengers' usual 80-minute commute into a four-hour nightmare.

The train's failure was among the winter lowlights for the Boston-area commuter rail system's fleet of 80 aging locomotives which, among other woes, have had trouble starting, keeping auxiliary power functioning for lighting systems and maintaining enough air pressure for braking systems, according to transit officials.

"I can't rely on it at all," said Frank Summers, who has been commuting to Boston from suburban Ashland for about seven years and believes service is declining. "It's always jammed-packed and rarely on time."

The commuter trains are run by a firm under a contract with the Massachusetts Bay Transportation Authority, known in Boston as the T. The T's equipment woes are hardly uncommon for big-city systems, and its financial struggles are shared by almost every transit system in the U.S., big and small.

The Great Recession and cuts in government subsidies have wreaked havoc on mass transit in America, even as rising gasoline prices have pushed up demand for reliable service. By one survey, more than 80 percent of U.S. transit systems had cut service, raised fares or both since the economic downturn started.

Cash-strapped and debt-ridden systems have put off new equipment purchases and other upgrades as they struggle to maintain daily operations. The Federal Transit Administration has pointed to tens of billions of dollars in deferred maintenance, a problem particularly acute for older urban systems.

William Millar, president of the Association of Public Transportation Agencies, said there are signs of financial improvement, but it's not enough to make up for the needs.

"We still have a significant majority of systems that are still running unfunded deficits, that are still going to have to consider further fare increases and further service cuts, though they certainly don't want to do those things," he said.

More riders represent a mixed bag for operators. Fare revenue goes up, of course, but the gains can easily be offset by the higher fuel costs that systems must incur.

Especially when ridership is growing. In Boston, for example, ridership is up 5 percent from last year. In an attempt to keep pace, the T bought two new commuter rail locomotives this year—the first new ones in 20 years—and is pledging to continue efforts to modernize the line, which includes the nation's oldest subway system.

"Almost universally, across the political spectrum, people are saying rising gas prices are making them nervous, that they really want to have more and better transit options," said David Goldberg, communications director for Transportation of America, a coalition representing the interests of transit users.

More riders represent a mixed bag for operators. Fare revenue goes up, of course, but the gains can easily be offset by the higher fuel costs that systems must incur.

An influx of riders also might generate greater political support for mass transit, but the added strain on aging and overtaxed equipment could frustrate commuters and leave them ready to return to their cars when gas prices ease.

A 2009 Federal Transit Administration study that examined the "state of good repair" of the nation's seven largest rail transit agencies—New York, Boston, Philadelphia, Washington, Chicago, San Francisco and the New Jersey Transit System—found anything but good repair.

The report found that 35 percent of all rail assets of those agencies were in subpar condition. Another 35 percent were deemed adequate, and only 30 percent were in good or excellent condition. Upgrades would cost the seven largest systems $50 billion, the agency estimated.

Add in the rest of the country's public transit systems, and the maintenance backlog mushrooms to $78 billion.

Millar's group surveyed its 1,500 agencies and found that at least 40 percent were delaying capital improvements.

"The problem is to try to keep fares to a reasonable level, to try to keep services at a reasonable level, they have had to let some maintenance practices slip," he said. "Of course they are concerned about safety, so they try hard not to defer anything of a major safety need."

It's not just the major systems that are being forced to scrimp.

The Transit Authority of River City, which provides bus service for five counties in the greater Louisville, Ky., region, laid off 42 operators and mechanics last year and 10 administrative employees the previous year.

The authority's executive director, J. Barry Barker, said the system also was forced to reduce service and raise fares by $1 to $2.50 for express buses. Preventing further cuts or steeper fare hikes has meant sacrificing some improvements.

"The feds have a guideline that you can replace a full-size, 40-foot bus every 12 years. Basically I don't know anybody in the business who is replacing them after 12 years, and it's typically 14–16 (years)," he said.

Over the last several years, the authority has purchased only about half the replacement buses needed to meet even the longer cycle.

Federal support for mass transit comes largely in the form of the gasoline tax, with 2.86 cents per gallon of the federal tax earmarked for transit. But revenue has been declining as fewer Americans drive and many who do have switched to more fuel-efficient vehicles.

Federal funding also has strings attached.

The financial crunch has prompted creative approaches to generate additional money for transit systems.

Transit systems in larger cities can apply it only toward capital improvements, while systems in areas with populations of 200,000 or less can use federal money to pay operating expenses. Federal stimulus money, now ending, provided a short-term boost with 1,072 grants worth $8.8 billion for special transit projects. That included the purchase of new buses and rail cars, according to the Federal Transit Administration.

Going to the ballot box has become a popular tool for systems trying to raise revenue, and voters have generally seemed receptive.

In 2010, voters nationwide approved 73 percent of transportation-related ballot questions, many calling for increases in sales or property taxes.

In Missouri, St. Joseph boasts of having one the nation's oldest public transit systems, dating to when horses pulled large coaches before the Civil War. But with revenue falling and costs increasing for fuel, health insurance and liability coverage, the system had to go to local voters for a one-quarter cent sales tax increase in 2008 to avoid shutting down some of its eight bus routes.

But it may be only a temporary patch.

"We raised our sales tax, but the people haven't been buying as much stuff. It's not producing the revenue we would have hoped," said Andrew Clements, assistant director for St. Joseph public works. "As the future looms, eight to 10 years from now, we may be looking at a much harder challenge."

The public transit system serving Grand Rapids, Mich., won voter approval of property tax measures in 2000, 2003 and 2007—allowing it to expand from 63 buses in 1999 to 105 buses this year at peak hours and more than double its ridership, said Peter Varga, chief executive officer of The Rapid.

The agency hasn't run a deficit in a decade, nor has it increased fares or cut service, he said, even as Michigan's economy has tanked.

The financial crunch has prompted creative approaches to generate additional money for transit systems.

To help close a projected $127 million operating deficit, the Boston-area system adopted a plan to sell bonds secured by future parking revenue and use proceeds to help cover operating expenses and pay off future debt. The agency also plans to sell more advertising space at stations and on trains and buses, and is moving its unionized employees to a more flexible state-run health insurance plan.

Passengers no longer will get a free ride if their bus or train is more than a half-hour late, but fare hikes, for now at least, are off the table.

Historically, fares have accounted for 30 percent to 40 percent of total transit revenue nationwide.

Experts who point to more modern and reliable systems around the world say U.S. cities must find ways to overcome financial hurdles and invest in public transit.

In Los Angeles, voters agreed in 2008 to pay a half-cent sales tax over the next 30 years to fund a massive expansion of public transportation. But Mayor Antonio Villaraigosa doesn't want to wait that long for the projects to be completed, so he's proposed borrowing billions from the federal government so the work can be done in just a decade.

"It's becoming clear that (cities) have to remain healthy and vital, and it's also becoming increasingly clear that a functioning transit system is a big part of that," said Robert Puentes, a transportation expert with the Brookings Institution.

Cuts in Federal Public Transportation Funding Could Further Limit Mass Transit

Keith Laing

Keith Laing is a reporter for The Hill, *a congressional newspaper that publishes daily whenever the US Congress is in session.*

Transportation advocates are wasting no time trying to convince lawmakers not to cut spending on public transit systems.

Though they have already secured stable funding through March of next year [2012], public transportation groups are worried Congress could impose significant cuts in a long-term highway bill, which would include public transportation funding.

On Tuesday [September 20, 2011], rallies were staged across subway and bus systems around the country to alert passengers to the potential cuts, dubbed "Don't X out public transit."

"Safe, reliable public transit is at risk," American Public Transportation Association President William Millar said Tuesday on a conference call with reporters.

Proposed Cuts in Public Transit

House Republicans have proposed a long-term bill that would maintain the same 80 percent-to-20 percent split between highway projects and public transportation funding, but would reduce overall spending to about $35 billion per year.

Transit advocates argue that would cut their portion of the budget pie by as much as a third, resulting in the loss of 620,000 transportation jobs in both the public and private sectors.

They also say such cuts would imperil daily commutes in cities large and small across the country at a time when passengers are already paying more for rides and communities are being forced to cut back services.

"We've already seen the highest fare increases and worst service cuts in 60 years," John Robert Smith, president and CEO of Reconnecting America and co-chairman of Transportation for America, said Tuesday.

The American Public Transportation Association and the Amalgamated Transit Union were also involved in Tuesday's effort.

The groups might not have to worry about further cuts for the time being.

The stagnant economy had already taken a broad hit on public transit funding at the local level. Budget cuts from Congress would only make matters worse.

Congress last week approved legislation to extend highway and aviation funding through March of next year. That bill would expire just as lawmakers are focusing more and more on the 2012 campaign, leading some to think further short-term extensions are likely.

But that isn't stopping public transportation groups from making their case now.

Smith said that the stagnant economy had already taken a broad hit on public transit funding at the local level. Budget cuts from Congress would only make matters worse, he said.

"Some may think we can't afford to invest in transit," Smith said. "I think the question is, can we afford not to?"

Long-Term Funding Issues

The House proposal for a long-term bill would spend $235 billion over six years on highways and public transit. GOP [Republican] lawmakers argue this figure is equal to the dollars raised by the federal gas tax, which is authorized by the highway bill.

The Senate has suggested a shorter, two-year, $109 billion bill, which increases current levels of funding for inflation.

Given the political climate, some think a long-term deal is not within reach, but Millar said political considerations could help advocates make their case.

"It's fashionable in Washington to look at the political season as negative, but most congressmen and senators are going to want to go home and say, 'I did something,'" he said in an interview with *The Hill*. "I don't know many congressmen who are going to want to go home and say, 'Guess what? I just cut the road budget by 30 percent.'"

While lawmakers face serious hurdles in winning a longer-term transportation bill, the issues aren't quite as thorny as the labor dispute that bogged down an extension of the Federal Aviation Administration's [FAA] authorization.

Mostly because of labor disputes, lawmakers have approved 22 short-term extensions of the FAA bill.

Asked if the highway bill might follow that pattern, Millar could only say he hoped not.

"I certainly hope we don't get to 22 extensions," he said. "To paraphrase an old TV show, I think eight is enough."

Millar said he was optimistic because "the issues are well-known" involving the transportation bill, and Democratic leaders in the Senate and Republican leaders in the House were personally involved in the short-term extension.

"I saw it as a good sign that Majority Leader [Harry] Reid [D-Nev.] and Speaker [John] Boehner [R-Ohio] were able to get together and get a six-month extension," he said. "I think that's a very good sign."

High-Speed Rail Is Too Expensive

Joel Kotkin

Joel Kotkin is a writer and author, a distinguished presidential fellow in urban futures at Chapman University in Orange, California, and executive editor of www.newgeography.com, a website that focuses on economic development, metropolitan demographics, and community leadership.

Perhaps nothing so illustrates President [Barack] Obama's occasional disconnect with reality than his fervent advocacy of high-speed rail. Amid mounting pressure for budget cuts that affect existing programs, including those for the inner city, the president has made his $53 billion proposal to create a national high-speed rail network as among his top priorities.

Our President may be an intelligent and usually level-headed man, but this represents a serious case of policy delusion. As Robert Samuelson pointed out in *Newsweek*, high-speed rail is not an appropriate fit for a country like the U.S. Except for a few areas, notably along the Northeast Corridor, the U.S. just lacks the density that would make such a system work. Samuelson calls the whole idea "a triumph of fancy over fact."

Extraordinary Costs

Arguably the biggest problem with high-speed rail is its extraordinary costs, which would require massive subsidies to keep operating. Unlike the Federal Highway Program, largely financed by the gas tax, high-speed rail lacks any credible source of funding besides taxpayer dollars.

Part of the pitch for high-speed rail is nationalistic. To be a 21st century super power, we must emulate current No. 2 China. But this is a poor reason to indulge in a hugely expensive program when the U.S. already has the world's most evolved highway, freight rail and airline system.

The prospect of mounting and uncontrollable costs has led governors to abandon high-speed projects in Ohio, Wisconsin and most recently Florida, where a battle to save the Tampa-Orlando line has begun.

Also, if the U.S. were to follow the Chinese model, as some have suggested, perhaps it should impose rule from a Washington version of a centralized authoritarian government. After all, dictatorships are often quite adept at "getting things done." But in a democracy "getting things done" means balancing interests and efficiencies, not following orders from above.

In China high-speed rail is so costly that the trains are too expensive for the average citizen. Furthermore, construction costs are so high the Chinese Academy of Sciences has already warned that its debts may not be payable. This experience with ballooning costs and far lower fare revenues have raised taxpayer obligations in Taiwan and Korea and added to heavily to the national debt in Japan.

The prospect of mounting and uncontrollable costs has led governors to abandon high-speed projects in Ohio, Wisconsin and most recently Florida, where a battle to save the Tampa-Orlando line has begun. In times of budget stress, the idea of building something new, and historically difficult to contain by costs, becomes a hard sell.

Oddly, the leaders of California, faced with one of the worst fiscal positions in the country, are determined to spend several billions on what *Sacramento Bee* columnist Dan Walters has dubbed a train to nowhere for 54 miles between Madera and Corcoran—two unremarkable and remote Central Valley towns. The proposal makes the former Alaska Sen. Ted Stevens' notorious "bridges to nowhere" project seem like frugal public policy.

California's train to nowhere has been justified as part of [a] wider project to construct a statewide system. But the whole idea makes little financial sense: The University of California's Institute for Transportation describes the high-speed proposal as based on an "inconsistent model" whose ridership projections are simply not "reliable."

Equally suspect are cost estimates, which have doubled (after adjustment for inflation) from 1999 to $42.6 billion last year and a new study says that the project could currently cost close to $65 billion. Costs for a ticket from Los Angeles to San Francisco, originally pegged at $55 one way, had nearly doubled by 2009, and now some estimates place it at about . . . $100 or perhaps [as] much as $190—considerably more than an advanced-purchase ticket on far faster Southwest Airlines.

There's growing political opposition to the system as well, and not just among penny-pinching right-wingers. Residents and local officials in the San Francisco peninsula, a wealthy and reliably liberal portion of Silicon Valley, largely oppose plans to route the line through their communities. This includes some prominent liberal legislators, such as San Mateo's Assembly member Jerry Hill, who has threatened to put high-speed rail back on the ballot if costs start to surpass initial estimates. Another Democrat, California Treasurer Bill Lockyer has doubts that the rail authority will be able to sell the deal to potential bond-buyers—due in part to a lack of consistent estimates in ridership or cost.

Powerful Supporters of High-Speed Rail

So why is Obama still so determined to push the high-speed boondoggle? Largely it's a deadly combination of theology and money. Powerful rail construction interests, notably the German giant Siemens, are spreading cash like mustard on a bratwurst to promote the scheme. Add to that construction unions and the ever voracious investment banks who would love to pocket fees for arranging to sell the bonds and you have interests capable of influencing either party.

High-speed rail is far more expensive than such things as fixing current commuter rail and subways or expanding both public and private bus service.

Then there's what might be called the "density lobby"— big city mayors, construction firms and the urban land owners. These magnates, who frequently extort huge public subsidies for their projects, no doubt think it grand to spend billions of public funds on something that might also increase the value of their real estate.

And finally there are the true believers, notably planners, academics, green activists and an army of rail fans. These are people who believe America should be more like Europe— denser, more concentrated in big cities and tied to the rails. "High speed rail is not really about efficient transport," notes California transit expert and accountant Tom Rubin. "It's all about shaping cities for a certain agenda."

A Chorus of Opposition

Yet despite their power, these forces face mounting obstacles. As transportation expert Ken Orski points out, the balance of power in the House [of Representatives] now lies with suburban and rural legislators, whose constituents would not benefit much from high-speed rail. And then there are governors, increasingly Republican and conservative, very anxious not to add potentially huge obligations to their already stressed budgets.

Gasoline

The most decisive opposition, however, could come from those who favor transit spending but understand the need to prioritize. High-speed rail is far more expensive than such things as fixing current commuter rail and subways or expanding both public and private bus service. Indeed, the money that goes to urban rail often ends up being diverted from other, more cost-effective systems, notably buses.

The choice between high-speed rail and more conventional, less expensive transit has already been presaged in the fight against expanding LA's expensive rail system by organizations representing bus riders. These activists contend that rail swallows funds that could be spent on buses

Much the same case is being made [in] the San Francisco peninsula. The opponents of high-speed rail on the San Francisco peninsula are outraged that the state would spend billions on a chancy potential boondoggle when the popular Caltrain commuter rail service is slated to be curtailed or even eliminated.

One can of course expect that anti-spending conservatives will be the biggest cheerleaders for high-speed rail's decline. But transit advocates may be forced to join the chorus of opposition, in order to steer transit spending towards more basic priorities [such] as buses in Los Angeles, subways in New York or commuter rail in the San Francisco Bay Area.

In an era of tough budgets, and proposed cutbacks on basic services, setting sensible transportation priorities is crucial. Spending billions on a conveyance that will benefit a relative handful of people and places is not just illogical. It's obscene.

CHAPTER 4

What Are the Keys to Oil and Gasoline Independence?

Chapter Preface

American President Barack Obama has identified energy independence as a major goal of his administration's energy policy. However, the president is also concerned about the environment and carbon emissions that contribute to global warming, so he has sought to achieve energy independence mainly by boosting alternative and clean energy technologies rather than by focusing solely on increasing the nation's production of fossil fuels such as oil and natural gas. Supporters see the Obama administration's energy positions as visionary because the United States can never drill enough oil to be free from foreign imports. Critics, on the other hand, think the Obama energy plan is a disaster and argue that alternative fuels are decades away and that America must seek to produce as much oil and natural gas as possible for the near future to minimize the nation's reliance on foreign producers. The issue may be somewhat moot, because the country's economic problems and debt crisis have made most of the administration's energy ideas impossible to achieve, at least during the president's first term.

President Obama was successful, however, in funding some clean energy projects during his first year in office. For example, Obama included a number of energy initiatives in the American Recovery and Reinvestment Act of 2009 (ARRA)—legislation enacted in response to the economic crisis then facing the country. The Act's purpose was to create jobs, spur economic activity, and fund long-term US investments in infrastructure. Many of the projects included in the law were for the development of clean energy and clean transportation—that is, renewable, low-carbon or emissions-free energy, such as solar, wind, and biofuels. According to some reports, the Act contained $70 billion in direct spending and tax credits for these types of projects.

One of the biggest ARRA-funded projects, for example, was a $3.4 billion Smart Grid Investment Grant designed to help utility companies and others to improve the US electrical grid. The program provided federal assistance to cover up to 50 percent of investments in so-called smart grid technologies with the goal of making the electrical system more efficient and more flexible in responding to energy demands. For example, a digitized grid would connect rural energy producers with urban power grids and would allow power companies to better manage demands for energy, by cutting electricity to non-essential uses during certain times of the day or during demand surges. Smart grid technology also would be better able to deliver electricity from various renewable sources and to accommodate new green technologies, such as plug-in electric cars. Smart grid technology, supporters also hope, will help repel security threats, such as cyber attacks, on the US electrical grid.

Another priority in ARRA was the Advanced Research Projects Agency-Energy (ARPA-E) project, which created a new government agency to promote and fund research and development of renewable energy technologies, such as solar, wind, geothermal, biofuels, and biomass energy crops. A host of related energy technologies also received grants, including energy efficiency projects, smart building technologies, and energy storage ideas, including improved lithium-ion batteries designed to power electric cars. About $400 million was budgeted for the first year, with plans to increase this to the $1 billion range in later years.

Other parts of ARRA funded a variety of additional energy initiatives. A weatherization program funded by ARRA, for example, allocated about $9.5 billion to weatherize 75 percent of federal buildings as well as more than one million private low-income homes around the country. ARRA also devoted funds to projects that train people for green jobs.

Apart from ARRA, the Obama administration also has taken several other actions to further its energy goals. The US Environmental Protection Agency (EPA) set new fuel economy standards for cars and light trucks that will raise the average fuel economy to 35.5 miles per gallon by 2016, and to 54.5 miles per gallon by 2025. The agency is also developing the first national fuel economy standards for heavier trucks, vans, and buses, designed to make those vehicles more fuel-efficient by 2018. In addition, as of January 2011, the EPA began regulating carbon emissions of companies operating in the United States as part of the Clean Air Act. The EPA was given this new authority as a result of a 2007 Supreme Court ruling granting the agency the authority to regulate emissions as a form of air pollution. Moreover, the Obama administration has suggested that it favors national Clean Energy Standards (CES) that would require 80 percent of US electrical power to be derived from zero- or low-carbon sources by 2035.

Although President Obama has also declared that environmentally friendly domestic oil production and nuclear power need to be part of the US energy mix, events have overtaken these initiatives. For example, the BP oil spill catastrophe in the Gulf of Mexico in 2010 caused President Obama to impose a moratorium on new oil drilling permits. The moratorium has been lifted but the administration still has been reluctant to issue deepwater drilling permits. Also, the president's support for nuclear power was made more difficult after the 2011 Japanese earthquake and tsunami, which destroyed the Fukushima nuclear facilities in that country. After the Japan disaster, the president continued to voice support for building more nuclear plants but this position increasingly is not supported by US public opinion because of concerns about the safety of nuclear power.

Many commentators predict that little action will be taken on energy issues given the gridlock in Congress, the focus on jobs and the national debt, and the upcoming 2012 presidential election. The president's cap-and-trade legislation died in the Senate in 2009, and his opponents in Congress have only grown more powerful since then. Unless President Obama is re-elected with majorities in both houses of Congress in 2012, many political pundits think it is unlikely that he will be able to achieve any energy goals that require legislation. Meanwhile, some opponents want to block the administration's regulatory energy efforts, such as the EPA's regulation of carbon emissions as part of the Clean Air Act. The authors of the following viewpoints present some of the differing views about the ways to achieve oil and gas independence.

The United States Must Increase Domestic Oil Production

Steve Huntley

Steve Huntley is a columnist for the Chicago Sun-Times, *an American newspaper.*

Predictions of $5 a gallon gasoline this summer [2011] are a stark reminder the nation doesn't have a comprehensive or even coherent energy policy to protect our economy in these uncertain times for a reliable, low-cost oil supply.

Obsessed with climate change, President [Barack] Obama and Democrats have made green energy the golden goal of U.S. energy strategy though many technological obstacles make wind, solar, hydrogen and electrical cars as mainstays of everyday life many years or even decades away.

Oil remains the lifeblood of the economy. It fuels our cars, the transportation system for moving products, the growing of food and the manufacture of products ranging from anesthetics to ballpoint pens to clothing to lipstick to paint to refrigerators to phones and on and on. We can't do without it.

Threats to Oil Markets

Libya is a relatively minor actor in oil production and the loss of much of its output from the civil war there has been offset by a drop in demand in Japan caused by its earthquake-tsunami disaster. But the enterprising Japanese will soon be rebuilding. China's booming economy slurps up 10 percent more oil than a year ago. The slowly gathering economic recovery here and in Europe will push up oil prices.

They have risen 20 percent since the Mideast uprisings started. No one knows how long Libyan oil will be off line. More critically, the contest between Iran and Saudi Arabia in Bahrain could become destabilizing. The Bahrain affair is not a carbon copy of pro-democracy movements elsewhere but one inflamed by sectarian passions—a ruling Sunni minority against a restive, resentful Shiite majority.

Mideast unpredictability and the potential of supply interruptions demand greater domestic oil and gas output.

That imbalance also is at play in Saudi Arabia. Riyadh is helping neighboring Bahrain suppress the protest movement out of fear revolt might spread to its own Shiite population. Strife in Saudi Arabia, with its huge petroleum reserves, could wreak chaos in oil markets.

The Need to Develop Domestic Oil

Obama recently boasted that U.S. oil production is up on his watch. That's disingenuous as it takes years to bring a well in production, so we're seeing the fruits of projects begun before he took office.

This week we witnessed the incoherent picture of an American president whose administration has impeded oil production in the Gulf of Mexico promoting Brazil's program to exploit its off-shore petroleum resources. "We want to help with technology and support to develop these oil reserves safely, and when you're ready to start selling, we want to be one of your best customers," Obama told an audience in Brasilia.

Mideast unpredictability and the potential of supply interruptions demand greater domestic oil and gas output. That means not just drilling in the Gulf but also developing oil shale resources such as the Green River Formation in the West. The U.S. Geological Survey estimates it holds 1.5 trillion barrels of oil, the largest shale deposits in the world.

Rather than outsource oil jobs to Brazil, the administration should be promoting them here. It's not just good energy policy, it's sound economic strategy. These are good-paying jobs at a time when our economy needs them. For example, mean salaries for oil and gas derrick and drill workers range from $43,000 to $59,000, the Bureau of Labor Statistics reports. Measuring the full range of oil and gas exploration and production jobs shows an average salary of $96,844, more than double the average annual salary of all occupations, according to the American Petroleum Institute.

I continue to believe we need to develop transportation alternatives to oil, such as the alcohol program promoted by the Set America Free coalition. That's not the current ethanol strategy that turns corn into ethanol, raising food prices. Rather it's the production of methanol from coal, natural gas and biomass that can be used in flex-fuel cars. It costs only $100 to make new autos flex-fuel capable.

Still, our dependence on oil is inescapable. We need to develop all domestic sources until the day green energy resources become a reliable, cost-effective alternative.

Oil Independence Is Impossible So Energy Independence Must Be the Goal

Swellsman

Swellsman is a frequent, anonymous blogger on the progressive website Daily Kos.

Something we've been hearing for decades now is that America needs to achieve "energy independence." However, while both Conservatives and Liberals deploy this phrase routinely, they usually intend it to function as shorthand for two very different policy prescriptions. For Conservatives, "energy independence" generally means independence from foreign sources of oil. For Liberals, "energy independence" usually means the creation of sustainable and renewable energy sources.

The two concepts are not the same, and it is a shame that a single phrase has been used to signal both. Although it is probably too late now, our national dialogue would be much improved by using different phrases to distinguish these two positions. What Conservatives are really seeking is "Oil Independence"—the ability to have as much oil as is wanted without being subject to the whims of other nations. What Liberals are really seeking is true "Energy Independence"—the ability to have as much energy as is needed without relying on finite energy sources.

A few recent news stories clearly demonstrate that not only is Energy Independence a more idealistic concept than is simply seeking Oil Independence, it is also much more practical.

Ending Oil Dependence by Force

There are only two ways for America to sever its dependence on oil producing nations: it can either invade those countries that still have sizeable caches of oil and seize those nations' oil fields for itself, or it can boost its domestic production until that production is sufficient to meet all of America's oil needs.

Now there are many who would claim that America already has engaged in the first course of action—and there probably is something to that assertion—but this approach to Oil Independence is clearly unworkable.

First, even setting aside the basic question of morality, a war of aggression to seize oil is incredibly difficult to pull off. It cannot be done openly, because it would result in the aggressor becoming a pariah nation; say whatever you want to about America's might, we still need trading partners. Which means that in order to succeed at something like that, the invading country has to find a pretext to invade a country, topple the government, and then arrange for a compliant successor government to "request" that it stay on and take over oil production (obviously, at extremely advantageous terms). This at least provides a patina of legality, but as the misadventure in Iraq proved it is incredibly difficult to occupy a country that does not really want you there.

Second, even assuming one pulls off a successful smash-n-grab on the international stage, wars of aggression are incredibly expensive ways to obtain any natural resource. What would have been cheaper? Lifting sanctions on Iraq and buying oil on the open market, or invading and occupying the country for decades while at the same time thumbing our nose at the rest of the world and declaring that Iraq's oil belongs to us now—as [business tycoon] Donald Trump actually argues we should do?

No matter how much Conservatives want to believe in "American Exceptionalism," no matter how much they may cling to the Green Lantern Theory of Geopolitics, the fact stubbornly remains (thank God) that neither America nor any other nation has the actual ability to attain Oil Independence by sheer force.

End Oil Dependence by Increasing Production

Exxon Mobile Corp. (XOM) announced it found the equivalent of 700 million barrels of oil beneath the Gulf of Mexico, the biggest discovery in the region in 12 years. The estimated size of the Hadrian field may increase as drilling continues, Exxon said in a statement today [June 16, 2011]. The discovery is about 250 miles (400 kilometers) southwest of New Orleans in 7,000 feet of water, Irving, Texas-based Exxon said. Wow! That certainly sounds big! But let's unpack those three sentences just a little.

First, let's note that the newly discovered Hadrian field is about 2,000 feet even *farther* below sea level than was the field being drilled during the Deepwater Horizon catastrophe last year. So, right there, drilling this oil field presents another possibility of ecologic catastrophe. After all, the reason it took so long to stop all of that oil gushing into the Gulf last year is because it is difficult to do pretty much *anything* that far down.

The United States needs to find about ten new domestic fields a year . . . and bring them online immediately. . . . This clearly is not going to happen.

Second, let's note the length of time that has passed since we last discovered an oil field this significant in the Gulf: 12 years. And one reason this field was not discovered earlier is almost certainly because no one had gone looking for it before; all things being equal, oil companies don't enthuse about drilling for oil a mile and a half below sea level. The only reason they are looking to drill there today is because they've essentially depleted the more easily obtainable oil located on land or in shallow water. The fact that Exxon Mobile is even looking for fields 1 ½ miles below sea level proves how finite a resource oil is. Once you've sucked your milkshake dry, the cup never magically refills; you've got to go find another one, and we've run out of cheap and easy "milkshakes" to exploit.

It doesn't necessarily mean that Exxon Mobile actually has access to 700 million barrels of oil, as it is not yet clear how much of this new find is actually recoverable. (You can never recover all of the oil out of a given field, because the pressure in an oil field decreases as the oil is pumped out of it; eventually, more than a barrel of oil's worth of energy is required to pump up a single barrel of the remaining oil.) But even if all 700 million barrels from this new find were instantly recoverable—and they are not, of course—what does that mean?

Well, according to the CIA [US Central Intelligence Agency] the United States consumed 18.69 million barrels of oil per day back in 2009. Even using this two year old figure, that means that Exxon Mobile's massive new find, the biggest in 12 years, could supply all of America's oil needs for ... 37 days. It means that to replace all of the oil America consumes every year the United States needs to find about ten new domestic fields a year—each one the size of Exxon Mobile's new "massive" discovery—and bring them online immediately. Only then could the United States claim to have truly achieved oil independence.

This clearly is not going to happen.

Right now, global demand for oil runs to about 89 million barrels a day. Which means this is the amount of new oil that needs to be found around the world—every day—just to keep from depleting current oil reserves. Obviously, that is a tall order. For example, even if the global demand for oil were to suddenly stop rising—which it won't—Exxon Mobile's new 700 million barrel oil field would only cover about one week's worth of global consumption. For that matter, Brazil's discovery last October [2011] of a new offshore field estimated at 8 billion barrels of recoverable oil can only meet the world's needs for about 3 months.

Dealing with Peak Oil

Indeed, last year the International Energy Agency [IEA] explicitly acknowledged the fact of "peak oil"—that is, the point at which the global supply of oil maxes out and then begins an inexorable decline—and provided a best estimate as to when it expects that point to be reached: 2035. But even that date, which is only about 24 years away—may be a bit optimistic.

The good people over at Energy Bulletin reviewed the IEA's 2010 World Energy Outlook and summarized the IEA's projections for future global oil production. . . .

Extending from around 2006 until 2035, the IEA estimates that the world's supply of crude oil—that is, oil the way we normally think of it, something liquid that can be pumped out of oil fields—will remain constant. Of course, this isn't great news since global *demand* will continue to rise. But it actually gets worse.

Look at how the IEA anticipates the world will maintain this constant rate of crude oil production. To begin with, the IEA acknowledges that we have begun to see a precipitous drop in production from all currently developed oil fields. The IEA expects that some already identified but as yet undeveloped fields will make up part of this shortfall, but it also acknowledges that production from these newly developed fields will also begin to drop precipitously around 2017.

In fact, the only way the IEA is able to claim that crude oil production will just remain constant until 2035 is by asserting that both of these expected shortfalls will be made up for by *oil fields that have not yet been discovered*—like, for example,

Exxon Mobile's "massive" Hadrian oil field, which can supply the world's needs for a whole week. . . .

The IEA's projections seem an exercise in wishful thinking: "sure, all known oil fields are quickly running out of that sweet, sweet crude, but we'll find some more *somewhere*." In fact, according to its own figures the only way the International Energy Agency avoids the conclusion that "peak oil" already has occurred is by suggesting both that if we clap loudly enough new fields will be discovered *and* that "natural gas liquids" and "unconventional oil"—the really expensive kind, produced from tar sands and shales—will make up the loss.

At least, y'know, for the next 20 years or so.

The United States Must Transition to Low-Carbon Fuels

David Burwell

David Burwell is the director of the Energy and Climate Program at the Carnegie Endowment for International Peace, a private nonprofit organization dedicated to advancing cooperation among nations and promoting active international engagement by the United States.

Four-dollar-a-gallon gas inevitably elicits calls of "drill-baby-drill" to ease the pain felt in Americans' wallets. But the present debate over how to fight high gas prices and whether or not to increase domestic oil production overlooks a key point—peak U.S. oil consumption has already been reached. We are looking at things backwards. The real question is not how much the U.S. can produce locally, but how fast domestic oil demand will decline and how public policy can support this transition. Demand destruction will do more for American national security, the environment, trade balances, and jobs, than ramping up production ever could.

Signs of Reduced Demand for Oil

Green shoots prophesying accelerated declines in American oil consumption are cropping up everywhere. Even before the recession, total domestic oil consumption was in decline and the trend accelerated as the economy lagged. And, importantly, the recovery has not led to the expected increase in consumption. The Energy Information Agency reports that gasoline consumption has declined for sixteen straight weeks compared to sales a year ago. Last week, the year-over-year weekly decline was 3.7 percent. While total travel has bounced back a bit as the economy has picked up, the most important measure of what's happening, vehicle miles traveled per capita, continues to decline.

U.S. vehicle sales also portend increasing declines in oil consumption. In 2008, auto sales, in the face of $4 gas and economic troubles, crashed to nine million vehicles annually. In the first quarter of 2011 they bounced back to a new rate of 13 million vehicles annually as consumers abandoned their gas guzzlers for Detroit's new line of gas sippers. As a result, the economy is exhibiting remarkable resilience amid this new oil price spike. President [Barack] Obama's directive that the entire federal vehicle fleet will be fuel efficient or rely on alternative fuels by 2015 will accelerate this transition.

Consumers are already "producing" new oil by reducing their need for it.

Oil and gas companies are also beginning to demonstrate new doubts about overreliance on oil. Even as oil prices—and profits—rise, windfall earnings are being re-invested more widely. ExxonMobil is only replacing 90 percent of the oil it produces through exploration or acquisition of new oil reserves, instead significantly increasing its investment in natural gas, algae, and other biofuels. BP is doing the same, announcing this week [May 26, 2011] an investment in Verdezyne, maker of a yeast that converts plant sugars to biofuels. Total, the big French oil company, has just bought a 60 percent interest in Sunpower, the largest U.S. solar energy company.

Regulatory policy is also nudging the energy industry off oil. New standards for fuel efficiency and renewable fuels mean that it doesn't take a chemical engineer to understand that oil, the source of 95 percent of transportation fuel, is about to face heavy competition in the fuels market.

Perhaps the most significant incentive driving reduction in oil demand is the price of oil itself. While current prices might be a short-term trend, long-term prices will remain high due to the rapid pace of motorization in China, India, and other developing countries. High world oil prices, while painful at the pump, accelerate turnover to a low-carbon vehicle fleet which, in turn, help reduce the marginal cost of travel even at higher fuel prices.

Moving Away from Oil

With the progress that has already been made, the choice is easy. Transitioning to low-carbon fuels and improving vehicle and system efficiency, promises higher returns in oil independence in the short term than a focus on increasing domestic production that only drains America's reserves faster.

Washington can [reduce demand] . . . by intensifying its efforts to increase fuel efficiency, establishing a low carbon fuel standard, investing in more travel choices, and ending subsidized sprawl.

Consider this: if America fully exploited all its known reserves to meet 100 percent of its domestic needs we would run out of oil within four years. Yes, we have more domestic oil to discover but we are increasingly tapped out on the production side.

History, as well as basic economics, demonstrates that increased domestic oil production does not necessarily lower prices for American consumers. After several years of aggressive incentives to boost domestic production, the percentage of oil the United States imports is 15 percent lower than it was in 2005 though the price of oil has doubled to over $100 a barrel. Obviously, further increases in domestic production will have little to no impact on gasoline prices.

Washington can accelerate demand destruction by intensifying its efforts to increase fuel efficiency, establishing a low carbon fuel standard, investing in more travel choices, and ending subsidized sprawl. It could also extend an olive branch to oil companies by offering to trade oil subsidies for investment tax credits in renewables, or by encouraging pooled energy R&D [research and development] efforts as it is already doing with China. The fact that oil companies are already testing the waters for alternative energy investments indicates that they may be ready to step up their efforts.

The road to oil independence is clear and straight: better to water the green shoots of demand destruction than feed our oil addiction through the chimera of "drill-baby-drill."

The United States Must Promote Electric Vehicles to Achieve Freedom from Oil

Sarah Hodgdon

Sarah Hodgdon is the director of conservation for the Sierra Club, an American environmental organization.

Imagine greater security for our service members abroad. Imagine freedom from the rising prices of the gas pump. Imagine freedom from massive oil spills like the one last year [2010] in the Gulf of Mexico or the one last week [July 1, 2011] in Yellowstone National Park. Imagine freedom from auto tailpipe emissions. Imagine greater economic freedom through reduced national debt and thousands of new clean tech jobs. Imagine freedom from oil altogether.

Promoting Electric Vehicles

This week, an unlikely group of more than 180 companies and organizations—large and small—from nearly every U.S. state joined together to issue a statement asking for comprehensive local, state, and federal programs that will promote plug-in electric vehicles (EVs) and drive us toward freedom from oil. This statement makes it clear more than ever before that there is widespread support for EVs in every part of the country and from a diverse set of economic, security, job growth, environmental, and public health interests.

Look at what our oil dependence is subjecting Americans to: The U.S. armed forces spend up to $83 billion annually protecting vulnerable infrastructure and patrolling oil transit routes. Earlier this year US Navy Secretary Roy Mabus said that "out of every 24 fuel convoys we use [in Afghanistan], a soldier or marine is killed or wounded guarding that convoy. That's a high price to pay for fuel."

Our nation sends up to a third of a trillion dollars overseas each year to purchase foreign oil, often produced by countries that are unstable or unfriendly to American interests. Foreign oil purchases are also responsible for about 50% of the U.S. trade deficit.

New EVs are on the market in select cities nationwide, and by next year, they will be available in nearly every state.

The statement we issued this week on freedom from oil includes companies and organizations with leaders who have served in our Armed Services—such as Brian Patnoe, Vice President of Fleet Sales at CODA Automotive, a Los Angeles, CA-based electric vehicle and battery company.

"I'm proud to be working for a company committed to supporting oil independence and the emerging EV supply chain," said Patnoe. "As a former Marine, it's also exciting for me to see successful business opportunities that support a prosperous oil-free future—from CODA's own parts manufacturers and assembly line workers to electrical workers installing EV chargers and the customers purchasing a whole new type of vehicle."

Necessary Policies

New EVs are on the market in select cities nationwide, and by next year, they will be available in nearly every state. Now, we need to put the right policies, infrastructure, and programs in place to support a cleaner and safer shift in the way we power our vehicles. This week's EV sign-on statement spells out some of the types of policies that will allow us to become EV-ready ASAP:

1. *Expand national, regional, and local efforts that help attract greater concentrations of electric vehicles in communities across the country.*

2. *Remove unnecessary bureaucratic and market obstacles to vehicle electrification nationwide through a variety of policies that:*

    • bolster nationwide installation of and access to basic charging infrastructure, both at people's homes and in public places;

    • incentivize the purchase of electric vehicles and EV charging equipment and streamline the permitting application process for EV charging equipment;

    • educate the public about the benefits of EVs and the costs, opportunities, and logistical considerations involved with EV charging infrastructure;

    • ensure appropriate training for workers installing EV charging equipment and for first responders;

    • encourage utilities to provide attractive rates and programs for EV owners and increase off-peak charging;

    • assist in deployment of clean energy, efficiency, and energy management technologies jointly with vehicle charging; and

    • accelerate advanced battery cost reduction by boosting EV use in fleets, in second use, and in stationary applications.

3. *Ensure US leadership in manufacturing of electric drive vehicles, batteries and components.*

EVs will help us achieve freedom from oil, and they also mean less air pollution. Emissions from EVs are at least 30% lower than those from traditional vehicles—and that's on today's electric grid. As we clean up our grid and rely more and more on renewable sources of power, EVs get even cleaner over time.

Natural Gas-Powered Vehicles Should Be the First Step Toward Energy Independence

David Fessler

David Fessler is the energy and infrastructure expert for Investment U, a website that publishes a daily newsletter and provides other products to help investors.

Why isn't the U.S. government doing more to get us off foreign oil?

Great question. It's one I ask myself all the time.

It was clearly on the minds of many attendees at the Investment U Conference in San Diego a couple of weeks ago [March 2010], too. I lost count of the number of times people asked me about it—and what the United States should be doing to address the problem.

So I decided to see what it would take to drastically cut our oil dependence.

How could we get to the point where we could get by on the oil we have here? To get to the point where it wouldn't be necessary to import it from anyone. Not even Canada. . . .

Getting America Off Foreign Oil . . . Now

Let's start with a few "crude" facts:

- The world produces about 85 million barrels of oil per day (BPD).

- Of that amount, the United States uses 25%, or about 21 million BPD.

David Fessler, "My Plan for Eliminating America's Dependence on Foreign Oil," *Investment U*, no. 1230, April 2, 2010. www.investmentu.com. Copyright © 2010 by Oxford Club/Agora Publishing. All rights reserved. Reproduced by permission.

- Breaking that down even further, the transportation sector gobbles up about 70% of the United States' daily use, or 14.7 million BPD.

Now, here's the crux of it. . . .

- We import about 75% of what we use, or about 16 million BPD. So it's easy to see that if the transportation sector can switch from oil to other fuels, we can get rid of 93% of our oil imports. But how?

The Mandate That Could Solve America's Oil Dependence Problem

When you think about the U.S. Congress, "energy" isn't the first thing that springs to mind.

And when it comes to the energy sector, our elected officials in Washington are in a collective slumber.

But let's assume for a crazy second that in a stroke of simplicity and common sense, Congress issues a mandate to all vehicle manufacturers.

The Mandate:

- Of the 10 million cars, SUVs, light trucks and heavy-duty trucks that will be produced in 2012, a minimum of 5% will operate on natural gas. (This is a much easier design issue than an all-electric vehicle, by the way.)

- It will also give auto manufacturers a tax credit of $1,000 per car over the first five years.

- Manufacturers must also increase their natural gas-powered vehicle production by 5% per year, with the goal that by 2015, natural gas will power 20% of all vehicles produced.

- The mandate increases by 20% per year, so that by 2019, all new vehicles produced will run on natural gas.

In Ten Years, America's Oil Imports Could Be Dramatically Reduced

The total U.S. vehicle fleet is roughly 254 million. Of that, 135 million are cars, 99 million are SUVs and/or pickup trucks and roughly nine million are larger trucks.

And with that mandate in place, 10 years from now, vehicles that run on natural gas will have replaced 76% of all the gasoline and diesel vehicles.

The result?

- We'll have shaved at least 13.8 million BPD—about 86%—off our daily oil imports.

- Our annual trade deficit will drop by about $94 billion, or 25%.

And what about the $10 billion in incentives that the government would shell out to auto companies?

We could phase in a progressive "legacy fuel" tax on gasoline and diesel to offset the tax incentives. It could either be phased out after five years, or left in place to continue to discourage gasoline and diesel use. That would hasten the switch to natural gas.

Of course, with all these natural gas vehicles, we'll need places to refuel them. So the 167,000 gas stations across the United States will need natural gas pumps alongside the gasoline ones.

In that regard, the government would offer incentives to gas station operators, right along with the ones to auto companies.

That means companies like Clean Energy Fuels can step up right now and begin installing their refueling stations around the country.

It's Time for "Somebody" to Get Going . . .

As the old saying goes, "This ain't rocket science."

Perhaps now that the focus on healthcare reform is behind us, we can get back to the business of addressing the rest of America's crucial issues. And undoubtedly, increasing our energy independence is one of them.

Unlike crude oil, the United States is awash in natural gas. We have nearly 2,100 tcf (Trillion Cubic Feet), which equates to a 100-year supply.

The crude oil import problem reminds me of the old joke about *"Everybody, Somebody, Anybody and Nobody."*

- *Everybody* thinks ending our dependence on foreign oil needs to be done.

- *Somebody* will do it.

- *Anybody* could put a plan together to end our dependence.

- But *Nobody* has.

The U.S. government needs to step up and be that *Somebody*.

My scenario is a simple way to solve it . . . right now. But we'll never get there if we don't get started.

C'mon, Congress . . . wake up. . . .

Why Natural Gas?

Unlike crude oil, the United States is awash in natural gas. We have nearly 2,100 tcf (Trillion Cubic Feet), which equates to a 100-year supply. That's 33% higher than just three years ago.

And you can bet that figure will rise further. In fact, with technological improvements, I fully expect that estimate to double over the next three to five years.

So how much gas do we need? One trillion cubic feet is enough to run 12 million cars per year. Replace 75% of the U.S. vehicle fleet (190 million vehicles) and we're still only talking 15 tcf per year.

While electric cars might be the ultimate alternative to fossil fuels, switching to natural gas-powered vehicles gets us a long way down the road towards energy independence.

More importantly, it buys America valuable time to replace power generation with alternatives, further reducing our dependence on fossil fuels.

The United States Must Increase Fuel Efficiency Standards

Jonathan Murray

Jonathan Murray, a veteran of the US Marines, is the former advocacy director for the Truman National Security Project, a national security leadership institute, and the former campaign director for Operation Free, a coalition of veterans and national security organizations that advocates for government action on climate change.

Congress is known for producing lots of "hot air." If some senators and representatives have their way during the new [2011] Congress, "hot air" could literally be the result of their work.

Certain senators and the new Republican-controlled House are attacking the Environmental Protection Agency's [EPA] authority to limit carbon pollution. This is likely to have devastating consequences for our environment and our national security.

National Security and Oil

Over the past 14 months, Operation Free and thousands of veterans across the country, from every generation, have worked to support a national clean energy policy. The Veterans for American Power tour visited hundreds of communities nationwide, meeting with thousands of Americans to deliver the message that U.S. national security is closely tied to our energy policy.

In Washington, veterans have met with scores of senators to ask for support for a climate and energy policy that reduces dependence on oil.

This oil dependence is among the most dangerous threats to U.S. national security. For years, senior military and intelligence officials have warned that too much of U.S. oil payments eventually trickle down to terrorists, who use it to buy the weapons used against our troops in Afghanistan and Iraq.

Ignoring all the warnings and security implications, the Senate failed to consider comprehensive climate and energy legislation last session.

Former CIA Director Jim Woolsey said it best: "This [the war on terror] is the first time since the Civil War where we are funding both sides of the war."

The Threat of Climate Change

Ignoring all the warnings and security implications, the Senate failed to consider comprehensive climate and energy legislation last session. To make matters worse, Congress will soon consider legislation to strip the EPA of its authority under the Clean Air Act. This would give polluters' free reign to emit as much carbon pollution as they want, speeding up the effects of climate change and risking national security.

If climate change continues unchecked, we will see millions of people displaced globally, countries destabilized and U.S. troops mobilized to address these new threats.

The Defense Department calls climate change a destabilizing influence and "threat multiplier." There is no better example of climate change as a destabilizing force than what happened in Pakistan last year [2010]. More than one-fifth of Pakistan was flooded by torrential rains and insurgents have pounced on the chaos-created opportunity to turn Pakistan into a breeding ground and safe haven for terrorist activity.

As predicted climate-related calamities occur—including drought and famine in unstable countries like Somalia, Sudan and Yemen—these are also likely to become breeding grounds for terror.

Fuel Efficiency Standards

While some senators attempt to move us in the wrong direction, the [Barack] Obama administration now has an opportunity to steer us back on track. Pushed by a diverse coalition that includes veterans and national security organizations, the EPA recently set new fuel efficiency standards of 60 miles per gallon by 2025.

Sixty miles per gallon by 2025 is an achievable goal that we must attain if we are to reduce dependence on oil and strengthen our national security. It will significantly cut demand for oil and drive prices down.

And by reducing the $1 billion a day that the United States spends on importing oil, the new standard would put less money into the pockets of Iranian leader Mahmoud Ahmadinejad, his nuclear program and his recently developed "Ambassador of Death" missile. It would also significantly hamper other regimes seeking to do us harm.

Most Americans don't think about climate change as a national security threat. But we must begin to focus on how it makes us vulnerable in a global context. Thousands of veterans, active duty troops, intelligence professionals and national security experts are doing this every day—and will continue the fight to secure America with clean energy.

It is in our national security interest to do so.

The Free Market, Rather Than Government, Should Govern Energy Choices

Conn Carroll

Conn Carroll is the assistant director for strategic communications for the Heritage Foundation, a conservative think tank, and he is the editor of The Foundry, *the organization's policy blog.*

Last Friday [January 28, 2011] on a conference call with reporters about the [Barack] Obama Administration's long-term energy proposals, Energy Secretary Steven Chu responded to a question about the situation in Egypt, saying: "Certainly any disruption in the Middle East means a partial disruption in the oil we import. It's a world market and [a disruption] could actually have real harm of the price. The best way America can protect itself against these incidents is to decrease our dependency on foreign oil, in fact to diversify our supply." This is a nice sentiment. Unfortunately, everything the Obama Administration is doing is only increasing our dependence on foreign sources of oil.

Blocking Oil Production and Promoting Energy Taxes

Secretary Chu is right: Oil does sell on a world market. But transportation and other distribution factors do segment oil markets somewhat. In fact, the United States is currently paying about $10 less for a barrel of oil than European and Asian nations are. Why? Because of U.S. access to oil refined from Canadian oil sands. Access to these vast natural resources is a great diversification of our oil supply. But now the Obama Administration is trying to make it harder for American consumers to get Canadian oil. The Obama Environmental Protection Agency [EPA] is stonewalling approval for the Keystone pipeline, which would increase the amount of oil the U.S. receives from Canada by over a million barrels per day. And that is not the only oil the Obama Administration is trying to keep out of American consumers' hands.

Offshore, the Obama Interior Department has blocked access to 19 billion barrels of oil in the Pacific and Atlantic coasts and the eastern Gulf of Mexico—and another 10 billion barrels estimated in the Chukchi Sea off the Alaskan coast. Onshore, federal leasing of oil and gas exploration in the western United States has dropped significantly in the past two years. According to data compiled by the Western Energy Alliance, the Bureau of Land Management offered 79 percent fewer leases for oil and natural gas development in Colorado, Montana, New Mexico, North Dakota, Utah, and Wyoming in 2010 than in 2005. And then there is the Arctic National Wildlife Reserve, where an estimated 10 billion barrels of oil lie beneath a few thousand acres that can be accessed with minimal environmental impact.

Government policies that ban economically feasible energy development while subsidizing economically unsustainable ones only raise energy costs.

Allowing Americans to develop these resources could easily produce at least 1 million new barrels of oil a day. The Heritage Foundation's Center for Data Analysis estimates that, if the United States managed to increase its domestic oil production by 1 million barrels a day, it would create an additional 128,000 jobs and generate $7.7 billion in economic activity.

As bad as these existing energy policies are, President Obama's planned energy policies are even worse. Today, the President is meeting with Senate Energy and Natural Resources Chairman Jeff Bingaman (D-NM) to plot passage of a clean energy standard (CES) bill. CES is just another cap-and-trade, energy-tax-like policy, except it's all cap and no trade. A CES would mandate that all electricity providers generate a certain percentage of energy from carbon-free sources. Just like cap and trade, this policy is fundamentally just an energy tax that would drive up everyone's electricity prices. Ironically, this would make electric vehicles even more expensive to operate, but we're sure the Obama Administration would offer another round of taxpayer-funded subsidies to fix that problem.

A Free-Market Approach

Government policies that ban economically feasible energy development while subsidizing economically unsustainable ones only *raise* energy costs rather than lowering them. What the U.S. economy really needs is a truly free-market energy approach, one that includes (1) real nuclear energy reform, not more loan guarantees; (2) predictable and sensible coal regulations; (3) reduced regulation on renewable energy; (4) an end to all energy subsidies; and (5) common-sense limits to environmental litigation.

Congress should not let unrest in the Middle East scare them into energy policies that would make all our energy only more expensive. More bans on energy development, more subsidies for economically unproven technologies, and expensive new alternative energy production mandates are not the answer. America needs a true free-market approach to energy, and we need it now.

Organizations to Contact

The editors have compiled the following list of organizations concerned with the issues debated in this book. The descriptions are derived from materials provided by the organizations. All have publications or information available for interested readers. The list was compiled on the date of publication of the present volume; the information provided here may change. Be aware that many organizations take several weeks or longer to respond to inquiries, so allow as much time as possible.

Cato Institute
1000 Massachusetts Ave. NW, Washington, DC 20001-5403
(202) 842-0200 • fax: (202) 842-3490
website: www.cato.org

Cato Institute is a nonprofit public policy research foundation that promotes a libertarian point of view that emphasizes principles of limited government, free markets, individual liberty, and peace. One of Cato's research areas is energy and the environment. Cato is committed to protecting the environment without sacrificing economic liberty, and the organization believes that those goals are mutually supporting, not mutually exclusive. Recent publications include *Oil Speculators Are Your Friends* and *The Case Against Government Intervention in Energy Markets*.

Center for Climate and Energy Solutions (C2ES)
2101 Wilson Blvd., Suite 550, Arlington, VA 22201
(703) 516-4146 • fax: (703) 516-9551
website: www.c2es.org

The Center for Climate and Energy Solutions (C2ES) succeeds the Pew Center on Global Climate Change, which was established in 1998 as a nonprofit, nonpartisan, and independent organization whose mission was to provide credible information, straight answers, and innovative solutions in the effort to address global climate change. In November 2011, the Pew Center was reestablished as the Center for Climate and Energy Solutions. The Center's website is an excellent source of publications, reports, fact sheets, articles, and speeches on all facets of the energy/climate change issue.

Environmental Literacy Council

1625 K St. NW, Suite 1020, Washington, DC 20006-3868
(202) 296-0390 • fax: (202) 822-0991
e-mail: info@enviroliteracy.org
website: www.enviroliteracy.org

The Environmental Literacy Council is an independent non-profit organization that helps teachers, students, policymakers, and the public find cross-disciplinary resources on the environment. The Council offers free background information on common environmental science concepts; vetted resources to broaden understanding; and curricular materials that give teachers the tools to augment their own backgrounds on environmental issues. The website contains a section on energy that provides information, recommended resources, and lesson plans relating to petroleum and US energy policies.

The Heritage Foundation

214 Massachusetts Ave. NE, Washington, DC 20002-4999
(202) 546-4400
website: www.heritage.org

The Heritage Foundation is a conservative think tank that promotes conservative public policies based on the principles of free enterprise, limited government, individual freedom, traditional American values, and a strong national defense. The group's staff conducts research on key policy issues and advocates conservative positions to members of Congress, congressional staff, policymakers in the executive branch, the news media, the academic community, and the public. Among the topics listed on the group's website is "Energy and Environment," a portal that leads to many articles and opinion pieces relating to fossil fuels, including, for example, *What to Do About High Oil Prices* and *Alternative Fuels as a Military Strategy*.

Institute for the Study of Energy and Our Future (ISEOF)
PO Box 270762, Fort Collins, CO   80527-0762
(303) 942-6209
e-mail: iseof.org
website: www.iseof.org

The Institute for the Study of Energy and Our Future (ISEOF) is a nonprofit corporation that conducts research and educates the public about energy issues and their impact on society. It publishes *The Oil Drum*, an online periodical devoted to discussions about energy and our future. According to the website, the world is near the point where new oil production cannot keep up with increased energy demand and older oil fields are nearly depleted, resulting in a decline of total world oil production. The website is an excellent source of analysis, research, and discussion of energy-related topics, such as peak oil, sustainable development and growth, and the implications of these ideas on politics.

International Energy Agency (IEA)
9 rue de la Fédération, 75739 Paris   Cedex 15
   France
+33 1 40 57 65 00/01 • fax: +33 1 40 57 65 09
e-mail: info@iea.org
website: www.iea.org

The International Energy Agency (IEA) is an intergovernmental organization that acts as energy policy advisor to twenty-eight member countries in their effort to ensure reliable, affordable, and clean energy for their citizens. Founded during the oil crisis of 1973–74, the IEA's initial role was to coordinate measures in times of oil supply emergencies, but that mandate has broadened to include promoting energy security, economic development, and environmental protection. The IEA's current work focuses on climate change policies, market reform, energy technology collaboration, and outreach to major consumers and producers of energy, such as China, India, Russia, and the OPEC countries. Publications available from IEA include *Energy Technology Transitions for Industry* and *Transport, Energy and CO$_2$: Moving towards Sustainability.*

Natural Resources Defense Council (NRDC)
40 West 20th St., New York, NY   10011
(212) 727-2700 • fax: (212) 727-1773
website: www.nrdc.org

Founded in 1970, the Natural Resources Defense Council (NRDC) is one of the nation's oldest environmental advocacy organizations. With a staff of more than three hundred and fifty lawyers, scientists, and policy experts, NRDC works to protect the planet's wildlife and wild places and to ensure a safe and healthy environment for all living things. Among the issues on NRDC's agenda are: curbing global warming, getting toxic chemicals out of the environment, moving America beyond oil, reviving our oceans, saving wildlife and wild places, and helping China go green. The group publishes a monthly newsletter, and the NRDC website is a good source of information about clean energy options. The website's energy section, for example, contains informative articles such as *Domestic Oil Drilling: Still Not a Solution to Rising Gas Prices*; *Grasping Green Car Technology*; *High Gas Prices: Supply and Demand*; and *Fighting Oil Addiction.*

Post Carbon Institute
613 4th St., Suite 208, Santa Rosa, CA   95404
(707) 823-8700 • fax: (866) 797-5820
website: www.postcarbon.org

The Post Carbon Institute is a nonprofit organization that helps individuals and communities understand and respond to the environmental, societal, and economic crises created by our dependence on fossil fuels. The group believes that world oil production has peaked and it aims to facilitate the process of transitioning to a more sustainable, post-carbon world. The group publishes the monthly *Post Carbon Newsletter*, featuring the latest news and information, and its website is a good source of articles, commentaries, reports, and books relating to oil depletion and the future of oil, energy, and the economy.

Resources for the Future (RFF)

1616 P St. NW, Suite 600, Washington, DC   20036
(202) 328-5000 • fax: (202) 939-3460
website: www.rff.org

Resources for the Future (RFF) is a nonprofit and nonpartisan organization that conducts independent research—rooted primarily in economics and other social sciences—on environmental, energy, natural resource, and public health issues. RFF was created at the recommendation of William Paley, then head of the Columbia Broadcasting System, who had chaired a presidential commission that examined whether the United States was becoming overly dependent on foreign sources of important natural resources and commodities. Today, one of the group's main areas of focus is energy and climate change. Examples of RFF publications include *An Economic Assessment of Eliminating Oil and Gas Company Tax Preferences* and *The Challenge of Climate for Energy Markets*.

US Department of Energy (DOE)

1000 Independence Ave. SW, Washington, DC   20585
(202) 586-5000 • fax: (202) 586-4403
e-mail: The.Secretary@hq.doe.gov
website: http://energy.gov

The US Department of Energy is the main federal agency responsible for ensuring America's security and prosperity by addressing its energy, environmental, and nuclear challenges through transformative science and technology solutions. The DOE website is a useful source of information about issues such as America's readiness to respond to oil disruptions, the national Strategic Petroleum Reserve, emerging technologies, and energy efficiency.

US Energy Information Administration (EIA)
1000 Independence Ave. SW, Washington, DC   20585
(202) 586-8800
e-mail: infoCtr@doe.gov
website: www.eia.gov

The US Energy Information Administration (EIA) is the statistical agency of the US Department of Energy (DOE) and is the nation's main source of unbiased energy data, analysis, and forecasting. Its mission is to provide policy-neutral data, forecasts, and analyses to promote sound policy making, efficient markets, and public understanding regarding energy and its interaction with the economy and the environment. The EIA website is a source of various reports and publications, such as *Petroleum Supply Monthly, Monthly Energy Review*, the *Annual Energy Review*, the *Short-Term Energy Outlook*, and the *Annual Energy Outlook*.

World Energy Council (WEC)
Regency House, 1-4 Warwick St., 5th Floor
London   W1B 5LT
   United Kingdom
(+44 20) 7734 5996 • fax: (+44 20) 7734 5926
e-mail: info@worldenergy.org
website: www.worldenergy.org

The World Energy Council (WEC) is the foremost multi-energy organization in the world today. WEC has member committees in nearly one hundred countries, including most of the largest energy-producing and energy-consuming nations. Established in 1923, the organization's mission is to promote the sustainable supply and use of energy for the greatest benefit of all people. Examples of WEC publications include *Assessment of Energy Policy and Practices, Energy Efficiency Policies*, and *Europe's Vulnerability to Energy Crisis*.

Bibliography

Books

Robert U. Ayres and Edward H. Ayres — *Crossing the Energy Divide: Moving from Fossil Fuel Dependence to a Clean-Energy Future.* Philadelphia: Wharton School Publishing, 2009.

Daniel B. Botkin — *Powering the Future: A Scientist's Guide to Energy Independence.* Upper Saddle River, NJ: FT Press, 2010.

Robert Bryce — *Gusher of Lies: The Dangerous Delusions of "Energy Independence."* New York: PublicAffairs, 2009.

Committee on Assessment of Resource Needs for Fuel Cell and Hydrogen Technologies and National Research Council — *Transitions to Alternative Transportation Technologies—Plug-in Hybrid Electric Vehicles.* Washington, DC: National Academies Press, 2010.

Council on Foreign Relations — *The New Arab Revolt: What Happened, What It Means, and What Comes Next.* Washington, DC: Council on Foreign Relations/Foreign Affairs, 2011.

Dan Dicker — *Oil's Endless Bid: Taming the Unreliable Price of Oil to Secure Our Economy.* Hoboken, NJ: Wiley, 2011.

Bradley L. Dunne   *Corporate Average Fuel Economy (CAFE) Standards and the Environmental Impact.* Hauppauge, NJ: Nova Science, 2011.

Y Ev   *Electric Vehicle EV, the Second Coming: What You Need to Know to "Go Green & Go Electric."* Charleston, SC: CreateSpace, 2011.

Philip G. Gallman   *Green Alternatives and National Energy Strategy: The Facts Behind the Headlines.* Baltimore, MD: The Johns Hopkins University Press, 2011.

Newt Gingrich and Vince Haley   *Drill Here, Drill Now, Pay Less: A Handbook for Slashing Gas Prices and Solving Our Energy Crisis.* Washington, DC: Regnery Publishing, 2008.

Michael J. Graetz   *The End of Energy: The Unmaking of America's Environment, Security, and Independence.* Cambridge, MA: The MIT Press, 2011.

Christopher B. Hummel   *Plug-in Hybrid Electric Vehicles and Energy Use.* Hauppauge, NY: Nova Science, 2011.

Antonia Juhasz   *The Tyranny of Oil: The World's Most Powerful Industry—and What We Must Do to Stop It.* New York: Harper Paperbacks, 2009.

Anne Korin and Gal Luft	*Turning Oil into Salt: Energy Independence Through Fuel Choice.* Charleston, SC: BookSurge Publishing, 2009.
Roger E. Meiners	*The False Promise of Green Energy.* Washington, DC: Cato Institute, 2011.
Kent Moors	*The Vega Factor: Oil Volatility and the Next Global Crisis.* Hoboken, NJ: Wiley, 2011.
Malcom R. Perdontis	*Battery Manufacturing and Electric and Hybrid Vehicles.* Hauppauge, NY: Nova Science, 2011.
Joseph M. Shuster	*Beyond Fossil Fools: The Roadmap to Energy Independence by 2040.* Edina, MN: Beaver's Pond Press, 2008.
Christopher Steiner	*$20 Per Gallon: How the Inevitable Rise in the Price of Gasoline Will Change Our Lives for the Better.* New York: Grand Central Publishing, 2009.

Periodicals and Internet Sources

| American Public Transportation Association | "Potential Impact of Gasoline Price Increases on U.S. Public Transportation Ridership, 2011–2012," March 14, 2011. www.apta.com. |

E. Calvin Beisner "Natural Gas a Natural Winner? Let the (Transportation) Market Decide!" *MasterResource*, May 24, 2011. www.masterresource.org.

Meteor Blades "Think Big: Transportation Overhaul Would Save Money, Create Jobs, Cut Pollution, Burn Less Oil," *Daily Kos*, June 19, 2011. www.dailykos.com.

Ben Casselman "Facing Up to End of 'Easy Oil,'" *Wall Street Journal*, May 24, 2011. http://online.wsj.com.

Gordon G. Chang "Oil Shock," *Forbes*, February 27, 2011. http://blogs.forbes.com.

Rory Cooper "10 Things You Need to Know About High Gas Prices and Obama's Oil Policy," *The Foundry*, February 23, 2011. http://blog.heritage.org.

Anthony H. Cordesman "US Oil and Gas Import Dependence: Department of Energy Projections in 2011," Center for Strategic & International Studies, April 29, 2011. http://csis.org.

Aaron Couch "Poll: With Gas Prices High, Americans Want 60 m.p.g. Fuel Efficiency," *Christian Science Monitor*, May 16, 2011. www.csmonitor.com.

Tanya Davis "The Effect of Rising Gas Prices on American Families," Cmvlive.com, June 2, 2011. http://cmvlive.com.

The Economist "The Gas-Price Debate," May 1, 2011. www.economist.com/blogs.

Jim Efstathiou Jr. and Kim Chipman	"Fracking: The Great Shale Gas Rush," *Bloomberg Businessweek*, March 3, 2011. www.businessweek.com.
Judah Flum	"Benefits to High Gas Prices?" JudahFlum.com, March 7, 2011. www.judahflum.com.
Merrill Goozner	"Oil Dependency: The Real Threat to National Security," *The Fiscal Times*, June 23, 2011. www.thefiscaltimes.com.
The Guardian	"Oil Prices: Green Light from the Black Stuff," March 5, 2011. www.guardian.co.uk.
Steve Hargreaves	"Gas Prices High—and Might Get Higher," *CNN Money*, January 21, 2011. http://money.cnn.com.
Ron Haynes	"12 Reasons Why High Gas Prices Are GOOD for America," *The Wisdom Journal*, May 13, 2008. www.thewisdomjournal.com.
The Independent	"An Opportunity to Kick Our Fossil-Fuel Addiction," January 6, 2011. www.independent.co.uk.
Jennifer Kho	"What High Gas Prices Mean for Renewable Energy," *Renewable Energy World*, May 31, 2011. www.renewableenergyworld.com.
Clifford Krauss	"Can We Do Without the Mideast?" *New York Times*, March 30, 2011.

David Kreutzer "Alternative Fuels as a Military Strategy," The Heritage Foundation, July 20, 2011. www.heritage.org.

Rebecca Lefton and Daniel J. Weiss "Oil Dependence Is a Dangerous Habit: Imports Threaten Our Security, Our Environment, and Our Economy," Center for American Progress, January 2010. www .americanprogress.org.

Ben Levisohn "Sizing Up the New Oil Spike," *Bloomberg Businessweek*, June 1, 2009.

David MacKay "Let's Get Real About Alternative Energy," *CNN*, May 13, 2009. www.cnn.com.

Jason Mick "FedEx CEO: 'Addiction' to Foreign Oil Is Costing the Economy, American Lives," *Daily Tech*, May 20, 2011. www.dailytech.com.

New Scientist "High Fuel Prices Could Slash US Emissions," May 8, 2008.

Cullen Roche "How Serious Is the Oil Price Threat to the US Recovery?" *Business Insider*, January 5, 2011. www.businessinsider .com.

Nansen G. Saleri "Our Man-Made Energy Crisis," *Wall Street Journal*, March 9, 2011. http://online.wsj.com.

Julia A. Seymour	"Rising Gas Prices Linked to Obama Drilling Ban in Just 1% of Evening News Stories," Business & Media Institute, April 19, 2011. www.mrc.org.
Time	"Getting Transit to Work," May 12, 2011.
Michael Totty and Spencer Swartz	"How to Kick Our Oil Addiction Despite Plunging Oil Prices," *Wall Street Journal*, March 1, 2009. http://online.wsj.com.

Index

Business Contracts Kit For Dummies®

Cheat Sheet

P9-DKF-383

Differences between Employees and Contractors

The following table summarizes some key areas in which independent contractors differ from employees. Many of these issues directly affect what forms you must fill out with respect to the worker.

Employer Responsibility	Employee	Independent Contractor
Make employer contribution to Social Security	Yes	No
Make employer contribution to Medicare taxes	Yes	No
Withhold applicable federal taxes	Yes	No
File Form 1099-MISC with IRS if you pay the person $600 or more	No	Yes
Carry Worker's Compensation Insurance for the person	Yes	No
Contribute to unemployment insurance fund and/or tax	Yes	No
Grant employee job benefits such as paid vacation, sick leave, holidays, and stock options	Yes	No
Pay employee for overtime	Yes	Generally no
Right to control how the worker performs the specific task for which he or she is hired	Generally yes	Generally no
Right to direct or control how the business aspects of the worker's activities are conducted	Generally yes	Generally no

What to Do When Concluding a Contract

Don't forget the following before you conclude an agreement:

✔ **Date and sign the agreement.** Date the agreement so that the parties can refer to it easily. The parties also should indicate the date they sign the agreement at the signature block. The parties don't have to sign the agreement on the same day, but unless the contract says when it will start, the contract is effective on the date of the last signature. It's a good idea to date the contract and then define that date as the "Effective Date." This way there will be no confusion about the start date of the contract regardless of who signs when.

✔ **Prepare two final copies of the contract.** Both parties should sign both copies, leaving each party with a signed original of the contract. Just sign the last page. You don't need to initial every single page unless you are worried about the other party changing the "final" copy without your knowledge.

✔ **Initial any handwritten last-minute changes.** If you make minor handwritten changes to the final copy before it is signed, both parties should put their initials next to the changes. This way, the parties will avoid claims that the handwritten changes are not legit.

✔ **Using fax signatures.** It's okay to sign a contract by fax, as long as neither side claims that the fax signature is a forgery. Because it's much easier to forge faxed signatures than "blue ink" original signatures, it's best to follow up fax signatures with originals sent by mail to each other for signature.

For Dummies: Bestselling Book Series for Beginners

Business Contracts Kit For Dummies®

Key Contract Definitions

Here are some common contract terms you may encounter:

- **Boilerplate:** Standard contract terms usually found at the end of the contract which are important but which do not reflect the essence of the deal. Examples of boilerplate terms include provisions describing notice, governing law, or payment of attorneys' fees.

- **Breach:** A claim by one party to a contract that the other party has failed to perform as required under the contract.

- **Conditions:** Provisions in a contract which deal with the certain events happening or not happening. Conditions are like triggers that, when pulled, cause some other part of the contract to come into effect.

- **Consideration:** A benefit or right that the parties to a contract exchange with each other in order to form the contract. Consideration can be a promise to do something (such as a promise to pay money or to lease your office space) or a promise not to do something (a promise not to lease your office space to your neighbor's biggest competitor), but whatever the parties exchange with each other, each party's consideration must be something of value to it.

- **Crappy:** Describes a contract that wasn't well drafted or negotiated. Just kidding.

- **Damages:** A type of remedy for a party's breach of a valid contract. Damages usually involve an award of money to the injured, non-breaching party.

- **Recitals:** Language at the beginning of the contract that describes why the parties are entering into the contract. Recitals are not always legally enforceable, so always repeat significant contract terms in the body of the contract after words such as "the parties agree as follows."

Lease Gotchas

Landlords often hand you a form lease that contains gotchas. *Gotchas* is a highly technical term for provisions that may cost you a lot of money or headaches in ways that you didn't plan. Your best bet is to negotiate them out of the lease. Here are some classic gotchas:

- The landlord's right to pass increased operating costs in the building on to the tenant without limitation

- The tenant's obligation to pay any increased taxes as a result of the landlord's selling the building

- The landlord's right to terminate your lease early for his or her convenience

- A disclaimer about the building and the services provided to tenants

- Severe limitations or prohibitions on subletting your space (you may need to sublet space if your business shrinks)

- Personal guarantees or payment of the rent required from the company's owners

Copyright © 2000 Wiley Publishing, Inc. All rights reserved.

Item 5236-8.

For more information about Wiley Publishing, call 1-800-762-2974.

For Dummies: Bestselling Book Series for Beginners

™

References for the Rest of Us!®

BESTSELLING BOOK SERIES

Do you find that traditional reference books are overloaded with technical details and advice you'll never use? Do you postpone important life decisions because you just don't want to deal with them? Then our *For Dummies*® business and general reference book series is for you.

For Dummies business and general reference books are written for those frustrated and hard-working souls who know they aren't dumb, but find that the myriad of personal and business issues and the accompanying horror stories make them feel helpless. *For Dummies* books use a lighthearted approach, a down-to-earth style, and even cartoons and humorous icons to dispel fears and build confidence. Lighthearted but not lightweight, these books are perfect survival guides to solve your everyday personal and business problems.

> *"More than a publishing phenomenon, 'Dummies' is a sign of the times."*
> — The New York Times

> *"A world of detailed and authoritative information is packed into them..."*
> — U.S. News and World Report

> *"...you won't go wrong buying them."*
> — Walter Mossberg, Wall Street Journal, on For Dummies books

Already, millions of satisfied readers agree. They have made For Dummies the #1 introductory level computer book series and a best-selling business book series. They have written asking for more. So, if you're looking for the best and easiest way to learn about business and other general reference topics, look to For Dummies to give you a helping hand.

Wiley Publishing, Inc.

Business
Contracts Kit
FOR
DUMMIES®

Business Contracts Kit

FOR DUMMIES®

by **Richard D. Harroch**

WILEY

Wiley Publishing, Inc.

Business Contracts Kit For Dummies®

Published by
Wiley Publishing, Inc.
111 River Street
Hoboken, NJ 07030
www.wiley.com

For general information on our other products and services or to obtain technical support, please contact our Customer Care Department within the U.S. at 800-762-2974, outside the U.S. at 317-572-3993, or fax 317-572-4002.

Wiley also publishes its books in a variety of electronic formats. Some content that appears in print may not be available in electronic books.

Library of Congress Cataloging-in-Publication Data:

Library of Congress Control Number: 99-69719

ISBN: 978-0-7645-5236-6

Manufactured in the United States of America

10 9 8 7 6

1O/RY/QT/QW/IN

About the Author

Richard Harroch is an attorney with over 20 years of experience in representing start-up and emerging companies, entrepreneurs, and venture capitalists. He is listed in the "Who's Who in American Law" and is a corporate partner in a major law firm in San Francisco, Orrick, Herrington & Sutcliffe LLP. He is a Phi Beta Kappa graduate of U.C. Berkeley and graduated from UCLA Law School, where he was managing editor of the *Law Review*. He has written a number of legal/business books, including *The Small Business Kit For Dummies; Start-Up and Emerging Companies: Planning, Financing and Operating the Successful Business;* and *Partnership and Joint Venture Agreements*. He also spearheaded the development of a premier legal agreements Web site on the Internet.

He has lectured extensively before various legal and business organizations, including the American Electronics Association, the Venture Capital Institute, the California Continuing Education of the Bar, the Corporate Counsel Institute, the San Francisco Bar, and the Practicing Law Institute (PLI).

Richard has served as the Chairman of the California State Bar Committee on Partnerships, the Co-Chairman of the Corporations Committee of the San Francisco Bar (Barristers), a member of the Executive Committee of the Business Law Section of the California State Bar, and Co-Chair of the *Law Journal* annual seminar in New York on "Joint Ventures and Strategic Alliances".

Richard has experience in the following areas: start-up and emerging companies, e-commerce, corporate financings, joint ventures, strategic alliances, venture capital financings, employment agreements, IPOs, leases, loans, online and Internet matters, license agreements, partnerships, preferred stock, confidentiality agreements, stock options, sales contracts, securities laws, and mergers and acquisitions. Richard can be reached by e-mail at rharroch@orrick.com.

Publisher's Acknowledgments

We're proud of this book; please send us your comments through our online registration form located at www.dummies.com/register.

Some of the people who helped bring this book to market include the following:

Acquisitions, Editorial, and Media Development

Senior Project Editor: Tim Gallan

Acquisitions Editor: Mark Butler

Copy Editors: Janet Withers, Corey Dalton

Acquisitions Coordinator: Lisa Roule

Technical Editor: James Malysiak

Editorial Manager: Pam Mourouzis

Editorial Assistant: Carol Strickland

Reprint Editor: Bethany André

Production

Project Coordinator: Maridee V. Ennis

Layout and Graphics: Angela Chaney-Granger, Barry Offringa, Tracy K. Oliver, Mary Jo Richards, Brent Savage, Brian Torwelle, Erin Zeltner

Proofreaders: Laura Albert, Corey Bowen, Marianne Santy, Jeannie Smith, Charles Spencer, Ethel Winslow

Indexer: Richard Shrout

Publishing and Editorial for Consumer Dummies

Diane Graves Steele, Vice President and Publisher, Consumer Dummies

Joyce Pepple, Acquisitions Director, Consumer Dummies

Kristin A. Cocks, Product Development Director, Consumer Dummies

Michael Spring, Vice President and Publisher, Travel

Brice Gosnell, Publishing Director, Travel

Suzanne Jannetta, Editorial Director, Travel

Publishing for Technology Dummies

Richard Swadley, Vice President and Executive Group Publisher

Andy Cummings, Vice President and Publisher

Composition Services

Gerry Fahey, Vice President of Production Services

Debbie Stailey, Director of Composition Services

Contents at a Glance

Cartoons at a Glance

By Rich Tennant

page 243

page 171

page 47

page 7

page 281

Fax: 978-546-7747
E-mail: richtennant@the5thwave.com
World Wide Web: www.the5thwave.com

Table of Contents

Introduction

•••

Many of you probably think that the key to running a successful business is hard work and good decision making. But look at what you spend a lot of your time doing. You probably spend way too much time filling out forms, drafting and negotiating contracts, and shuffling papers. Paperwork is the key to business, believe it or not, and although none of us may be happy with this state of affairs, this book can certainly make your life a little easier.

If you have big bucks and don't really care about saving money, you can probably hire a lawyer to draft contracts and other legal documents for you. Now don't get me wrong, I'm an attorney, and there are definitely times when you need the expertise of a good attorney. But, with or without a good attorney, you have to understand what is really important in negotiating a contract, and I'm here to help you figure that out.

I don't mind telling you that contracts, forms, and other legal documents are incredibly important but also can be difficult to decipher. This book and its accompanying CD-ROM provide you with the many and varied sample forms that can help you in your business. Sure, you will need to revise a number of the documents I've put together for you, but at least I can give you a start, and with any luck, I'm sure I'll be saving you a few headaches.

How to Use This Kit

You've bought more than a book (assuming, of course, that you bought it and aren't borrowing it). You bought yourself a high-tech gizmo called a CD-ROM that you can cram into your Windows computer or Macintosh to access over 200 business forms and contracts.

What this means is that once you read my insightful explanations regarding all the myriad forms and contracts that the typical business needs to be using, you can grab the same forms and contracts off the CD to use for yourself. Cool, aye?

Uh oh. You know how Spider Man says that his "spider sense" is tingling when something bad is going to happen? Right now, my "lawyer sense" is kicking in. I won't tell you which body part of mine is tingling, but I will state this book is not intended to give you specific legal advice, and although the forms in this book are good, laws do change and can vary from place to place. Furthermore, the forms may not be appropriate to your particular transaction. Seek legal counsel when you have questions, especially when big bucks (or your reputation) are involved. End of disclaimer.

What I Assume about You

First, I don't assume that you have a legal background. Throughout this book, I define the terms that appear in the contracts and forms I present, and I'm always offering advice so that you can draft contracts that are clear and concise. If you're a legal expert, you can still benefit from this book. Why write contracts from scratch when you can use what I've done to get you started?

I do assume that you have an interest in making your business run smoothly and safely, and many of the forms and contracts throughout this book perform the CYA function — that is, cover your, um, butt. You want to stay out of legal trouble, and you want to make sure that how you do business is spelled out clearly to your employees, vendors, and customers. I help you to avoid legal pitfalls by giving you the kinds of business contracts that will assist you in covering that butt of yours.

Finally, I don't assume that you want to expect to know enough to pass the Bar exam after you read this book. I don't bore you with too much jargon, and I try to explain things in non-lawyerly language. I expect that you want to get in, get what you need, and get out.

How to Use This Book

If you take a look at the Table of Contents, you'll see that I've organized this book so that each chapter deals with the forms or contracts for a discrete aspect of business. What that means is that you don't need to read this book from cover to cover. It's a reference, and you really only need to read the chapters that interest you. If, say, you're launching a Web site, you ought to take a look at Chapters 15 and 16. If your company is about to sell stock, flip to Chapter 5. The chapters are self-contained, so don't worry if you don't have a need to read about real estate leases in Chapter 10 if that doesn't interest you.

I would say, though, that if you're completely new to the wonderful world of drafting forms and contracts, then you may want to take a crack at the first three chapters of this book. They present the basics, which will help you as you use the forms that appear later in the book.

How This Book Is Organized

As I said, the chapters are self-contained, and related chapters are grouped together in parts. Here are summaries of what's covered in each part:

Part I: The Basics

In this part, I show the important and necessary parts of a typical contract. I also give you some guidelines on how to draft trouble-free forms and contracts, and I provide you with some common boilerplate language that you'll probably see in all kinds of contracts.

Part II: Forms for Businesses Big and Small

If you're running a business, you need the forms in this part. Believe it or not, whether you're a guy running a lawnmower repair shop with two employees or an executive at Microsoft, you have to deal with many of the same issues. You have to let your employees and customers know what your policies are. You have to know how to deal with contractors. And you have to know what to do when it comes to acquisitions and stock options. (Okay, maybe not if you're running a lawnmower repair shop, but who knows?)

Part III: Money: Leases, Licenses, and Loans (Oh My!)

I cover everything from real estate leases, to license agreements, loan agreements, service contracts, and confidentiality agreements. It's all stuff that has to do with money. Your business earns you money; these contracts make sure you keep it.

Part IV: The Brave New World of the Web

Doing business on the Internet presents all kinds of challenges. Truth is, many legal questions haven't been answered yet when it comes to things like copyrights, fair use, and linking. Heaven knows you don't want your business on the wrong end of a lawsuit that helps decide what the laws are going to be, so your best bet is to cover your butt. The forms in this part can help.

Part V: The Part of Tens

Every *For Dummies* book ends with top-ten lists, and this one is no exception. Here, you can find ten mistakes to avoid, ten great resources for forms, and ten key contracts for small businesses.

Icons Used in This Book

A signature feature of *For Dummies* books, besides top-notch authors and the catchy yellow and black covers, is the use of icons, which are little pictures we like to throw next to pieces of important text. Here's what the icons mean:

A suggestion that can save you time and money.

A note that will keep you out of trouble, especially legal trouble.

A more general concept that you shouldn't forget.

Lets you know that the document I'm talking about is on the CD-ROM that's stuck to the inside cover of this book.

A Note about the CD-ROM

You can read much more about the contents of the CD in the "About the CD" appendix, but I wanted to mention here that the CD offers you two versions of every document:

- ✔ A PDF that you can view and print with Adobe Acrobat Reader (included on the CD).

- ✔ An RTF that you can actually edit with most major word processors. I put these documents together using Microsoft Word, so they'll look best, I imagine, if you use that particular program.

The upshot is that you can't edit the PDFs, but you can view and print them. I include the RTF versions of the documents so that you can edit the documents however you like, which I think is a great feature of this book. Remember, the forms are only a starting place and you alone (or with your attorney) will have to decide the necessary changes and deletions.

Where to Go from Here

It's up to you. Take a look at the Table of Contents and see what catches your eye. Or maybe look up a topic that interests you in the Index. Or start reading Chapter 1 and don't stop until you reach the end. It's up to you. Have fun.

Part I

The Basics

The 5th Wave   By Rich Tennant

"Does our insurance cover a visit from Mike Wallace?"

In this part . . .

1 get you started. I show you the important and necessary parts of a typical contract. I also give you some guidelines on how to draft trouble-free forms and contracts, and I provide you with some common boilerplate language that you'll probably use in many of your own contracts.

Chapter 1

Contract Essentials

. . . .

In This Chapter

▶ Knowing when you need a contract

▶ Creating a contract

▶ Using oral versus written contracts

▶ Using a standard form contract

▶ Using a letter agreement

. . . .

Any time you enter into an agreement that can affect the future of your business, you need a business contract. Your business contracts are like turkey at Thanksgiving dinner — someone's bound to feel disappointed if you don't have a good one.

In this chapter, I explain what you always need to include in your contracts, no matter what your business. I also talk about why it's worth the effort to put your agreement in writing. And I discuss when and why you can feel comfortable using a pre-prepared standard form contract.

Do You Even Need a Contract (Not to Mention This Book)?

Business contracts are used to memorialize important agreements you (or your business) enter into with others. So what's an "important" agreement? Any agreement on which you are relying and that can affect the future of your business.

Sure, small business owners operate all the time on informal understandings that they may never write down or even completely verbalize to the other party. But it's often worthwhile for you to take the time to draw up a formal contract. Contracts allow the parties the opportunity to

✔ Clearly define their obligations to and expectations of each other.

✔ Limit their liability.

> ✔ Lay out payment terms.
>
> ✔ Divide up business risks.
>
> ✔ Make sure each side understands its responsibilities.

Here's a quick rule: If you've spent more than five minutes worrying about whether you need a contract, guess what? You probably do.

Legal Requirements for a Contract

So, what makes a contract a contract? A contract is an agreement between parties, with terms and conditions that describe the agreement, that constitutes a legal obligation. A valid contract typically requires the following four elements:

> ✔ **A meeting of the minds between the parties** demonstrating they both understand and agree to the essentials of the deal
>
> ✔ **Consideration** (something of value exchanged by each of the parties, such as cash, goods, or a promise to do something)
>
> ✔ **An agreement to enter into the contract** (typically evidenced by both parties signing a written contract, although oral contracts can be valid, too, in some situations)
>
> ✔ **The legal competence of each party,** meaning the parties are not minors and are of sound mind

Meeting of the minds

The first step in creating a contract is making sure that both parties are talking about the same deal, so that when they subsequently agree to enter into the contract they are both agreeing to the same thing. Seems obvious, right? Until you realize that the "vintage red car" you planned on buying from your brother-in-law isn't the Ferrari, it's his Pinto. Take the time to communicate your understanding of the deal to the other party, and listen carefully when he or she talks back.

Consideration

After the parties reach a "meeting of the minds" regarding the deal, they must both exchange something of value in order to create a contract. Often one party provides its goods or services in exchange for the cash of the other party. But consideration can take many other forms, as long as each party is giving up something of value to it to convince the other party to enter into the contract.

You can read law treatises defining *consideration* until the cows come home, but in the real world your biggest issues related to consideration are *how much* and *when*.

If cash is exchanging hands in your contract (unlike one of my first high school contracts when I swapped a few hours of yard work for a chance to drive the Mustang), think through any assumptions you are making about the way payment will be made.

✔ If you expect to be paid at the time the contract is signed, say so.

✔ If one of the parties will be paying after the contract is signed, say whether the payment will be in cash, by check, by cashier's check or by wire transfer. It's better to be explicit about the way the money will change hands. For example, you likely want a cashier's check if you're turning over title to a car or other significant assets.

✔ If payments will be made over time or based on external factors such as the amount of business done, you may need to define the payment schedule by using a formula. Keep the formula simple and feel free to put examples of how the formula works right in the body of the contract.

✔ If you have to use a complex royalty or other payment formula, test the formula with the other side to be sure you both understand it.

Be wary of *gift contracts,* where someone gets something for nothing. If the value one party is receiving is truly free, so that only the other side is giving up something of value, then they probably haven't formed a contract. You usually can't make someone give you a true gift, no matter how many times the giver promised to do so.

Agreement to enter into the contract

After both parties understand the deal and understand what type of consideration will be exchanged by each party, they are ready to form an agreement. Usually, the parties demonstrate that negotiations have ended and an agreement has been reached when the parties sign the contract. (I discuss oral agreements, which are created without any written, signed contract, in the section "Oral Contracts," later in this chapter.)

In business as in opera, it's not over until the fat lady sings — I mean *signs.* It's fine, within reason, to negotiate changes in a written contract up until the moment you sign it.

Key contract definitions

Here are some common contract terms you may encounter. Many are discussed at greater length throughout the rest of this book.

✔ **Boilerplate:** Standard contract terms usually found at the end of the contract that are important but that do not reflect the essence of the deal. Examples of boilerplate terms include provisions describing notice, governing law, or payment of attorneys' fees.

✔ **Breach:** A claim by one party to a contract that the other party has failed to perform as required under the contract.

✔ **Conditions:** Provisions in a contract that deal with the certain events happening or not happening. Conditions are like triggers that, when pulled, cause some other part of the contract to come into effect.

✔ **Consideration:** A benefit or right that the parties to a contract exchange with each other in order to form the contract. Consideration can be a promise to do something

(such as a promise to pay money or to lease your office space) or a promise not to do something (a promise not to lease your office space to your neighbor's biggest competitor), but whatever the parties exchange with each other, each party's consideration must be something of value to it.

✔ **Crappy:** Describes a contract that wasn't well drafted or negotiated. Just kidding.

✔ **Damages:** A type of remedy for a party's breach of a valid contract. Damages usually involve an award of money to the injured, non-breaching party.

✔ **Recitals:** Language at the beginning of the contract that describes why the parties are entering into the contract. Recitals are not always legally enforceable, so always repeat significant contract terms in the body of the contract after words such as "the parties agree as follows."

Legal competence

Be sure that the party you're working with is legally competent to enter into a contract. Otherwise, your signed contract may be void and unenforceable (as in worth zippo). Even if the other guy wears a lampshade on his head, he may be legally competent. But watch out for the following situations:

✔ **Minors** cannot enter into contracts without the additional signature of their parents or guardians. In most states, a minor is a person under the age of 18.

✔ **Persons lacking sound mind** usually cannot enter into contracts because, the reasoning goes, they lack the ability to understand what they are doing and to create a "meeting of the minds." Persons lacking sound mind generally are those who are mentally handicapped or impaired by the use of drugs or alcohol to such an extent that they cannot understand the significance of their acts. So try not to do deals at your local watering hole late into Saint Patrick's Day.

✔ **Persons who lack authority** to act on behalf of someone else may not be able to legally bind that other person or company. So make sure that the person signing on behalf of a company or other person has the legal authority to do so.

Oral Contracts

Oral contracts can be as binding as written contracts. But have fun proving what you've agreed to without a written record. If your deal goes south, you may feel like Sylvester to the other party's Tweetie Bird, endlessly chasing the truth. Make it easy on yourself and write up an agreement.

Often, parties enter into agreements that are partially oral and partially written, based on a handshake and a few letters or memos that may indicate some of the aspects of the agreement without actually being contracts themselves. In this case, the agreement is contained partly in the oral agreement and partly in the letters and memos. It's best to put all of the information relating to your agreement in one place — a single, clear, and complete written contract.

Offer and acceptance

Legal scholars often discuss contract formation in terms of *offer and acceptance.* But you're not likely to use these terms yourself unless you're auditioning for *Ally McBeal.* . . .

Contract law focuses on figuring out which types of promises between parties should be enforced by law and which types of promises should not be enforced by law. To form a contract (in other words, to form a promise that can be enforced) there must be a bargained exchange between the parties for legally sufficient consideration. Often, when the parties to the contract enter into this "bargained exchange for consideration," it is in the form of an offer by one party and an acceptance of that offer by another party. Fair enough.

One of the most common examples of offer and acceptance occurs in the real estate context.

For example, Madonna may offer to purchase a Beverly Hills home for 2 million dollars with a closing to occur in 60 days. She makes it on a preprinted form of contract containing various terms and conditions. If the seller accepts every one of the terms and conditions by countersigning the offer, then a contract has occurred.

But if the seller doesn't like the price offered or some of the terms, he or she may counter, say at 8 million dollars with closing to occur in 30 days. This *counteroffer* acts as a rejection of Madonna's offer. If she accepts the counteroffer, then the contract comes into existence. If she rejects it, makes a counteroffer herself, or doesn't respond within the time required, there is no acceptance of the seller's counteroffer and thus no contract.

Attack of the killer handshake

It's true that a written agreement is not final until signed — unless you indicate your agreement to the deal otherwise; say, with a handshake. Don't let an oral agreement sneak up on you by verbally agreeing to a deal before you are really ready to sign it.

A couple of oil companies found this out the hard way in 1987, when a court upheld a handshake deal between Getty Oil and Pennzoil, created when an attorney from Pennzoil shook hands with the directors of Getty Oil over a written agreement that was never signed. A jury found that Getty Oil and Pennzoil did have a valid contract, and further found that Texaco had interfered with this contract when Texaco tried to lure Getty Oil into a better deal at Pennzoil's expense. The jury awarded damages of 10.6 billion dollars for interference with the Pennzoil-Getty contract. Yup, that was a *b,* as in billion.

Message to take home: Even world-class attorneys and businesspeople can have trouble understanding what the heck they are doing without a written, signed contract.

In case you still aren't getting the message, here are a few lousy reasons to use an oral contract instead of a written contract:

- ✔ **I'm too busy to write it down.** Overworked businesspeople fail just as often as lazy ones. Find the time.

- ✔ **The other party won't agree to write it down.** News flash — you may be entering into an unstable business relationship. The world is full of honest people, and none of them mind putting what they promise in writing.

- ✔ **I trust the other party.** Uhmmm, hello?! We're all nice people here, but remember the old Richard Nixon line: "Trust everyone, but cut the cards."

- ✔ **The deal is too complicated to write down.** Odds are that it's not too complicated; you just don't understand it. Take the time to write out the deal and hash out any unclear points with the other party as you go along. If you don't understand, how will a judge or jury understand it when you try to enforce it?

- ✔ **It's a great deal for me — I don't want the other party to think it through too much.** Guess what? The other guy is thinking the same thing about you.

Some oral contracts are unenforceable. These four types of contracts typically must be in writing by law.

- ✔ Contracts for the sale or purchase of land

- ✔ Contracts for the sale or purchase of goods priced at $500 or more (with some significant exceptions that I don't discuss here)

✔ Marital settlement contracts (a promise to do something swapped for a promise to marry, such as a promise by Dad to give the groom a job after the groom marries his daughter) or prenuptial contracts

✔ Contracts that cannot be performed within one year of the time the contract is made (such as a contract to buy your office 13 months in the future)

Letter Agreements

One common way that you can form a contract is by use of a letter agreement. This takes the form of a letter from one party to the other that includes all of the important terms and conditions of the agreement.

The end of the letter then has a sentence that says that if the other side agrees with the terms of the letter, he or she can simply sign at the bottom of the letter, where there is an "Agreed and Accepted" line and signature space for the other party, and return it to the sender.

Letter agreements have the advantage of being less intimidating-looking than a formal contract and thus may be easier to get signed.

But letter agreements, because of their informal nature, tend to skip some important provisions, including "boilerplate" provisions. Don't get into hot water because of that missing legalese. Check out Chapter 3 on boilerplate.

E-Mail Contracts

Much business today is conducted by e-mail. It's even possible to bind yourself to a contract through e-mail communications, either deliberately or inadvertently.

If an e-mail or chain of e-mails clearly evidences an offer for entering into a deal with all of the material terms, and the other side responds by e-mail accepting the terms, then there is a good chance that a valid contract has been formed in spite of the fact that no signatures have been exchanged.

So be careful in your e-mail. If all that you intend by the e-mail exchanges is to negotiate the issues leading to a formal, written, and signed contract accepted by both parties, make sure you say precisely that in your e-mails.

Chapter 2

Contract Drafting Tips

• •

• •

*N*ow that you know what it takes to make a contract a contract, you may want to review the basics of contract drafting. In this chapter, I make sure that the contract describes the real deal between the parties, and I go over some tried and true drafting tips.

Later in the chapter, I review provisions you can put in your contract to limit your exposure to the other party. After you master these basics, I show you how to make your own standard form for your business.

What You Want from the Draft

Your goal when drafting a contract is to create a clear, concise, and complete description of the deal. That's it. No hocus-pocus or lawyer mumbo-jumbo needed. Of course, "clear, concise, and complete" is easier said than done — so the following sections explain exactly what that means.

Clarity

Clarity is at the heart of any well-written contract. As the lawyer in me would say, "the terms of an agreement must be sufficiently definite and certain to be legally enforceable."

Recitals

Recitals are one tool used for drafting clarity. They are the paragraphs at the beginning of the contract *before* words such as "the parties agree as follows," and often start with a fancy "Whereas." You can use recitals to summarize the agreement or to provide background information related to the deal. Recitals are not a mandatory part of any contract, and some contracts skip them entirely. But they can be useful as a touchy-feely description of what the parties intend to do in the contract and can assist outsiders who are trying to understand the contract. Legally, the contract begins after the recitals, after "the parties agree as follows." So don't put any important contract terms in the recitals unless you clearly repeat them in the body of the contract.

Remember, it's not enough for the parties to understand the deal in their own minds. An outsider should be able to understand the deal from reading the contract. Otherwise, how can a judge enforce it?

You may be tempted to take shortcuts here, especially when both sides believe that they understand the deal, without writing out the finer points. The other side owns a building, and you are buying it — what could be simpler? But clarity is important from the perspective of enforcement. If things go wrong later, it's always best to have a definitive written description to which the parties can refer. So don't write a contract to buy "the seller's building." What if, unbeknownst to you, the seller is the Donald Trump of your hometown and later claims that you intended to buy his dog of a shack, not the prime office space you wanted?

Make sure that both your responsibilities and the other side's obligations are carefully and clearly described. Ambiguous language in a contract can lead to misunderstandings, delays, frustration, and litigation.

Conciseness

You often don't need a 100-page contract to get the job done. In fact, very long contracts can delay getting a business deal done. The trick is making sure that you have sufficiently described what you expect. My preference is for shorter, concise contracts — get to the essential points right away.

Completeness

Many contracts fail because they are incomplete. That is, you may fail to put in some important terms or expectations. Some people assume that the terms are understood and don't need to be spelled out. Wrong! Make sure that if you are relying on something important when entering into a contract (such as a promise or guarantee from the other side) that this information is actually included in the draft.

When drafting your contract be sure to write down exactly what you mean and include all the relevant points, including

- ✔ An accurate description of the parties
- ✔ The price, including the amount paid, and when and how it will be paid
- ✔ A thorough description of the goods or services to be bought or sold

A contract checklist is shown as Form 2-1.

Key Provisions to Focus On

Good contracts focus on the key elements — such as the payment terms, the various obligations of the parties, representations and warranties, conditions to closing the deal, liability issues, remedies, and termination rights.

Payment terms

In some contracts, payment terms are easy to describe, such as "IDG Books hereby promises to pay the author $1 million on signing of this contract for him to prepare *Business Contracts For Dummies.*" (I wish.) But make sure that your payment-terms provision answers these questions:

- ✔ How much is being paid, by whom, and to whom?
- ✔ When is the payment to be made?
- ✔ What steps have to occur before payment is required?
- ✔ What is the form of payment? Is it by check, wire transfer, promissory note, or something else?

Contract Checklist

1. <u>Identity of Parties</u>

    • Name
    • Type of entity of each party (corporation, LLC, etc.)
    • Addresses

2. <u>Recitals</u>

    • Background of agreement
    • Purpose for entering into the contract
    • Key assumptions for the contract

3. <u>Obligations of the Parties</u>

    • What is each side required to do?
    • By what date?
    • If something has to be delivered, whose obligation is it and at whose cost

4. <u>Term of the Contract</u>

    • Is the contract a one-shot situation or will it last for some designated time period?
    • How can the term be renewed or extended?

5. <u>Price</u>

    • What is the price for the product or service?
    • Is it a fixed price, determined by a formula, by a project fee, or some other manner?
    • Who pays any tax?

6. <u>Payment Terms</u>

    • When is payment due?
    • Will there be installment payments?
    • Will interest be charged?
    • Is there a penalty for late payment?

Form 2-1: Contract Checklist.

7. Representations and Warranties

  - What representations and warranties are to be made by the parties?
  - Are certain warranties disclaimed (e.g., merchantability or fitness for a particular purpose)?
  - How long are any warranties good for?

8. Liability

  - What limitations of liability exist (e.g., no liability in excess of payment received, or no liability for consequential damage or lost profits)?
  - Under what circumstances is one party liable (e.g., material breach of agreement or grossly negligent in performing services)?

9. Termination of Contract

  - When can one party terminate the contract early?
  - What are the consequences of termination?
  - What post-termination obligations are there?

10. Confidentiality

  - What confidentiality obligations are there?
  - What are the exclusions from confidentiality?

11. Default

  - What are the events of default?
  - Does a party have a period to cure a default?
  - What are the consequences of a default?

12. Disputes

  - How are disputes to be handled – litigation, mediation, or arbitration?
  - If arbitration, what rules will govern? (e.g., JAMS/Endispute or the American Arbitration Association)
  - If arbitration, how many arbitrators and how will they be picked?
  - If arbitration, will there be procedures for discovery and what the arbitrator can and can't do?
  - If litigation, where can or must the litigation be brought?

13. Indemnification

  - Is there indemnification for certain breaches or problems?
  - What is the procedure required to obtain indemnification?
  - Is there a cap on or exclusions from indemnification?

(continued)

14.   <u>Miscellaneous</u>

- Governing law
- Attorneys fees
- Modification of Agreement
- Notice
- Entire Agreement
- Severability
- Time of the Essence
- Survival
- Ambiguities
- Waiver
- Headings
- Necessary Acts and Further Assurances
- Execution
- Jury Trial Waivers
- Specific Performances
- Representation on Authority of Parties
- Force Majuere
- Assignment

15.   <u>Signatures</u>

- What authority is required for one party to sign the contract (e.g., Board of Directors approval)?
- How many signatures are required?
- Are the signature blocks correct? For corporations, this is a typical appropriate signature block:

ABC, Inc.

By:_____
       John Smith, President

Obligations of the parties

Besides payment obligations, a business contract usually spells out various obligations of each party. So make sure that you have addressed these:

- ✔ What is each party obligated to do?
- ✔ By what date must the obligations be performed?
- ✔ What quality standards must be met for the obligations to be deemed fully completed?

This is an area that leads to frequent litigation — where one party expected the other side to do something more, better, or different than the other side expected. So be detailed and clear here as to what you really expect the other side to deliver.

Conditions

A number of contracts have "conditions" or "conditions precedent." This phrase is just a complicated way to say that certain things have to occur before the other side is obligated to do something.

Here's an example: In contracts to buy a business, the buyer usually insists that as a condition to his making payment for the business, the seller will already

- ✔ Have made various representations and warranties about the business.
- ✔ Have ensured that those representations and warranties are true at the closing.
- ✔ Have delivered all transfer documents to the buyer.
- ✔ Have made sure that no litigation or legal roadblocks to the closing exist.

Conditions are essential for many contracts to ensure that everything you expect to happen will happen before you are stuck with performing your side of the bargain.

Default and breach

The *default* or *breach* section of a contract addresses when a party is in violation of the contract and what the innocent party's rights are in such an event.

If the breach is a small one (not material to the deal), then the remedies are usually limited in the contract or by law.

If the breach or default is material, then the contract or the law could provide for some or all of the following rights (or *remedies*) to the nonbreaching (innocent) party:

- ✔ The right to recover damages for the breach
- ✔ The right to suspend further performance
- ✔ The right to terminate the contract
- ✔ The right to get *injunctive relief* (stopping the other side from continuing doing the breaching act) or *specific performance* (forcing the breaching party to live up to its obligations under the contract)

Limiting your risk

You also need to look at the portions of a contract designed to protect your behind and minimize the risks created when you enter into a contract. Lawyers use these sections of the contract to *shift risk* from one party to the other.

There are four primary ways in which the parties shift risk between each other: limitation of liabilities, indemnification, disclaimers, and warranties. Don't worry — I assume all responsibility for explaining this jargon to you!

Limitation of liabilities

Limitation of liabilities limits the liability of one party to the contract to the other. One common limitation of liability provides that neither party will be responsible for indirect or consequential damages to the other party arising out of the contract. Another provision could also set the maximum dollar amount of liability of either party to the other, under the agreement. For example, the parties may provide that no matter what happens in connection with the agreement, one will have no liability in excess of the amount to be received under the contract. The parties also may agree that their liability will be limited to certain assets (such as the assets of a partnership, but not the individual assets of the partners themselves).

Liquidated damages are a special type of limitation of liability. A liquidated damages provision allows the parties to agree up front when the contract is signed that the damages paid on a breach will be a fixed, predetermined amount. This provision is one step away from a roulette wheel in Vegas, because the actual damages suffered by the injured party some time in the future may be more or less than the liquidated damages payment that the parties agreed to when the contract was signed. If the actual damages are less than the liquidated damages amount, the injured party still gets the entire liquidated damages amount and may enjoy a windfall (maybe enough for a trip to Vegas).

Liquidated damages clauses are common in residential real estate purchase contracts. Such clauses can be beneficial to a buyer by limiting his or her legal exposure to a specified amount (such as 3 percent of the purchase price).

Liquidated damages provisions must be a reasonable estimate of the actual damages that the parties could suffer in the future. Figuring out what the heck this means can involve complicated analysis unique to each contract, so check with an attorney before drafting a liquidated damages provision.

Indemnification

Indemnification provides that if a *third party* brings a claim against the contracting party, the *other contracting party* will be responsible for it. Generally, the other party agrees to pay for all the costs of defending any lawsuit brought by a third party, as well as any settlement paid to the third party or any damages the third party wins at trial.

The indemnity section shifts "third party" risks from one contracting party to the other.

Hang on — it's not you! This concept really is a bit complicated, so here's an example. Say you own and lease out a mother lode of commercial real estate in New York City, but you work in Albuquerque, New Mexico. How can you know about or control what your tenants are doing in or to your property each and every moment? And why should you be liable if one of your tenants decides to hold an office party on the roof? If an employee blows off the roof and sues you, the deep-pocketed owner, why should you be liable? An indemnity provision between the owner of the property and the tenant of the property provides that the lessee has to compensate the building owner for any costs and expenses incurred by the owner when a third party sues the owner for claims "arising out of" the tenant's occupation of the property.

Indemnity provisions typically are found in leases, construction contracts (where the construction company indemnifies the owner of the land against any injuries to third parties during construction), and agreements with manufacturers, distributors, licensors, and sellers of goods (for example, where the purchaser indemnifies the manufacturer against injury to any third party arising out of the use of the goods after they were sold).

Indemnification clauses also can be drafted to protect one party from acts or wrongdoings of the other party.

Take a look at some sample indemnity language on Form 2-5 on the CD-ROM accompanying this book.

A word about representations and warranties

Representations and warranties are statements made in the contract by either party that refer to past or present facts or matters that are important to the contract. For example, if you're opening a restaurant, the party selling you your dishwashers may warrant in the purchase contract that the dishwashers are not defective. Your contract may then go on to provide that if he is wrong about the warranty (in legalspeak, if he breaches the warranty), that you have certain remedies, such as the right to return the dishwashers and get your money back.

The idea here is for each of the parties to think about the facts and circumstances it has relied on in entering the contract and to write them down in the representations and warranties section of the contract. This process allows one party to reflect on and identify the crucial statements or assumptions it relied on when it decided to enter into the contract and requires the other party to expressly state these facts or matters in the contract — and then stand behind its representations or pay the price for breaching them.

Representations and warranties are critical to contracts for the sale of goods, and Article 2 of the Uniform Commercial Code sets out all kinds of complicated rules on this subject, including implied warranties that you may be making without even knowing it (ouch!). Take a look at Form 2-2 on the CD-ROM for sample representations and warranties.

Disclaimer

A *disclaimer* does away with an underlying *obligation* of a contracting party. This is a common way to shift risk. For example, manufacturers often attempt to disclaim warranties of merchantability or fitness for a particular purpose when they sell goods.

Waiver

A *waiver* does away with a *right* of a contracting party. For example, one party may waive its rights under a law that would otherwise apply to the contract. A common waiver is one in which a party gives up the right to sue for lost profits and consequential damages.

Courts are not always eager to enforce waivers, especially in contracts where one of the parties is a merchant and the party waiving its rights under law is a consumer.

Boilerplate

These are the miscellaneous clauses at the end of a contract, such as the attorneys' fees clause, the jurisdiction clause, and the other important clauses that I discuss in Chapter 3.

Drafting and Negotiating Tips

Okay, here are some tips that I don't normally give away for free to help you arrive at a great contract.

Take charge of the draft

You always want to write the first draft yourself. Doing so can give you a tremendous advantage in shaping the negotiations. Writing the first draft allows you to

- ✔ Define the issues to be addressed in the contract.
- ✔ Set the tone of the business negotiations.
- ✔ Potentially limit the issues raised by the other party because she may respond to the points raised in your draft before raising deal points of her own.
- ✔ Structure the deal based on your own wish list, with payment and delivery terms most beneficial to you.
- ✔ Avoid the hassle of renegotiating the other party's draft, which may be more time-consuming than preparing your own first draft.

 Preparing the first draft of a contract can be a ton of work, but it is worth the effort.

Look at sample contracts and forms

The best way to start drafting a contract is to look at several sample forms that may be similar to your situation. If the sample forms are any good, they can alert you to issues that you may not have even thought about, and they can provide you with good language for your contract. Review the sample forms I've included with this book or look for forms on the Web or in forms books.

Don't be too reliant on a "standard" form or sample contract

On the other hand, don't make the mistake of being *too* reliant on some form you may find. Often, the form may not really be applicable to your situation, may be drafted for the benefit of the wrong side, or may be just plain lousy. Most forms are simply a starting place and need to be revised to reflect your particular transaction.

Make your own standard form

If you plan to enter into the same type of contract over and over, take the time to make your own standard form for that type of contract. This way, you can present the other party with your ideal contract terms and then negotiate from this strong position.

If you are just getting started, it can be tough to get a sense of what you should put in your standard form. The other party definitely isn't going to tell you what you should ask for, and your competitors won't be falling all over themselves to help you, either. Call professional associations and friends in your business for sample contracts written from your perspective — not the other side's.

When you are starting out, it may be worthwhile to pay a lawyer to draft an initial standard form contract for you. A business attorney usually reviews many more contracts than his or her clients', and may have a good sense of the latest developments in your area of business. But be sure to use a lawyer with direct experience in your field, on your side of the competitive fence.

Here are some tips for drafting your own standard form:

✔ Don't use the other party's contract terms as a model for your standard form. I guarantee you those guys haven't been up nights writing contracts with your best interests at heart.

✔ Don't be afraid to ask for too much in the standard form, within reason. You can always revise aggressive contract terms at the request of the other side (and come out looking quite generous).

✔ On the other hand, do stay within the boundaries of commercially reasonable behavior. *Aggressive* doesn't mean *offensive*. If 30-day payment terms are the standard in your field, sending out a standard form with 3-day payment terms will only create ill will and slow down negotiations. And you'll feel silly when you have to admit that your "standard form" isn't the standard at all.

✔ Make your standard form look as official as possible by formatting it with a professional-looking font. (Most basic word processors have a nice range available.)

Put your wish list of commercially reasonable terms in your standard form, and let the other party tell you what it is not willing to do.

Take two and call me in the morning

You can avoid some headaches by following these two simple tips:

✔ Make sure everyone knows your draft is just that — and not a final copy waiting to be signed. Put a header or footer that states "Draft for discussion purposes only. Not intended as a legal binding document." Include the date the draft was prepared in the header or footer so that you can keep track of earlier and later versions of the document.

✔ If you revise the other party's draft, be sure you indicate how you've changed it by striking though words that you want to delete and by underlining new text. It's plain snotty (if not bad faith) to revise someone else's draft without pointing out the changes you've made. Most word processing programs will track changes to a document as they are made, marking the changes with strike-outs and underlines.

Be aware of legal requirements

Certain types of provisions in a contract may be questionable legally (such as non-competition clauses, in certain instances). Some provisions (such as limitations of liability or waivers of warranties) may need to be boldfaced or in all capital letters to be effective. A good business lawyer can point these out to you.

Use exhibits

Sometimes your best bet to ensure clarity is to use *exhibits* (also called *attachments* or *addendums*) to a contract. That way, you can use your base contract over and over, and all the details that are specific to the transaction, such as a description of goods to be sold or the method of payment, can be put in an exhibit. Just make sure to number or letter each exhibit and to refer to each exhibit in the main contract. You don't have to sign the exhibits, just the main contract.

Last Call for Concluding the Contract

Don't forget the following before you call it a day:

✔ **Date and sign the agreement.** Date the agreement so that the parties can refer to it easily. The parties also should indicate the date they sign the agreement at the signature block. The parties don't have to sign the agreement on the same day, but unless the contract says when it will start, the contract is effective on the date of the last signature. It's a good idea to date the contract and then define that date as the "Effective Date." This way, there will be no confusion about the start date of the contract, regardless of who signs when.

- **Prepare two final copies of the contract.** Both parties should sign the contract (or perhaps even two copies so that each side has a signed copy). Just sign the last page. You don't need to initial every single page unless you are worried about the other party changing the "final" copy without your knowledge. Exhibits to the contract are fine and don't need to be initialed or signed.

- **Initial any handwritten last-minute changes.** If you make minor, handwritten changes to the final copy before it is signed, both parties should put their initials next to the changes. This way, the parties will avoid claims that the handwritten changes are not legit.

- **Using fax signatures.** It's okay to sign a contract by fax, as long as neither side claims that the fax signature is a forgery.

Forms on the CD-ROM

Form 2-1:	**Contract Checklist**	A checklist of points to consider when drafting and negotiating a contract
Form 2-2:	**Sample Representations and Warranties**	Sample representation and warranty clauses
Form 2-3:	**Sample Payment Terms**	A variety of sample payment forms for contracts
Form 2-4:	**Sample Limitations of Liability**	Sample language for limiting one party's liability under a contract
Form 2-5:	**Sample Indemnification Provisions**	Sample provisions indemnifying and holding harmless a party

Chapter 3

Boilerplate

● ●

In This Chapter

▶ The importance of boilerplate

▶ Key provisions from attorney fees to arbitration

● ●

*B*oilerplate provisions or clauses usually appear at the end of a contract. Sometimes they are referred to as the "Miscellaneous" provisions. Because they are at the end, people sometimes don't think that these clauses are important and don't read or pay any attention to them. Big mistake, bucko!

Boilerplate provisions are important because they affect your legal rights under the contract as much as all other clauses. The purpose of boilerplate provisions is to save the parties and drafters of contracts time with commonly used language. (Well, it's common in legal contracts, anyway — maybe not so common in the checkout line at the supermarket.)

What the Heck Is Boilerplate?

The common understanding of the term *boilerplate* is apparently standard clauses or language in a legal document.

 Get a glass of merlot, a beer, or a double, low-fat, low-foam latte, and read through *all* the sections, even the boilerplate at the end, of any contract you are about to sign. Ask questions and make comments. Boilerplate provisions are essential to the effective enforcement of your rights under the contract, and in some instances may grant or take away important rights.

Isn't it all standard?

Absolutely not. Boilerplate language is used to save time, but it is nevertheless important to understand the meaning and effect of these provisions in order to choose which ones are important for your particular contract.

Although boilerplate provisions may seem "standard," they can still be tailored to meet your specific contracting requirements. Every clause of every contract may be negotiated — even the boilerplate provisions.

Do I really need all that boilerplate?

No, you don't need every single boilerplate provision in every contract. Some of the key boilerplate provisions that should be included in every contract are discussed in the following sections, and several more are included on the CD-ROM. Aside from the key provisions, whether a particular boilerplate provision is used in your contract will depend upon the type of transaction documented in your contract.

Key Boilerplate Provisions

In this section, I discuss some of the more important boilerplate provisions. Note that you don't have to put boilerplate provisions in any particular order in a contract.

Attorney fees

This clause provides that the prevailing party in any dispute arising under the agreement shall be awarded his or her reasonable attorney fees and costs. The *prevailing party* is typically the party who recovers the greater relief in any action brought to enforce his or her rights under the agreement. For example, if Joe sues Fred for breach of contract and wins a damage award, Joe will be the prevailing party and will be awarded his reasonable attorneys' fees that he incurred if the attorney fees clause is included in the contract. A court determines the "reasonableness" of attorney fees and costs.

Any party who brings an action for breach of contract (or any other action based on the agreement) will likely incur substantial legal costs in seeking to recover damages. Not only will that party incur the cost of attorney fees, but may also incur a multitude of other costs associated with bringing a lawsuit, including expert witness fees, payments for court reporters, fees for filing documents with the court, as well as costs of travel, printing, photocopying, postage, telephone, and messenger services.

The general rule is that, without a contractual provision, statute, or case law to the contrary, attorney fees and other litigation costs are generally not recoverable by the prevailing party in a breach of contract case. Given that harsh rule, it's wise to include an attorney fees provision in your contracts.

If an attorney fees clause is not included, then each party has to bear the cost of paying his or her attorney fees and costs and expenses. What this means is, without this clause, you could end up having to pay your own attorney fees and costs — even if you win.

Here is a sample attorney fees clause:

> **Attorney Fees. In any litigation, arbitration, or other proceeding by which one party either seeks to enforce its rights under this Agreement (whether in contract, tort, or both) or seeks a declaration of any rights or obligations under this Agreement, the prevailing party shall be awarded its reasonable attorney fees, and costs and expenses incurred.**

A *tort,* by the way, is not the cake you ate to celebrate the contract signing; it's a civil cause of action for things such as negligence by one party.

Notice

A *notice* clause states how the parties will communicate with each other in written form. It may seem too simple and obvious to include in your contract, but if you don't lay it out, you may leave yourself open to problems.

It is important that notice is "effective upon delivery," and that delivery must be evidenced in some provable manner. When communications are sent between parties, you don't want the other party to be able to claim that he or she did not receive something you sent. This clause avoids that situation. Increasingly, notices may also be valid through e-mail communications.

So here is a sample notice provision:

> **Notice. Any notices required or permitted to be given hereunder shall be given in writing and shall be delivered (a) in person, (b) by certified mail, postage prepaid, return receipt requested, (c) by facsimile, or (d) by a commercial overnight courier that guarantees next day delivery and provides a receipt, and such notices shall be addressed as follows:**
>
> **If to _____: _____**
> **_____**
> **_____**
> **Attention:**
> **Fax:**
>
> **If to _____: _____**
> **_____**
> **_____**
> **Attention:**
> **Fax:**

or to such other address as either party may from time to time specify in writing to the other party. Any notice shall be effective only upon delivery, which for any notice given by facsimile shall mean notice that has been received by the party to whom it is sent as evidenced by confirmation slip.

Sometimes you want the "Attention" line to be directed to an officer (such as a CEO or General Counsel) instead of to a particular individual. After all, individuals do leave companies.

Modification of agreement

The *modification of agreement* clause states that the agreement may only be modified in writing. As important as it is to have your contract in writing, it's equally important to require any modifications (that is, additions, deletions, or changes in wording) to be in writing. You usually don't want someone claiming that a conversation or telephone call that you had with the other side modified your written contract.

Here is a sample clause:

> **Modification of Agreement. This Agreement may be supplemented, amended, or modified only by the mutual agreement of the parties. No supplement, amendment, or modification of this Agreement shall be binding unless it is in writing and signed by all parties.**

Entire agreement

The purpose of this clause, sometimes known as a *merger,* or *integration* clause, is to prohibit the introduction of any other evidence, oral or written, to vary or add to the terms of the agreement. The presence of this clause in your contract is designed to be conclusive evidence that it is the final, entire, and complete agreement and that nothing else (such as a letter of intent, earlier drafts of the agreement, or oral testimony of the other party) may be introduced in court to demonstrate otherwise.

Here is a sample clause:

> **Entire Agreement. This Agreement and all other agreements, exhibits, and schedules referred to in this Agreement constitute the final, complete, and exclusive statement of the terms of the agreement between the parties pertaining to the subject matter of this Agreement and supersedes all prior and contemporaneous understandings or agreements of the parties. This Agreement may not be contradicted by evidence of any prior or contemporaneous statements or agreements. No**

party has been induced to enter into this Agreement by, nor is any
party relying on, any representation, understanding, agreement, commitment or warranty outside those expressly set forth in this
Agreement.

Time of the essence

Unless *a time is of the essence* clause is included in your contract, a "reasonable" time for performance is implied if a problem arises as to any timing
issue. If the subject matter of your contract (for example, perishable goods,
meeting a critical deadline, and so on) requires split-second timing, then this
clause should be included. By including this clause in your contract, you
have made the precise timing of performance critical, and if this timing is not
met, then you can claim a breach of the contract. This clause can be tailored
to reflect specific timing issues within your contract.

Here is a sample clause:

> **Time of the Essence. Time is of the essence with respect to all provi-
> sions of this Agreement that specify a time for performance; provided,
> however, that the foregoing shall not be construed to limit or deprive a
> party of the benefits of any grace or use period allowed in this
> Agreement.**

Waiver

The *waiver* clause deals with the possibility of a waiver of contractual obligations; the purpose of this clause is to avoid the troublesome situations that
arise with alleged oral waivers, or unintended waivers arising from a party's
conduct.

Require that all waivers be in writing, and you can save yourself a lot of trouble.

For example, a waiver could occur where one party's performance is broken
into several parts. Say, a home remodeling contractor is doing some remodeling for you in stages. If the party receiving the performance accepts a late
performance by the other party the first time (the summer porch takes
longer to build than anticipated), that party (the contractor) might assert
that there was a waiver of the timing of performance for the remaining performance (completing the fireplace before winter). With this clause, an
attempted assertion of a waiver can be avoided.

Additionally, this clause can avoid the possibility of one party (mis)interpret-
ing the other party's conduct as constituting a waiver by requiring any
waiver to be in writing.

Here is a sample clause:

> <u>Waiver</u>. **No waiver of a breach, failure of any condition, or any right or remedy contained in or granted by the provisions of this Agreement shall be effective unless it is in writing and signed by the party waiving the breach, failure, right, or remedy. No waiver of any breach, failure, right, or remedy, whether or not similar, shall constitute a continuing waiver unless the writing so specifies.**

Necessary acts/further assurances

This is a catchall clause that can be used to require a party to sign a document or perform some act that is not specifically required elsewhere in the contract. This clause can be particularly useful for two reasons: (1) it can be used to require an act in the future not anticipated at the time the agreement was signed; and (2) it allows the parties not to have to draft the contract down to the most excruciatingly detailed points.

But watch out! This clause can't be used in place of some really important provision that you may have failed to include in the contract.

This clause also provides that if one party becomes wary of the other party's ability to perform any aspect of the contract, that party can request "assurances" from the other party that this is not the case. For example, if one party reads in the paper that the other party is experiencing financial difficulties, this clause allows that alert party to request and (hopefully) receive assurances from the other party that there are no financial problems.

Here is a sample clause:

> <u>Necessary Acts, Further Assurances</u>. **The parties shall at their own cost and expense execute and deliver such further documents and instruments and shall take such other actions as may be reasonably required or appropriate to evidence or carry out the intent and purposes of this Agreement.**

Consent to jurisdiction and forum selection

This clause states where any disputes relating to the agreement may take place. This is a critical clause, particularly when parties to a contract reside in or do business in two different states, different countries, or in the case of large states (such as Texas or California), two different counties.

Ideally, you want to have any action or proceeding take place where you reside or do business. If there's a dispute, you don't want to be hauled into court or into an arbitrator's office 3,000 or even 300 miles away. And this clause is particularly important if you're dealing with companies in foreign countries.

Here is a sample clause:

> **Consent to Jurisdiction and Forum Selection**. The parties hereto agree that all actions or proceedings arising in connection with this Agreement shall be tried and litigated exclusively in the State and Federal courts located in the County of San Francisco, State of California. The aforementioned choice of venue is intended by the parties to be mandatory and not permissive in nature, thereby precluding the possibility of litigation between the parties with respect to or arising out of this Agreement in any jurisdiction other than that specified in this paragraph. Each party hereby waives any right it may have to assert the doctrine of forum non conveniens or similar doctrine or to object to venue with respect to any proceeding brought in accordance with this paragraph, and stipulates that the State and Federal courts located in the County of San Francisco, State of California shall have in personam jurisdiction and venue over each of them for the purpose of litigating any dispute, controversy, or proceeding arising out of or related to this Agreement. Each party hereby authorizes and accepts service of process sufficient for personal jurisdiction in any action against it as contemplated by this paragraph by registered or certified mail, return receipt requested, postage prepaid, to its address for the giving of notices as set forth in this Agreement. Any final judgement rendered against a party in any action or proceeding shall be conclusive as to the subject of such final judgement and may be enforced in other jurisdictions in any manner provided by law.

To put it plainly, this clause says that the parties have agreed that any disputes will be litigated solely in San Francisco, even if it's inconvenient for one party, and that any final judgment can be enforced anywhere else desirable.

Representation on authority of parties/signatories

This clause states that the parties who sign the agreement have the authority to bind the parties to the agreement. When you sign your contract with another party, you aren't asking for this person's autograph — you want the signature to certify that that party has the authority to sign the contract and have it be legally binding.

Signatures may seem to be the easiest part of any contract, but they are botched often enough to require some attention. If you have entered into a contract with a corporation, it's not enough only to obtain the signature of some individual representative. With only that person's signature, it's possible that only that individual and not the corporation itself can be held liable under the contract. It's also possible that you could obtain the signature of a person who doesn't have authority to sign the contract. This clause is intended to avoid these possibilities.

Make sure you obtain the signature of the appropriate individual representing a company. For example, the signature line for a corporation typically reads:

Woohoo, Inc.,

a California corporation

_____

By: Joe Woohoo

Title: Chief Executive Officer

Here is a sample clause:

> **Representation on Authority of Parties/Signatories. Each person signing this Agreement represents and warrants that he or she is duly authorized and has legal capacity to execute and deliver this Agreement. Each party represents and warrants to the other that the execution and delivery of the Agreement and the performance of such party's obligations hereunder have been duly authorized and that the Agreement is a valid and legal agreement binding on such party and enforceable in accordance with its terms.**

Force majeure

Force majeure is defined in *Black's Law Dictionary* as "that part of a contract which cannot be performed due to causes which are outside the control of the parties and could not be avoided by the exercise of due care."

This includes an "act of God," which *Black's Law Dictionary* defines as "an act, event, happening, or occurrence, due to natural causes and inevitable accident, or disaster; a natural and inevitable necessity which implies entire exclusion of all human agency which operates without interference or aid from man and which results from natural causes and is in no sense attributable to human agency."

This clause states that the parties shall not be liable for failure to perform the contract's obligations under the agreement due to causes out of their control and is based on the concept that parties to an agreement desire to protect themselves from risks posed by unpredictable events.

The following sample clause specifically mentions the possibilities of mechanical, electronic, or communications failure, which are particularly important in the electronic age.

> **Force Majeure. No party shall be liable for any failure to perform its obligations in connection with any action described in this Agreement, if such failure results from any act of God, riot, war, civil unrest, flood, earthquake, or other cause beyond such party's reasonable control**

(including any mechanical, electronic, or communications failure, but excluding failure caused by a party's financial condition or negligence).

Ambiguities

This clause says that any ambiguous language in the contract shall be interpreted for its fair meaning and not strictly for or against any party. This is particularly important if you draft the contract, because ambiguities in a contract are typically construed against the drafter. On the other hand, if the other party drafts the contract, you may not want to include this clause.

Here is a sample clause:

> **Ambiguities. Each party and its counsel have participated fully in the review and revision of this Agreement. Any rule of construction to the effect that ambiguities are to be resolved against the drafting party shall not apply in interpreting this Agreement. The language in this Agreement shall be interpreted as to its fair meaning and not strictly for or against any party.**

Assignment

Assignment clauses deal with how and when a party wishing to transfer its rights or obligations under the contract to another party may do so. Most assignment clauses prohibit an assignment without the other party's consent. In some situations, though, you may want some specific rights to assign the contract (as in connection with the sale of your business).

This clause helps avoid the situation of having to deal with a third party who was not a party to the contract.

Here is a sample clause:

> **Assignment and Delegation. Neither party shall voluntarily, by operation of law or otherwise, assign any of its rights or delegate any of its duties, hypothecate, give, transfer, mortgage, sublet, license, or otherwise transfer or encumber all or part of its rights, duties, or other interests in this Agreement or the proceeds thereof without the other party's written consent. Any attempt to make an assignment or delegation in violation of this provision shall be a material default under this Agreement and any assignment or delegation in violation of this provision shall be null and void.**

Arbitration

This clause states that all disputes will be handled by arbitration rather than litigation. With growing court congestion, prolonged discovery, and pretrial tactics driving up the cost of litigation, arbitration has become an increasingly popular form of alternate dispute resolution. *Arbitration* is allowing an independent arbiter to settle a dispute rather than putting it before court in a lawsuit. Without an agreement like this in the contract, parties are not required to submit disputes to arbitration (although they may still do so).

Advantages of arbitration

Arbitration has several advantages, including the following:

- Arbitration can be faster than litigation.
- Arbitration can be cheaper than litigation.
- Arbitration is less formal.
- Arbitrators tend to be more sophisticated and knowledgeable than juries.

Disadvantages of arbitration

Arbitration has some disadvantages, including the following:

- If you get a bad decision from the arbitrator, there usually is nothing you can do about it (no appeals are generally allowed in arbitration).
- You may get stuck with a lousy arbitrator.
- You have less chance to really investigate your case (through discovery) than you do in litigation. *Discovery* means the opportunity to discover information from the other side in a dispute, such as through written questions or depositions.

I'm not a big fan of arbitration, after once having been stuck with an ignorant nincompoop arbitrator and finding out there was nothing I could do about it.

You should negotiate the specifics of any arbitration clause. For example, you may want to provide for three arbitrators instead of one or require that certain rules have to be followed.

If you think arbitration is best for you, here is a sample clause. (I put in JAMS as the arbitrator because those arbitrators in my experience are very good.)

<u>Arbitration</u>. Any controversy, claim or dispute arising out of or relating to this Agreement, shall be settled by binding arbitration in San Francisco, California. Such arbitration shall be conducted in accordance with the then prevailing commercial arbitration rules of JAMS/Endispute ("JAMS"), with the following exceptions if in conflict: (a) one arbitrator shall be chosen by JAMS; (b) each party to the arbitration will pay its pro rata share of the expenses and fees of the arbitrator, together with other expenses of the arbitration incurred or approved by the arbitrator; and (c) arbitration may proceed in the absence of any party if written notice (pursuant to the JAMS' rules and regulations) of the proceedings has been given to such party. The parties agree to abide by all decisions and awards rendered in such proceedings. Such decisions and awards rendered by the arbitrator shall be final and conclusive and may be entered in any court having jurisdiction thereof as a basis of judgment and of the issuance of execution for its collection. All such controversies, claims or disputes shall be settled in this manner in lieu of any action at law or equity; provided however, that nothing in this subsection shall be construed as precluding the bringing an action for injunctive relief or other equitable relief. The arbitrator shall not have the right to award punitive damages or speculative damages to either party and shall not have the power to amend this Agreement. The arbitrator shall be required to follow applicable law. IF FOR ANY REASON THIS ARBITRATION CLAUSE BECOMES NOT APPLICABLE, THEN EACH PARTY, TO THE FULLEST EXTENT PERMITTED BY APPLICABLE LAW, HEREBY IRREVOCABLY WAIVES ALL RIGHT TO TRIAL BY JURY AS TO ANY ISSUE RELATING HERETO IN ANY ACTION, PROCEEDING, OR COUNTERCLAIM ARISING OUT OF OR RELATING TO THIS AGREEMENT OR ANY OTHER MATTER INVOLVING THE PARTIES HERETO.

A Final Word on Boilerplate

It is critical to include the appropriate boilerplate provisions in your contracts. Although you don't necessarily need every clause, check out all the clauses presented here and contained in Form 3-1 on the CD-ROM accompanying this book for sample language.

IMPORTANT BOILERPLATE PROVISIONS FOR CONTRACTS

Miscellaneous

(a)   Choice of Law. This Agreement, and any dispute arising from the relationship between the parties to this Agreement, shall be governed by *[e.g., California]* law, excluding any laws that direct the application of another jurisdiction's laws.

(b)   Attorney Fees Provision. In any litigation, arbitration, or other proceeding by which one party either seeks to enforce its rights under this Agreement (whether in contract, tort, or both) or seeks a declaration of any rights or obligations under this Agreement, the prevailing party shall be awarded its reasonable attorney fees, and costs and expenses incurred.

(c)   Notice. Any notices required or permitted to be given hereunder shall be given in writing and shall be delivered (a) in person, (b) by certified mail, postage prepaid, return receipt requested, (c) by facsimile, or (d) by a commercial overnight courier that guarantees next day delivery and provides a receipt, and such notices shall be addressed as follows:

If to _____: _____
                        _____
                        _____
                        Attention:
                        Fax:

If to _____: _____
                        _____
                        _____
                        Attention:
                        Fax:

or to such other address as either party may from time to time specify in writing to the other party. Any notice shall be effective only upon delivery, which for any notice given by facsimile shall mean notice which has been received by the party to whom it is sent as evidenced by confirmation slip.

(d)   Modification of Agreement. This Agreement may be supplemented, amended, or modified only by the mutual agreement of the parties. No supplement, amendment, or modification of this Agreement shall be binding unless it is in writing and signed by all parties.

(e)   Entire Agreement. This Agreement and all other agreements, exhibits, and schedules referred to in this Agreement constitute(s) the final, complete, and exclusive statement of the terms of the agreement between the parties pertaining to the subject matter of this Agreement and supersedes all prior and contemporaneous understandings or agreements of the parties. This Agreement may not be contradicted by evidence of any prior or contemporaneous statements or agreements. No party has been induced to enter into this Agreement by, nor is any

Form 3-1: Sample boilerplate.

party relying on, any representation, understanding, agreement, commitment or warranty outside those expressly set forth in this Agreement.

(f)   <u>Severability of Agreement</u>. If any term or provision of this Agreement is determined to be illegal, unenforceable, or invalid in whole or in part for any reason, such illegal, unenforceable, or invalid provisions or part thereof shall be stricken from this Agreement, and such provision shall not affect the legality, enforceability, or validity of the remainder of this Agreement. If any provision or part thereof of this Agreement is stricken in accordance with the provisions of this section, then this stricken provision shall be replaced, to the extent possible, with a legal, enforceable, and valid provision that is as similar in tenor to the stricken provision as is legally possible.

(g)   <u>Separate Writings and Exhibits</u>. The following [*e.g., agreements, exhibits, schedules, or other separate writings*] constitute a part of this Agreement and are incorporated into this Agreement by this reference: [*List separate writings by name and date*]. Should any inconsistency exist or arise between a provision of this Agreement and a provision of any exhibit, schedule, or other incorporated writing, the provision of this Agreement shall prevail.

(h)   <u>Time of the Essence</u>. Time is of the essence in respect to all provisions of this Agreement that specify a time for performance; provided, however, that the foregoing shall not be construed to limit or deprive a party of the benefits of any grace or use period allowed in this Agreement.

(i)   <u>Survival</u>. Except as otherwise expressly provided in this Agreement, representations, warranties, and covenants contained in this Agreement, or in any instrument, certificate, exhibit, or other writing intended by the parties to be a part of this Agreement, shall survive for ___ years after the date of this Agreement.

(j)   <u>Ambiguities</u>. Each party and its counsel have participated fully in the review and revision of this Agreement. Any rule of construction to the effect that ambiguities are to be resolved against the drafting party shall not apply in interpreting this Agreement. The language in this Agreement shall be interpreted as to its fair meaning and not strictly for or against any party.

(k)   <u>Waiver</u>. No waiver of a breach, failure of any condition, or any right or remedy contained in or granted by the provisions of this Agreement shall be effective unless it is in writing and signed by the party waiving the breach, failure, right, or remedy. No waiver of any breach, failure, right, or remedy, whether or not similar, nor shall any waiver constitute a continuing waiver unless the writing so specifies.

(l)   <u>Headings</u>. The headings in this Agreement are included for convenience only and shall neither affect the construction or interpretation of any provision in this Agreement nor affect any of the rights or obligations of the parties to this Agreement.

(continued)

(m)   <u>Necessary Acts, Further Assurances</u>. The parties shall at their own cost and expense execute and deliver such further documents and instruments and shall take such other actions as may be reasonably required or appropriate to evidence or carry out the intent and purposes of this Agreement.

(n)   <u>Execution</u>. This Agreement may be executed in counterparts and by fax.

(o)   <u>Consent to Jurisdiction and Forum Selection</u>. The parties hereto agree that all actions or proceedings arising in connection with this Agreement shall be tried and litigated exclusively in the State and Federal courts located in the County of_____, State of____. The aforementioned choice of venue is intended by the parties to be mandatory and not permissive in nature, thereby precluding the possibility of litigation between the parties with respect to or arising out of this Agreement in any jurisdiction other than that specified in this paragraph. Each party hereby waives any right it may have to assert the doctrine of forum non conveniens or similar doctrine or to object to venue with respect to any proceeding brought in accordance with this paragraph, and stipulates that the State and Federal courts located in the County of __ _____, State of _____ shall have in personam jurisdiction and venue over each of them for the purpose of litigating any dispute, controversy, or proceeding arising out of or related to this Agreement. Each party hereby authorizes and accepts service of process sufficient for personal jurisdiction in any action against it as contemplated by this paragraph by registered or certified mail, return receipt requested, postage prepaid, to its address for the giving of notices as set forth in this Agreement. Any final judgement rendered against a party in any action or proceeding shall be conclusive as to the subject of such final judgement and may be enforced in other jurisdictions in any manner provided by law.

(p)   <u>Jury Trial Waivers</u>. To the fullest extent permitted by law, and as separately bargained-for-consideration, each party hereby waives any right to trial by jury in any action, suit, proceeding, or counterclaim of any kind arising out of or relating to this Agreement.

(q)   <u>Specific Performance</u>. The parties acknowledge that it will be impossible to measure in money the damage to them caused by any failure to comply with the covenants set forth in Section __, that each such covenant is material, and that in the event of any such failure, the injured party will not have an adequate remedy at law or in damages. Therefore, the parties consent to the issuance of an injunction or the enforcement of other equitable remedies against them at the suit of the other, without bond or other security, to compel performance of all of the terms of Section __, and waive the defense of the availability of relief in damages.

(r)   <u>Representation on Authority of Parties/Signatories</u>. Each person signing this Agreement represents and warrants that he or she is duly authorized and has legal capacity to execute and deliver this Agreement. Each party represents and warrants to the other that the execution and delivery of the Agreement and the performance of such party's obligations hereunder have been duly authorized and that the Agreement is a valid and legal agreement binding on such party and enforceable in accordance with its terms.

(s)   <u>Force Majeure</u>. No party shall be liable for any failure to perform its obligations in connection with any action described in this Agreement, if such failure results from any act of God, riot, war, civil unrest, flood, earthquake, or other cause beyond such party's reasonable control (including any mechanical, electronic, or communications failure, but excluding failure caused by a party's financial condition or negligence).

(t)   Assignment. Neither party shall voluntarily or by operation of law assign, hypothecate, give, transfer, mortgage, sublet, license, or otherwise transfer or encumber all or part of its rights, duties, or other interests in this Agreement or the proceeds thereof (collectively, "Assignment"), without the other party's prior written consent. Any attempt to make an Assignment in violation of this provision shall be a material default under this Agreement and any Assignment in violation of this provision shall be null and void.

[(u)   Arbitration. Any controversy, claim or dispute arising out of or relating to this Agreement, shall be settled by binding arbitration in [City], [State]. Such arbitration shall be conducted in accordance with the then prevailing commercial arbitration rules of JAMS/Endispute ("JAMS"), with the following exceptions if in conflict: (a) one arbitrator shall be chosen by JAMS; (b) each party to the arbitration will pay its pro rata share of the expenses and fees of the arbitrator, together with other expenses of the arbitration incurred or approved by the arbitrator; and (c) arbitration may proceed in the absence of any party if written notice (pursuant to the JAMS' rules and regulations) of the proceedings has been given to such party. The parties agree to abide by all decisions and awards rendered in such proceedings. Such decisions and awards rendered by the arbitrator shall be final and conclusive and may be entered in any court having jurisdiction thereof as a basis of judgment and of the issuance of execution for its collection. All such controversies, claims or disputes shall be settled in this manner in lieu of any action at law or equity; [provided however, that nothing in this subsection shall be construed as precluding the bringing an action for injunctive relief or other equitable relief]. The arbitrator shall not have the right to award punitive damages or speculative damages to either party and shall not have the power to amend this Agreement. The arbitrator shall be required to follow applicable law. [IF FOR ANY REASON THIS ARBITRATION CLAUSE BECOMES NOT APPLICABLE, THEN EACH PARTY, TO THE FULLEST EXTENT PERMITTED BY APPLICABLE LAW, HEREBY IRREVOCABLY WAIVES ALL RIGHT TO TRIAL BY JURY AS TO ANY ISSUE RELATING HERETO IN ANY ACTION, PROCEEDING, OR COUNTERCLAIM ARISING OUT OF OR RELATING TO THIS AGREEMENT OR ANY OTHER MATTER INVOLVING THE PARTIES HERETO.]]

Forms on the CD

Form 3-1	**Sample Boilerplate**	Sample boilerplates or miscellaneous clauses that can be added to the end of a contract

Part II
Forms for Businesses Big and Small

The 5th Wave   By Rich Tennant

"You can become a 'corporation' or a 'sole proprietor,' Mr Holk. But there's simply no legal way of filing yourself as a 'formidable presence.'"

In this part . . .

1f you're running a business, you need the forms in this part. Believe it or not, whether you're a manager at a lawnmower repair shop with two employees or an executive at Microsoft, you have to deal with many of the same issues. You have to let your employees and customers know what your policies are. You have to know how to deal with contractors. And you have to know what to do when it comes to acquisitions and stock options. (Okay, maybe not if you're running a lawnmower repair shop, but who knows?)

Chapter 4

Incorporation Forms and Agreements

Many businesses today are established as *corporations*. Corporations are separate legal entities that are typically used to operate a business. Corporations give you the advantage of *limited liability* — meaning that you risk only the amount you invest in the company, provided that you properly operate the corporation.

Corporations are not that complicated to set up. However, you do have to follow some important steps and create a number of documents. In this chapter, I provide you with the key documents for creating a corporation. Other documents and forms are included on the CD-ROM and may be referred to in this chapter.

A Corp Is Born

Forming a corporation requires you to take some basic steps. Corporations are subject to state statutes, and the rules and procedures for creating corporations vary from state to state. Make sure that you consult your state's laws for the precise rules.

Playing the name game

Choosing a name for your corporation isn't something you want to do during a commercial break in a rerun of *Seinfeld* (or even *60 Minutes*). Your company's name is a serious decision that impacts your ability to create the documents necessary to properly form the corporation. Not only does the name you choose affect your customers' image of your company, but the uniqueness of your name can also affect future trademarks, service marks, and your ability to conduct business in your own state and in other states.

Before you choose a name for your corporation, conduct the following searches:

- ✔ Has another company filed a conflicting trademark or service mark with the U.S. Patent and Trademark Office?

- ✔ Is your proposed name available in key states in which you intend to do business? A conflict in another state generally prevents the company from qualifying to do business in that state under that corporate name. (You can do this by calling the Secretary of State in the state you are concerned about.)

- ✔ Can you get the desired domain name if you decide to set up a Web site?

Have a couple of names in mind

Unfortunately, many names are already taken, so be prepared to check the availability of several names at once. Also, remember that the state corporation statute typically requires that your corporation's name include the word "Corporation," "Company," "Inc.," or "Incorporated." Similarly, many laws prohibit the use of certain words, such as "Bank" or "Insurance," in the corporate name unless the corporation qualifies as such an entity.

After a name is cleared . . .

After you receive a clearance on a name, you can either incorporate right away with the name or reserve it for a while (time periods vary) by filing for a *Name Reservation*. The Secretary of State's office can provide you with the procedure.

Choosing a state of being

Because the laws that affect corporations vary from state to state, many people ask in which state to incorporate their businesses. As a practical matter, most of the time the answer is to incorporate under the laws of the state in which the corporation intends to conduct its principal business. Thus, if you are a California business, then a California incorporation probably makes sense.

If you intend to incorporate in California, check out Forms 4-1 and 4-2 on the CD-ROM. Form 4-1 is a checklist for incorporating in the state of California. Form 4-2 is a guide for operating a California corporation. If you incorporate in a state other than California, familiarize yourself with this checklist and guide anyway because understanding the general issues can help when you consult your corporate attorney.

Delaware, which has a well-developed body of corporate law, is also a favorite haven for incorporation. However, if you are doing business in another state and incorporate under Delaware law, you will have extra filings and costs. Delaware may make sense if the company is backed by a venture capitalist with a clear goal of going public.

Most states have pamphlets on how to incorporate, with sample forms that you can order by calling up the Secretary of State's office.

Creating the Articles of Incorporation

After you select the corporate name and state of incorporation, you must file the official document creating the corporation with the Secretary of State. This document is called the *Articles of Incorporation* or the *Certificate of Incorporation,* depending on the state.

The Articles are typically short — two to three pages long. The key sections are as follows:

- ✓ **The Corporate Name.** This section of the Articles identifies the formal name of the corporation.

- ✓ **The Purpose of the Corporation.** Many states, including California and Delaware, allow this section to simply state that the purpose of the corporation is to engage in any lawful activity for which corporations may be organized in that state. You usually fare better when this clause is more general because you then have flexibility to expand your business into almost any area.

✔ **Duration.** Most state statutes provide that the corporation can have a perpetual duration. You generally don't want the Articles to provide for a fixed term of existence.

✔ **The Authorized Capital.** This section must set forth the total number of shares that the corporation can issue, the par value per share, and the different classes of stock. Typically, you have only one class of common stock, but sometimes you can issue both common stock and preferred stock. This section should authorize a sufficient number of shares to cover the founders' shares plus shares that may be issued to future employees or investors. If the state doesn't charge you extra, think about authorizing 10,000,000 shares.

✔ **Name and Address of Registered Agent.** Most states require the corporation to designate the name and address of a registered agent for service of process in the state. The registered agent is the person given notice of lawsuits filed against your company. If you are incorporating in a state other than where you maintain your principal office, you can designate various professional registered agent companies for a fee.

✔ **Other Required Provisions.** Depending on the state law, some provisions, such as preemptive right to purchase future shares, must also be contained in the Articles to be effective.

Form 4-3C shows a sample Articles of Incorporation for a California corporation (you can also find the form on the CD-ROM accompanying this book). Form 4-3D is a similar document for a Delaware corporation. Forms 4-4C and 4-4D are transmittal letters to send to the Secretary of States of California and Delaware, respectively. (All are available on the CD-ROM.)

Capitalizing the corporation

The corporation needs to sell stock to its founding shareholders as part of properly organizing the corporation. This stock sale is sometimes referred to as *capitalizing the corporation,* and the purpose of the sale is to inject start-up funds into the corporation to get it going. Although no minimum amount of money needs to be contributed in order to properly form a corporation, you should consider capitalizing the company with sufficient funds to meet its anticipated early needs in order to avoid potential personal financial risk to the shareholders.

Forms 4-49 through 4-50 on the CD-ROM deal with securities law filings and S corporation elections for a California corporation.

ARTICLES OF INCORPORATION

OF

[NAME OF CORPORATION]

ARTICLE I

The name of this corporation is: [Corporation Name].

ARTICLE II

The purpose of this corporation is to engage in any lawful act or activity for which a corporation may be organized under the General Corporation Law of California other than the banking business, the trust company business, or the practice of a profession permitted to be incorporated by the California Corporations Code.

ARTICLE III

The name and complete business address in the State of California of this corporation's initial agent for service of process is:

      [Agent]
      [Building]
      [Street]
      [City, State Zip]

Form 4-3C: Sample Articles of Incorporation for a California Corporation.

(continued)

ARTICLE IV

This corporation is authorized to issue only one class of shares of stock which shall be designated Common Stock, $.001 par value; and the total number of shares which this corporation is authorized to issue is _____.

ARTICLE V

(a)   The liability of directors of this corporation for monetary damages shall be eliminated to the fullest extent permissible under California law.

(b)   This corporation is authorized to provide indemnification of agents (as defined in Section 317 of the California Corporations Code) through bylaw provisions, agreements with agents, vote of shareholders or disinterested directors, or otherwise, to the fullest extent permissible under California law.

(c)   Any amendment, repeal or modification of any provision of this Article V shall not adversely affect any right or protection of an agent of this corporation existing at the time of such amendment, repeal or modification.

_____

[Incorporator]

Classy classes of stock

You can provide many types of securities to investors in exchange for the capital that they make available. Two of the most common securities are *common stock* and *preferred stock,* and you need to know the differences between these two types of securities:

- **Common stock.** Shares in a corporation that have no preferences or priorities over other classes of stock. The rights to distributions, number of votes per share, liquidation rights, and other rights are the same for all shareholders on a share-by-share basis.

- **Preferred stock.** Shares that give the holders various benefits over the common stock holders. Many professional investors, including venture capitalists, prefer preferred stock to common stock. Preferred stock often has the following rights:

  - A priority on the business's assets upon liquidation

  - A priority on any dividends

- Special voting or veto rights

- A right to force the company to buy back the shares at some point in the future (known as *redemption rights*)

- A right to convert to common stock based on a formula

- Protection against certain stock splits, stock dividends, and future cheap issuances of stock (known as *anti-dilution* rights)

- A possible separate right to elect a designated number of directors

Issuing stock

In issuing shares to its initial shareholders, the corporation must ensure that it complies with both state and federal securities laws. These laws apply whenever you issue a "security," such as common or preferred stock. Typically, the issuance of shares to a small number of founding shareholders qualifies for a "private placement" type of exception from the registration requirements of securities laws. But double-check with your lawyer.

When you sell the stock, you need to issue a stock certificate. Form 4-54 on the CD-ROM is a sample common stock certificate. Form 4-55 on the CD-ROM is a sample preferred stock certificate.

Keeping a Stock Ledger

The company must keep good records of stock issuances, showing the amount of stock issued, dates issued, and funds received. A Stock Ledger can help the company organize this information. Keeping copies of all the stock certificates that the company issues is generally a good idea, at least while the company is privately held.

(Lights . . . camera . . .) Action of Incorporator

The *incorporator* is the person who initially organizes the corporation. The incorporator uses a document called an Action of Incorporator to perform important functions like adopting bylaws, electing directors (if they are not named in the Articles of Incorporation), and signing the Articles of Incorporation. The incorporator can be a lawyer, a prospective shareholder, or another interested individual.

Unless the Articles of Incorporation name the initial directors, you *must* create an Action of Incorporator to name the corporation's first board of directors and permit the corporation to transact business lawfully. Make sure that the document is dated or effective on or after the date after the date of incorporation, and insert the document in the corporation's minute book.

You can find a sample Action of Incorporator form for a California corporation (Form 4-5C) and for a Delaware corporation (Form 4-5D) on the CD-ROM.

The owners and operators

The *shareholders* of the corporation are the "owners" of the corporation, the investors who receive ownership in the corporation in return for money or assets they invest. The shareholders elect a *board of directors,* the "operators" of the corporation, who have overall responsibility for the business of the corporation. The board, in turn, elects the officers of the corporation (president, vice president, secretary, and chief financial officer, typically). The officers handle the day-to-day affairs of the corporation.

The board of directors

The directors must act in connection with the best interests of the corporation and its shareholders. Board members can provide valuable wisdom and experience in guiding a company to success.

The board members maintain a *fiduciary* relationship with the company (a relationship founded in trust and confidence).

The size of the board is up to the discretion of the shareholders. Generally, you want to avoid an unwieldy number of directors or an even number of directors (to avoid deadlock). The board should meet on a regular basis. After filing the incorporation papers with the Secretary of State, the board needs to adopt organizational resolutions (either at a meeting or by unanimous written consent). These organizational resolutions concern preliminary matters for properly establishing the corporation, as described in the following section.

Initial actions by the board of directors

The board of directors can accomplish the organizational resolutions of the corporation by adopting them in a meeting that they call in accordance with the corporation's bylaws or by unanimous written consent. Generally, the directors authorize the following:

- ✔ Adoption or ratification of the bylaws
- ✔ Designation of principal office
- ✔ The election of the initial officers
- ✔ The selection of a specimen stock certificate for the corporation's common stock
- ✔ The designation of the corporation's bank or banks
- ✔ The issuance of the stock to initial shareholders
- ✔ The election of S Corporation status, if desirable
- ✔ The payment of organizational expenses
- ✔ The authorization of any Buy-Sell Agreement, leases, or other material contracts

Form 4-7C on the CD-ROM shows sample organizational board resolutions for California corporations; Form 4-7D on the CD-ROM shows sample organizational board resolutions for Delaware corporations.

Ongoing actions by the board of directors

The board is required to hold annual meetings but typically meets more often than that. Some of the actions that may be necessary or desirable for the board to approve on an ongoing basis include the following:

- ✔ Issuing securities and granting warrants, options, or other rights to purchase securities
- ✔ Adopting a Stock Option Plan
- ✔ Amending the Articles of Incorporation or bylaws
- ✔ Entering into major contracts, leases, or other obligations
- ✔ Declaring distributions, dividends, or stock splits
- ✔ Borrowing significant sums and providing the security for the loans
- ✔ Entering into Employment Agreements with key employees
- ✔ Electing officers of the company and setting or changing their compensation and terms of employment
- ✔ Adopting or amending employee benefit plans
- ✔ Calling shareholders' meetings
- ✔ Buying or selling significant assets
- ✔ Adopting company policies

The CD-ROM offers an extensive array of forms (Forms 4-8 to 4-31) that you can use for your board minutes or consents.

The shareholders

The founders of the business typically buy stock in the company and are the first shareholders. Later on, investors can contribute money or other assets and also become shareholders.

Various actions of the corporation require action by the shareholders, and these actions must be reflected in minutes of meetings or by appropriate written consents. A corporation is typically required to hold annual meetings of shareholders, the principal purpose of which is to elect the members of the board of directors.

Some of the actions for which shareholder approval may be required or desirable include the following:

- ✔ Merger or reorganization of the corporation
- ✔ Amendment to the Articles of Incorporation
- ✔ Amendment of the bylaws (other than an amendment settling the exact number of directors within the range established by the bylaws or Articles of Incorporation)
- ✔ Sale or transfer of all or substantially all of the corporation's assets
- ✔ Approval of contracts with interested directors
- ✔ Authorization of indemnity of a corporate agent for liability incurred when acting on behalf of the company
- ✔ Issuance of certain securities
- ✔ Adoption of stock option plans
- ✔ Dissolution or winding up of the corporation

Form 4-32C is a form for Action by Written Consent of Stockholders of a California corporation used for the shareholders' part of the initial formation of the corporation. Form 4-32D is a similar form for Delaware. For ongoing Shareholders' resolutions in the forms of minutes, consents, and resolutions, see Forms 4-33 through 4-38 on the CD-ROM.

Let Bylaws Be Bylaws

The bylaws of a corporation contain the rules and procedures that govern the rights and powers of shareholders, directors, and officers. Most lawyers have a prepared "standard" set of template bylaws that may be modified to meet your company's specific requirements.

The bylaws are typically adopted by the incorporator or by the board of directors in the organizational meting or the written consent in place of the organizational meeting. This organizational meeting or written consent is the first action taken by the board of directors in connection with the formation of the corporation (listed earlier in this chapter, under "Initial actions by the board of directors").

The bylaws cover the following:

- ✔ The size of the board of directors
- ✔ When and how board meetings are called (including notice)
- ✔ When and how shareholder meetings are called (including notice)
- ✔ Duties and responsibilities of directors and officers
- ✔ Procedures for exercising voting rights
- ✔ Regulation of the transfer of corporate stock
- ✔ Indemnification obligations for officers, directors, and agents (*indemnification* refers to protection from lawsuits and claims)
- ✔ The company's fiscal year
- ✔ General corporate matters

Bylaws generally may be adopted, amended, or repealed by the board of directors or by a vote of the shareholders; and the bylaws may limit the board's powers in this respect.

Form 4-6C on the CD-ROM accompanying this book shows some sample bylaws for a California corporation. Form 4-6D on the CD-ROM shows sample bylaws for a Delaware corporation.

Protecting the Directors

It's particularly important to offer *protection* to the directors, the people running and managing your corporation. This is normally done by including clauses offering *indemnification* of directors, and by maintaining *Directors & Officers Insurance*. Contact your insurance agent for information about D&O Insurance.

Buy! Sell! Agreement

A Buy-Sell Agreement provides for the buying and selling of the stock in a corporation (usually a small, closely held corporation) of a withdrawing shareholder. This agreement benefits both the corporation and its owners. (Sometimes a Buy-Sell Agreement includes a Right of First Refusal Agreement, which I discuss in the "Right of First Refusal Agreement" section, later in this chapter.)

Reasons for withdrawing

A shareholder may either want to (or need to) withdraw from the corporation for a number of reasons, including the following:

- Wanting to sell (needs the money)
- Death
- Disability (mental or physical)
- Expulsion from the business
- Termination of employment
- Bankruptcy
- Retirement
- Voluntary or involuntary dissolution of the corporation

Let's make a deal (setting the price)

Setting the price of the interest to be bought and sold is both the most important and most difficult part of the Buy-Sell Agreement. Valuing a closely held business is fraught with potential difficulties, but it's a critical part of the agreement. You can choose from different valuation methods, such as capitalized earnings formula, book value, appraisal, or agreed price with arbitration, among others.

Key provisions of the Buy-Sell Agreement include the following:

- ✔ Restrictions on transfer of shares
- ✔ Permitted transfers
- ✔ Mandatory repurchase in certain cases
- ✔ Optional repurchase by the company or the other shareholders
- ✔ Obligations of transferees
- ✔ Possible purchase on death, total disability (physical or mental), or termination of employment
- ✔ Valuation (price and terms of sale)
- ✔ Dissolution of corporation
- ✔ Termination of agreement
- ✔ Spouse's (partner's) consent

Hire a lawyer to draft the agreement!

Don't attempt to draft a Buy-Sell Agreement by yourself. Hire a lawyer for this! This agreement can be extremely complicated and is very important for maintaining the continuity of your company.

Right of First Refusal Agreement

Shareholders of start-up companies often enter into a *Right of First Refusal Agreement* requiring shareholders to give the company or the other shareholders the priority right to match any offers to buy shares in the company. This right arises when a shareholder wishes to sell his or her stock. Such an agreement is usually desirable to try to keep stock in friendly hands and maintain the continuity of the corporation. This agreement is sometimes included within the Buy-Sell Agreement.

Key provisions of the Right of First Refusal Agreement (which are similar to provisions in the Buy-Sell Agreement) include the following:

- ✔ Restrictions on transfer
- ✔ Right of first refusal
- ✔ Legend on stock certificate
- ✔ No transfer to competitors

> ✓ Term of agreement
>
> ✓ Will provisions
>
> ✓ Spouse's (partner's) consent

A sample Right of First Refusal Agreement for a California corporation is found as Form 4-57 on the CD-ROM.

Forms on the CD-ROM

The following list contains forms on the CD-ROM pertaining to corporate formalities. (*Note:* Forms ending in a C or D are the same form for use in California or Delaware, respectively.)

Form 4-1	**Checklist for Formation of a California Corporation**	A checklist of issues to consider when forming a California corporation
Form 4-2	**Guide to Operation of Newly Formed California Corp.**	A comprehensive guide and discussion for forming a California corporation
Form 4-3C	**Articles of Incorporation (California corp.)**	Sample Articles to be filed with the California Secretary of State for forming the corporation
Form 4-3D	**Certificate of Incorporation (Delaware corp.)**	Sample Certificate of Incorporation to be filed with the Delaware Secretary of State necessary for forming the corporation
Form 4-4C	**Transmittal Letter Enclosing Articles of Incorporation to the California Secretary of State**	A sample letter to send to the California Secretary of State enclosing the Articles of Incorporation
Form 4-4D	**Transmittal Letter Enclosing Certificate of Incorporation to the Delaware Secretary of State**	A sample letter forwarding the Certificate of Incorporation for filing with the Delaware Secretary of State's office

Form 4-5C	**Action of Incorporator (California corp.)**	A form where the incorporator appoints initial directors for a California corporation
Form 4-5D	**Action of Incorporator (Delaware corp.)**	A form where the incorporator appoints initial directors for a Delaware corporation
Form 4-6C	**Bylaws (California corp.)**	Sample form bylaws for a California corporation
Form 4-6D	**Bylaws (Delaware corp.)**	Sample bylaws for a Delaware corporation
Form 4-7C	**Action by Unanimous Written Consent of Board of Directors in Lieu of Organizational Meeting (California corp.)**	A form of written consent of the board of directors of a California corporation adopting various important organizational resolutions
Form 4-7D	**Action by Unanimous Consent of the Board of Directors in Lieu of Organizational Meeting (Delaware corp.)**	A form of written consent of the board of directors of a Delaware corporation adopting various important organizational resolutions
Form 4-8	**Notice of Meeting of Board of Directors**	A form of written notification of a board of directors meeting
Form 4-9	**Declaration of Mailing Notice of Board Meeting**	A sample form for the corporate records showing that proper notice was given for a board of directors meeting
Form 4-10	**Waiver of Notice and Consent to Holding Meeting of Board of Directors**	A form for the board of directors to sign waiving requirement of a written notice for a meeting
Form 4-11	**Action by Unanimous Written Consent of Board of Directors**	Template for actions by unanimous written consent rather than at a meeting
Form 4-12	**Minutes of Meeting of the Board of Directors**	Template for recording the actions taken at a board of directors meeting

Form 4-13	**Board Resolution Approving Agreement**	Sample resolution to be approved by the board of directors approving the corporation entering into an agreement
Form 4-14	**Board Resolution Approving Borrowing**	Sample resolution to be approved by the board of directors approving the corporation making a certain borrowing
Form 4-15	**Board Resolution Approving Sale of Common Stock**	Sample resolution to be approved by the board of directors approving the sale of stock by the corporation
Form 4-16	**Board Resolution Approving a Stock Option Plan**	Sample resolution to be approved by the board of directors approving a stock option plan
Form 4-17	**Board Resolution Approving Amendment of Bylaws**	Sample resolution to be approved by the board of directors approving amendment of the corporate bylaws
Form 4-18	**Board Resolution Approving Articles of Incorporation**	Sample resolution to be approved by the board of directors approving amendment of the Articles of Incorporation
Form 4-19	**Board Resolution Approving an Employment Agreement**	Sample resolution to be approved by the board of directors approving execution of an employment agreement with a senior-level employee
Form 4-20	**Board Resolution Appointing Officers**	Sample resolution to be approved by the board of directors appointing officers for the corporation
Form 4-21	**Board Resolution Approving an Acquisition**	Sample resolution to be approved by the board of directors approving the acquisition of a business

Form 4-22	**Board Resolution Approving Dividends**	Sample resolution to be approved by the board of directors declaring dividends to be distributed to the shareholders
Form 4-23	**Board Resolution Approving Establishing a Committee of the Board**	Sample resolution to be approved by the board of directors that establishes a precisely named committee of the board
Form 4-24	**Board Resolution Approving Accountants**	Sample resolution to be approved by the board of directors appointing accountants for the corporation
Form 4-25	**Board Resolution Approving a Stock Split**	Sample resolution to be adopted by the board of directors approving a stock split
Form 4-26	**Board Resolution Approving a Lease**	Sample resolution to be approved by the board of directors approving the corporation entering into a lease
Form 4-27	**Board Resolution Approving Purchase of Property**	Sample resolution to be approved by the board of directors approving the purchase of a particular property
Form 4-28	**Board Resolution Approving Sale of Series A Preferred Stock**	Sample resolution to be approved by the board of directors approving the offer and sale of Series A preferred stock of the corporation
Form 4-29	**Board Resolution Approving S Corporation Election**	Sample resolution to be approved by the board of directors approving the corporation electing to be taxed as an S corporation

Form 4-30	**Board Resolution Regarding Annual Shareholders Meeting**	Sample resolution to be approved by the board of directors establishing the date of the annual meeting of the shareholders and other related matters
Form 4-31	**Board Resolution Regarding Qualification to Do Business**	Sample resolution to be approved by the board of directors authorizing the corporation to qualify to do business in appropriate states
Form 4-32C	**Action by Written Consent of Shareholders (California corp.)**	A form of written consent for initial actions or documents to be approved by the shareholders
Form 4-32D	**Action by Written Consent of Stockholders (Delaware corp.)**	A form of written consent for initial actions or documents to be approved by the stockholders
Form 4-33	**Notice of Annual Meeting of Shareholders**	A notice to be sent to shareholders of a corporation informing them of the date and place of the Annual Meeting of Shareholders
Form 4-34	**Declaration of Mailing Notice of Shareholders Meeting**	A form for the Secretary or Assistant Secretary of a corporation to complete and sign, declaring that a form of Notice of Shareholders Meeting in the form was attached and sent to all shareholders
Form 4-35	**Notice of Special Meeting of Shareholders**	A form to be sent to the shareholders notifying them of the date, place, and purpose of a special meeting of the shareholders

Form 4-36	**Waiver of Notice and Consent to Holding Meeting of Shareholders**	A form of waiver, to be signed by shareholders, consenting to a meeting of the shareholders without notice required by the corporation's bylaws
Form 4-37	**Action by Written Consent of the Shareholders**	A template for action to be taken by the written consent of the shareholders of a corporation, in place of action taken at a meeting
Form 4-38	**Minutes of Meeting of Shareholders**	A template for minutes of a shareholders meeting of a corporation
Form 4-39	**Shareholder Resolution Appointing Directors**	A sample shareholder resolution for appointing the directors of the corporation
Form 4-40	**Shareholder Resolution Confirming Accountants**	A sample shareholder resolution confirming and approving the designation of accountants of the corporation
Form 4-41	**Shareholder Resolution Approving Amendment of Bylaws**	A sample shareholder resolution for approval of the amendment of the corporate bylaws
Form 4-42	**Shareholder Resolution Approving Amendment of Articles of Incorporation**	A sample shareholder resolution for approval of the amendment of the Articles of Incorporation
Form 4-43	**Shareholder Resolution Approving an Acquisition**	A sample shareholder resolution for approving the acquisition of a business
Form 4-44	**Shareholder Resolution Approving a Stock Option Plan**	A sample shareholder resolution for approving an employee Stock Option Plan

Form 4-45	**Shareholder Resolution Approving an Agreement**	A sample shareholder resolution for approving the corporation entering into an agreement
Form 4-46	**Shareholder Resolution Approving Sale of Stock**	A sample shareholder resolution for approving the sale of common stock by the corporation
Form 4-47	**Shareholder Resolution Approving Increasing the Size of the Board**	A sample shareholder resolution for approving an amendment to the corporate bylaws to increase the size of the board of directors and to elect new directors for the new seats
Form 4-48	**Shareholder Resolution Appointing Director to Fill Vacancy**	A sample shareholder resolution for appointing a new director to fill a vacant seat on the corporation's board of directors
Form 4-49	**California Form 1502 (Statement by Domestic Stock Corporation)**	The form that the California Secretary of State requires new California corporations to fill out
Form 4-50	**Transmittal Letter to California Secretary of State Enclosing Form 1502**	The form required to be filed with the California Secretary of State by new corporations
Form 4-51	**California Form 25102(f) (Notice to California Department of Corporations)**	The form that can be filed with the California Department of Corporations in connection with the issue of private placement stock
Form 4-52	**Transmittal Letter to Department of Corporations Enclosing Form 25102(f)**	A sample letter forwarding the Form 25102(f) to the California Department of Corporations

Form 4-53	**Transmittal Letter to Franchise Tax Board Enclosing S Corporation Election Form**	A sample letter forwarding the California S corporation election form to the California Franchise Tax Board
Form 4-54	**Stock Certificate — Common Stock**	Sample common stock certificate for a privately held company
Form 4-55	**Stock Certificate — Preferred Stock**	Sample preferred stock certificate for a privately held company
Form 4-56	**Stock Ledger and Capitalization Summary**	This is a sample form to be used to keep track of the issue of stock, preferred stock, options, and warrants
Form 4-57	**Right of First Refusal Agreement (California corp.)**	A sample agreement where the shareholders have to offer a California corporation a right of first refusal on any transfer of their shares

Chapter 5

Stock Purchase Agreements

● ●

In This Chapter

▶ Selling stock in your company

▶ Understanding the securities laws

▶ Documenting stock sales

▶ Exploring venture capital financings

▶ Allying with strategic partner equity investors

● ●

*S*tart-up and emerging companies often need to raise capital to fund their businesses.

If you're interested in selling stock in your company, whether to angel investors, professional investors, or venture capitalists, this chapter outlines some of the key documents necessary.

I also help you try to avoid some of the legal liabilities associated with selling stock.

Placing Your Stock on the Auction Block

Raising funding through the sale of *stock* (or other equity interest) means selling ownership in your business in exchange for capital. The upside of stock sales is that the capital you raise typically doesn't have to be paid back in the same way a loan does. The downside is that you may have to relinquish some of the control over your company to the investors.

Regardless of whom you intend to sell your stock to, run through the items on the checklist shown in Form 5-1 on the CD-ROM to make sure that you remember the key points about issuing stock.

Checklist for issuing stock

If you are planning to issue stock, you need to undertake a number of important steps, including the following:

- ✔ **Obtain board approval.** The board of directors of the company should approve the offer and sale of the stock, any agreements for the sale, and the filing of any needed governmental documents. This can be accomplished through resolutions adopted at a board meeting or by written unanimous consent. See the forms discussed in Chapter 4.

- ✔ **Obtain shareholder approval.** Approval of the shareholders may also be necessary, especially if the Articles of Incorporation of the company are being amended. Amendment of the Articles typically requires approval by the holders of the majority of the outstanding shares, either by resolutions adopted at a meeting or by written consent. See the forms discussed in Chapter 4.

- ✔ **Review the company charter.** Your company needs to review its charter (Articles of Incorporation or Certificate of Incorporation) to ensure that it has enough shares authorized to allow the new issuance.

- ✔ **Review compliance with securities laws.** Before an offer or sale of stock can be made, you need to ensure that the proper steps have been taken to comply with the federal securities laws and the securities laws of the states where the offers or sales of stock are made. Typically, you want to find a private placement type of exemption to avoid the costly procedures of conducting a registered offering.

- ✔ **Prepare appropriate agreements.** The sale of the stock should be documented by appropriate agreements. When the transaction is not really negotiated, such as the sale of common stock to friends and family, a Subscription Agreement may be appropriate. If the transaction involves venture capitalists or strategic investors, then a more detailed negotiated Stock Purchase Agreement is necessary.

- ✔ **Review how the sale will affect future action.** The company needs to review how this stock offering may affect future financings. Ideally, the stock issuance should not unduly restrict the ability of the company to issue additional stock in the future.

- ✔ **Establish price and number of shares.** The company and the investors need to negotiate the appropriate price for the shares and the number of shares to be issued. Because issuing new stock will dilute the percentage ownership of the existing shareholders, the company and the shareholders need to determine together that such a dilution is acceptable.

- ✔ **Make securities law filings.** Make the required filings with the SEC and any state securities administrators, generally within 15 days of the stock sale. I include the SEC form for a Regulation D offering as Form 5-5 on the CD-ROM, with the cover letter to the SEC on Form 5-6.

✔ **Issue a stock certificate.** After the sale, the company needs to issue a stock certificate, signed by the appropriately authorized officers of the company. Keep a copy of the stock certificate in the company records. Each stock certificate should be dated and numbered. Sample common stock and preferred stock certificates are included as Forms 5-2 and 5-3 on the CD-ROM. The certificate must include any appropriate *legends* (notices alerting a potential share buyer about restrictions on the shares), such as those included in Form 5-22 on the CD-ROM.

✔ **Record the certificate in the Stock Ledger.** Record the issuance of stock on the company's Stock Ledger, showing the date issued, consideration paid, name and address of each shareholder, certificate number, and other relevant information. A sample Stock Ledger is included as Form 5-15 on the CD-ROM.

Different Stocks for Different Folks

You can provide many types of securities to investors in exchange for the capital that they make available. Two of the most common securities are *common stock* and *preferred stock,* and you need to know the differences between these two types of securities:

✔ **Common stock:** Shares in a corporation that have no preferences or priorities over other classes of stock. The rights to distributions, number of votes per share, liquidation rights, and other rights are the same for all shareholders on a share-by-share basis. Form 5-2 on the CD-ROM shows a stock certificate for common stock.

✔ **Preferred stock:** Shares that give the holders various benefits over the common stock holders. Many professional investors, including venture capitalists, prefer preferred stock to common stock. Form 5-3 on the CD-ROM shows a stock certificate for preferred stock. Preferred stock often has the following rights:

A priority on the business's assets upon liquidation

A priority on any dividends

Special voting or veto rights

A right to force the company to buy back the shares at some point in the future (known as *redemption rights*)

A right to convert to common stock based on a formula

Protection against certain stock splits, stock dividends, and future cheap issuances of stock (known as *anti-dilution rights*)

A possible separate right to elect a designated number of directors

Securities Laws 101

If you plan to sell shares of stock, limited partnership interests, LLC interests, promissory notes, or other interests that may constitute a "security," you have to be concerned about the requirements of federal and state securities laws.

Federal securities laws

The federal securities laws generally provide that you need to register the offering of any securities with the Securities and Exchange Commission (SEC), which is the governmental body that monitors compliance with the federal securities laws. Registering a security can be a time-consuming and expensive process, requiring that you file a complete document with the SEC (containing your company's financial statements and other information).

Who was that masked investor?

Some investors who typically look for an equity stake in your company are

- **Angel investors.** Investors who are interested in funding start-up or early-stage companies in exchange for equity in the company. These investors often do not take an active role in the running of the company. A simple Stock Subscription Agreement (Form 5-10 on the CD-ROM) may be appropriate for them.

- **Venture capitalists.** Professional investment firms that invest primarily in high-growth companies. Venture capitalists can provide significant amounts of funding, management advice, business strategy, and contacts and introductions to other companies. Venture capitalists expect to share in the company's equity and typically insist on a significant say or veto power in the running of the business. Venture capitalists expect more thorough documentation to memorialize their investment, as described

later in this chapter in the section "Venture Capital Financings."

- **Strategic partners.** A *strategic partnership* or joint venture with another company can provide financing, resources, technology, or information. A *strategic alliance* can involve a minority equity investment in your company, which can add both cash and credibility (if the partner is well known). These deals typically require both investment-related documents and marketing, distribution, or licensing agreements.

- **Private placements through placement agents or finders.** As your company grows, you may consider hiring a placement agent, finder, or broker-dealer to help raise money. They find investors for the company through their contacts and receive a commission or fee for the sale of the company's securities. Check out Form 5-26 for a sample form Finder's Fee Agreement.

A security by any other name

Although stocks are the most typical kinds of securities, the following can also be securities and thus also subject to securities laws:

✔ **Warrants:** A warrant is a right, exercisable for a stated period of time, that allows the holder to purchase a stated amount of shares for a designated price. For example, a warrant may state that the holder has the right to purchase 10,000 shares of common stock, at $1 per share, for up to two years. This is, in essence, an option to purchase shares. And if the value of the company's stock later goes up (say, to $10), the warrant becomes very valuable because the investor can buy the stock for the $1 price. Warrants are sometimes given to investors as an "equity kicker" or "equity sweetener" to make the investment more attractive to them. Check out the sample Warrant Purchase Agreement in Form 5-25 on the CD-ROM.

✔ **Promissory notes:** Promissory notes provide evidence of a loan made to the business and are more in the nature of debt financing than equity financing. The key terms of promissory notes are the due date, interest payments, interest rate, and whether any security is pledged for the promissory note.

✔ **Convertible notes:** A convertible note is a debt instrument (essentially a loan), but it has the additional right to convert to company stock on predetermined terms. For example, the loan may be for $25,000, but at the lender's option, the loan can convert into 25,000 shares of the company's common stock. Some people like convertible notes because this option gives them the protection of being a lender while adding the potential upside available to equity investors.

✔ **Profit participation:** Sometimes capital can be raised by giving a right to profit participation on the sale of a certain product or line of business. For example, in exchange for $100,000 of capital to fund new software development, the company can give the investor 10 percent of all profits derived from the product's sale. This is sometimes more beneficial for the company because you are neither giving the investor a percentage in the entire company nor any voting rights.

✔ **Stock options:** Many start-up companies find it desirable to grant employees stock options, which allow the employee to buy company stock at a fixed price. This incentive tool is particularly common in Silicon Valley.

The purpose of the federal securities laws is to protect investors. These laws require that you follow some strict rules as to the manner and sale of a stock offering and that you provide a prospectus containing material and detailed information about your company and the stock that you're offering.

Luckily, you can sell stock using one of a number of exemptions from the registration statement requirements of the federal securities laws (see "Every rule has an exemption," later in this chapter, for details).

Even if an offering is exempt from registration, the issuance of securities is also subject to so-called *anti-fraud laws*. These laws impose liability on the company (and perhaps certain officers or directors) if in connection with the sale of the securities, the company makes an untrue statement of a material fact, omits disclosing material information to the investor, or provides misleading material information to the investor.

State securities laws

A company selling securities also has to worry about the securities laws of all the states in which the securities are offered or sold (sometimes referred to as *"Blue Sky" laws*).

Similar to federal law, a number of exemptions are available under each state's law, but you have to jump through various hoops and make some special filings to get them.

Generally, if you can qualify under SEC Rule 506 of Regulation D (check out the following section, "Every rule has an exemption"), you can obtain an exemption from the state securities registration laws. Be prepared to make some filings, however.

Every rule has an exemption

Because registered public offerings are so expensive and complicated, most start-up businesses try to take advantage of one or more of the exemptions from the federal and state registration requirements. Most private companies try to take advantage of a private placement or limited offering exemption.

In order for an exemption work, you have to follow a fair number of technical rules, which you have to prove that the company has met. Keep track of whom you're soliciting, whether they're sophisticated and able to bear the risk of the investment, and to whom you're sending out Private Placement Memorandums (see the section "Private Placement Memorandums," later in this chapter). Check out the Control Sheet for Private Placement Memorandums (Form 5-7 on the CD-ROM), the Subscription Agreement (which I describe in the section "Stock Subscription Agreements," later in this chapter), and the Stock Subscription Package (Form 5-8 on the CD-ROM) for ideas of how you can prepare proof of the compliance of your offering with these exemptions.

Stock Sale Documents

If the company is planning to sell common stock to individual investors, you need to consider preparing four key documents (each of which is described in more detail later in this section):

- ✔ **Stock Subscription Agreement:** This is a simple form of agreement where the prospective investor agrees to subscribe for stock in the company. This agreement is more suitable for simple deals involving individuals already known to the company or the officers of the company.

- ✔ **Stock Purchase Agreement:** This is a lengthier and more thorough form of agreement, where the investors are more sophisticated and expect various representations, warranties, and covenants from the company.

- ✔ **Private Placement Memorandum:** This document discloses to prospective investors important information about the company and highlights appropriate risk factors.

- ✔ **Right of First Refusal Agreement:** This agreement is signed by the investors and gives the company a right of first refusal on transfer of shares held by the investors.

Stock Subscription Agreements

The Subscription Agreement is an essential document for selling stock or other securities to individual investors. The idea behind this document is to have the prospective investor offer to purchase securities from the company. A thorough Subscription Agreement also protects the company with various representations and warranties by a prospective investor.

The Subscription Agreement can also serve to solicit information concerning the investor's sophistication, past investment experience, income, net worth, and other relevant information. The company needs to analyze this information in order to determine whether the prospective investor is qualified under any applicable exemption from the securities laws. Because the company must have a reasonable basis for its decision as to whether an investor is appropriate for the company in connection with securities laws, many Subscription Agreements are tailored to provide the company with the necessary information.

The Subscription Agreement should also require that the prospective investor represent that he or she

- ✔ Has relied only on the information contained in the Private Placement Memorandum or other information document provided by the company.

✔ Has the knowledge and experience necessary to evaluate the investment adequately.

✔ Has had an opportunity to review any documents he or she requested concerning the offering.

✔ Has had prior personal or business relationships with the company, its officers, or directors; or has the business sense to protect his or her own interest in the transaction.

✔ Realizes that the securities are sold pursuant to an exemption from the securities laws and are not freely transferable.

A good Subscription Agreement also requires prospective investors to indemnify the company and its affiliates from and against any loss, damage, or liability due to breach of their representations or warranties contained in the Subscription Agreement.

Form 5-10 shows a sample Stock Subscription Agreement for the sale of common stock in a private company.

Stock Purchase Agreements

In instances involving more sophisticated investors, a Stock Purchase Agreement is used in lieu of a Subscription Agreement. The key ingredients of these agreements are as follows:

✔ **Type of security:** The type of security (for example, common stock or preferred stock) is set forth.

✔ **Price and number of shares:** The price per share and number of shares being sold is identified

✔ **Representations and warranties:** A list of the representations and warranties made to the investors by the company is included.

The agreement's representations and warranties are important. Here, the company must present a truthful picture of the business's financial and operational state. A breach of the company's representations and warranties (a false or misleading statement) can lead to a real problem for the company, giving the investors various remedies. (See also the sidebar on "Representations and warranties.")

✔ **Covenants:** Any promises by the company to do various things are often set forth.

✔ **Conditions:** Any conditions to closing of the deal are set forth (for example, various certificates or opinion letters to be delivered).

✔ **Closing date:** The date and place where the closing is to occur are set forth, together with how the money or other consideration will be delivered to the company.

Representations and warranties

Representations and warranties from the company are almost always present as part of a full-blown Stock Purchase Agreement. These can go on for pages and pages because the investor wants to make sure that he or she flushes out any "warts" with the business.

Here are the most important ones you may expect the investor to ask:

✔ The exact outstanding capitalization of the company

✔ That the company's financial statements are true and correct in all material respects and have been prepared in accordance with generally accepted accounting procedures

✔ That the company has no liabilities other than those reflected in its latest balance sheet and those that have occurred in the ordinary course of business since the date of the last balance sheet

✔ That the company owns all of the assets it purports to own, without liens or encumbrances except those disclosed

✔ That the company's intellectual property and products don't infringe the rights of others

✔ That the company is in compliance with all laws in connection with its operations

Private Placement Memorandums

Preparing a Private Placement Memorandum when selling stock or other securities is almost always desirable for the company (or required to obtain an exemption from the securities laws). The purpose of a Private Placement Memorandum is to disclose the material information about the company and its business — especially the risk factors associated with the investment in the company — to prospective investors.

The Private Placement Memorandum may not be technically required in very small stock offerings to a few individuals who are sophisticated and who have access to all the information they need about the company. However, a Private Placement Memorandum is a useful way, in all circumstances, to prove that the company provided all important information to investors (in case the investment goes bad and investors insist on having their money refunded).

A complete Private Placement Memorandum needs to follow several important rules, so make sure to consult with an experienced securities attorney when putting one together. The following list contains some fundamental principles to adhere to when creating a Private Placement Memorandum:

✔ Be certain that your statements are true.

✔ Don't mislead potential investors in any way.

✔ Don't omit any information that may affect the investor's decision.

    ↙ Lay out the risks to the potential investor.

    ↙ Provide proof of your statements.

    ↙ Don't exaggerate facts or projections.

If you don't follow the rules to the letter, a number of adverse consequences can follow, including possible civil and criminal penalties and the investor's right to demand his or her money back. The advice of a good securities lawyer is absolutely essential in this area.

The specific contents of a Private Placement Memorandum can be quite detailed. Form 5-4 on the CD-ROM provides a checklist of the information desirable for a Private Placement Memorandum. For examples of the types of disclosures made by public companies in a *prospectus* (the public offering equivalent of a Private Placement Memorandum), check out the SEC documents contained in the online EDGAR database at `www.sec.gov`.

Before you go through the time and expense of preparing a full-blown Private Placement Memorandum, you may want to prepare a shorter *Pre-Offering Summary*. You can use this document to lay out the basics of your company and gauge the potential receptiveness of investors.

Form 5-9 on the CD-ROM is a sample Pre-Offering Summary for a hypothetical company.

Right of First Refusal Agreements

Your company may want the investors who buy stock in the company to execute a Right of First Refusal Agreement. This agreement typically requires the shareholder to grant the company a right to match any offers for their stock, and thus to preempt any other buyers. Such an agreement may help to keep your company's stock in friendly hands.

The Right of First Refusal Agreement can also be expanded to provide the option or the obligation for the company to buy back shares of a shareholder who has died or left the employment of the company.

Sometimes, investors may insist on a Right of First Offer Agreement in lieu of a Right of First Refusal Agreement. This agreement provides that the shareholder can first come to the company with a proposed price and terms for the shares to be sold. If the company turns down the offer, then the shareholder is free to sell the stock to any third party, as long as the price is the same as or greater than that offered to the company. This type of agreement may be somewhat more appealing to an investor than a Right of First Refusal Agreement.

The Right of First Refusal Agreement almost always terminates on an IPO (initial public offering) or after a certain number of years.

A sample Right of First Refusal Agreement for a California corporation is found as Form 5-27 on the CD-ROM.

Venture Capital Financings

Venture capital is a widely used phrase that doesn't have an exact definition. Typically, venture capital refers to an investment fund or partnership (the "venture capitalist" or "venture fund") that focuses on investing in promising start-up and emerging companies. Venture capitalists have invested in some of today's most famous companies, including Yahoo!, Apple, Genentech, Intel, and Compaq. Typically, this investment is in company stock (the venture capitalist gets a share in the company for the money put up).

The venture capitalist, in addition to supplying the company with money, also assists in its business planning, bringing industry knowledge to the table, as well as experience in growing businesses and expertise in taking the company public someday. The venture capitalist's primary motive is to make *a lot* of money on their investment. The track record of venture capitalists directly relates to the success they have in raising money for their partnership to invest in promising companies.

Beware — venture capitalists are only interested in businesses that can grow very BIG! So if you're a corner grocery store, sushi bar, or lemonade stand, forget it (unless you plan to grow to a chain of 500).

What venture capitalists want

Venture capitalists receive vast numbers of business plans and proposals from companies that want funding. If you want to stand out from the rest, you have to accomplish two things: Interest venture capitalists enough to meet with you and knock their socks off when they do.

Here are some tips for increasing the chance that a venture capitalist may pay attention to your proposal:

- ✔ Gather information about different venture capitalists (see the sidebar "Venture capital matchmaking" in this chapter).

- ✔ Prepare a top-notch business plan.

- ✔ Find a reputable third party (such as your lawyer, colleague, or accountant) to deliver your business plan or make an introduction.

When you meet with the venture capitalist, be prepared to communicate the following:

- ✔ You have a clear understanding of your business.
- ✔ You have a clear understanding of the hurdles facing your business.
- ✔ You have a vision for the company's growth.
- ✔ You have a sound company strategy and business plan.
- ✔ Your management team has drive and ambition.
- ✔ Your management team has relevant experience.
- ✔ Your target market is substantial and growing rapidly.
- ✔ Your business has a proprietary or differentiated product.
- ✔ Your business can realize significant gross profit margins in the long term.
- ✔ Your business has the potential to be a "home run" investment.

Form 5-12 is a sample of the type of form that venture capitalists use when deciding whether to invest in a company. Before you meet the venture capitalist, fill out this form and think about whether *you* would invest in your company.

Venture capital matchmaking

Venture capitalists focus on particular industries and particular stages of company development. When conducting your research for venture capital sources, try to identify venture capitalists who specialize in the industry and development stage that match your company.

Industries that venture capitalists currently favor include software, biotech, medical instruments, health care, retail, networking, computers, and online and Internet.

The stages of company development that a venture capitalist may look for include:

- ✔ **Seed round:** The company is still a very early start-up.

- ✔ **First round:** The company has refined its business plan, has some of its management team in place, and is starting to develop products and sales.

- ✔ **Second round:** The company has made good progress on its plan, sales have started to increase, and the business is expanding.

- ✔ **Third round:** The company has done well, attacked its market, refined its product, and is now gearing up for an initial public offering or other major progress.

Business due diligence

Before the venture capitalist forks over cash to invest in your business, it has to get comfortable with your business and the management team. As part of getting comfortable with your company, the venture capitalist conducts a *business due diligence*. This business due diligence often includes

- ✔ A review of the market for the company's product.
- ✔ A background check on the founders and key management team.
- ✔ The company's competition.
- ✔ Discussions with the company's key customers or prospective customers.
- ✔ An analysis of financial projections for the business.
- ✔ A review of any holes in the management team.

Legal due diligence

The venture capitalists also have their lawyers conduct a *legal due diligence*. This legal due diligence involves the lawyers checking that your company doesn't have significant legal problems and is being properly operated. You can expect to receive a Due Diligence Checklist from the venture capitalist's lawyers asking for lots of documents and information about the company.

Responding to a Due Diligence Checklist can be time-consuming. Make sure that all your legal documents are in order. If they are not, financing can be delayed or even killed. So also make sure that your lawyer is experienced and knows what to expect.

Here are some of the main documents you may need to hand over quickly:

- ✔ Key contracts
- ✔ Employment agreements
- ✔ Minutes and consents of the board of directors and shareholders
- ✔ Confidentiality and Invention Assignment Agreements with employees
- ✔ Corporate charter and bylaws
- ✔ Litigation-related documents
- ✔ Patents, copyrights, and other intellectual property-related documents.

For a complete sample Due Diligence Checklist, see Form 4-15 on the CD-ROM. By reviewing and preparing the documents on this list, you can help expedite closing a deal.

Term sheets

After getting comfortable with the company and its plans, the venture capitalist submits a *term sheet,* a summary of the proposed terms and conditions for the investment. Normally, the term sheet isn't binding. Nevertheless, the term sheet is a serious show of interest by the venture capitalist and typically covers

- ✔ The proposed valuation that the venture capitalist places on the company.
- ✔ How much the venture capitalist proposes to invest in the company and for what percentage ownership in the company.
- ✔ The form of investment.
- ✔ The rights to participate on the company's board.
- ✔ The rights to register the venture capitalist's share in a public offering.
- ✔ The conditions to the investment (completion of due diligence, definitive agreements in a form satisfactory to the venture capitalist, and so on).
- ✔ How the money is to be used.

At this stage, the company can typically negotiate some of the key terms. You need a good lawyer to help with the intricacies of this negotiation — find one who is an expert in venture financings.

Forms 5-13 and 5-14 on the CD-ROM contain sample term sheets. With careful review, you can see the numerous rights that the venture capitalist typically expects to get.

Venture capital Stock Purchase Agreements

After the company and the venture capitalist agree on the term sheet, either side can prepare the definitive agreements reflecting the transaction. If it's the first round of venture capital financing, the venture capitalist's counsel typically prepares the documents. In later rounds of financing, it's typically the company's counsel who prepares them. The main agreement is the venture capital *Stock Purchase Agreement,* which typically contains the following:

- ✔ The price of the stock to be sold and number of shares to be purchased
- ✔ The company's representations and warranties
- ✔ Various covenants by the company
- ✔ Conditions to closing the deal

- A requirement to reimburse the venture capitalist's legal fees
- Exhibits and related agreements, which contain other rights for the venture capitalist

Sometimes the venture capitalist *stages* the investment — that is, some money is invested right away and then additional monies come as the company meets certain milestones. For the company's benefit, these milestones must be clearly defined and reasonably obtainable.

Most venture capital financings take the form of an agreement to sell *convertible preferred stock* to the venture capitalist. Because the stock is preferred stock, the venture capitalist gets preference over the common shareholders in the event of a liquidation or merger. Because the stock is convertible, the venture capitalist can convert the stock into common stock at its option. In certain events, such as an initial public offering (IPO) of the company, the convertible preferred stock automatically converts to common stock because this simplifies the company's capital structure and facilitates the IPO.

A sample form of a Venture Capital Stock Purchase Agreement is included as Form 5-28 on the CD-ROM. This form tends to be more pro-company-oriented.

Investors' Rights Agreements

The venture capitalist also typically expects to get the following rights associated with its investment, which are often contained in an Investors' Rights Agreement:

- The right to elect one or more directors to the company's board of directors
- The right to receive various reports, financial statements, and information
- The right to have its stock registered for sale in a public offering at the company's cost
- The right to maintain its percentage share ownership in the company by participating in future stock issuances
- The right to participate in the sale of any shares made by the founders of the company (a so-called "co-sale" right that is embodied in a separate agreement).

A sample form Investors' Rights Agreement is contained as Form 5-31 on the CD-ROM.

Articles of Incorporation

The company's Articles of Incorporation (or Certificate of Incorporation, in some states) spells out various rights of the preferred stock to be obtained by the venture capitalist, including the following:

- ✔ Dividends
- ✔ Liquidation preference on liquidation or merger of the company
- ✔ Anti-dilution protection in the event of the issuance of stock at a price lower than the price paid by the investor (with various stock issuances being excluded)
- ✔ Redemption of the stock
- ✔ Voting rights
- ✔ Rights and obligations regarding conversion of the preferred stock into common stock

This document is very complicated, and you need an experienced corporate lawyer drafting or reviewing this.

Strategic Partner Equity Investments

Many large and established companies, as well as smaller companies, are investing in start-up and early-stage companies. These deals are often coupled with a license, marketing, distribution, or some other form of strategic alliance agreement.

The company receiving the investment can gain many advantages from such a deal: money, access to a larger partner's distribution and marketing departments, credibility, and more. And the larger company can gain access to a profitable investment, cutting-edge technology, or other business synergies.

Although these deals are complicated and can have many different structures, here are some key elements:

- ✔ Investment in stock of the company, often in preferred stock
- ✔ Right to participate in future stock offerings of the company
- ✔ Participation on the board of directors or, alternatively, board "observation" rights (rights to attend board meetings and receive board-related information)
- ✔ Warrants in the company, giving the strategic investor the option to invest more in the company in the future at a predetermined price

   ╻ ✔ A revenue share on any co-marketing or distribution agreements

   ╹ ✔ License rights to certain technology

A sample term sheet for a Strategic Partner Equity Investment is included as Form 5-24 on the CD-ROM and a sample Warrant Purchase Agreement (with related Warrant) is contained in Form 5-25.

Forms on the CD-ROM

Check out the following forms that deal with raising capital for your business:

Form 5-1	**Checklist for Issuing Stock**	A sample checklist of key items to consider before issuing stock
Form 5-2	**Stock Certificate — Common Stock**	A sample certificate for common stock
Form 5-3	**Stock Certificate — Preferred Stock**	A sample certificate for preferred stock
Form 5-4	**Checklist for Contents of Private Placement Memorandums**	A checklist of items to be considered for inclusion in a Private Placement Memorandum for a securities offering
Form 5-5	**SEC Form D**	The Form required by the Securities and Exchange Commission to be filed for a stock offering under SEC Regulation D
Form 5-6	**Transmittal Letter to SEC Enclosing Form D**	Cover letter to the SEC to enclose with Form D
Form 5-7	**Control Sheet for Private Placement Memorandums**	A sample sheet to keep track of the distribution of Private Placement Memorandums
Form 5-8	**Stock Subscription Package**	Several forms to be used in connection with larger private placement stock offerings
Form 5-9	**Pre-Offering Summary**	A summary of a company's proposed securities offering to ascertain the interest level from prospective investors

Form 5-10	**Stock Subscription Agreement**	A form of simple agreement for subscribing to the purchase of stock
Form 5-11	**Investment Analysis Summary Used by Venture Capitalists**	A sample form used by some venture capitalists in summarizing their analyses as to whether to invest in a company
Form 5-12	**Due Diligence Checklist**	A sample checklist of documents and information that a venture capitalist requests from a company in which it is interested in investing
Form 5-13	**Short Form Venture Capital Term Sheet**	A short form sample term sheet for a venture capital investment in a company
Form 5-14	**Long Form Venture Capital Term Sheet**	A long form, annotated sample term sheet for a venture capital investment in a company
Form 5-15	**Stock Ledger and Capitalization Summary**	A sample form ledger to keep track of stock, option, and warrant issuances with a summary of the company's capitalization
Form 5-16	**Stock Option and Incentive Plan (with Stock Option Agreement)**	A form of agreement granting an employee the option to buy stock in the company
Form 5-17	**Stock Assignment Separate From Certificate**	A sample form to assign a stock certificate
Form 5-18	**Short Form Transfer of Stock Agreement**	A short form agreement to sell stock
Form 5-19	**Irrevocable Proxy**	A form of irrevocable proxy given with respect to stock
Form 5-20	**Revocable Proxy**	A form of revocable proxy with respect to stock
Form 5-21	**Affidavit of Lost Stock Certificate**	An affidavit to be signed by a shareholder who has lost his or her stock certificate, in order to allow the company to issue a replacement certificate

Form 5-22	**Sample Legends For Stock Certificates**	Sample legends that may be appropriate to place in a stock certificate
Form 5-23	**Statement of Investment Representation**	A statement to be signed by the stock purchaser to help comply with applicable securities laws
Form 5-24	**Strategic Partner Equity Investment Term Sheet**	A term sheet for purchase of a minority stock interest by a strategic partner
Form 5-25	**Warrant Purchase Agreement**	An agreement to purchase a warrant with related sample form warrant
Form 5-26	**Finder's Fee Agreement**	An agreement where a fee is paid to a party who brings an investor to the company
Form 5-27	**Right of First Refusal Agreement (California)**	An agreement for a California corporation granting the corporation the right of first refusal on transfer of stock by a shareholder
Form 5-28	**Venture Capital Stock Purchase Agreement**	A sample agreement for the sale of Series A Preferred Stock in a California corporation to a venture capitalist

Chapter 6

Buying a Business

• •

In This Chapter

▶ Types of deals (assets versus stock)

▶ Confidentiality agreements

▶ Letters of intent

▶ Due diligence

▶ Key provisions of asset purchase agreements

▶ Key provisions of stock purchase agreements

▶ Non-competition agreements

• •

*O*nce you've decided you want to buy a business, your dream is more likely to come true if you develop an organized plan, do your homework, gather information, and obtain and draft the essential documents. There's no guarantee that you'll be listed in the *Forbes* Top 100 Business List in the first year or even after 30 years, but a well thought-out and executed plan can help the chances of your business being a financial success.

In this chapter, I guide you through the basic steps to take and documents to prepare after you decide to take the plunge and pursue your own American dream.

The Big Picture

When contemplating purchasing a business, you have some major issues to sort through, including the following:

✔ **Type of deal:** What kind of deal will it be — purchasing the assets of the business or purchasing the stock? See "Types of Deals (Assets versus Stock)," later in this chapter.

✔ **Confidentiality:** If the seller will be sharing confidential information, such as financial statements and customer lists, the buyer probably will be asked to sign a Confidentiality Agreement. See "Confidentiality Agreements," later in this chapter.

✔ **Letters of Intent:** Consider whether signing a Letter of Intent makes sense before you invest a great deal of time and money. See "Letters of Intent," later in this chapter.

✔ **Due Diligence (Don't Buy a Pig in a Poke):** Make sure you have thoroughly checked out the business you are buying — its financial performance, assets, liabilities, contracts, employees, and more. See "Due Diligence," later in this chapter.

✔ **Definitive agreement:** You will need a comprehensive definitive agreement setting forth the terms of the acquisition. See "Asset Purchase Agreements" and "Key Provisions of Stock Purchase Agreements," later in this chapter.

Form 6-1 on the CD-ROM is a comprehensive Checklist of Issues in Acquiring a Privately Held Company.

Types of Deals (Assets versus Stock)

There are basically two types of deals when purchasing a business — either a purchase of the assets of the business, or the purchase of the stock of the company (assuming it's a corporation). In addition, a merger is a special type of stock acquisition, discussed in the section "Mergers," later in this chapter. Generally, a seller prefers to sell the stock of his or her business, whereas a buyer often prefers to purchase the assets.

Purchase of assets

The purchase of assets is a popular type of acquisition. You have four distinct advantages when purchasing the assets of a business rather than the stock. The purchase of assets

✔ Allows you to avoid some or all of the liabilities of the existing business.

✔ Gives you tax advantages.

✔ Lets you avoid acquiring undesirable assets.

✔ Helps you avoid taking on hidden or unknown problems.

The buyer of the assets of a business does not generally inherit the liabilities of the business, whereas the stock purchaser does. This is a critical factor in deciding which type of deal is best for you.

Purchase of stock

Some particular situations can tip the scales in favor of the purchase of stock. For instance, if you find a company that looks very good to you, having done all of your research (see "Due Diligence (Don't Buy a Pig in a Poke)," later), but the company has a favorable, long-term lease that is not freely assignable, then you may need to purchase the stock of the company in order to benefit from the lease. Or if the business is involved in any other type of contract that is not assignable, then the purchase of stock can avoid that potential problem.

Engaging in due diligence helps you determine whether the business's contracts are assignable and whether the contracts can continue if you purchase the stock of the company. Many contracts with major companies, businesses, and vendors have specific clauses dealing with the event of a sale of the assets of that company and the event of the sale of the stock.

Most sellers of a business prefer selling the stock, too, because they are often able to obtain tax-favored capital gains treatment on the sale.

Mergers

Stock acquisitions can be accomplished through direct stock purchases from all of the selling shareholders or through a *merger*.

A merger is a creature of state law (so you have to follow the legal rules in your state) that results in one entity being combined (or "merged") into another entity. After the merger, the merged-out entity no longer exists, and the business of the combined entities continues in one company.

Mergers can have certain tax advantages. For example, you may be able to accomplish a *tax-free* merger, where the selling shareholders receive stock in another company and don't have to pay immediate tax on the sale of their shares. Mergers also have the advantage of not requiring that every shareholder approve the deal.

But mergers are complicated, and you definitely need the help of an experienced corporate attorney here.

Confidentiality Agreements

In most transactions involving the purchase of a business, a confidentiality or mutual non-disclosure agreement is important to have in place before beginning negotiations and exchanging documents and information. The agreement needs to define precisely what is confidential, what is excluded from confidential treatment (such as matters already publicly known), and how long the confidentiality obligations last.

Form 6-2 on the CD-ROM is a form of Confidentiality Agreement where only one party provides confidential information, and Form 6-3 is a form of Mutual Non-Disclosure Agreement. Also check out Chapter 14 for more information on Confidentiality and Non-Disclosure Agreements.

Letters of Intent

Entering into a letter of intent is sometimes very helpful in approaching a particular acquisition. A *letter of intent* allows the parties to indicate that they are seriously interested in doing a deal and wish to explore discussions further. The letter of intent lays out the principal terms of the proposed purchase to make sure that the parties have a "meeting of the minds" before they devote the greater amount of time, effort, and money it takes to enter into and consummate a definitive acquisition agreement.

The "intent" of the letter of intent

Here are some of the questions the letter of intent attempts to answer:

- ✔ **Structure:** What is the basic structure of the deal? For example, is the deal a purchase of assets or a purchase of stock?

- ✔ **Price and terms:** How much money is involved? Will the payment be in cash at the closing or spread out over time?

- ✔ **Main obligations:** What are each side's key obligations?

- ✔ **Closing:** By what date will the parties sign a definitive contract and close the deal? Your letter can also say that if a definitive contract is not signed by that date, then both sides are free to go elsewhere or continue discussions, at their option.

- ✔ **Exclusivity:** Will the negotiations between the parties be exclusive for a period of time? If the seller agrees to exclusive negotiations, he or she will probably want this to last only for a limited period of time, such as 21 days or a month. Agreements for exclusive negotiations can be legally binding on a seller. Buyers often like to get exclusive negotiation provisions because they can get some leverage in the later negotiations.

> ✔ **Conditions:** What key conditions have to occur before a final agreement can be executed? For example, buyers typically want at least two conditions — that they are satisfied with their review of the business and that they have obtained whatever financing is needed to close the deal.

Short and sweet versus lengthy and comprehensive

Opinion is divided about the best way to write a letter of intent. One view is that letters of intent should be short and sweet, highlighting only the really important points. In that way, the parties feel that they have momentum toward a deal, but without devoting the greater energy needed to reach an agreement on every important point.

The other view is that letters of intent should be relatively long, with every major point of the deal addressed in the letter. The feeling is that, with such a letter, the parties will be less likely to encounter stumbling blocks when they later put together a definitive contract. The approach you take depends on the circumstances and your personal preferences, and in many deals you may want no letter of intent at all. If you want to make sure you have a true "meeting of the minds" for a deal, then opt for the more detailed approach. If you are in a hurry and believe that you can work out any issues that come up, then a shorter version may work.

Binding versus nonbinding

You need to decide whether you want the letter of intent, or certain provisions of the letter of intent, to be *binding* or *nonbinding*. What obligations in the letter of intent are intended to legally bind the parties? You want to be *extremely careful* here because the buyer doesn't necessarily want something in the letter to bind him or her to move forward on the deal. *Typically,* the buyer (and often the seller, as well) wants to say that the parties are *not bound in any way* except with respect to the confidentiality obligations and perhaps the exclusive negotiation clause.

Form 6-4 on the following page is a sample Letter of Intent for the purchase of the assets of a business that illustrates some of these points. This sample is also included in the CD-ROM as Form 6-4.

[Date]

_____
_____
_____
_____

Dear _____:

This letter confirms your and our mutual intentions with respect to the potential transaction described herein between _____ ("Buyer") and _____ ("Seller").

1. **Prices and Terms**. We envision that the principal terms of the proposed transaction would be substantially as follows:

    (a) **Business to be Acquired; Liabilities to be Assumed**. We would acquire substantially all of the assets, tangible and intangible, owned by Seller that are used in, or necessary for the conduct of, its software development business, including, without limitation: (i) the _____ software, subject to any obligations contained in disclosed license agreements and all related intellectual property; (ii) the fixed assets of Seller; (iii) any and all customer lists; and (iv) the goodwill associated therewith, all free and clear of any security interests, mortgages or other encumbrances.

    (b) **Consideration**. The aggregate consideration for the assets and business to be purchased would be $_____; provided, however, that the working capital (current assets less current liabilities) of the business to be purchased equals or exceeds $0, as shown on a closing date balance sheet prepared in accordance with generally accepted accounting principles.

    (c) **Due Diligence Review**. Promptly following the execution of this letter of intent, you will allow us to complete our examination of your financial, accounting and business records and the contracts and other legal documents and generally to complete due diligence. Any information obtained by us as a result thereof will be maintained by us in confidence subject to the terms of the Confidentiality Agreement executed by the parties and dated _____ (the "Confidentiality Agreement"). The parties will cooperate to complete due diligence expeditiously.

    (d) **Conduct in Ordinary Course**. In addition to the conditions discussed herein and any others to be contained in a definitive written purchase agreement (the "Purchase Agreement"), consummation of the acquisition would be subject to having conducted your business in the ordinary course during the period between the date hereof and the date of closing and there having been no material adverse change in your business, financial condition or prospects.

Form 6-4: Letter of Intent to Purchase a Business.

(e) **Definitive Purchase Agreement**. All of the terms and conditions of the proposed transaction would be stated in the Purchase Agreement, to be negotiated, agreed and executed by you and us. Neither party intends to be bound by any oral or written statements or correspondence concerning the Purchase Agreement arising during the course of negotiations, notwithstanding that the same may be expressed in terms signifying a partial, preliminary or interim agreement between the parties.

(f) **Employment Agreement**. Simultaneously with the execution of the Purchase Agreement, we would enter into employment agreements with Paul Smith and John Halper on such terms and conditions as would be negotiated and agreed by them and us, including mutually agreeable provisions regarding term, base and incentive compensation, confidentiality, assignment to us of intellectual property rights in past and future work product and restrictions on competition. We would also offer employment to substantially all of Seller's employees and would expect the management team to use its reasonable best efforts to assist us to employ these individuals.

(g) **Timing**. We and you would use all reasonable efforts to complete and sign the Purchase Agreement on or before _____ and to close the transaction as promptly as practicable thereafter.

2. **Expenses**. You and we will pay our respective expenses incident to this letter of intent, the Purchase Agreement and the transactions contemplated hereby and thereby.

3. **Public Announcements**. Neither you nor we will make any announcement of the proposed transaction contemplated by this letter of intent prior to the execution of the Purchase Agreement without the prior written approval of the other, which approval will not be unreasonably withheld or delayed. The foregoing shall not restrict in any respect your or our ability to communicate information concerning this letter of intent and the transactions contemplated hereby to your and our, and your and our respective affiliates', officers, directors, employees and professional advisers, and, to the extent relevant, to third parties whose consent is required in connection with the transaction contemplated by this letter of intent.

4. **Broker's Fees**. You and we have represented to each other that no brokers or finders have been employed who would be entitled to a fee by reason of the transaction contemplated by this letter of intent.

5. **Exclusive Negotiating Rights**. In order to induce us to commit the resources, forego other potential opportunities, and incur the legal, accounting and incidental expenses necessary properly to evaluate the possibility of acquiring the assets and business described above, and to negotiate the terms of, and consummate, the transaction contemplated hereby, you agree that for a period of [45] days after the date hereof, you, your affiliates and your and their respective officers, directors, employees and agents shall not initiate, solicit, encourage, directly or indirectly, or accept any offer

(continued)

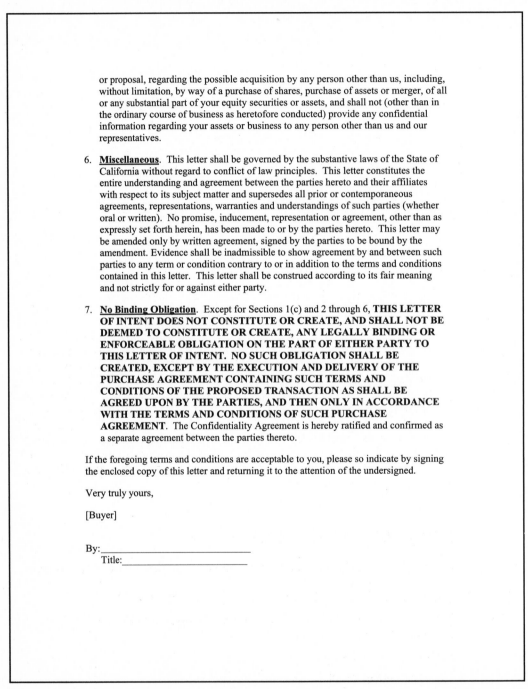

or proposal, regarding the possible acquisition by any person other than us, including, without limitation, by way of a purchase of shares, purchase of assets or merger, of all or any substantial part of your equity securities or assets, and shall not (other than in the ordinary course of business as heretofore conducted) provide any confidential information regarding your assets or business to any person other than us and our representatives.

6. **Miscellaneous**. This letter shall be governed by the substantive laws of the State of California without regard to conflict of law principles. This letter constitutes the entire understanding and agreement between the parties hereto and their affiliates with respect to its subject matter and supersedes all prior or contemporaneous agreements, representations, warranties and understandings of such parties (whether oral or written). No promise, inducement, representation or agreement, other than as expressly set forth herein, has been made to or by the parties hereto. This letter may be amended only by written agreement, signed by the parties to be bound by the amendment. Evidence shall be inadmissible to show agreement by and between such parties to any term or condition contrary to or in addition to the terms and conditions contained in this letter. This letter shall be construed according to its fair meaning and not strictly for or against either party.

7. **No Binding Obligation**. Except for Sections 1(c) and 2 through 6, **THIS LETTER OF INTENT DOES NOT CONSTITUTE OR CREATE, AND SHALL NOT BE DEEMED TO CONSTITUTE OR CREATE, ANY LEGALLY BINDING OR ENFORCEABLE OBLIGATION ON THE PART OF EITHER PARTY TO THIS LETTER OF INTENT. NO SUCH OBLIGATION SHALL BE CREATED, EXCEPT BY THE EXECUTION AND DELIVERY OF THE PURCHASE AGREEMENT CONTAINING SUCH TERMS AND CONDITIONS OF THE PROPOSED TRANSACTION AS SHALL BE AGREED UPON BY THE PARTIES, AND THEN ONLY IN ACCORDANCE WITH THE TERMS AND CONDITIONS OF SUCH PURCHASE AGREEMENT.** The Confidentiality Agreement is hereby ratified and confirmed as a separate agreement between the parties thereto.

If the foregoing terms and conditions are acceptable to you, please so indicate by signing the enclosed copy of this letter and returning it to the attention of the undersigned.

Very truly yours,

[Buyer]

By:_____
   Title:_____

(continued)

ACCEPTED AND AGREED

[Seller]

By: _____

Title: _____

Due Diligence (Don't Buy a Pig in a Poke!)

Buying a business is an arduous, yet potentially rewarding, process and can take weeks or months. Because buying a business involves investing a fair amount of money and time, do your homework diligently when gathering information about the business. This process is commonly referred to as conducting *due diligence*. In most purchases of small businesses, the buyer wants to learn everything possible about a business before signing the purchase agreement. (Alternatively, if there isn't time to do that, then the buyer needs to make sure that the representations of the seller concerning the business are quite comprehensive and that the definitive agreement allows him or her to back out of the deal if the due diligence done after signing the definitive agreement is not satisfactory.)

Why do due diligence?

Conducting *due diligence* can help the buyer avoid the following problems:

- ✔ Purchase price of the business turns out to be too high
- ✔ Misunderstandings as to the type and condition of the business being bought
- ✔ Bad financial situation
- ✔ Bad management
- ✔ Pending lawsuits
- ✔ Contingent liabilities

Doing your homework

Following is a list of some of the main documents you may expect to receive from the seller in the course of your due diligence:

- ✔ Key contracts
- ✔ Financial statements
- ✔ Customer lists
- ✔ Employment agreements
- ✔ Minutes and consents of the board of directors and shareholders
- ✔ Confidentiality and Invention Assignment Agreements with employees
- ✔ Corporate charter and bylaws
- ✔ Litigation-related documents
- ✔ Patents, copyrights, and other intellectual property related documents
- ✔ Licenses and permits related to operation of the business

What to do

For a complete sample Due Diligence Checklist, see Form 6-5. By requesting from the seller and then reviewing the documents on this checklist, the buyer can help expedite signing and closing a deal. The checklist is used in connection with businesses that are structured as corporations, and if you are buying a business in partnership or LLC form, additional or different documents may be appropriate.

Due Diligence Checklist

In connection with a potential acquisition transaction, please provide us with the following materials or information relating to _____, and any subsidiaries (together, the "Company"). Upon review, we may request additional documents. If compiling any of the requested items would be unduly burdensome, please let us know so that we may arrange a less burdensome alternative. If you have already delivered any of the information, please so indicate and you need not provide an additional copy.

(A) **Corporate Documents of the Company and Subsidiaries**

(1) Articles of Incorporation and all amendments thereto.

(2) Bylaws and all amendments thereto.

(3) Minutes of all Board of Directors, committee and shareholders meetings and all consents to actions without meeting.

(4) List of states and jurisdictions in which qualified to do business and in which the Company has offices, holds property or conducts business.

(5) Material information or documents furnished to shareholders and to directors during the last two years.

(6) Most recently obtained good standing certificates for all states and jurisdictions where the Company is qualified to do business.

(B) **Previous Issuances of Securities**

(1) All applications and permits for issuance/transfer of securities.

(2) Sample copy of stock certificates, warrants and options.

(3) Stockholder information, indicating number of shares held, dates of issuance, and consideration paid.

(4) All stock option, stock purchase and other employee benefit plans and forms of agreements.

(5) List of any outstanding stock options and warrants.

Form 6-5: Due Diligence Checklist.   *(continued)*

(6)   Any voting trust agreements, buy/sell agreements, stockholder agreements, warrant agreements, proxies, or right of first refusal agreements.

(7)   Any registration rights or pre-emptive rights agreements.

(8)   Powers of attorney on any matter.

(9)   Convertible debt instruments.

(10)   Other contracts, arrangements, or public or private documents or commitments relating to the stock of the Company.

(11)   Any debt arrangements, guarantees or indemnification between officers, directors or the shareholders and the Company.

(C)   Material Contracts and Agreements

(1)   List of banks or other lenders with whom Company has a financial relationship (briefly describe nature of relationship — lines of credit, equipment lessor, etc.).

(2)   Credit agreements, debt instruments, security agreements, mortgages, financial or performance guaranties, indemnifications, liens, equipment leases or other agreements evidencing outstanding loans to which the Company is a party or was a party within the past two years.

(3)   All material correspondence with lenders during the last three years, including all compliance reports submitted by the Company or its accountants.

(4)   List of major clients and their locations.

(5)   Any other material contracts.

(D)   Litigation

(1)   Copies of _any_ pleadings or correspondence for pending or prior lawsuits involving the Company or the Founders.

(2)   Summary of disputes with suppliers, competitors, or customers.

(3)   Correspondence with auditor or accountant regarding threatened or pending litigation, assessment or claims.

(4)   Decrees, orders or judgments of courts or governmental agencies.

(5)   Settlement documentation.

(E)   <u>**Employees and Related Parties**</u>

(1)   A management organization chart and biographical information.

(2)   Summary of any labor disputes.

(3)   Correspondence, memoranda or notes concerning pending or threatened labor stoppage.

(4)   List of negotiations with any group seeking to become the bargaining unit for any employees.

(5)   All employment and consulting agreements, loan agreements and documents relating to other transactions with officers, directors, key employees and related parties.

(6)   Schedule of all compensation paid to officers, directors and key employees for most recent fiscal year showing separately salary, bonuses and non-cash compensation (i.e. use of cars, property, etc.).

(7)   Summary of employee benefits and copies of any pension, profit sharing, deferred compensation and retirement plans.

(8)   Summary of management incentive or bonus plans not included in (7) above, as well as other non-cash forms of compensation.

(9)   Confidentiality agreements with employees.

(10)   Description of all related party transactions which have occurred during the last three years (and any currently proposed transaction) and all agreements relating thereto.

(continued)

(F) **Financial Information**

(1) Audited financial statements since inception (unaudited if audited financials are unavailable).

(2) Quarterly income statements for the last two years and the current year (to date).

(3) Financial or operating budgets or projections.

(4) Business plan and other documents describing the current and/or expected business of the Company including all material marketing studies, consulting studies or reports prepared by the Company.

(5) A description of all changes in accounting methods or principles during the last three fiscal years.

(6) Any documents relating to material write-downs or write-offs other than in the ordinary course.

(7) Revenue, gross margin and average selling price by product or service.

(8) Management letters or special reports by auditors and any responses thereto for the last three fiscal years.

(9) Letters of counsel to the Company delivered to auditors for the last three fiscal years.

(10) Aging schedules for accounts receivable for the last two years.

(11) Breakdown of G&A expenses for the last two years.

(12) Copies of any valuations of the Company's stock.

(13) Description of all contingent liabilities.

(G) **Property**

(1) List of real and material personal property owned by the Company.

(2) Documents of title, mortgages, deeds of trust and security agreements pertaining to the properties listed in (1) above.

(3)   All outstanding leases with an original term greater than one year for real and personal property to which the Company is either a lessor or lessee.

(4)   Documents pertaining to proprietary technology developed/owned by the Company, including any copyright or patent filings. This will also include information confirming that the Company's systems, software and technology is owned solely by the Company and does not infringe on any other party's rights.

(H)   <u>Taxation</u>

(1)   Any notice of assessment, revenue agents' reports, etc. from federal or state authorities with respect to any currently "open" years.

(2)   Federal and state income tax returns for the last three years.

(3)   Evidence of Company being current on sales tax, unemployment, social security, and other tax payments.

(I)   <u>Insurance and Liability</u>

(1)   Schedule or copies of all material insurance policies of the Company covering property, liabilities and operations, including product liabilities.

(2)   Schedule of any other insurance policies in force such as "key man" policies or director indemnification policies.

(3)   All other relevant documents pertaining to the Company's insurance and liability exposure, including special reserve funds and accounts.

(J)   <u>Acquisition, Partnership or Joint Venture Agreements</u>

(1)   All acquisition, partnership or joint venture agreements.

(2)   Documents pertaining to potential acquisitions or alliances.

(3)   Any agreements regarding divestiture or assets.

(continued)

(K)   <u>**Governmental Regulations And Filings**</u>

(1)   Summary of OSHA inquiries for past three years.

(2)   Summary of federal and state EPA, EEO, or other governmental agency inquiries during the past three years.

(3)   Material reports to government agencies for past three years (<u>e.g.</u>, OSHA, EPA).

(4)   Copies of all permits and licenses necessary to conduct the Company's business.

(5)   Summary of applicable federal, state and local laws, rules and regulations.

(L)   <u>**Miscellaneous**</u>

(1)   Press releases during the last two years.

(2)   Articles and other pertinent marketing studies or reports relating to the Company or the industry.

(3)   Information regarding competitors.

(4)   Customer satisfaction surveys, if any.

(5)   Current brochures and sales materials describing the Company's services.

Please provide copies of all documents to:

_____

_____

_____

_____

Phone: _____

Fax: _____

Key Provisions of Asset Purchase Agreements

When you buy the assets of a business, the definitive purchase agreement is generally known as an Asset Purchase Agreement. Here are the key points to keep in mind when drafting or negotiating an Asset Purchase Agreement:

- ✔ **Specific Assets Acquired:** The assets of a business generally consist of inventory, fixed assets (such as equipment, furniture, and fixtures), and intangible assets (such as a trade name, customer list and goodwill, intellectual property, and a lease). In the agreement, set forth specifically the assets to be acquired. It may also be a good idea to specifically list the assets that will not be acquired. The buyer typically wants to make sure that all assets used in the business are transferred.

- ✔ **Price and Terms of Payment:** Clearly set forth the price for the assets. You have many possibilities for payment terms in the purchase of a business. Some of these include: full payment in cash; down payment in cash and then monthly, quarterly, or yearly installment payments; and *earn-outs,* which are payments based on future performance of the business. Tax considerations and the desires of the seller and buyer play a large role as to the final terms.

- ✔ **Representations and Warranties (of Seller):** The seller gives representations and warranties to the buyer to reassure him or her about the state of affairs of the business being sold. Some of the representations and warranties that the seller of the assets of a business may make in the Asset Purchase Agreement are that: (1) the seller is a corporation in good standing or some other legal entity; (2) the seller has the authority to enter into the agreement and perform his or her obligations under the agreement; (3) all financial statements provided were prepared in accordance with generally accepted accounting principles and fairly represent the financial condition of the company; (4) a completely accurate list of all tangible and intangible assets to be transferred is provided; (5) the seller has good and marketable title to all tangible and intangible assets to be transferred, free of liens and encumbrances; (6) there are no undisclosed liabilities; (7) there are no other contracts outstanding except those that have been disclosed pursuant to the agreement; and (8) the business is not in violation of any federal, state, or local laws.

- ✔ **Representations and Warranties (of Buyer):** The buyer generally warrants that: (1) the buyer is a company in good standing, or a private individual; (2) the buyer has the authority to enter into the agreement and perform his or her obligations under the agreement; and (3) the buyer has had the opportunity to inspect the assets and agrees to accept the assets, except any assets specifically excluded from the agreement.

✔ **Accounts Receivable:** Determine whether accounts receivable after the date of closing will go to the buyer, or if the purchase price needs to be reduced to reflect that the seller will be retaining such accounts receivable. Buyers may also ask for some representations or guarantees as to the collectability of the accounts receivable.

✔ **Bulk Sales Law Compliance:** If you are purchasing the assets of a business that involves the sale of merchandise from stock that is kept on hand, you may need to consider the *bulk sales* law of your state. These laws apply whenever there is any transfer in bulk, not in the ordinary course of business, of a major part of the materials, supplies, merchandise, or other inventory of a business. These laws generally do not cover businesses that primarily sell personal services rather than merchandise, but check your state's laws in this area. A seller covered under the bulk sales law must provide the buyer with a list (sworn under penalty of perjury) of all business creditors and the amounts due each one. The buyer then sends notice to the named creditors to inform them of the purchase of the business, and may also be required to publish notice of the sale in a local newspaper.

✔ **Assumption of Liabilities:** Your agreement needs to address what obligations and liabilities of the business will be assumed by the buyer or paid off or kept by the seller. The buyer generally wants to avoid taking any unknown liabilities.

✔ **Preservation of Business in Normal Course:** This provision gives assurances to the buyer that, pending the closing of the purchase of the business, the seller will not enter into any unusual transactions; alter its method of conducting business; or deplete the business's cash position.

✔ **Tax Issues:** Many tax consequences to buying the assets of a business exist. You certainly want to address who pays for any transfer or sales taxes and who is responsible for any past income taxes of the business.

✔ **Employment-Related Issues:** An Asset Purchase Agreement usually contains several employment-related provisions, including issues dealing with retaining employees, continuation or alteration of employee benefits, collective bargaining agreement issues, and termination of employees.

✔ **Corporate and Shareholder Approvals:** This provision addresses what types of approvals are required for the sale of the assets of a business, including approval of directors and/or shareholders, when the approvals will be obtained, and when they will be delivered to the buyer.

✔ **Conditions to Closing:** The purchase agreement needs to address the buyer's and seller's conditions to closing the deal. Typical closing conditions include: that all representations and warranties are true and correct; that all consents have been obtained; that all covenants have been complied with; and that various certificates, documents, and legal opinions from the lawyer to the seller have been delivered that give the buyer comfort on various legal issues.

✔ **Expenses:** Unless one party has agreed to pay the other's expenses, it's a good idea to have a provision stating that each party will bear its own expenses incurred in negotiating and preparing the Asset Purchase Agreement, and in closing and carrying out the transactions contemplated within the agreement.

✔ **Continuing Services of Key Employees:** This provision provides for hiring of key employees as consultants to the business after the assets have been sold. It's sometimes a good idea to do this, especially for the period of transition between the old ownership and the new. The consulting agreement is typically separate from the purchase agreement. Alternatively, employment agreements may be appropriate.

✔ **The Closing:** This provision sets forth the time and date of the closing of the deal and may include conditions under which the closing date may be modified. Both parties should be very cautious about allowing extensions of time for closing the deal.

The CD-ROM has a number of forms helpful for asset purchases, including an Option Agreement to Purchase Assets (Pro-Buyer) (Form 6-6). The following additional forms for specific asset purchases are also included in the CD-ROM: Patent Assignment (Form 6-7); Copyright Assignment (Form 6-8), and Trademark Assignment (Form 6-9).

Key Provisions of Stock Purchase Agreements

When you buy the stock of a business, the definitive purchase agreement is generally known as a Stock Purchase Agreement. Following are the key points to keep in mind when drafting or negotiating a Stock Purchase Agreement.

✔ **Number of Shares and Purchase Price:** This provision sets forth the number of shares being sold and the purchase price of the stock.

✔ **Representations and Warranties (of Seller):** The seller of the stock of a business typically makes warranties that (1) the seller is a company in good standing or a private individual; (2) the seller has the authority to enter into the agreement and perform his or her obligations under the agreement; (3) all financial statements of the business provided were prepared in accordance with generally accepted accounting principles and fairly present the financial condition of the business; (4) the seller has provided a completely accurate list of all tangible and intangible assets of the business; (5) the business has good and marketable title to all tangible and intangible assets it purports to own; (6) there are no undisclosed liabilities; (7) there are no contracts outstanding except those that have been disclosed pursuant to the agreement; and (8) the business is not in violation of any federal, state, or local laws. The seller of stock further warrants and represents that the shares being sold were validly issued, fully paid, and nonassessable; that they have been issued in full compliance with all federal and state laws; and that the buyer will receive the shares free of any liens or encumbrances.

✔ **Representations and Warranties (of Buyer):** As with the purchase of the assets of a business, the buyer of the stock of a business generally warrants that (1) the buyer is a company in good standing or a private individual; and (2) the buyer has the authority to enter into the agreement and perform its obligations under the agreement. Additional warranties of the buyer of stock depend upon whether the purchase is cash or noncash. Purchases for cash generally do not require the buyer to make representations concerning its financial wherewithal or ability to pay the purchase price. But if the purchase of stock includes a promissory note or is to be paid in the future, then the buyer typically makes representations and warranties regarding its financial position.

✔ **Tax Issues:** The tax consequences of the purchase of the stock of a business are very different from the purchase of assets. The seller typically tries to get capital gains treatment for the sale. Contact your attorney as to how tax matters need to be addressed in the agreement.

✔ **Consent of Shareholders:** If the sale is structured as a merger, the consent of the shareholders and directors of the business being acquired are required. If the sale is a direct stock sale by the shareholders, then all of the shareholders need to sign the agreement.

✔ **Employment-Related Issues:** The agreement also likely contains several employment-related provisions, including issues dealing with retaining employees, continuation or alteration of employee benefits; collective bargaining agreements (if any); and termination of employees.

✔ **Closing Conditions:** Conditions to the deal closing also need to be addressed. As with Asset Purchase Agreements, closing conditions may include: that all representations and warranties are true and correct; that all consents have been obtained; that all covenants have been complied with; that all government consents or permits necessary have been obtained; and that various certificates, documents, and legal opinions have been delivered.

✔ **Special Concerns about Corporate Liabilities:** Unlike the purchase of the assets of a business (assuming that related liabilities are not also assumed), the purchase of the stock of a business subjects the buyer to the effect of corporate liabilities. So the Stock Purchase Agreement needs to carefully describe the liabilities of the company being acquired. The buyer should require that the seller warrant that there are no other liabilities not specifically listed. Then, even though the buyer (by purchasing stock) may inherit unknown liabilities, it may have recourse back to the seller for not disclosing such liabilities.

> ✔ **Litigation:** A provision stating the nature and extent of any litigation affecting the company is generally used to protect the buyer if unknown and unanticipated litigation or antitrust or other governmental regulatory problems arise in the future.
>
> ✔ **The Closing:** This provision sets forth the time and date of the closing of the deal and may include conditions under which the closing date and time may be modified.

Non-Competition Agreements

Sometimes it's important to have the seller of the business sign a Non-Competition Agreement with the buyer of the business. These are also referred to as *covenants not to compete.* This covenant is to avoid the situation where you buy a business and the seller opens another competing business down the street or across town (or, in the case of an Internet-related business, possibly anywhere in the world). A Non-Competition Agreement is typically a separate agreement, but its form is attached to and referenced within the Purchase Agreement.

What is a covenant not to compete?

In a Non-Competition Agreement, the seller covenants (promises) not to compete directly or indirectly with the buyer in the type of business just purchased.

Geographic limitation

It's wise to place reasonable geographic limitations in the Non-Competition Agreement because courts often do not enforce restrictions that they perceive to be unreasonable in scope. What a *reasonable* geographic limitation is depends on the size of the area in which the business is located and how large the city, county, or state is. What may be considered a reasonable geographic limitation in Rhode Island may not be reasonable in California. Essentially, the geographic limitation in a Non-Competition Agreement cannot be stated to unreasonably limit the seller's ability to earn a living, and how this is determined varies from state to state. You need to talk to a good lawyer on this point.

Time limitation

It's also wise to place a time limit in the Non-Competition Agreement to make it more likely that a court will find it reasonable. Determine whether one year, two years, or five years suits your purposes. And as with geographic limitations, the time limit may not unreasonably limit the seller's right to earning a living. What is a reasonable time limit may also vary from state to state.

Key provisions in a covenant not to compete

Although no specific language or terminology must be included in a Non-Competition Agreement, consider the following list of key provisions:

- ✔ Statement of the type of business
- ✔ Seller's covenant not to compete *directly* with buyer
- ✔ Seller's covenant not to compete *indirectly* with buyer
- ✔ Reasonable geographic limitation of covenant
- ✔ Reasonable time limitation of covenant
- ✔ Rights to injunctions for specific performance of the agreement

You must know the legal limits your state imposes in these types of agreements, so consultation with an experienced business attorney is crucial.

Form 6-10 on the CD-ROM is a sample Non-Competition Agreement.

Forms on the CD-ROM

Form 6-1	**Checklist of Issues in Acquiring a Privately Held Company**	A sample checklist of issues to consider when acquiring a privately held business
Form 6-2	**Confidentiality Agreement**	A sample Confidentiality Agreement where one party will be sharing confidential information with another party
Form 6-3	**Mutual Non-Disclosure Agreement (Short Form)**	An agreement allowing two companies to exchange confidential information with mutual protection obligations

Form 6-4	**Letter of Intent to Purchase a Business**	A sample letter of intent for the purchase of the assets of a business
Form 6-5	**Due Diligence Checklist**	A sample checklist of documents and information that a buyer needs to request from a company that it wants to purchase
Form 6-6	**Option Agreement to Purchase Assets (Pro-Buyer)**	A form of agreement granting the holder of the option a favorable right to buy assets
Form 6-7	**Patent Assignment**	An agreement for assigning a patent
Form 6-8	**Copyright Assignment**	An agreement for assigning a copyright
Form 6-9	**Trademark Assignment**	An agreement for assigning a trademark
Form 6-10	**Non-Competition Agreement**	A form of non-competition agreement for the seller or key owners of a business being sold

Chapter 7

Employment Agreements and Forms

- -

In This Chapter

▶ Interview questions and job offers

▶ Documents for new hires

▶ Job offer letters

- -

Good employees can be the most important ingredient in a successful business. But finding and hiring good employees can be among the most challenging aspects of running a business.

Numerous federal and state laws govern the various processes of soliciting employees, including advertising, interviewing, and hiring. If you don't follow the rules, you may find yourself the defendant in a lawsuit over your hiring (or nonhiring) practices. Or, you may get stuck with a very costly and unproductive employee whom you have trouble firing.

In this chapter, I give you some tips for the procedures and agreements involved in hiring employees.

Parlez-Vous Interview?

Before you hire an employee, you usually interview him or her. Most people have gone through the sweaty-palmed experience of sitting through an interview at some time. This section gives you some sample questions that can give you good information on which to base your decision and warns you about inappropriate questions that can land you in court if you don't avoid them.

Questions to ask

Form 7-1 shows a list of questions that may be appropriate to ask when interviewing a prospective employee.

Questions not to ask

You probably have many questions that you want to ask a prospective employee. But certain questions can only get you in trouble (yes, you can trip over many laws in interviews). The following list contains the top ten questions that you may *not* ask:

- ✔ How old are you?
- ✔ Do you have any disabilities?
- ✔ Are you pregnant?
- ✔ Are you married with children?
- ✔ Have you ever been arrested?
- ✔ Would you be willing to sleep with the boss?
- ✔ What is your religious affiliation?
- ✔ What is your sexual orientation?
- ✔ What ethnic background are you?
- ✔ Who played Lumpy on "Leave It to Beaver"?

So what the heck can you ask? Generally, the focus of the questions should be on the skill and experience of the candidates and the qualifications needed to perform the job.

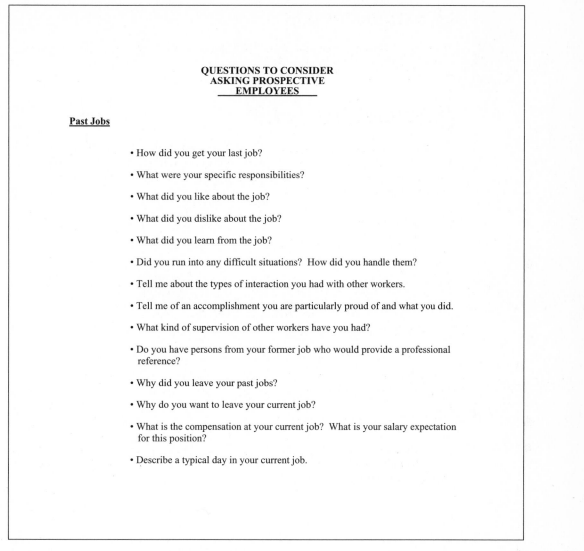

**QUESTIONS TO CONSIDER
ASKING PROSPECTIVE
EMPLOYEES**

<u>**Past Jobs**</u>

• How did you get your last job?

• What were your specific responsibilities?

• What did you like about the job?

• What did you dislike about the job?

• What did you learn from the job?

• Did you run into any difficult situations? How did you handle them?

• Tell me about the types of interaction you had with other workers.

• Tell me of an accomplishment you are particularly proud of and what you did.

• What kind of supervision of other workers have you had?

• Do you have persons from your former job who would provide a professional reference?

• Why did you leave your past jobs?

• Why do you want to leave your current job?

• What is the compensation at your current job? What is your salary expectation for this position?

• Describe a typical day in your current job.

Form 7-1: Questions to Consider Asking Prospective Employees.

(continued)

<u>**The New Job**</u>

• What would be your specific goals for this job?

• What experience do you have that you think will be helpful for this job?

• This job will require a lot of [describe]. Will that be a problem for you?

• This job will require interacting with [describe the types of people]. What experience do you have working with such people?

• What would you like to get from this new job?

• One requirement of this job is writing various types of reports -- e.g., weekly, monthly, projections, goals, employee evaluation, etc. What relevant experience have you had on your previous job? Do you have any writing samples you could provide us with?

• This job will require a certain amount of new client development. Have you had much experience? Tell me how you have gone about this.

<u>**Education**</u>

• What subjects did you do well in school?

• What was your major?

• Where did you attend high school, college or post-graduate school?

• Did you work at an outside job while going to school? Describe the job.

• Are you interested in continuing your education?

• Did you have any school honors?

General Information

- What do you consider your strong points?

- What do you consider your weak points?

- What specific kind of work do you particularly enjoy doing?

- What is your long term career objective?

Physical Condition

- Do you think you will be able to handle the physical aspects of this job?

- Do you currently use any illegal drugs?

- If offered a job, will you submit to a medical examination?

- This job requires annual medical evaluation which includes urinalysis for drug testing, etc. Do you have any objection to this?

Experience and Skills

- What special skills do you have?

- How proficient are you in using PCs?

- Are there software applications you are particularly familiar with?

(continued)

<u>**Outside Activities**</u>

- What kind of job-related organizations or professional societies do you belong to (you may omit those that indicate your race, religion, color, national origin, ancestry, sex or age)?

- How will your involvement in these activities affect your job here?

<u>**Nepotism Information**</u>

- Do you have any relatives already employed by our company? If so, who are they and what is their relationship to you?

- Do you have any relatives employed by a competitor of this company? If so, who are they and what is there relationship to you?

* * * * *

Checking 'em out

Okay, suppose you think that you have interviewed the perfect person for the job. Do you extend an offer now? No! Before you make any definite job offer, you need to perform a background and reference check on the person.

Ideally, the prospective employee has signed your handy-dandy "Background Check Permission Form" (Forms 7-2 or 7-3 on the CD-ROM), which allows you to get reference information from prior employers and even do a credit check.

If you want to formally request information in writing from a prior employer, use the "Reference Check Letter" (Form 7-4 on the CD-ROM). Of course, make sure that the prospective employee has given you permission to do so.

You may find that past employers are reluctant to give you much information other than confirming employment, position, and salary (for fear of getting sued by those damage-hungry lawyers should the company say anything bad about the former employee). And yes, your company should have the same policy with respect to your departing employees.

Here are the steps you can take to confirm a candidate's background:

- ✔ **Check out school experience.** Some people lie about the degrees that they have earned or where they went to school. Definitely check these out.

- ✔ **Talk to the candidate's former supervisors.** If you can, talk to the candidate's former supervisors — they may provide much more meaningful information than that company's Human Resources Department.

- ✔ **Check for felony convictions.** For sensitive jobs, check to see if the candidate has any past felony convictions.

- ✔ **Verify past employment.** Verify that the employee worked at each of the companies listed, at the position listed, and the dates of employment.

Remember, lying about any of the above may be a tip-off of bigger problems.

Avoiding job offer mistakes

When you make job offers oral or written, you need to be careful not to mislead the applicant or promise something that you can't deliver.

You need to especially avoid statements that give the applicant a false sense of security, or that the applicant may understand to be a long-term promise of employment. Avoid phrases like the following:

- ✔ "We expect you will have a long and prosperous career here."

- ✔ "You can expect your salary to increase by at least 5 percent each year."

- ✔ "After a probationary period, you will enjoy the benefits the company provides to its long-term employees."

You also want to be careful about extending to an applicant different benefits from those available to other employees. This action may be seen as discriminatory.

If you are going to offer the employee stock or stock options in the company, make sure that the stock only *vests,* or is earned, after some significant period of continued employment.

If you plan to offer a commission, bonus, or profit-sharing arrangement to the employee, make sure that the percentage or amount is reasonable and doesn't make the employee unprofitable for your business.

Hiring Documents

Hiring employees can be a document-intensive exercise. In this section, I describe some important agreements and forms you should consider having.

Employment applications

Think about requiring all of your prospective employees to fill out an Employment Application. An application solicits lots of information to help you make decisions on whether to hire the person.

Be careful what the application contains because some questions are illegal. A good Employment Application form asks for prior work experience, special skills, educational background, and also gives consent to the company to check references.

Keep employment applications on file. The application can be helpful later if you decide to fire an employee after discovering that he or she lied about the information on the form.

Attach the employee's résumé to the application and keep it in your files. You may want to refer to the résumé later if problems arise with the employee.

Form 7-5 on the CD-ROM shows a sample Employee Application form.

Offer letters

After you find the perfect employee (or at least one who satisfies your desperation standards), you are ready to make the job offer.

You could just call him (or her) over the phone and say "We want you; we have to have you; we promise you the moon if only you will grace us with your presence." Or, you can try to protect yourself from misunderstanding — and those nasty lawyers later on — by sending a formal job offer letter like the one shown in Form 7-6.

[Company Name and Address]

[Date]

_____
_____
_____

Re: <u>Terms of Employment</u>

Dear _____:

      We are pleased to inform you that after careful consideration, _____ (the "Company") has decided to make you this offer of employment. This letter sets forth the terms of the offer which, if you accept, will govern your employment.

      Position; Duties. Your position will be _____, reporting to the _____ of the Company. Your duties and responsibilities will be as designated by the Company, with an initial focus on (i) _____ and (ii) _____.

      Full Time Employment. The employment term will begin on _____, ____.

      Compensation. Your compensation will be $_____ a year, paid twice monthly consistent with the Company's payroll practices. Your package will include participation in the health and other benefit plans of the Company pursuant to their terms as may be amended by the Company from time to time[; until the Company's health plan is adopted, your reasonable COBRA payments will be reimbursed (subject to a maximum of $200 per month)]. You will be entitled to _____ week's paid vacation (equivalent of ___ business days) for each year of full employment.

      Stock Options. You will be granted options to acquire _____ shares of the Company's Common Stock, vesting over a [four (4)] year term with one (1) year cliff vesting for 1/4th of the options. The options will be granted at a strike price of $_____ per share. The terms and conditions of your stock options are contained in a Stock Option Agreement of even date herewith and must be executed by you and returned to us immediately to be effective.

      Employment at Will. Our employment relationship is terminable at will, which means that either you or the Company may terminate your employment at any time, and for any reason or for no reason.

      Confidentiality and Invention Assignment Agreement. You will be subject to the Company's Confidentiality and Invention Assignment Agreement, which is enclosed with this letter and must be signed and returned by you before any employment relationship will be effective.

Form 7-6: Job offer letter.

(continued)

Certain Acts. During employment with the Company, you will not do anything to compete with the Company's present or contemplated business, nor will you plan or organize any competitive business activity. You will not enter into any agreement, which conflicts with your duties or obligations to the Company. You will not during your employment or within one (1) year after it ends, without the Company's express written consent, directly or indirectly solicit or encourage any employee, agent, independent contractor, supplier, customer, consultant or any other person or company to terminate or alter a relationship with the Company.

No Inconsistent Obligations. You represent that you are aware of no obligations legal or otherwise, inconsistent with the terms of this Agreement or with your undertaking employment with the Company. You will not disclose to the Company, or use, or induce the Company to use, any proprietary information or trade secrets of others. You represent and warrant that you have returned all proprietary and confidential information belonging to all prior employers.

Miscellaneous. Upon your acceptance, this letter will contain the entire agreement and understanding between you and the Company and supersedes any prior or contemporaneous agreements, understandings, term sheets, communications, offers, representations, warranties, or commitments by or on behalf of the Company (oral or written). The terms of your employment may in the future be amended, but only by writing and which is signed by both you and, on behalf of the Company, by a duly authorized executive officer. In making this offer, we are relying on the information you have provided us about your background and experience, including any information provided us in any Employment Application that you may have submitted to us. The language in this letter will be construed as to its fair meaning and not strictly for or against either of us. The party prevailing in any dispute between us shall be awarded reasonable attorney's fees and cost from the non-prevailing party. In the event a dispute does arise, this letter, including the validity, interpretation, construction and performance of this letter, shall be governed by and construed in accordance with the substantive laws of the State of [California or other State]. Jurisdiction for resolution of any disputes shall be solely in [City] [State].

If these terms are acceptable, please sign in the space provided below and return this letter to us. Again, we're very excited to have you join the Company.

Yours truly,

[Name]
[Title]

Agreed and Accepted:

_____
[Name]

Employment Agreements

You may want some high-level employees to sign a formal Employment Agreement (or they may ask for one). A well-drafted Employment Agreement addresses the following key issues:

- ✔ The job description: title and role
- ✔ Whether the employer can change the position
- ✔ The length of the agreement
- ✔ The salary, bonus, and benefits
- ✔ Whether the employee gets stock or stock options in the company (remember, the employee should typically earn these over time)
- ✔ When the employee can be terminated for good cause
- ✔ What "good cause" means
- ✔ When the employee can be terminated without good cause and what severance payment will be due
- ✔ The employee's job responsibilities
- ✔ The employee's confidentiality obligations
- ✔ Where and how disputes will be handled

Form 7-7 (a pro-employer-oriented form that begins on the following page) shows an Employment Agreement for a senior-level employee. If you are the employee negotiating the Employment Agreement, check out the comprehensive "Checklist of Employment Agreement Issues from the Perspective of the Employee" in Form 7-8 on the CD-ROM.

Confidentiality and Invention Assignment Agreements

Your employees, especially if the business is high-tech-oriented, will have access to lots of the company's confidential information. You also expect your employees to come up with ideas, work product, and inventions that are useful to the business.

To make sure that your employees keep the company's proprietary information confidential, you should require them to sign a Confidentiality and Invention Assignment Agreement. This agreement deals with the confidentiality issue, but it can also provide that the ideas, work product, and inventions that the employee creates related to the business of the company belong to the company — not to the employee.

This agreement is discussed in more detail in Chapter 14. Form 7-9 on the CD-ROM shows a sample Confidential Information and Invention Assignment Agreement for Employee.

CONFIDENTIAL INFORMATION AND INVENTION ASSIGNMENT AGREEMENT FOR EMPLOYEE

This CONFIDENTIAL INFORMATION AND INVENTION ASSIGNMENT AGREEMENT (the "Agreement") is made between _____ (the "Company") and the undersigned employee.

In consideration of my employment with the Company (which for purposes of this Agreement shall be deemed to include any subsidiaries or Affiliates of the Company), the receipt of confidential information while associated with the Company, and other good and valuable consideration, I, the undersigned individual, agree that:

1. <u>Term of Agreement</u>. This Agreement shall continue in full force and effect for the duration of my employment by the Company (the "Period of Employment") and shall continue thereafter as otherwise provided in this Agreement.

2. <u>Confidentiality</u>.

(a) <u>Definitions</u>. "Proprietary Information" is all information and any idea whatever form, tangible or intangible, pertaining in any manner to the business of the Company, or any of its Affiliates, or its employees, clients, consultants, or business associates, which was produced by any employee or consultant of the Company in the course of his or her employment or consulting relationship or otherwise produced or acquired by or on behalf of the Company. All Proprietary Information not generally known outside of the Company's organization, and all Proprietary Information so known only through improper means, shall be deemed "Confidential Information." By example and without limiting the foregoing definition, Proprietary and Confidential Information shall include, but not be limited to:

(1) formulas, research and development techniques, processes, trade secrets, computer programs, software, electronic codes, mask works, inventions, innovations, patents, patent applications, discoveries, improvements, data, know-how, formats, test results, and research projects;

(2) information about costs, profits, markets, sales, contracts and lists of customers, and distributors;

_____

For purposes of this agreement, "Affiliate" shall mean any person or entity that directly or indirectly controls, is controlled by, or is under common control with the Company.

(3) business, marketing, and strategic plans;

(4) forecasts, unpublished financial information, budgets, projections, and customer identities, characteristics and agreements; and

(5) employee personnel files and compensation information.

Confidential Information is to be broadly defined, and includes all information that has or could have commercial value or other utility in the business in which the Company is engaged or contemplates engaging, and all information of which the unauthorized disclosure could be detrimental to the interests of the Company, whether or not such information is identified as Confidential Information by the Company.

(b) <u>Existence of Confidential Information</u>. The Company owns and has developed and compiled, and will develop and compile, certain trade secrets, proprietary techniques and other Confidential Information which have great value to its business. This Confidential Information includes not only information disclosed by the Company to me, but also information developed or learned by me during the course of my employment with the Company.

(c) <u>Protection of Confidential Information</u>. I will not, directly or indirectly, use, make available, sell, disclose or otherwise communicate to any third party, other than in my assigned duties and for the benefit of the Company, any of the Company's Confidential Information, either during or after my employment with the Company. In the event I desire to publish the results of my work for the Company through literature or speeches, I will submit such literature or speeches to the President of the Company at least 10 days before dissemination of such information for a determination of whether such disclosure may alter trade secret status, may be highly prejudicial to the interests of the Company, or may constitute an invasion of its privacy. I agree not to publish, disclose or otherwise disseminate such information without prior written approval of the President of the Company. I acknowledge that I am aware that the unauthorized disclosure of Confidential Information of the Company may be highly prejudicial to its interests, an invasion of privacy, and an improper disclosure of trade secrets.

(d) <u>Delivery of Confidential Information</u>. Upon request or when my employment with the Company terminates, I will immediately deliver to the Company all copies of any and all materials and writings received from, created for, or belonging to the Company including, but not

Form 7-9: Confidential Information and Invention Assignment Agreement for Employee.

limited to, those which relate to or contain Confidential Information.

(e) <u>Location and Reproduction</u>. I shall maintain at my work station and/or any other place under my control only such Confidential Information as I have a current "need to know." I shall return to the appropriate person or location or otherwise properly dispose of Confidential Information once that need to know no longer exists. I shall not make copies of or otherwise reproduce Confidential Information unless there is a legitimate business need of the Company for reproduction.

(f) <u>Prior Actions and Knowledge</u>. I represent and warrant that from the time of my first contact with the Company I held in strict confidence all Confidential Information and have not disclosed any Confidential Information, directly or indirectly, to anyone outside the Company, or used, copied, published, or summarized any Confidential information, except to the extent otherwise permitted in this Agreement.

(g) <u>Third-Party Information</u>. I acknowledge that the Company has received and in the future will receive from third parties their confidential information subject to a duty on the Company's part to maintain the confidentiality of such information and to use it only for certain limited purposes. I agree that, during the Period of Employment and thereafter, I will hold all such confidential information in the strictest confidence and not to disclose or use it, except as necessary to perform my obligations hereunder and as is consistent with the Company's agreement with such third parties.

(h) <u>Third Parties</u>. I represent that my employment with the Company does not and will not breach any agreements with or duties to a former employer or any other third party. I will not disclose to the Company or use on its behalf any confidential information belonging to others and I will not bring onto the premises of the Company any confidential information belonging to any such party unless consented to in writing by such party.

3. <u>Proprietary Rights, Inventions and New Ideas</u>.

(a) <u>Definition</u>. The term "Subject Ideas or Inventions" includes any and all ideas, processes, trademarks, service marks, inventions, designs, technologies, computer hardware or software, original works of authorship, formulas, discoveries, patents, copyrights, copyrightable works products, marketing and business ideas, and all improvements, know-how, data, rights, and claims related to the foregoing that, whether or not patentable, which are conceived, developed or created which: (1) relate to the Company's current or contemplated business or activities; (2) relate to the Company's actual or demonstrably anticipated research or development; (3) result from any work performed by me for the Company; (4) involve the use of the Company's

equipment, supplies, facilities or trade secrets; (5) result from or are suggested by any work done by the Company or at the Company's request, or any projects specifically assigned to me; or (6) result from my access to any of the Company's memoranda, notes, records, drawings, sketches, models, maps, customer lists, research results, data, formulae, specifications, inventions, processes, equipment or other materials (collectively, "Company Materials").

(b) <u>Company Ownership</u>. All right, title and interest in and to all Subject Ideas and Inventions, including but not limited to all registrable and patent rights which may subsist therein, shall be held and owned solely by the Company, and where applicable, all Subject Ideas and Inventions shall be considered works made for hire. I shall mark all Subject Ideas and Inventions with the Company's copyright or other proprietary notice as directed by the Company and shall take all actions deemed necessary by the Company to protect the Company's rights therein. In the event that the Subject Ideas and Inventions shall be deemed not to constitute works made for hire, or in the event that I should otherwise, by operation of law, be deemed to retain any rights (whether moral rights or otherwise) to any Subject Ideas and Inventions, I agree to assign to the Company, without further consideration, my entire right, title and interest in and to each and every such Subject Idea and Invention.

(c) <u>California Labor Code (If Applicable)</u>. However, Section 3(b) shall not apply if and to the extent that California Labor Code Section 2870 lawfully prohibits the assignment of rights in such intellectual property. I acknowledge that I understand the limits placed on this definition by California Labor Code Section 2870, if applicable to me, which provides:

(1) "Any provision in an employment agreement which provides that an employee shall assign, or offer to assign, any of his or her rights in an invention to his or her employer shall not apply to an invention that the employee developed entirely on his or her own time without using the employer's equipment, supplies, facilities, or trade secret information except for those inventions that either:

a. Relate at the time of conception or reduction to practice of the invention to the employer's business, or actual or demonstrably anticipated research or development of the employer; or

b. Result from any work performed by the employee for the employer.

(2) To the extent a provision in an employment agreement purports to require an employee to assign an invention otherwise excluded from being required to be assigned under subdivision (a), the provision is

(continued)

against the public policy of this state and is unenforceable."

(d) <u>Burden</u>. I understand that I bear the full burden of proving to the Company that an Invention qualifies fully under Section 2870. I agree to disclose promptly to the Company full details of any and all Subject Ideas and Inventions.

(e) <u>Maintenance of Records</u>. I agree to keep and maintain adequate and current written records of all Subject Ideas and Inventions and their development made by me (solely or jointly with others) during the term of my employment with the Company. These records will be in the form of notes, sketches, drawings, and any other format that may be specified by the Company. These records will be available to and remain the sole property of the Company at all times.

(f) <u>Determination of Subject Ideas and Inventions</u>. I further agree that all information and records pertaining to any idea, process, trademark, service mark, invention, technology, computer hardware or software, original work of authorship, design, formula, discovery, patent, copyright, product, and all improvements, know-how, rights, and claims related to the foregoing ("Intellectual Property"), that I do not believe to be a Subject Idea or Invention, but that is conceived, developed, or reduced to practice by the Company (alone by me or with others) during the Period of Employment and for one (1) year thereafter, shall be disclosed promptly by me to the Company (such disclosure to be received in confidence). The Company shall examine such information to determine if in fact the Intellectual Property is a Subject Idea or Invention subject to this Agreement.

(g) <u>Access</u>. Because of the difficulty of establishing when any Subject Ideas or Inventions are first conceived by me, or whether it results from my access to Confidential Information or Company Materials, I agree that any Subject Idea and Invention shall, among other circumstances, be deemed to have resulted from my access to Company Materials if: (1) it grew out of or resulted from my work with the Company or is related to the business of the Company, and (2) it is made, used, sold, exploited or reduced to practice, or an application for patent, trademark, copyright or other proprietary protection is filed thereon, by me or with my significant aid, within one year after termination of the Period of Employment.

(h) <u>Assistance</u>. I further agree to assist the Company in every proper way (but at the Company's expense) to obtain and from time to time enforce patents, copyrights or other rights or registrations on said Subject Ideas and Inventions in any and all countries, and to that end will execute all documents necessary:

(1) to apply for, obtain and vest in the name of the Company alone (unless the Company otherwise directs) letters patent, copyrights or other analogous protection in any country throughout the world and when so obtained or vested to renew and restore the same; and

(2) to defend any opposition proceedings in respect of such applications and any opposition proceedings or petitions or applications for revocation of such letters patent, copyright or other analogous protection; and

(3) to cooperate with the Company (but at the Company's expense) in any enforcement or infringement proceeding on such letters patent, copyright or other analogous protection.

(i) <u>Authorization to Company</u>. In the event the Company is unable, after reasonable effort, to secure my signature on any patent, copyright or other analogous protection relating to a Subject Idea and Invention, whether because of my physical or mental incapacity or for any other reason whatsoever, I hereby irrevocably designate and appoint the Company and its duly authorized officers and agents as my agent and attorney-in-fact, to act for and on my behalf and stead to execute and file any such application, applications or other documents and to do all other lawfully permitted acts to further the prosecution, issuance, and enforcement of letters patent, copyright or other analogous rights or protections thereon with the same legal force and effect as if executed by me. My obligation to assist the Company in obtaining and enforcing patents and copyrights for Subject Ideas and Inventions in any and all countries shall continue beyond the termination of my relationship with the Company, but the Company shall compensate me at a reasonable rate after such termination for time actually spent by me at the Company's request on such assistance.

(j) <u>Exhibit</u>. I acknowledge that there are no currently existing ideas, processes, inventions, discoveries, marketing or business ideas or improvements which I desire to exclude from the operation of this Agreement, unless a reference thereto has been attached as an exhibit hereto. To the best of my knowledge, there is no other contract to assign inventions, trademarks, copyrights, ideas, processes, discoveries or other intellectual property that is now in existence between me and any other person (including any business or governmental entity).

(k) <u>No Use of Name</u>. I shall not at any time use the Company's name or any the Company trademark(s) or trade name(s) in any advertising or publicity without the prior written consent of the Company.

4. Competitive Activity.

(a) <u>Acknowledgment</u>. I acknowledge that the pursuit of the activities forbidden by Section 4(b) below would necessarily involve the use, disclosure or misappropriation of Confidential Information.

(b) <u>Prohibited Activity</u>. To prevent the above-described disclosure, misappropriation and breach, I agree that during my employment and for a period of one (1) year after termination of the Period of Employment, without the Company's express written consent, I shall not, directly or indirectly, (i) employ, solicit for employment, or recommend for employment any person employed by the Company (or any Affiliate); and (ii) engage in any present or contemplated business activity that is or may be competitive with the Company (or any Affiliate) in any state where the Company conducts its business, unless I can prove that any action taken in contravention of this subsection (ii) was done without the use in any way of Confidential Information.

5. <u>Representations and Warranties</u>. I represent and warrant (i) that I have no obligations, legal or otherwise, inconsistent with the terms of this Agreement or with my undertaking a relationship with the Company; (ii) that the performance of the services called for by this Agreement do not and will not violate any applicable law, rule or regulation or any proprietary or other right of any third party; (iii) that I will not use in the performance of my responsibilities for the Company any materials or documents of a former employer; and (iv) that I have not entered into or will enter into any agreement (whether oral or written) in conflict with this Agreement.

6. Termination Obligations.

(a) Upon the termination of my relationship with the Company or promptly upon the Company's request, I shall surrender to the Company all equipment, tangible Proprietary Information, documents, books, notebooks, records, reports, notes, memoranda, drawings, sketches, models, maps, contracts, lists, computer disks (and other computer-generated files and data), any other data and records of any kind, and copies thereof (collectively, "Company Records"), created on any medium and furnished to, obtained by, or prepared by myself in the course of or incident to my employment, that are in my possession or under my control.

(b) My representations, warranties, and obligations contained in this Agreement shall survive the termination of the Period of Employment.

(c) Following any termination of the Period of Employment, I will fully cooperate with the Company in all matters relating to my continuing obligations under this Agreement.

(d) In the event that I leave the employ of the Company I hereby grant consent to notification by the Company to my new employer about my rights and obligations under this Agreement.

(e) Upon termination of the Period of Employment, I will execute a Certificate acknowledging compliance with this Agreement in the form reasonably provided by the Company.

7. <u>Injunctive Relief</u>. I acknowledge that my failure to carry out any obligation under this Agreement, or a breach by me of any provision herein, will constitute immediate and irreparable damage to the Company, which cannot be fully and adequately compensated in money damages and which will warrant preliminary and other injunctive relief, an order for specific performance, and other equitable relief. I further agree that no bond or other security shall be required in obtaining such equitable relief and I hereby consent to the issuance of such injunction and to the ordering of specific performance. I also understand that other action may be taken and remedies enforced against me.

8. <u>Modification</u>. No modification of this Agreement shall be valid unless made in writing and signed by both parties.

9. <u>Binding Effect</u>. This Agreement shall be binding upon me, my heirs, executors, assigns and administrators and is for the benefit of the Company and its successors and assigns.

10. <u>Governing Law</u>. This Agreement shall be construed in accordance with, and all actions arising under or in connection therewith shall be governed by, the internal laws of the State of _____ (without reference to conflict of law principles).

11. <u>Integration</u>. This Agreement sets forth the parties' mutual rights and obligations with respect to proprietary information, prohibited competition, and intellectual property. It is intended to be the final, complete, and exclusive statement of the terms of the parties' agreements regarding these subjects. This Agreement supersedes all other prior and contemporaneous agreements and statements on these subjects, and it may not be contradicted by evidence of any prior or contemporaneous statements or agreements. To the extent that the practices, policies, or procedures of the Company, now or in the future, apply to myself and are inconsistent with the terms of this Agreement, the provisions of this Agreement shall control unless changed in writing by the Company.

(continued)

12. Employment at Will. This Agreement is not an employment agreement. I understand that the Company may terminate my association or employment with it at any time, with or without cause, subject to the terms of any separate written employment agreement executed by a duly authorized officer of the Company.

13. Construction. This Agreement shall be construed as a whole, according to its fair meaning, and not in favor of or against any party. By way of example and not limitation, this Agreement shall not be construed against the party responsible for any language in this Agreement. The headings of the paragraphs hereof are inserted for convenience only, and do not constitute part of and shall not be used to interpret this Agreement.

14. Attorneys' Fees. Should either I or the Company, or any heir, personal representative, successor or permitted assign of either party, resort to legal proceedings to enforce this Agreement, the prevailing party (as defined in California statutory law) in such legal proceeding shall be awarded, in addition to such other relief as may be granted, attorneys' fees and costs incurred in connection with such proceeding.

15. Severability. If any term, provision, covenant or condition of this Agreement, or the application thereof to any person, place or circumstance, shall be held to be invalid, unenforceable or void, the remainder of this Agreement and such term, provision, covenant or condition as applied to other persons, places and circumstances shall remain in full force and effect.

16. Rights Cumulative. The rights and remedies provided by this Agreement are cumulative, and the exercise of any right or remedy by either the Company or me (or by that party's successor), whether pursuant hereto, to any other agreement, or to law, shall not preclude or waive that party's right to exercise any or all other rights and remedies. This Agreement will inure to the benefit of the Company and its successors and assigns.

17. Nonwaiver. The failure of either the Company or me, whether purposeful or otherwise, to exercise in any instance any right, power or privilege under this Agreement or under law shall not constitute a waiver of any other right, power or privilege, nor of the same right, power or privilege in any other instance. Any waiver by the Company or by me must be in writing and signed by either myself, if I am seeking to waive any of my rights under this Agreement, or by an officer of the Company (other than me) or some other person duly authorized by the Company.

18. Notices. Any notice, request, consent or approval required or permitted to be given under this Agreement or pursuant to law shall be sufficient if it is in writing, and if and when it is hand delivered or sent by regular mail, with postage prepaid, to my residence (as noted in the Company's records), or to the Company's principal office, as the case may be.

19. Date of Effectiveness. This Agreement shall be deemed effective as of the commencement of my employment with the Company.

20. Agreement to Perform Necessary Acts. I agree to perform any further acts and execute and deliver any documents that may be reasonably necessary to carry out the provisions of this Agreement.

21. Assignment. This Agreement may not be assigned without the Company's prior written consent.

22. Compliance with Law. I agree to abide by all federal, state, and local laws, ordinances and regulations.

23. Employee Acknowledgment. I acknowledge that I have had the opportunity to consult legal counsel in regard to this Agreement, that I have read and understand this Agreement, that I am fully aware of its legal effect, and that I have entered into it freely and voluntarily and based on my own judgment and not on any representations or promises other than those contained in this Agreement.

IN WITNESS WHEREOF, the undersigned have executed this Agreement as of the date set forth below.

CAUTION: THIS AGREEMENT CREATES IMPORTANT OBLIGATIONS OF TRUST AND AFFECTS THE EMPLOYEE'S RIGHTS TO INVENTIONS AND OTHER INTELLECTUAL PROPERTY THE EMPLOYEE MAY DEVELOP DURING HIS OR HER EMPLOYMENT.

Dated: _____

_____
Employee Signature

Printed Name of Employee: _____

[Name of Company]

By: _____

Name: _____

Title: _____

New employee paperwork

When the new employee shows up for the first day of work, make sure that you have all of the appropriate paperwork for him or her to sign.

The CD-ROM includes the following paperwork for the employee to sign on the first day:

- ✔ **Employee handbook:** If you have an employee handbook, get a receipt that the employee has received and reviewed it (Form 7-10).

- ✔ **IRS Form W-4:** Each employee must complete this form for the company to determine the appropriate level of tax withholding (Form 7-11).

- ✔ **Employee benefit elections:** If your business provides employee benefit programs such as medical insurance or pension plans, the employee should sign up and provide relevant information (identifying dependents, making required elections, and so on). See Chapter 8 for more on these forms.

- ✔ **Confidentiality and Invention Assignment Agreement:** This agreement requires the employee to keep company information confidential (Form 7-9).

- ✔ **Emergency notification:** This form advises the company of whom to contact in the event of an emergency (Form 7-12).

Forms on the CD-ROM

Form 7-1	**Questions to Consider Asking Prospective Employees**	A list of questions to consider asking prospective employees
Form 7-2	**Background Check Permission (Comprehensive)**	A form that the prospective employee signs, which gives the employer permission to check references
Form 7-3	**Background Check Permission (Simple)**	A simpler consent form from a prospective employee for the employer to perform a background check
Form 7-4	**Reference Check Letter**	Letter to prior employer of prospective employee requesting reference information
Form 7-5	**Employment Application for Prospective Employees**	Form for prospective employees to fill out

(continued)

Form 7-6	**Offer Letter to Prospective Employee**	Letter providing terms of employment offer to prospective employee
Form 7-7	**Employment Agreement**	Agreement for executive-level employee
Form 7-8	**Checklist of Employment Agreement Issues from the Perspective of the Employee**	A checklist of issues for an employee to consider when negotiating an Employment Agreement
Form 7-9	**Confidentiality and Invention Assignment Agreement for Employee**	Agreement in which the employee agrees to keep company information confidential and to assign to the company business-related inventions developed by the employee
Form 7-10	**Employee Handbook and At Will Employee Status Acknowledgement**	A form in which the employee acknowledges receiving the employee handbook and the "at will" notice of his or her employment
Form 7-11	**IRS Form W-4**	IRS Employee's Withholding Allowance Certificate
Form 7-12	**Employee Emergency Notification Form**	Form that the employee fills out, identifying the person to contact in the event of an emergency

Chapter 8

Rewarding and Managing Employees

*E*mployees are key to the success of any business. So you really need to properly manage and motivate your employees. In this chapter, I discuss some programs and plans to motivate employees together with guidance on properly managing employees.

Digging through the Employee Incentive Tool Kit

You have a good number of employee incentive plans available for your business — including a stock option plan, bonus arrangements, 401(k) plans, and profit-sharing plans. You can also think about providing some unusual perks for your employees. In the following sections, I discuss some incentive arrangements.

Table 8-1 contains a chart of the key employee benefit plans and programs that many companies choose from.

Table 8-1	Chart of Key Employee Benefit Plans and Programs
Plan Type	**Summary**
Cafeteria Plan	Provides employees with a choice of different benefits (or sometimes a cash option instead)
Defined Benefit Pension Plan	Provides employees with a specific amount of payment upon retirement, depending on the employee's length of service and level of compensation
Defined Contribution Pension Plan	Provides that the employer will contribute a prescribed amount into a pension plan each year
Disability Plan	Provides employees with certain payments on disability
Health and Medical Plan	Provides employees coverage for certain health, medical, and accident occurrences
Life Insurance Plan	Provides group-term life insurance for employees
Phantom Stock Plan	Gives employees the economic advantages (without actually issuing stock) of stock in the employer if the stock appreciates
Profit-Sharing Program	Allows employees to share a percentage of the profits from the business
Retention Agreements	Provides for cash bonuses or other payment if the employee stays employed for a designated period of time
Section 401(k) Plan	Provides employees with an incentive savings plan wherein employee and employer contributions are not taxed until withdrawn or when employees reach certain age levels
SIMPLE Plan	Offers a simple form of pension plan for companies with no more than 100 eligible employees

Plan Type	Summary
Stock Bonus Plan	Gives the company the right to award stock as a bonus to employees
Stock Option Plans	Gives the company the right to grant stock options to employees, directors, officers, and consultants
Stock Purchase Plan	Allows the employee to purchase stock in the employer

Stock Option Plans

Stock Option Plans are an extremely popular method of attracting, motivating, and retaining employees, especially when the company is unable to pay high salaries. A Stock Option Plan gives the company the flexibility to award stock options to employees, officers, and consultants, allowing these people to buy stock in the company when they exercise the option.

Stock Option Plans permit employees to share in the company's success without requiring a start-up business to spend precious cash. In fact, Stock Option Plans can actually contribute capital to a company as employees pay the exercise price for their options.

The primary disadvantage of Stock Option Plans for the company is the possible dilution of other shareholders' equity when employees exercise the stock options. For employees, the main disadvantage of stock options in a private company — compared to cash bonuses or greater compensation — is the lack of liquidity. Until the company creates a public market for its stock or is acquired, the options will not be the equivalent of cash benefits. And, if the company does not grow bigger and its stock does not become more valuable, the options may ultimately prove worthless.

Thousands of people have become millionaires through stock options, making these options very appealing to employees. (Indeed, Microsoft has reportedly made over 1,000 employees into millionaires from stock options.) The spectacular successes of Silicon Valley companies and the resulting economic riches of employees who held stock options have made Stock Option Plans a powerful motivational tool for employees to work for the company's long-term success.

Getting rich on stock options

The following example shows how stock options are granted and exercised:

1. ABC, Inc., hires employee John Smith.

2. As part of his employment package, ABC grants John options to acquire 40,000 shares of ABC's common stock at 25 cents per share (the fair market value at the time of grant).

3. The options are subject to a four-year, yearly vesting, which means that John has to stay employed with ABC for one year before he gets the right to exercise 10,000 of the shares, another year for the second 10,000 shares, and so on.

4. If John leaves ABC or is fired before the end of his first year, he doesn't get any of the options.

5. After his shares are "vested" (become exercisable), he has the option to buy the stock at 25 cents per share, even if the share value has gone up dramatically.

6. After four years, all 40,000 of his option shares are vested if he has continued to work for ABC.

7. ABC becomes successful and goes public. Its stock trades at $20 per share.

8. John exercises his options and buys 40,000 shares for $10,000 ($40,000 × 25 cents).

9. John turns around and sells all 40,000 shares for $800,000 (40,000 times the $20 per share price), making a nice profit of $790,000.

A company needs to address a number of key issues before adopting a Stock Option Plan and issuing options. Generally, the company wants to adopt a plan that gives it maximum flexibility. Here are some of the important considerations:

- **Total number of shares:** The Stock Option Plan must reserve a maximum number of shares to be issued under the plan. This total number is generally based on what the board of directors believes is appropriate, but typically ranges from 5 percent to 30 percent of the company's outstanding stock. Of course, not all options reserved for issuances have to be granted.

- **Plan administration:** Although most plans appoint the board of directors as administrator, the plan should also allow the board to delegate responsibilities to a committee. The board or the committee should have broad discretion as to the optionees, the types of options granted, and other terms.

- **Vesting:** Most plans allow the company to impose *vesting* periods for the options. For example, the options don't become exercisable unless the employee continues to be employed with the company. The board or committee typically has broad latitude to determine appropriate vesting schedules and even waive vesting. Typically, companies set the vesting period between three and five years with a *pro rata* percentage vesting either each month or year that the optionee maintains his or her relationship with the company.

✔ **Consideration:** The plan should give the board of directors maximum flexibility in determining how the exercise price can be paid, subject to compliance with applicable corporate law. So, for example, the consideration can include cash, deferred payment, promissory note, or stock. A "cashless" feature can be particularly attractive, where the optionee can use the *buildup* in the value of his or her option (the difference between the exercise price and the stock's fair market value) as the currency to exercise the option.

✔ **Shareholder approval:** The company should generally have shareholders approve the plan, both for securities law reasons and to cement the ability to offer tax-advantaged incentive stock options.

✔ **Right to terminate employment:** To prevent giving employees an implied promise of employment, the plan should clearly state that the grant of stock options does not guarantee any employee a continued relationship with the company.

✔ **Right of first refusal:** The plan (and related Stock Option Agreement) can also provide that in the event the option is exercised, the shareholder grants the company a right of first refusal on transfers of those shares. Doing so allows the company to keep share ownership in the company to a limited group of shareholders.

✔ **Financial reports:** For securities law reasons, the plan may require that periodic financial information and reports are delivered to option holders.

✔ **Vesting:** How do the options vest? Most companies provide a *vesting schedule,* where the employee or advisor has to continue to work for the company for some period of time before the optionee's rights *vest.* For example, an employee may be awarded options to acquire 30,000 shares, vesting in three equal annual installments as long as the company still employs him or her at the end of each one-year anniversary of the date the option was granted.

✔ **Exercise price:** How much does the optionee have to pay for the stock when he exercises his option? Typically, the price is set at the stock's fair market value at the time the option is granted. If the stock's value goes up, the option becomes valuable because the optionee has the right to buy the stock at the cheaper price.

✔ **Term of option:** How long does the optionee have the right to exercise the option? The Stock Option Agreement typically sets a date when the option must be exercised (the date is usually shortened on termination of employment or death).

✔ **Transferability restrictions:** What restrictions apply to the transfer of the option and underlying stock? Most Stock Option Agreements provide that the option is nontransferable. The agreements also state that the stock purchased by exercising the option may be subject to rights of repurchase or rights of first refusal on any potential transfers.

Form 8-2 on the CD-ROM provides a sample Stock Option and Incentive Plan (with a form of stock option agreement). Check with your lawyer, as it will need to be tailored to your situation and conform with applicable securities laws.

Profit-Sharing Programs

Profit-Sharing Programs are employee incentives in which the company announces that a portion of the business's profits will be set aside at year-end and distributed to the employees. To be effective, these programs need to address the following issues:

✔ **Profit threshold:** Establish a designated profit level as a company goal. For example, the Profit-Sharing Program may say that the program kicks in after the company has achieved at least $100,000 in profits for the year.

✔ **Percentage of profits:** Establish the percentage of profits to be shared with the employees and articulate this decision in advance. For example, you may say that 10 percent of all profits over $100,000 will be set aside for the Profit-Sharing Program.

✔ **Eligible participants:** Determine which employees will be eligible to participate — all employees or only certain staff members (such as the sales employees)? Or you may decide that although the amount of the profit-sharing pool is fixed in advance, the recipients will be picked individually by the company's management.

✔ **Continuing employment:** The program may also state that to be eligible, the employee needs to have been employed the entire year and also employed at the time the profit-sharing amounts are to be distributed. You want to avoid giving a profit-sharing award to someone whom you no longer employ.

Make sure to integrate your program into your other benefit programs so that your total benefits package is attractive and motivates employees.

Bonuses

Sometimes the greatest motivational tool is a cash bonus for a job well done when the company has had a good year. Or consider awarding extra vacation time, extra personal leave time, or a gift. Even small, unexpected bonuses or gifts can be real morale boosters for employees.

Cafeteria Plans

Cafeteria Plans are employer-sponsored benefit packages that offer employees a choice between taking cash and receiving qualified benefits (such as accident and health coverage, group-term life insurance coverage, or coverage under a dependent care program). No amount is included in a participant's income if she chooses among the plan's benefits; however, if a participant chooses cash, it can be included in gross income as compensation. If the employee chooses qualified benefits, they are excludable from taxes to the extent allowed by law.

Cafeteria Plans are especially popular among employees because of the flexibility they provide. For example, if one spouse is already working at another company that provides health coverage, the employee can choose to instead obtain group-term life insurance, dental or vision coverage, or even cash.

A human resources professional or labor law attorney should design any Cafeteria Plan to make sure that it complies with all the legal requirements.

401(k) Plans

401(k) Plans are retirement plans that are designed to encourage long-term retirement savings by employees. 401(k) Plans need to meet a variety of rules contained in Section 401(k) of the Internal Revenue Code. But these plans are very popular among companies and employees.

Here are the key features of such plans:

✔ **Employer contributions:** The employer can contribute to the plan (subject to certain limits) for the employee's benefit, and the employee doesn't have to pay immediate income tax on that contribution.

✔ **Employee contributions:** The employee can elect to contribute a portion of his or her salary to the plan, and then the employee doesn't have to pay immediate income tax on that contributed salary.

✔ **Investment of contributions:** The employee can choose how to invest contributed money (in stocks, bonds, and other qualifying investments, for example).

✔ **Tax deferral:** The taxes on the contributions and the plan's investment earnings are deferred until the employee withdraws them (generally, at retirement).

✔ **Loan:** In some instances, a participant may be able to take a loan against the 401(k) account, and as long as the employee repays the loan before taking a distribution from the plan, the funds remain tax-deferred.

✔ **Withdrawals:** Unless the employee is age 59½ or another exception applies (such as total disability), withdrawals by an employee may be subject to *both* a 10 percent penalty and regular income tax.

✔ **Rollovers:** Penalties and taxes generally do not apply if the employee changes jobs and *rolls over* his or her sums in the plan to the new employer's qualified plan that accepts rollovers. Penalties and taxes can also be avoided in certain circumstances for rollovers into an IRA (Individual Retirement Account).

The nature of a 401(k) Plan can be drafted to accommodate certain employer needs, subject to qualifying with the appropriate tax rules.

Unusual perks

You may not want or be able to spend the money for the benefits that I discuss in this chapter. Yet, you are probably still concerned about employee morale. So how about coming up with some unusual employee perks that don't cost an arm, a leg, and a bank loan?

Here are some ideas that other companies use:

- ✔ **Laundry service:** Employees at Netscape can drop off their laundry at the office and have it returned the next day.
- ✔ **Massages:** At Intuit, Inc., workers can get neck and back massages at their desks.
- ✔ **Car washes:** At Intel, employees can make appointments to have their cars picked up at work and washed and detailed while they work.
- ✔ **On-site dental visits:** At Cisco, a dentist makes on-site visits to the company, and employees can make advance appointments.
- ✔ **Day care facilities:** A number of companies provide on-site day care facilities.
- ✔ **Health club memberships:** A number of companies provide various employees memberships at nearby health clubs.
- ✔ **On-site health services:** Some companies offer on-site doctor checkups, mammograms, and other nontraditional health services.
- ✔ **Beer and pizza parties:** Beer and pizza parties are a fixture at a number of Silicon Valley companies.
- ✔ **Office meal delivery:** Some companies offer meal-delivery services for employees working late into the night.

These perks enhance productivity and morale and provide convenience and accessibility to the employees. The cost of such perks may be worth the benefits gained from improved work conditions for employees — employees who are less distracted can focus more on the job at hand.

Form 8-3 on the CD-ROM contains a Certificate of Employee of the Month and Form 8-4 includes an Employee Satisfaction Survey.

Going by the Handbook

You need to treat workers fairly and with respect. And they need to understand the rules of the workplace and the policies to which you expect them to adhere.

Maintaining good written policies helps you in the event that an unhappy employee sues you or makes a complaint to a governmental entity (such as the Equal Employment Opportunity Commission).

An employee handbook can be the central place where company policies and employee benefits and rights are laid out. Consider including the following company policies in your employee handbook:

- ✔ Normal working hours and overtime pay
- ✔ Your vacation policy
- ✔ Your sick days policy
- ✔ Your policy prohibiting the use of illegal drugs or alcohol
- ✔ Your sexual harassment policy
- ✔ Your disciplinary policy
- ✔ Your *at will employment* policy (the company reserves its rights to terminate employees for any reason or no reason)
- ✔ Your non-discrimination policy
- ✔ Your e-mail policy
- ✔ Your employee safety policy

Check out the Checklist for Employee Handbooks shown in Form 8-5 on the CD-ROM.

Have each employee sign an acknowledgement and agreement form on his or her first day of work. This form states that the employee has read and understands your employee handbook. (See the example in Form 8-6 on the CD-ROM.) Make sure to keep a signed copy of this acknowledgement in the employee's personnel file.

Non-discrimination policy

A great number of federal and state laws prohibit various forms of discrimination against employees and prospective employees.

Your employee handbook should contain a non-discrimination policy, such as the one shown in Form 8-7.

NON-DISCRIMINATION POLICY STATEMENT

Overall Policy

It is the policy of [ABC Inc.] (the "Company") to maintain a working environment free of all forms of unlawful discrimination. In recognition of the importance of good employee relations, all applicants are extended an equal opportunity to gain employment and all employees are extended an equal opportunity to progress in their field of endeavor.

Equal Opportunity

The Company affords equal opportunity to all employees and prospective employees without regard to race, color, sex, religion, age, marital status, disability, veteran status or national origin in the following employment practices: recruitment, hiring, placement, transfer, promotion, demotion, selection for training, layoff, termination, determination of service, rate of pay, benefit plans, compensation, and other personnel actions.

Disability

The Company will not discriminate against any employee or applicant for employment because of disability in regard to any position for which the employee or applicant for employment is qualified.

Complaint Procedure

Any individual, whether an employee or applicant for employment who believes that he or she has been discriminated against unlawfully should bring any complaint to _____ in the [Human Resources Department]. Complaints may be lodged in writing or in person. Persons who file complaints will be advised, as is appropriate, regarding any investigation, action or resolution of the problem.

Consequences

The Company will not tolerate any form of discrimination and will take appropriate disciplinary action, including possibly termination, of any person determined to have engaged in unlawful conduct under this policy.

No Retaliation

The Company will not retaliate nor discriminate against any employee or applicant because he or she has opposed any unlawful employment practice or filed a charge of employment discrimination, testified, assisted, or participated in any manner in an investigation, proceeding, or hearing related to employment practices.

* * *

Form 8-7: Non-Discrimination Policy.

Sexual harassment policy

Your company can be held liable for sexual harassment committed by your employees, so consider adopting a sexual harassment policy and placing it in your handbook. Illegal sexual harassment occurs when one employee experiences unwelcome sexual advances, requests for sex, and other acts or statements of a sexual nature from another employee that create a hostile or abusive workplace.

Take steps to notify employees that your company doesn't tolerate sexual harassment. Your company should also do the following:

- ✔ Take reasonable steps to prevent sexual harassment.
- ✔ Investigate every complaint promptly.
- ✔ Consider disciplinary action or termination of employment for an offender.
- ✔ Take all allegations seriously.
- ✔ Establish procedures for how complaints can be made.
- ✔ Consider an in-house seminar to raise employee awareness of the issues surrounding sexual harassment.

Form 8-8 shows an example of a sexual harassment policy that you can modify to fit the particular circumstances of your business.

By adopting affirmative and reasonable steps designed to show that sexual harassment is not tolerated, three important things happen:

- ✔ The occurrence of sexual harassment decreases.
- ✔ You can try to deal with sexual harassment before it heads to litigation.
- ✔ The company can argue more effectively that it shouldn't be held liable for sexual harassment.

Your employees can also be sexually harassed by nonemployees — such as clients, customers, vendors, and so on. Be prepared to take affirmative steps to deal with such acts.

Sexual Harassment
Policy

In order to provide a productive and pleasant working environment, it is important that we at [ABC, Inc.] endeavor to maintain a workplace characterized by mutual respect. Accordingly, sexual harassment in our workplace will not be tolerated.

Prohibited Activities

Sexual harassment has been defined as a form of sex discrimination, consisting of unwanted sexual advances. Examples of prohibited sexual harassment include:

- Supervisors or managers explicitly or implicitly suggesting sex in return for a hiring, compensation, promotion or retention decision.

- Verbal or written sexually suggestive or obscene comments, jokes, or propositions

- Unwanted physical contact, such as touching, grabbing, or pinching

- Displaying sexually suggestive objects, pictures, or magazines

- Continual expression of sexual or social interest after an indication that such interest is not desired

- Conduct with sexual implications when such conduct interferes with the employee's work performance or creates an intimidating work environment

- Suggesting or implying that failure to accept a request for a date or sex would adversely affect the employee in respect to a performance evaluation or promotion

Harassment by Nonemployees

We will endeavor to protect employees, to the extent possible, from reported harassment by non-employees such as from customers, vendors and other parties who have workplace contact with our employees.

Complaint Procedure

An employee who feels that he or she has been harassed is strongly urged to immediately bring the subject to the attention of the appropriate supervisor or to the Head of Human Resources. Inquiries and/or complaints will be investigated as quickly as possible. Any investigation will be conducted in as confidential manner as is compatible with a thorough investigation of the complaint.

Discipline

Any employee found to have harassed another employee or applicant for employment will be subject to appropriate disciplinary procedure action, including reprimands, suspension or termination of employment.

Form 8-8: Sexual Harrassment Policy.

A person committing sexual harassment may also be held legally liable for his or her actions under applicable law.

Responsibility

Each manager is responsible for implementing this policy within his or her area of supervision.

E-mail policy

If you provide employees with computers, consider adopting an e-mail policy. These rules should be clear and comprehensive. You want the employees to know that e-mail is only to be used for appropriate business purposes.

Too many times, employees consider e-mail very informal and write things that can later come back to haunt the company (for example, dirty jokes to a coworker, statements of discrimination, and so on).

Sexual harassment 101

In recent years, lots of litigation has arisen claiming sexual harassment. Here are some sample allegations made by employees:

- Telling dirty jokes

- Making remarks that concern an employee's breasts

- Commenting inappropriately on an employee's outfit

- Asking an uninterested employee out repeatedly

- Suggesting that the way to advance in the company is to sleep with the supervisor

- Posting or circulating nude or explicitly sexual pictures

- Keeping pornographic Web sites on a computer terminal within view of coworkers

- Touching, pinching, or other physical contact that is unwelcome

Here are some guidelines for what your e-mail policy should say:

- ✔ E-mail should at all times be professional and courteous.
- ✔ E-mail is to be used for business purposes and not for personal reasons.
- ✔ E-mail is not private or personal to the sender or recipient and management of the company has access to all e-mail sent to or from company computers.
- ✔ All e-mail is company property.
- ✔ E-mail must not contain any illegal, libelous, or offensive statements.
- ✔ All harassing statements (sexual or otherwise) are prohibited — sex jokes are also inappropriate.
- ✔ E-mail that is deleted can still be retrieved from the company's system.
- ✔ Any violation of the company's e-mail policy subjects an employee to disciplinary measures or termination of employment.

Form 8-9 on the following page shows a sample E-Mail Policy.

Drug-free work policy

Make sure that employees know about your strong policy regarding illegal drugs. Consider including a policy statement such as the one shown in Form 8-10 in each new employee's first-day packet of documents to sign.

Appraising Away

Employee performance appraisals are important tools for small and growing businesses. The appraisals can be crucial in developing employees, reinforcing good performance, and pointing out areas of improvement. Appraisals provide an opportunity to formally communicate expectations for future performance.

Yet many businesses dread doing appraisals or do an inadequate job of giving them. Here are some tips for doing good performance appraisals:

- ✔ Convey the good and the bad concerning past performance.
- ✔ Set clear goals.
- ✔ Outline areas for improvement.
- ✔ Give detailed feedback — vague generalities don't help the employee.
- ✔ Set new goals.
- ✔ Establish procedures for ongoing feedback — not just once or twice a year through a formal performance appraisal process.

<u>**Sample E-Mail Policy**</u>

This document sets forth the policy of _____ (the "Company") with respect to e-mail. All employees who use the Company's e-mail system are required to comply with this policy statement.

1. <u>Business Use</u>. The e-mail system is to be used solely for business purposes of the Company and not for personal purposes of the employees.

2. <u>Ownership</u>. All information and messages that are created, sent, received or stored on the Company's e-mail system is the sole property of the Company.

3. <u>E-mail Review</u>. All e-mail is subject to the right of the Company to monitor, access, read, disclose and use such e-mail without prior notice to the originators and recipients of such e-mail. E-mail may be monitored and read by authorized personnel for the Company for any violations of law, breaches of Company policies, communications harmful to the Company, or for any other reason.

4. <u>Prohibited Content</u>. E-mails may not contain statements or content that are libelous, offensive, harassing, illegal, derogatory, or discriminatory. Foul, inappropriate or offensive messages such as racial, sexual, or religious slurs or jokes are prohibited. Sexually explicit messages or images, cartoons or jokes are prohibited.

5. <u>Security</u>. The e-mail system is only to be used by authorized persons, and an employee must have been issued an e-mail password in order to use the system. Employees shall not disclose their codes or passwords to others and may not use someone else's code or password without express written authorization from the Company.

6. <u>No Presumption of Privacy</u>. E-mail communications should not be assumed to be private and security cannot be guaranteed. Highly confidential or sensitive information should not be sent through e-mail.

7. <u>Certain Prohibited Activities</u>. Employees may not, without the Company's express written authorization transmit trade secrets or other confidential, private or proprietary information or materials through e-mail.

8. <u>Message Retention and Creation</u>. Employees should be careful in creating e-mail. Even when a message has been deleted, it may still exist in printed version, be recreated from a back-up system, or may have been forwarded to someone else. Please note that appropriate electronic messages may need to be saved. And, the Company may be required to produce e-mail in litigation.

Form 8-9: E-Mail Policy. *(continued)*

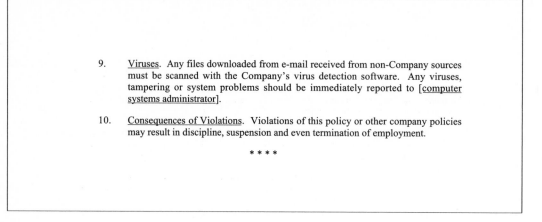

9.   Viruses. Any files downloaded from e-mail received from non-Company sources must be scanned with the Company's virus detection software. Any viruses, tampering or system problems should be immediately reported to [computer systems administrator].

10.   Consequences of Violations. Violations of this policy or other company policies may result in discipline, suspension and even termination of employment.

* * * *

Good documentation — such as performance appraisals showing poor performance — is useful evidence if you ever get involved in a lawsuit with an employee over what you felt was a justified firing.

Form 8-11 on the CD-ROM is a sample Employee Appraisal Form.

Employee Terminations

If your company has a dispute with a fired employee or if you want to avoid litigation, then you may want to enter into a Settlement Agreement with the employee. Settlements can often be cheaper than protracted litigation. And a settlement can help you avoid the distractions of the potentially disruptive effect on management time and attention to litigation.

Of course, the scope of any settlement depends on an analysis of the strength of the employee's case. Your attorney can advise you of the hazards and risks you may face if the case actually goes to trial.

What kind of payments or benefits should you consider giving the employee? Here are some of the more frequently requested items:

- Severance payment
- Continuation of benefits for some amount of time (if allowed under your employee benefit plans)
- Vesting of any unvested stock options
- Allowing the employee to keep his company computer, cellular phone, or other tools

Drug-Free Workplace Policy

The following policy is required by the Drug-Free Workplace Act and complies with applicable law concerning drug use in the workplace.

1. Employees are expected and required to report to work on time and in appropriate mental and physical condition for work. It is our intent and obligation to provide a drug-free, healthful and safe work environment.

2. The unlawful manufacture, distribution, possession or use of a controlled substance on the Company's premises or while conducting the Company's business off its premises is absolutely prohibited. Violations of this policy will result in disciplinary action, up to and including termination, and may have legal consequences.

3. Employees must report any conviction under a criminal drug statute for violations occurring on or off the Company's premises while conducting company business. A report of a conviction must be made within seven (7) days after the conviction.

4. The Company recognizes drug dependency as an illness and a major health problem. The Company also recognizes drug abuse as a potential health, safety and security problem. Employees needing help in dealing with such problems are encouraged to use our employee assistance program and health insurance programs. (Further information about these programs is available from the Personnel Department.) Conscientious efforts to seek such help will not jeopardize any employee's job and will not be noted in any personnel record.

I have read, understand and agree to the Company's Drug-Free Workplace Policy.

_____
Print Name

_____
Sign Name

_____
Date

Form 8-10: Drug-Free Workplace Policy.

✔ Payment for outplacement services

✔ A favorable reference letter for future employees (but watch out — this can come back to be a problem with a future employer)

✔ Reimbursement of moving or relocation expenses

Of course, if you give an ex-employee some of these benefits, then you should expect to get back some or all of the following in a Settlement Agreement:

✔ A release by the employee of all claims, known or unknown, that the employee may have against the company, its officers, or other employees related to the employee's employment and termination of employment

✔ An agreement that the employee will not make disparaging remarks about the company, its officers, and other employees

✔ A commitment to keep all company proprietary information confidential

✔ An agreement not to solicit any of the company's employees or customers for at least one or two years

Form 8-12 on the CD-ROM shows excerpts from a sample Settlement Agreement with a terminated employee. The terminated employee agrees to release any claims against the company in exchange for a lump sum payment.

Some companies make a practice of having a formal interview with all employees who decide to leave the company (or are fired). Such an interview can serve several purposes, including the following:

✔ Finding out why the person is leaving, if voluntary

✔ Reminding the employee of his or her confidentiality obligations

✔ Getting feedback on company operations and policies to spot any needed areas of improvement

Form 8-13 shows a sample form that you can use to conduct an employee exit interview.

Forms on the CD-ROM

Form 8-1	**Chart of Key Employee Benefit Plans and Programs**	A chart summarizing different employee benefit plans and programs
Form 8-2	**Stock Option and Incentive Stock Plan (with Stock Option Agreement)**	A sample stock option plan with stock option agreement

Form 8-3	**Certificate of Employee of the Month**	A sample certificate to be given to an employee in appreciation of good work
Form 8-4	**Employee Satisfaction Survey**	A sample form to be given to employees to gauge employee satisfaction
Form 8-5	**Checklist for Employee Handbooks**	A checklist of items to consider including an employee handbook
Form 8-6	**Employee Handbook and At Will Employee Status Acknowledgement**	A sample acknowledgment covering the employee handbook and At Will Employment Status for employees to sign
Form 8-7	**Non-Discrimination Policy**	A sample policy prohibiting unlawful discrimination in the workplace
Form 8-8	**Sexual Harassment Policy**	A sample policy giving guidance to employees and prohibiting sexual harassment
Form 8-9	**E-Mail Policy**	A sample policy concerning how e-mail should and should not be used on company computers
Form 8-10	**Drug-Free Workplace Policy**	A sample policy — to be signed by the employee — concerning the company's policy against illegal drugs
Form 8-11	**Employee Appraisal Form**	A sample form to be used to record an employee appraisal
Form 8-12	**Employee Settlement and Release Agreement**	A sample agreement where the employee releases any claims against the employer in exchange for some payment
Form 8-13	**Employee Exit Interview**	A sample form to be used in connection with a departing employee

Chapter 9

Independent Contractor and Consultant Agreements

• •

In This Chapter

▶ Independent contractor and consulting agreements

▶ Key tax forms for independent contractors and consultants

• •

*B*usinesses can benefit from hiring independent contractors or consultants rather than employees. You must carefully document the agreement with the independent contractor or consultant, however, to avoid some really nasty problems with the Internal Revenue Service. And if you contract with the independent contractor or consultant to develop a product, software, a book or manual, or intellectual property, you really need to document what rights you expect to retain in the end product.

In this chapter, I provide valuable forms and agreements to use when working with independent contractors and consultants. I also tell you a bit about the key business and tax issues that necessitate these forms.

Forming Relationships with Independent Contractors and Consultants

You can reap some rewards by contracting with independent contractors and consultants. Consider the following advantages:

✔ You get special expertise.

✔ You use them as needed.

✔ You save on tax contributions.

✔ You save on benefits.

✔ You have flexibility in the relationship.

But using independent contractors is not all roses and champagne. Consider the following disadvantages:

- ✔ You run the risk of tax problems.
- ✔ You may not have the same continuity in the relationship that you would have with an employee.
- ✔ You may have to pay high fees to the contractor.
- ✔ You have limited control over the contractor.

Before you hire an independent contractor or consultant, you may want to get background information to determine if he or she is the right person for the job. Form 9-1 on the CD-ROM offers questions that you may want to ask. If you want to check out the answers you get, have the consultant or independent contractor sign a background check form such as the samples given in Forms 9-2 and 9-3 on the CD-ROM.

Independent Contractor Agreements

Your business must have a good form of agreement when hiring independent contractors. A good agreement covers the following:

- ✔ **Services to be performed:** This part of the contract should carefully spell out the services to be performed. Make sure that you have spelled out all of the things you expect the independent contractor to do for his compensation.
- ✔ **Timing:** The contract should spell out when the services are to be performed. Also consider a late-penalty fee if the services are not performed on time, or a bonus if finished early.
- ✔ **Payment:** The payment clause of the contract should address the amount to be paid, the manner payment is to be paid (on an hourly basis? on a project basis?), and when payments are due. From the company's perspective, it wants to ensure that it's reasonably satisfied with the quality and scope of services rendered by the contractor before being obligated to pay the entire amount.
- ✔ **Reporting:** The contract can also address how often the contractor needs to report progress made, and to whom to report. Be careful here, because excessive control over the activities of the contractor may result in him or her being deemed an "employee" for tax purposes.
- ✔ **Confidentiality obligations:** The contract needs to make clear that the contractor must keep proprietary information about the company confidential and not use such information other than for the benefit of the company.

✔ **Work for hire:** The contract should typically provide that the work product developed by the contractor for the company will be deemed *work for hire* under the copyright laws and owned solely by the company (and not the contractor).

✔ **Warranties:** Spell out any warranties from the contractor, such as the contractor warranty that the services be performed in a high-quality, professional, and timely manner.

✔ **Subcontractors:** If the contractor expects to use any subcontractors, consider providing that you have approval over these subcontractors and that they execute an appropriate agreement with you.

Form 9-4 is a good sample Independent Contractor Agreement.

<u>INDEPENDENT CONTRACTOR AGREEMENT</u>

This Independent Contractor Agreement (the "Agreement") is made and entered between _____, an independent contractor hereafter referred to as "Contractor", and _____, hereafter referred to as "Company".

In consideration of the covenants and conditions hereinafter set forth, Company and Contractor agree as follows:

1. <u>SERVICES</u>

    Contractor shall perform the following services for the Company (the "Work").
    _____
    _____
    _____

2. <u>REPORTING</u>

    Contractor shall report to _____. Contractor shall provide a weekly written report to the Company on his progress on assignments.

3. <u>TERM</u>

    This Agreement shall commence on _____, ____ and shall expire on _____, ____. Contractor agrees to perform services for the Work to Company on or before the expiration of the term set forth above. The Company may terminate the use of Contractor's services at any time without cause and without further obligation to Contractor except for payment due for services prior to date of such termination. Termination of this Agreement or termination of services shall not affect the provisions under Sections 5-11, hereof, which shall survive any termination.

4. <u>PAYMENT</u>

    Contractor will be paid for Work performed under this Agreement as follows:
    _____
    _____
    _____

    Contractor will submit an invoice for the Work on _____. Invoices shall be paid by the Company within 15 business days of receipt.

5. <u>CONFIDENTIALITY AND OWNERSHIP</u>

    (a)   Contractor recognizes and acknowledges that the Company possesses certain confidential information that constitutes a valuable, special, and unique asset. As used herein, the term "confidential information" includes all information and materials belonging to, used by,

Form 9-4: Independent Contractor Agreement.

or in the possession of the Company relating to its products, processes, services, technology, inventions, patents, ideas, contracts, financial information, developments, business strategies, pricing, current and prospective customers, marketing plans, and trade secrets of every kind and character, but shall not include (a) information that was already within the public domain at the time the information is acquired by Contractor, or (b) information that subsequently becomes public through no act or omission of the Contractor. Contractor agrees that all of the confidential information is and shall continue to be the exclusive property of the Company, whether or not prepared in whole or in part by Contractor and whether or not disclosed to or entrusted to Contractor's custody. Contractor agrees that Contractor shall not, at any time following the execution of this Agreement, use or disclose in any manner any confidential information of the Company.

(b)   To the extent any inventions, technologies, reports, memoranda, studies, writings, articles, plans, designs, specifications, exhibits, software code, or other materials prepared by Contractor in the performance of services under this Agreement include material subject to copyright protection, such materials have been specially commissioned by the Company and they shall be deemed "work for hire" as such term is defined under U.S. copyright law. To the extent any such materials do not qualify as "work for hire" under applicable law, and to the extent they include material subject to copyright, patent, trade secret, or other proprietary rights protection, Contractor hereby irrevocably and exclusively assigns to the Company, its successors, and assigns, all right, title, and interest in and to all such materials. To the extent any of Contractor rights in the same, including without limitation any moral rights, are not subject to assignment hereunder, Contractor hereby irrevocably and unconditionally waives all enforcement of such rights. Contractor shall execute and deliver such instruments and take such other actions as may be required to carry out and confirm the assignments contemplated by this paragraph and the remainder of this Agreement. All documents, magnetically or optically encoded media, and other tangible materials created by Contractor as part of its services under this Agreement shall be owned by the Company.

6.   RETURN OF MATERIALS

Contractor agrees that upon termination of this Agreement, Contractor will return to the Company all drawings, blueprints, notes, memoranda, specifications, designs, writings, software, devices, documents and any other material containing or disclosing any confidential or proprietary information of the Company. Contractor will not retain any such materials.

7.   WARRANTIES

Contractor warrants that:

(a)   Contractor's agreement to perform the Work pursuant to this Agreement does not violate any agreement or obligation between Contractor and a third party; and

(b)   The Work as delivered to the Company will not infringe any copyright, patent, trade secret, or other proprietary right held by any third party; and

(continued)

(c)   The services provided by Contractor shall be performed in a professional manner, and shall be of a high grade, nature, and quality. The services shall be performed in a timely manner and shall meet deadlines agreed between Contractor and the Company.

8.   INDEMNITY

Contractor agrees to indemnify, defend, and hold the Company and its successors, officers, directors, agents and employees harmless from any and all actions, causes of action, claims, demands, cost, liabilities, expenses and damages (including attorneys' fees) arising out of, or in connection with any breach of this Agreement by Contractor.

9.   RELATIONSHIP OF PARTIES

Contractor is an independent contractor of the Company. Nothing in this Agreement shall be construed as creating an employer-employee relationship, as a guarantee of future employment or engagement, or as a limitation upon the Company' sole discretion to terminate this Agreement at any time without cause. Contractor further agrees to be responsible for all of Contractor's federal and state taxes, withholding, social security, insurance, and other benefits. Contractor shall provide the Company with satisfactory proof of independent contractor status.

10.   OTHER ACTIVITIES

Contractor is free to engage in other independent contracting activities, provided that Contractor does not engage in any such activities which are inconsistent with or in conflict with any provisions hereof, or that so occupy Contractor's attention as to interfere with the proper and efficient performance of Contractor's services thereunder. Contractor agrees not to induce or attempt to influence, directly or indirectly, any employee at the Company to terminate his/her employment and work for Contractor or any other person.

11.   MISCELLANEOUS

(a)   Attorneys' Fees. Should either party hereto, or any heir, personal representative, successor or assign of either party hereto, resort to legal proceedings in connection with this Agreement or Contractor's relationship with the Company, the party or parties prevailing in such legal proceedings shall be entitled, in addition to such other relief as may be granted, to recover its or their reasonable attorneys' fees and costs in such legal proceedings from the non-prevailing party or parties.

(b)   Governing Law. This Agreement shall be governed by and construed in accordance with the laws of the State of _____ without regard to conflict of law principles.

(c)   Entire Agreement. This Agreement contains the entire agreement and understanding between the parties hereto and supersedes any prior or contemporaneous written or oral agreements, representations and warranties between them respecting the subject matter hereof.

(d)   Amendment. This Agreement may be amended only by a writing signed by Contractor and by a duly authorized representative of the Company.

(e)   Severability. If any term, provision, covenant or condition of this Agreement, or the application thereof to any person, place or circumstance, shall be held to be invalid, unenforceable or void, the remainder of this Agreement and such term, provision, covenant or condition as applied to other persons, places and circumstances shall remain in full force and effect.

(f)   Construction. The headings and captions of this Agreement are provided for convenience only and are intended to have no effect in construing or interpreting this Agreement. The language in all parts of this Agreement shall be in all cases construed according to its fair meaning and not strictly for or against either party.

(g)   Rights Cumulative. The rights and remedies provided by this Agreement are cumulative, and the exercise of any right or remedy by either party hereto (or by its successor), whether pursuant to this Agreement, to any other agreement, or to law, shall not preclude or waive its right to exercise any or all other rights and remedies.

(h)   Nonwaiver. No failure or neglect of either party hereto in any instance to exercise any right, power or privilege hereunder or under law shall constitute a waiver of any other right, power or privilege or of the same right, power or privilege in any other instance. All waivers by either party hereto must be contained in a written instrument signed by the party to be charged and, in the case of the Company, by an officer of the Company or other person duly authorized by the Company.

(i)   Remedy for Breach. The parties hereto agree that, in the event of breach or threatened breach of any covenants of Contractor, the damage or imminent damage to the value and the goodwill of the Company's business shall be inestimable, and that therefore any remedy at law or in damages shall be inadequate. Accordingly, the parties hereto agree that the Company shall be entitled to injunctive relief against Contractor in the event of any breach or threatened breach of any of such provisions by Contractor, in addition to any other relief (including damages) available to the Company under this Agreement or under law.

(j)   Notices. Any notice, request, consent or approval required or permitted to be given under this Agreement or pursuant to law shall be sufficient if in writing, and if and when sent by certified or registered mail, with postage prepaid, to Contractor's residence (as noted below), or to the Company's principal office, as the case may be.

(k)   Assistance. Contractor shall, during and after termination of services rendered, upon reasonable notice, furnish such information and proper assistance to the Company as may reasonably be required by the Company in connection with work performed by Contractor; provided, however, that such assistance following termination shall be furnished at the same level of compensation as provided in Section 4.

(l)   Disputes. Any controversy, claim or dispute arising out of or relating to this Agreement or the relationship, either during the existence of the relationship or afterwards, between the parties hereto, their assignees, their affiliates, their attorneys, or agents, shall be

(continued)

litigated solely in state or federal court in _____, _____. Each party (1) submits to the jurisdiction of such court, (2) waives the defense of an inconvenient forum, (3) agrees that valid consent to service may be made by mailing or delivery of such service to the _____ Secretary of State (the "Agent") or to the party at the party's last known address, if personal service delivery can not be easily effected, and (4) authorizes and directs the Agent to accept such service in the event that personal service delivery can not easily be effected. EACH PARTY, TO THE FULLEST EXTENT PERMITTED BY APPLICABLE LAW, HEREBY IRREVOCABLY WAIVES ALL RIGHT TO TRIAL BY JURY AS TO ANY ISSUE RELATING HERETO IN ANY ACTION, PROCEEDING, OR COUNTERCLAIM ARISING OUT OF OR RELATING TO THIS AGREEMENT OR ANY OTHER MATTER INVOLVING THE PARTIES HERETO.

Company: Contractor:

By:_____   By:_____
                                              [Signature]
Title:_____
                                       Name: _____
                                                  (Print)

                                       _____
                                       Social Security #

Date: _____   Address:_____

                                       _____

                                       _____

Form 9-5 on the CD-ROM provides a similar agreement for consulting services.

Confidentiality and Invention Assignment Agreements

Your consultants, especially if the business is high-tech-oriented, may have access to lots of the company's confidential information. And you may expect the consultants to come up with ideas, work product, and inventions useful to your business.

In areas where you are particularly sensitive about confidentiality and the company's ownership of the product developed, you should require consultants to sign a *Confidentiality and Invention Assignment Agreement*. This agreement deals with the confidentiality issue, but can also provide that the ideas, work product, and inventions the consultant creates in connection with services performed for your business belong to the company (not the consultant). This agreement is more detailed and protective than the Independent Contractor Agreement that I discuss in the preceding section. It is best used with the Consulting Agreement in Form 9-5 on the CD-ROM..

Form 9-6 shows a sample Confidentiality and Invention Assignment Agreement for Consultants. This form is very extensive and pro-company-oriented.

CONFIDENTIAL INFORMATION AND INVENTION ASSIGNMENT AGREEMENT
FOR CONSULTANT

This CONFIDENTIAL INFORMATION AND INVENTION ASSIGNMENT AGREEMENT (the "Agreement") is made between _____ (the "Company") and the undersigned consultant.

In consideration of my relationship with the Company (which for purposes of this Agreement shall be deemed to include any subsidiaries or Affiliates[*] of the Company), the receipt of confidential information while associated with the Company, and other good and valuable consideration, I, the undersigned individual, agree that:

1. <u>Term of Agreement</u>. This Agreement shall continue in full force and effect for the duration of my relationship with the Company and shall continue thereafter until terminated through a written instrument signed by both parties.

2. <u>Confidentiality</u>.

(a)   <u>Definitions</u>. "Proprietary Information" is all information and any idea whatever form, tangible or intangible, pertaining in any manner to the business of the Company, or any of its Affiliates, or its employees, clients, consultants, or business associates, which was produced by any employee or consultant of the Company in the course of his or her employment or consulting relationship or otherwise produced or acquired by or on behalf of the Company. All Proprietary Information not generally known outside of the Company's organization, and all Proprietary Information so known only through improper means, shall be deemed "Confidential Information." By example and without limiting the foregoing definition, Proprietary and Confidential Information shall include, but not be limited to:

(1)   formulas, research and development techniques, processes, trade secrets, computer programs, software, electronic codes, mask works, inventions, innovations, patents, patent applications, discoveries, improvements, data, know-how, formats, test results, and research projects;

(2)   information about costs, profits, markets, sales, contracts and lists of customers, and distributors;

(3)   business, marketing, and strategic plans;

(4)   forecasts, unpublished financial information, budgets, projections, and customer identities, characteristics and agreements; and

(5)   employee personnel files and compensation information.

Confidential Information is to be broadly defined, and includes all information that has or could have commercial value or other utility in the business in which the Company is engaged or contemplates engaging, and all information of which the unauthorized disclosure could be detrimental to the interests of the Company, whether or not such information is identified as Confidential Information by the Company.

(b)   <u>Existence of Confidential Information</u>. The Company owns and has developed and compiled, and will develop and compile, certain trade secrets, proprietary techniques and other Confidential Information which have great value to its business. This Confidential Information includes not only information disclosed by the Company to me, but also information developed or learned by me during the course of my relationship with the Company.

(c)   <u>Protection of Confidential Information</u>. I will not, directly or indirectly, use, make available, sell, disclose or otherwise communicate to any third party, other than in my assigned duties and for the benefit of the Company, any of the Company's Confidential Information, either during or after my relationship with the Company. In the event I desire to publish the results of my work for the Company through literature or speeches, I will submit such literature or speeches to the President of the Company at least 10 days before dissemination of such information for a determination of whether such disclosure may alter trade secret status, may be prejudicial to the interests of the Company, or may constitute an invasion of its privacy. I agree not to publish, disclose or otherwise disseminate such information without prior written approval of the President of the Company. I acknowledge that I am aware that the unauthorized disclosure of Confidential Information of the Company may be highly prejudicial to its interests, an invasion of privacy, and an improper disclosure of trade secrets.

(d)   <u>Delivery of Confidential Information</u>. Upon request or when my relationship with the Company terminates, I will immediately deliver to the Company all copies of any and all materials and writings received from, created for, or belonging to the Company including, but not limited to, those which relate to or contain Confidential Information.

(e)   <u>Location and Reproduction</u>. I shall maintain at my workplace only such Confidential Information as I have a current "need to know." I shall return to the appropriate person or location or otherwise properly dispose of Confidential Information once that need to know no longer exists. I shall not make copies of or otherwise reproduce

_____

[*] For purposes of this Agreement, "Affiliate" shall mean any person or entity that shall directly or indirectly controls, is controlled by, or is under common control with the Company.

Form 9-6: Confidentiality Information and Invention Assignment Agreement for Consultant.

Confidential Information unless there is a legitimate business need of the Company for reproduction.

(f) <u>Prior Actions and Knowledge</u>. I represent and warrant that from the time of my first contact with the Company I held in strict confidence all Confidential Information and have not disclosed any Confidential Information, directly or indirectly, to anyone outside the Company, or used, copied, published, or summarized any Confidential information, except to the extent otherwise permitted in this Agreement.

(g) <u>Third-Party Information</u>. I acknowledge that the Company has received and in the future will receive from third parties their confidential information subject to a duty on the Company's part to maintain the confidentiality of such information and to use it only for certain limited purposes. I agree that I will at all times hold all such confidential information in the strictest confidence and not to disclose or use it, except as necessary to perform my obligations hereunder and as is consistent with the Company's agreement with such third parties.

(h) <u>Third Parties</u>. I represent that my relationship with the Company does not and will not breach any agreements with or duties to a former employer or any other third party. I will not disclose to the Company or use on its behalf any confidential information belonging to others and I will not bring onto the premises of the Company any confidential information belonging to any such party unless consented to in writing by such party.

3. Proprietary Rights, Inventions and New Ideas.

(a) <u>Definition</u>. The term "Subject Ideas or Inventions" includes any and all ideas, processes, trademarks, service marks, inventions, designs, technologies, computer hardware or software, original works of authorship, formulas, discoveries, patents, copyrights, copyrightable works products, marketing and business ideas, and all improvements, know-how, data, rights, and claims related to the foregoing that, whether or not patentable, which are conceived, developed or created which: (1) relate to the Company's current or contemplated business; (2) relate to the Company's actual or demonstrably anticipated research or development; (3) result from any work performed by me for the Company; (4) involve the use of the Company's equipment, supplies, facilities or trade secrets; (5) result from or are suggested by any work done by the Company or at the Company's request, or any projects specifically assigned to me; or (6) result from my access to any of the Company's memoranda, notes, records, drawings, sketches, models, maps, customer lists, research results, data, formulae, specifications, inventions, processes, equipment or other materials (collectively, "Company Materials").

(b) <u>Company Ownership</u>. All right, title and interest in and to all Subject Ideas and Inventions, including but not limited to all registrable and patent rights which may subsist therein, shall be held and owned solely by the Company, and where applicable, all Subject Ideas and Inventions shall be considered works made for hire. I shall mark all Subject Ideas and Inventions with the Company's copyright or other proprietary notice as directed by the Company and shall take all actions deemed necessary by the Company to protect the Company's rights therein. In the event that the Subject Ideas and Inventions shall be deemed not to constitute works made for hire, or in the event that I should otherwise, by operation of law, be deemed to retain any rights (whether moral rights or otherwise) to any Subject Ideas and Inventions, I agree to assign to the Company, without further consideration, my entire right, title and interest in and to each and every such Subject Idea and Invention.

(c) <u>Disclosure</u>. I agree to disclose promptly to the Company full details of any and all Subject Ideas and Inventions.

(d) <u>Maintenance of Records</u>. I agree to keep and maintain adequate and current written records of all Subject Ideas and Inventions and their development made by me (solely or jointly with others) during the term of my relationship with the Company. These records will be in the form of notes, sketches, drawings, and any other format that may be specified by the Company. These records will be available to and remain the sole property of the Company at all times.

(e) <u>Determination of Subject Ideas and Inventions</u>. I further agree that all information and records pertaining to any idea, process, trademark, service mark, invention, technology, computer hardware or software, original work of authorship, design, formula, discovery, patent, copyright, product, and all improvements, know-how, rights, and claims related to the foregoing ("Intellectual Property"), that I do not believe to be a Subject Idea or Invention, but that is conceived, developed, or reduced to practice by the Company (alone by me or with others) during my relationship with the Company and for one (1) year thereafter, shall be disclosed promptly by me to the Company. The Company shall examine such information to determine if in fact the Intellectual Property is a Subject Idea or Invention subject to this Agreement.

(f) <u>Access</u>. Because of the difficulty of establishing when any Subject Ideas or Inventions are first conceived by me, or whether it results from my access to Confidential Information or Company Materials, I agree that any Subject Idea and Invention shall, among other circumstances, be deemed to have resulted from my access to Company Materials if: (1) it grew out of or resulted from my work with the Company or is related to the business of the Company, and (2) it is made, used, sold, exploited or reduced to practice, or an application for patent, trademark, copyright or other proprietary protection is filed thereon, by me or with my significant aid, within one year after termination of my relationship with the Company.

(g) <u>Assistance</u>. I further agree to assist the Company in every proper way (but at the Company's expense) to obtain and from time to time enforce patents, copyrights or other rights or registrations on said Subject Ideas and Inventions in any and all countries, and to that end will execute all documents necessary:

(1) to apply for, obtain and vest in the name of the Company alone (unless the Company otherwise directs) letters patent, copyrights or other analogous protection in any country throughout the world and when so obtained or vested to renew and restore the same; and

(2) to defend any opposition proceedings in respect of such applications and any opposition proceedings or petitions or applications for revocation of such letters patent, copyright or other analogous protection; and

(3) to cooperate with the Company (but at the Company's expense) in any enforcement or infringement proceeding on such letters patent, copyright or other analogous protection.

(h) <u>Authorization to Company</u>. In the event the Company is unable, after reasonable effort, to secure my signature on any patent, copyright or other analogous protection relating to a Subject Idea and Invention, whether because of my physical or mental incapacity or for any other reason whatsoever, I hereby irrevocably designate and appoint the Company and its duly authorized officers and agents as my agent and attorney-in-fact, to act for and on my behalf and stead to execute and file any such application, applications or other documents and to do all other lawfully permitted acts to further the prosecution, issuance, and enforcement of letters patent, copyright or other analogous rights or protections thereon with the same legal force and effect as if executed by me. My obligation to assist the Company in obtaining and enforcing patents and copyrights for Subject

(continued)

Ideas and Inventions in any and all countries shall continue beyond the termination of my relationship with the Company, but the Company shall compensate me at a reasonable rate after such termination for time actually spent by me at the Company's request on such assistance.

(i)   Acknowledgement. I acknowledge that there are no currently existing ideas, processes, inventions, discoveries, marketing or business ideas or improvements which I desire to exclude from the operation of this Agreement. To the best of my knowledge, there is no other contract to assign inventions, trademarks, copyrights, ideas, processes, discoveries or other intellectual property that is now in existence between me and any other person (including any business or governmental entity).

(j)   No Use of Name. I shall not at any time use the Company's name or any the Company trademark(s) or trade name(s) in any advertising or publicity without the prior written consent of the Company.

4. Competitive Activity.

(a)   Acknowledgment. I acknowledge that the pursuit of the activities forbidden by Section 4(b) below would necessarily involve the use, disclosure or misappropriation of Confidential Information.

(b)   Prohibited Activity. To prevent the above-described disclosure, misappropriation and breach, I agree that during my relationship and for a period of one (1) year thereafter, without the Company's express written consent, I shall not, directly or indirectly, (i) employ, solicit for employment, or recommend for employment any person employed by the Company (or any Affiliate); and (ii) engage in any present or contemplated business activity that is or may be competitive with the Company (or any Affiliate) in any state where the Company conducts its business, unless I can prove that any action taken in contravention of this subsection (ii) was done without the use in any way of Confidential Information.

5. Representations and Warranties. I represent and warrant (i) that I have no obligations, legal or otherwise, inconsistent with the terms of this Agreement or with my undertaking a relationship with the Company; (ii) that the performance of the services called for by this Agreement do not and will not violate any applicable law, rule or regulation or any proprietary or other right of any third party; (iii) that I will not use in the performance of my responsibilities for the Company any confidential information or trade secrets of any other person or entity; and (iv) that I have not entered into or will not enter into any agreement (whether oral or written) in conflict with this Agreement.

6. Termination Obligations.

(a)   Upon the termination of my relationship with the Company or promptly upon the Company's request, I shall surrender to the Company all equipment, tangible Proprietary Information, documents, books, notebooks, records, reports, notes, memoranda, drawings, sketches, models, maps, contracts, lists, computer disks (and other computer-generated files and data), any other data and records of any kind, and copies thereof (collectively, "Company Records"), created on any medium and furnished to, obtained by, or prepared by myself in the course of or incident to my relationship with the Company, that are in my possession or under my control.

(b)   My representations, warranties, and obligations contained in this Agreement shall survive the termination of my relationship with the Company.

(c)   Following any termination of my relationship with the Company, I will fully cooperate with the Company in all matters relating to my continuing obligations under this Agreement.

(d)   I hereby grant consent to notification by the Company to any of my future employers or companies I consult with about my rights and obligations under this Agreement.

(e)   Upon termination of my relationship with the Company, I will execute a Certificate acknowledging compliance with this Agreement in the form reasonably requested by the Company.

7. Injunctive Relief. I acknowledge that my failure to carry out any obligation under this Agreement, or a breach by me of any provision herein, will constitute immediate and irreparable damage to the Company, which cannot be fully and adequately compensated in money damages and which will warrant preliminary and other injunctive relief, an order for specific performance, and other equitable relief. I further agree that no bond or other security shall be required in obtaining such equitable relief and I hereby consent to the issuance of such injunction and to the ordering of specific performance. I also understand that other action may be taken and remedies enforced against me.

8. Modification. No modification of this Agreement shall be valid unless made in writing and signed by both parties.

9. Binding Effect. This Agreement shall be binding upon me, my heirs, executors, assigns and administrators and is for the benefit of the Company and its successors and assigns.

10. Governing Law. This Agreement shall be construed in accordance with, and all actions arising under or in connection therewith shall be governed by, the internal laws of the State of California (without reference to conflict of law principles).

11. Integration. This Agreement sets forth the parties' mutual rights and obligations with respect to proprietary information, prohibited competition, and intellectual property. It is intended to be the final, complete, and exclusive statement of the terms of the parties' agreements regarding these subjects. This Agreement supersedes all other prior and contemporaneous agreements and statements on these subjects, and it may not be contradicted by evidence of any prior or contemporaneous statements or agreements. To the extent that the practices, policies, or procedures of the Company, now or in the future, apply to myself and are inconsistent with the terms of this Agreement, the provisions of this Agreement shall control unless changed in writing by the Company.

12. Not Employment. This Agreement is not an employment agreement as I am an independent consultant. I understand that the Company may terminate my association with it at any time, with or without cause, subject to the terms of any separate written consulting agreement executed by a duly authorized officer of the Company.

13. Construction. This Agreement shall be construed as a whole, according to its fair meaning, and not in favor of or against any party. By way of example and not limitation, this Agreement shall not be construed against the party responsible for any language in this Agreement. The headings of the paragraphs hereof are inserted for convenience only, and do not constitute part of and shall not be used to interpret this Agreement.

14. Attorneys' Fees. Should either I or the Company, or any heir, personal representative, successor or permitted assign of either party, resort to legal proceedings to enforce this Agreement, the prevailing party (as defined in California statutory law) in such legal proceeding shall be awarded, in addition to such other relief as may be granted, attorneys' fees and costs incurred in connection with such proceeding.

15. Severability. If any term, provision, covenant or condition of this Agreement, or the application thereof to any person, place or circumstance, shall be held to be invalid, unenforceable or void, the

remainder of this Agreement and such term, provision, covenant or condition as applied to other persons, places and circumstances shall remain in full force and effect.

16. <u>Rights Cumulative</u>. The rights and remedies provided by this Agreement are cumulative, and the exercise of any right or remedy by either the Company or me (or by that party's successor), whether pursuant hereto, to any other agreement, or to law, shall not preclude or waive that party's right to exercise any or all other rights and remedies. This Agreement will inure to the benefit of the Company and its successors and assigns.

17. <u>Nonwaiver</u>. The failure of either the Company or me, whether purposeful or otherwise, to exercise in any instance any right, power or privilege under this Agreement or under law shall not constitute a waiver of any other right, power or privilege, nor of the same right, power or privilege in any other instance. Any waiver by the Company or by me must be in writing and signed by either myself, if I am seeking to waive any of my rights under this Agreement, or by an officer of the Company (other than me) or some other person duly authorized by the Company.

18. <u>Notices</u>. Any notice, request, consent or approval required or permitted to be given under this Agreement or pursuant to law shall be sufficient if it is in writing, and if and when it is hand delivered or sent by regular mail, with postage prepaid, to my residence (as noted in the Company's records), or to the Company's principal office, as the case may be.

19. <u>Agreement to Perform Necessary Acts</u>. I agree to perform any further acts and execute and deliver any documents that may be reasonably necessary to carry out the provisions of this Agreement.

20. <u>Assignment</u>. This Agreement may not be assigned without the Company's prior written consent.

21. <u>Compliance with Law</u>. I agree to abide by all federal, state, and local laws, ordinances and regulations.

22. <u>Acknowledgment</u>. I acknowledge that I have had the opportunity to consult legal counsel in regard to this Agreement, that I have read and understand this Agreement, that I am fully aware of its legal effect, and that I have entered into it freely and voluntarily and based on my own judgment and not on any representations or promises other than those contained in this Agreement.

IN WITNESS WHEREOF, the undersigned have executed this Agreement as of the dates set forth below.

CAUTION: THIS AGREEMENT CREATES IMPORTANT OBLIGATIONS OF TRUST AND AFFECTS THE CONSULTANT'S RIGHTS TO INVENTIONS AND OTHER INTELLECTUAL PROPERTY THE CONSULTANT MAY DEVELOP.

Dated: _____

_____
Consultant Signature

Printed Name of Consultant: _____

[Name of Corporation]

By: _____

Name: _____

Title: _____

Tiptoe through the Tax Forms

Tax laws allow you to treat employees and contractors differently. In fact, decreased tax liability is one of the greatest benefits your company can realize from using an independent contractor or consultant. You must be especially vigilant, however, to correctly fill out your forms and agreements to avoid having the IRS disagree with your assessment of a worker as an independent contractor.

Table 9-1 summarizes some key areas in which independent contractors differ from employees. Many of these issues directly affect what forms you must fill out with respect to the worker. (Table 9-1 is available on the CD-ROM as Form 9-7.)

Table 9-1	Withholding, Benefit, and Legal Differences between Employees and Contractors		
Employer Responsibility		*Employee*	*Independent Contractor*
Make employer contribution to Social Security		Yes	No
Make employer contribution to Medicare taxes		Yes	No
Withhold applicable federal taxes		Yes	No
File Form 1099-MISC with IRS if you pay the person $600 or more		No	Yes
Carry Worker's Compensation Insurance for the person		Yes	No
Contribute to unemployment insurance fund and/or tax		Yes	No
Grant employee job benefits such as paid vacation, sick leave, holidays, and stock options		Yes	No
Pay employee for overtime		Yes	Generally no
Right to control how the worker performs the specific task for which he or she is hired		Generally yes	Generally no
Right to direct or control how the business aspects of the worker's activities are conducted		Generally yes	Generally no

Using a contractor takes determination

Determining whether you can properly characterize a worker as an employee or an independent contractor is absolutely necessary before you enter into an independent contractor agreement. If you have the right to direct or control the specific tasks and business aspects of the worker's activities, the IRS will probably consider the worker an employee, no matter what title or label you may use.

To determine whether a worker is an employee or an independent contractor see Form 9-8 on the CD-ROM. Also, check out the *Small Business Kit For Dummies* for more on this topic.

Go directly to jail: Do not pass Go or collect $200

The kooky, fun-loving people at the IRS prefer to classify workers as employees rather than independent contractors. Coincidentally, the IRS also collects more tax revenue if the worker is an employee than if the worker is an independent contractor.

The IRS requires employers to do the following for each employee (but not for each contractor):

✔ **Withhold** income taxes and the employee's share of Social Security and Medicare contributions

✔ **Pay** the employer's share of the Social Security and Medicare contributions

If the IRS determines that a worker should have been classified as an employee, rather than an independent contractor, it can assess the following penalties:

✔ Payment of federal income tax that should have been withheld from the employee

✔ Payment of Medicare contributions that should have been withheld

✔ Interest on taxes that should have been withheld

✔ A penalty for failure to properly file tax returns and pay taxes

✔ A big penalty if the IRS determines that the behavior was negligent, intentional, or fraudulent

✔ Criminal sanctions, including imprisonment and fines up to $100,000

    ✔ Personal liability for corporate officers, up to 100 percent of the amount that the employer should have withheld from the employee's compensation

    ✔ Send you to bed without supper

Okay, I assume that these horrendous penalties have your full attention. (And these are only the IRS penalties. Other governmental entities — such as the State Employment Department or the National Labor Relations Board — may also impose penalties.) So don't mess this up.

Tax forms of the rich and famous (not poor and nameless)

Here are two IRS forms that you need to worry about when dealing with independent contractors.

IRS Form W-9

Require all your independent contractors to complete IRS Form W-9, which gives you various information, including their Social Security numbers or their Employer I.D. numbers. You will need this information when you make filings with the IRS. If you don't get this information, you may have to withhold taxes from the independent contractor.

IRS Form 1099-MISC

If you pay an independent contractor $600 or more in a year, you need to send an IRS Form 1099-MISC at the end of the year to the IRS and to the independent contractor.

You can find IRS Form 1099-MISC included on the CD-ROM as Form 9-9.

Forms on the CD-ROM

Form 9-1	**Questions to Consider Asking Prospective Consultants or Independent Contractors**	Questions that may be useful to ask prospective consultants or independent contractors
Form 9-2	**Background Check Permission (Simple)**	A sample simple form, to be signed by a prospective consultant or independent contractor, giving permission for a background check

Form 9-3	**Background Check Permission (Comprehensive)**	A sample comprehensive form, to be signed by a prospective consultant or independent contractor, giving permission for a background check
Form 9-4	**Independent Contractor Agreement**	A sample, pro-company oriented Independent Contractor Agreement
Form 9-5	**Consulting Agreement**	A sample, pro-company oriented form agreement to be used for a consultant
Form 9-6	**Confidentiality and Invention Assignment Agreement for Consultant**	A form of agreement that requires the consultant to keep company information confidential, and to assign ownership of inventions and materials developed as part of the work for the company over to the company
Form 9-7	**Chart of Key Differences between Employees and Independent Contractors**	A summary chart showing the key differences in a worker being classified as an employee or independent contractor
Form 9-8	**IRS Publication 15-A**	Illustrative examples of key differences in the classification of employees and independent contractors
Form 9-9	**IRS Form 1099-MISC**	The IRS form to be filed for independent contractors

Part III
Money: Leases, Licenses, and Loans (Oh My!)

The 5th Wave   By Rich Tennant

"...and that's not the worst of it, your Honor. It appears the good doctor is not even <u>licensed</u> to practice re-animation of the dead in this village!"

In this part . . .

1 cover everything from real estate leases, to license agreements, loan agreements, service contracts, and confidentiality agreements. I should have called this part "Potpourri." Too bad it doesn't smell all that great.

Chapter 10

Real Estate Leases

· ·

· ·

Most businesses require leased space. And as your business grows, you may need to add space for more people or increased operations. A lease agreement constitutes a significant financial commitment for a business. Yet many people blindly sign leases that bind their business for many years without any meaningful attempt to negotiate the terms of the lease.

In this chapter, I tell you what to look out for when signing a lease and what you want to negotiate in a good lease. However, having an experienced real estate attorney review the lease before you sign it is always a good practice.

Negotiating an Office Lease Contract

When you find a great space for the business and are ready to lease, the landlord typically hands you a preprinted agreement that looks (for all the world) just the way leases were meant to look. The landlord is likely to call this the *standard lease,* as if the perfect form of a lease agreement had been chiseled in stone eons ago.

Pay attention here: This form is undoubtedly totally one-sided in favor of the landlord. No "standard" lease exists. And regardless of whether the form looks standard or preprinted, don't be afraid to carefully review and negotiate the lease.

Your ability to negotiate changes to an office lease depends on how much leverage you have. Are other companies vying for the space? Has the space been vacant a long time? Are you willing to pay a good rent? Let's face it: If Microsoft and General Motors are about to engage in a bidding war for the same prime space you're interested in, all of your negotiating skills mean zilch (zero, in technical legal terms).

Lease gotchas

Landlords often hand you a form lease that contains gotchas. *Gotchas* is a highly technical term for provisions that may cost you a lot of money or headaches in ways that you didn't plan. Your best bet is to negotiate them out of the lease. Here are some classic gotchas:

✔ The landlord's right to pass increased operating costs in the building on to the tenant without limitation

✔ The tenant's obligation to pay any increased taxes as a result of the landlord's selling the building

✔ The landlord's right to terminate your lease early for his or her convenience

✔ A disclaimer about the building and the services provided to tenants

✔ Severe limitations or prohibitions on subletting your space (you may need to sublet space if your business shrinks)

✔ Personal guarantees or payment of the rent required from the company's owners

Assuming that you do have some leverage, the following sections detail the key provisions of an office lease.

Form 10-1 on the CD-ROM shows a checklist of issues to consider when negotiating an office lease.

CHECKLIST FOR OFFICE LEASES

1. Space
   (a) What is the rentable square footage?
   (b) What is the usable square footage?
   (c) Is rent based on usable or rentable square footage?
   (d) Verify square footage number provided by the landlord.

2. Permitted Uses of the Premises
   (a) What uses of the premises are permitted?
   (b) Is the permitted use clause broad enough for possible changes in the business?
   (c) Is the permitted use clause broad enough for potential assignments or subleases?
   (d) Can the use clause be drafted to include "any lawful purposes"?
   (e) Can uses be changed with landlord's consent, which consent can't be unreasonably withheld or delayed?

3. Primary lease term
   (a) What is the commencement date of the lease?
   (b) What happens if the space is not ready on the commencement date? Is there rent abatement, monetary damages, right to cancel the lease, or other remedies specified?
   (c) What is the termination date?
   (d) Does the landlord have the right to terminate early without cause?
   (e) Does the tenant have the right to terminate early by payment of a fee?

4. Rentals
   (a) What is the base rent for the primary term?
   (b) Are there escalation clauses?
   (c) Are there cost of living increases?
   (d) Is there a cap on any rent increases?
   (e) Is there a reasonable grace period and written notice before a late charge is imposed?

5. Common area maintenance, HVAC, and Operating costs
   (a) What does the tenant have to contribute for common area maintenance, ventilating, heating, air conditioning, and other building operation costs?
   (b) Is there a cap?
   (c) Can the amount be increased each year?
   (d) Real estate taxes and other impositions:
       (i) Does the tenant have to pay a portion of the real estate taxes?
       (ii) What increases over base year (the first year of the lease) can the landlord impose?
       (iii) Is there a cap on tax increases?

Form 10-1: Checklist for Office Leases.

(continued)

        (iv)   Does the tenant have to pay increased taxes that may occur on sale of the building?

(e)   Are there any special provisions or exceptions on the payment of these expenses?

(f)   When is payment due?

(g)   What detailed reports does the landlord have to provide the tenant showing the actual expenses?

(h)   What audit rights does the tenant have to review the landlord's books and records?

(i)   Are there provisions made for weekend and holiday service? What are the charges?

(j)   Does the tenant have a remedy for service interruption?

6.   <u>Tenant Improvements</u>

(a)   What tenant improvements will be necessary?

(b)   What is the cost?

(c)   How much time will it take to complete the tenant improvements?

(d)   Will the landlord contribute to the cost for the tenant improvements?

(e)   What approvals will be necessary?

(f)   What permits will be necessary?

(g)   Does the landlord or the tenant own any improvements?

7.   <u>Repairs and replacements:</u>

(a)   What responsibility does the tenant have for repairs or replacements?

(b)   What responsibility does the landlord have for repairs or replacements?

(c)   At the end of the tenancy, is tenant's obligation to return the premises in same condition at the beginning of tenancy, excluding (1) ordinary wear and tear, (2) damage by fire and other unavoidable casualty, and (3) alterations previously approved by landlord?

8.   <u>Utilities:</u>

(a)   Direct supply or individually metered?

(b)   Method of computing payment?

9.   <u>Assignment and subletting:</u>

(a)   Is the landlord's written approval required?

(b)   What standard is there for approval? absolute discretion? reasonable approval?

(c)   Does the landlord have the right to cancel the lease if notified of a proposed assignment of sublease?

(d)   If the assignment or sublet is at a higher price than the base rent, who keeps the excess? or what split is there?

(e)   Can the lease be assigned to affiliates of the tenant without landlord approval?

(f)   Can the landlord terminate the lease if the stock ownership of the tenant changes?

10. <u>Subordination and attornment</u>:
    (a)   All present or future mortgages?
    (b)   Execution of estoppel certificates required?
    (c)   Tenant agrees to attorn to landlord's successor in interest?

11. <u>Destruction</u>:
    (a)   Is there a right of cancellation for the tenant in the event of destruction?
    (b)   What obligation does the landlord have to rebuild?
    (c)   Does the tenant share in any proceeds from insurance?

12. <u>Indemnity and Disclaimer</u>:
    (a)   Indemnity mutual or tenant only?
    (b)   Waiver of claims mutual or tenant only?
    (c)   Waiver of subrogation (rights related to insurance)?
    (d)   Landlord liability limited to interest in property?

13. <u>Default</u>:
    (a)   Does the tenant have a cure period after notice of a breach?
    (b)   What remedies are available for breach?

14. <u>Landlord's warranties</u>:
    (a)   Quiet enjoyment of the premises by the tenant?
    (b)   First class services?
    (c)   Security building?
    (d)   Ownership of building?

15. <u>Option to renew</u>
    (a)   Does the tenant have the option to renew the lease?
    (b)   How long is the renewal option?
    (c)   How far in advance must the option be exercised?
    (d)   How is rent determined for the renewal period?

16. <u>Right of first refusal or first offer for additional space</u>
    (a)   What is the scope of any right of first offer or first refusal?
    (b)   How is rent determined?
    (c)   How long does the tenant have before exercising the right?

17. <u>Security deposit</u>:
    (a)   What is the amount?
    (b)   Can it be a letter of credit?
    (c)   Will the tenant receive interest on the security deposit?
    (d)   Does the lease provide for the return of the tenant's security deposit within a set number of days after termination of the lease?

(continued)

18. Guaranty:
    (a)   Is a personal guaranty required?
    (b)   When does the guaranty terminate?

19. Can any mortgages adversely affect the tenant's rights if foreclosed upon?

20. Free rent:
    (a)   Will the landlord grant a free rent period?
    (b)   When does it have to be returned (e.g., on breach of lease)?

21. Are there any peculiar landlord obligations that should be included?

22. Compliance With Law:
    (a)   Does landlord warrant that the premises are in compliance with the law?
    (b)   If tenant is obligated to comply with applicable law, does it exclude matters that should more properly be the responsibility of the landlord (e.g., asbestos problems, disability access)?
    (c)   Is landlord obligated to comply with all laws applicable to its control of the building?

23. Insurance:
    (a)   What insurance is the tenant required to maintain?
    (b)   What insurance is the landlord required to maintain?
    (c)   Has the tenant reviewed the insurance requirements in the lease?

24. Rules and Regulations for the Building:
    (a)   Are there specific rules and regulations in existence?
    (b)   Can the rules be changed without approval of tenant?
    (c)   Is the landlord required to enforce the rules against other tenants?
    (d)   Are there any rules that interfere with the operations of the tenant?

25. Rights of Entry:
    (a)   Exclusive of emergencies, what notice must the landlord give in advance for entry into the tenant's premises?
    (b)   Are there any restrictions on landlord interfering with tenant's business in showing the premises to buyers, lenders or prospective tenants?

26. What signage is the tenant allowed to put in or about the building and premise?

27. Parking:
    (a)   How many parking spaces will be available to the tenant?
    (b)   At what cost?

Rent

A cost analysis between buildings is essential for your business to properly estimate its future rental costs.

Any analysis of a given space's desirability typically begins with the fixed rent that the landlord quotes you. But this starting point must be evaluated in light of other factors. For example, landlords may quote a monthly lease rate of $2 per square foot, typically meaning rentable square footage. The actual usable square footage of the premises is the space that you actually can use for your business operations.

Usable square footage is less than rentable square footage, because you calculate what's "usable" by deducting common areas such as public corridors, elevators, lobbies, and bathrooms from the total space. So, to compare apples to apples, you have to know the exact usable square footage of each space you are considering.

The structure of the lease payments may also be important. For example, a start-up business without much capital may want two or three months of free rent at the beginning of the lease, with a lower rental for the first year and increasing rentals for the second and third years.

When analyzing the cost of space, you also need to take into account other operating costs that the landlord may pass on to you, the tenant. Some leases require the tenant to pay for all cleaning, building security, air-conditioning, maintenance, and so on (a so-called *Triple Net Lease*). And some leases require the landlord to provide and pay for basic services while the tenant pays a pro rata share of any cost increases the landlord incurs for such services over the initial base year of the lease.

Keep in mind that different buildings have different costs, and landlords may charge for services in a different manner. So the types and amounts of the costs that the landlord passes on to the tenant can have a big impact on the economics of a lease.

Permitted uses

The lease typically has a section that sets forth the permitted uses of the leased space.

It's to your advantage as the tenant to make this permitted use clause as broad as possible, even if your intended purpose is initially narrow. Because your business may grow and your plans may change, you want the flexibility to use the space in any reasonable, legal manner.

Also, a narrow permitted use clause can often serve as a restriction on your ability to assign or sublet the space.

So what's the best permitted use clause? Find out whether you can get the landlord to agree to something like the following:

Tenant is permitted to use the premises for any legal purpose or business.

If the landlord doesn't go for that, at least spell out all of your expected or potential uses.

You may also want to take a look at Form 10-2 on the CD-ROM — an Addendum to Real Estate Lease that benefits the tenant.

The term of the lease

The length of the lease has a significant impact on the rental rate. Landlords typically like longer-term leases and are more willing to make concessions for such leases. With a long lease, the landlord enjoys the financial security of a regular rental stream over a number of years. And the landlord can avoid the hassle and expense of re-leasing the space.

From the tenant's side, a long-term lease has both benefits and risks. The benefit is knowing that the premises are available at a predictable cost for the long term. The risk is that the company may outgrow the space, may need less space as its business contracts, or is locked into paying what turns out to be above-market rent if demand for rentals subsequently declines.

If you can get it, the best of all worlds is a shorter-term lease with renewal options. You are usually much better off getting a 2-year lease with four 2-year renewal options rather than getting stuck in a 10-year lease.

Rent escalations

Fixed rent over longer-term leases is relatively rare, because landlords often build in rent escalation provisions.

Sometimes, landlords insist on annual increases based upon the percentage increases in the Consumer Price Index (CPI). If you are confronted with such a request, try two things. First, you may arrange that the CPI does not kick in for at least two years. Second, you may get a cap on the amount of each year's increase (for example, no more than a 3 percent increase in any year). Here is a sample clause for doing that:

Any rent increases under this Lease shall commence no earlier than two (2) years after the date of the commencement of this Lease. The maximum amount that the rent may be increased in any one year (starting in the third year of this Lease) shall be three percent (3%) over the beginning base rent under this Lease.

If you have to live with a rent escalation clause, consider a predetermined fixed amount, like

- ✔ $2,000 a month for the first year
- ✔ $2,200 a month for the second year
- ✔ $2,400 a month thereafter

Such a provision gives you more predictability in planning your business. *Note:* Make sure that your business plan projections adequately reflect such increases.

Operating costs

The starting point for determining your operating costs is identifying what services the landlord provides, what services the tenant must get directly, and who bears the cost. The following are common costs for office space:

- ✔ Heating, ventilating, and air-conditioning (commonly referred to as HVAC)
- ✔ Cleaning and janitorial services
- ✔ Electricity
- ✔ Repairs
- ✔ Security

If the landlord is charging you separately for such services, negotiate a fixed fee or cap on the amount.

If the landlord pays for basic services but charges you for increases in the cost of rendering those services, ask how the landlord calculates that increase. For example, some landlords may figure the base year for calculating the starting point of costs as one in which the building is not fully occupied (heat not necessarily fully on, not all lights on, and so on). In this case, your company's moving in will naturally cause cost increases. Get the landlord to count the base-year costs as if the building were fully occupied and operational.

Landlords often want tenants to pay for increases in property taxes on the building. Watch out for this cost because if the property has been held for a long time before being sold, the value of the property may be significantly higher for property tax purposes. The end result is a higher property tax that you may be stuck paying. Tell the landlord that having to pay for such an increase is not fair to you.

Landlords also sometimes throw in items as operating expenses that should really be capital expenses (and thus not properly chargeable to a tenant). So make sure that the definition of operating expenses that you may be liable for doesn't include capital improvements, financing charges, and other capital costs.

In addition, some landlords charge extra for services supplied other than on "business days" or "after hours." So look at this clause carefully and limit charges for extra services to those that are truly extraordinary and that won't be incurred on a regular basis. This provision can be of particular importance for a start-up business when employees are often working nights and weekends.

Tenant improvements and alterations

Most form leases provide that the tenant can't make any alterations or improvements to the premises without the landlord's consent. Those provisions are typically too restrictive, so negotiate changes ahead of time. For example, you want the right to make nonstructural changes or changes costing less than $2,500 without needing the landlord's consent.

Before you can occupy the space, the premises may need some improvements or alterations to make it appropriate for your business needs. Here are some key questions to answer about the initial tenant improvements and alterations:

- ✔ What is the scope of necessary changes?
- ✔ What is the cost?
- ✔ How much time is needed to complete the improvements?
- ✔ What permits or approvals do you need?
- ✔ Will the landlord contribute to the payment for the improvements?
- ✔ Who will own the improvements after the lease is terminated?

If possible, get a clause stating that you are allowed to remove any trade fixtures and alterations that you pay for, provided that you repair any damages to the premises.

If you anticipate the need to make alterations or improvements in the future, the lease should provide that you may make them with the landlord's consent, but that the landlord cannot unreasonably withhold or delay the consent.

Also, be aware of the clause that says that at the end of the lease you have to return the premises in their original condition. Instead, negotiate a clause that states something like the following:

> **The premises will be returned to the Landlord at the end of the tenancy in the same condition as at the beginning of the tenancy, excluding (1) ordinary wear and tear, (2) damage by fire and unavoidable casualty not the fault of the Tenant, and (3) alterations previously approved by the Landlord.**

Assignment and subletting

The assignment and subletting clause of the lease can become a very important provision. Typically, the landlord's lease form states that the tenant may not assign or sublet the lease without the landlord's prior consent, with such consent to be granted or withheld at the landlord's sole discretion.

Attempt to modify such a clause in several ways. The ideal change provides that an assignment or sublease requires the landlord's consent, but that the consent cannot be unreasonably withheld or delayed. (A landlord is unlikely to give you the total right to assign or sublease without some kind of approval procedure.)

If the landlord does give you a reasonableness standard on your proposed assignment or sublease, she may insist upon *a recapture right*. That is, the landlord may want to recapture the space for her own use or re-leasing. This condition may be acceptable as long as the landlord pays you any profit you expect to make on the assignment or sublease.

If an assignment or subletting comes with potential profit, then the landlord typically expects to share that profit. Often, the split is 50/50, but make sure to recoup any expenses you incur in getting an assignee or subtenant before a profit split.

A tenant should also negotiate enough flexibility in the assignment and subletting clause to allow for the possibility that the tenant may undergo mergers, reorganizations, and share ownership changes.

Find out whether you are allowed to freely assign and sublet the lease to your company's subsidiaries and affiliates.

Be particularly leery of a clause that says a change in more than 50 percent of the company's stock ownership is considered an assignment that is prohibited without the landlord's approval. A prohibited assignment can result in the landlord terminating a favorable lease. As the company grows and new people invest in it, the company may inadvertently trigger this clause.

On the CD-ROM, you can find a sample Assignment of Lease (Form 10-3) and a sample Office Sublease (Form 10-4).

Renewal options

Because your company's future space needs are uncertain, renewal options for the lease can be quite helpful. But some landlords may be reluctant to grant such options because doing so limits their flexibility to market the space to prospective tenants.

If you can get a renewal option, request that the option rent be fixed at a predetermined rental. Avoid the options that are based on "fair market rent" at the time of renewal.

Here are the key issues for renewal options:

- ✔ How many renewal options can you get?
- ✔ How long is each renewal option?
- ✔ What is the rent for each renewal option?
- ✔ How much notice do you have to give in advance to exercise the option?

Form 10-5 on the CD-ROM contains various sample clauses that you can use for a renewal option in a lease.

Option to expand

The right to expand into additional or adjoining space in a building can be very valuable. After all, you are planning to have your business grow, aren't you?

These expansion options have several variations. First, you can have a fixed expansion option, where the tenant has a defined period of time in which to exercise the option. Here is an example of this type of option:

> **Tenant shall have the right to occupy that certain space adjacent to its existing leased space, of approximately 1,000 square feet, for an additional monthly rent of $500. Tenant must exercise this expansion option within 120 days of the date of this Lease by giving written notice to Landlord. In that event, all other terms of this Lease shall apply to this expansion space.**

Form 10-6 on the CD-ROM is a sample letter offering to expand space in a building that you lease.

Alternatively, the tenant can have a Right of First Offer on any space that becomes available in the building. The landlord under this alternative is obligated to first present any space available to the tenant before marketing it to third parties.

Finally, you can ask for a Right of First Refusal on space. That obligates the landlord to bring to you first any deals he is willing to sign with third parties for space in the building and allow you to match the deal and preempt the third party.

Any expansion option can be helpful, so get what you can.

Security deposits

The landlord typically requires you to post a security deposit for performance of your lease obligations. This security deposit is generally equal to one or two months' rent, but a landlord may insist on more if the company is new or financially unstable.

From the tenant's perspective, you want the following:

- ✔ Interest on the security deposit
- ✔ A reduction in the amount of the security deposit if the tenant has been paying the rent on time for at least a year
- ✔ A provision that says the security deposit must be returned within 15 days of the termination of the tenancy

You may be able to obtain the clauses above in an amendment to the landlord's lease. Form 10-7 on the CD-ROM is a sample Lease Amendment that you can use.

Some landlords may insist on a personal guarantee from the business founders if the tenant is a corporation or other entity. Avoid this situation — it puts your personal, as well as business, assets at risk.

Rules and regulations of the building

Landlords often have separate rules and regulations that are applicable to the building. These rules may contain a number of restrictions and limitations as to what you can do in the building.

Make sure to review these rules and regulations before you sign the lease, and, if possible, get your lease to include the following:

- ✔ The terms of the lease govern if any inconsistencies arise between your lease and the landlord's rules and regulations.
- ✔ The rules must be reasonable, and no new rules may be adopted that are not reasonable.
- ✔ The landlord will enforce these rules against all of the building's tenants.

And of course, if some of the rules and regulations are problematic for your business, make sure that your lease gives you the needed waiver or flexibility.

Offer Letter

Okay, so say that you've found some space that looks ideal for the business. How do you begin negotiations? Well, one way is to submit an Offer Letter to the landlord, laying out the terms that are acceptable to you. From there, you can commence the negotiations and move to a definitive lease. Form 10-8 shows a sample Offer Letter.

Forms on the CD-ROM

Form 10-1	**Checklist for Office Leases**	A checklist of issues to look out for in analyzing office leases
Form 10-2	**Addendum to Real Estate Lease (For the Benefit of the Tenant)**	A sample Addendum designed to give some protections and benefits to the tenant from the standard form of lease provided by the landlord
Form 10-3	**Assignment of Lease**	A form of assignment of lease by a tenant
Form 10-4	**Office Sublease**	A sample office sublease
Form 10-5	**Option to Renew Real Estate Lease**	Sample provisions to add to a real estate lease granting the tenant a right to renew the lease at the end of the term
Form 10-6	**Option to Expand Space Leased in Building**	A sample provision for a tenant to expand a lease to include additional space in the building
Form 10-7	**Amendment to Lease**	Form used to amend a lease
Form 10-8	**Offer to Lease Space**	A sample letter offering to lease space

Form 10-9	**Consent by Lessor to Assignment of Lease**	A consent by the landlord to the assignment of a lease
Form 10-10	**Consent by Lessor to Sublease**	A consent by a landlord to a pro-posed sublease
Form 10-11	**Demand for Rent**	A sample letter firmly demanding rent payment from a tenant
Form 10-12	**Notice of Change in Rent**	A sample letter notifying a tenant of an impending rent change

Chapter 11

License Agreements

A license gives you the right to use someone else's assets. A *License Agreement* spells out the precise terms of those rights.

The party that gives someone use of a right or license is the *licensor;* the party that receives the use of that asset is the *licensee.*

A common example of a License Agreement concerns the use of software. When you buy a software product, you only buy the right to use the software in limited ways — you don't buy "ownership" of the software. The License Agreement that comes along with the software sets forth these limits. Some other typical License Agreements include Trade Name License, Patent License, Software License, and Copyright License. This chapter gives you advice for negotiating such agreements.

Key Points in License Agreements

If you are negotiating to obtain a license or if you find yourself in the situation of providing a license for someone else, the License Agreement should address the following key points:

✔ **Exclusivity/Nonexclusivity:** The license can be exclusive or nonexclusive. Licensors typically resist giving exclusive licenses. If the license grants exclusivity, over what areas is the license exclusive? If the license is exclusive, under what circumstances does the license convert to a nonexclusive one?

- ✔ **Term:** The License Agreement needs to explicitly spell out the length of the license, plus any renewal rights.

- ✔ **Payment:** The License Agreement needs to clearly state any up-front payments and any periodic payments required to maintain the license. A particular use of the license may also require an increase in payments. (For example, Software Licenses often require greater payment as the number of users increases.)

- ✔ **Restrictions on use of the license:** Licensors often place a number of restrictions on use of the license, such as use in certain geographic areas, or for designated purposes. (For example, a trade name licensor may grant the right to use a name, but only in a certain city.)

- ✔ **Infringement:** The licensee may require the licensor to represent that the licensor actually owns the licensed item and that it does not infringe on the rights of third parties. Licensors will resist making such statements—rightfully so, in many instances.

- ✔ **Termination:** The licensor typically defines various circumstances that allow him or her to terminate the License Agreement early, especially if the licensee breaches the License Agreement.

- ✔ **Assignment and sublicense:** Depending on the agreement, the licensee may be able to assign or sublicense the license. An *assignment* typically means a transfer of all of your rights in the license, whereas a *sublicense* involves giving someone the right to use a portion of your rights in the license. Most License Agreements prohibit assignment or sublicensing without the licensor's approval. Licensees may want to negotiate for broader rights if their business necessitates sublicensing the product.

- ✔ **Requirments of the licensee:** Licensors will often require the licensee to do a number of ongoing things for the benefit of the licensor. The licensee's failure to comply with these items often can be a material breach of the License Agreement.

Software License Agreements

When you purchase a software product (such as Windows or Quicken), you do not actually get *ownership* of the product. Rather, the owner of the software merely *licenses* you the right to use the software under certain terms and conditions contained in a *Software License Agreement.*

If the software is an off-the-shelf product like Microsoft Office, it comes with a Software License Agreement that you actually don't sign. Instead, opening the box containing the software or using the software is your assent to the terms of the Software License Agreement. People sometimes call such agreements *shrink-wrap licenses* because the box containing the software also contains the license.

Shrink wrap licenses are not negotiable — either you accept the terms or don't buy (or license) the product. For an example of a shrink-wrap Software License Agreement, see Form 11-1.

SOFTWARE LICENSE AGREEMENT

Important:	Do not use the software accompanying this Agreement (the "Software") until you have carefully read the following Agreement. Opening the sealed Software package and/or using the Software (or authorizing any other person to do so) indicates your acceptance of the terms and conditions contained in this Agreement. If you do not agree with the terms and conditions of this Agreement, promptly return the unopened Software and accompanying items to the place of purchase within 60 days of purchase and your money will be refunded. This Agreement sets forth the terms and conditions for licensing of the Software from _____ ("Licensor").
License and Certain Restrictions	You are granted a non-exclusive license to use one copy of the Software only on a single computer and a single terminal. Although you are encouraged to make a backup copy of the Software for your own use, you are not allowed to make more than two copies for backup purposes. The Software (including any images, icons, graphics, animations, video, audio, music, and text incorporated into the Software) is protected by copyright laws. You may not make copies of the Software except for backups. You may not give copies to another person, or duplicate the Software by any other means, including electronic transmission. You may not copy the printed materials accompanying the Software, nor print copies of any user documentation. The Software contains trade secrets, and in order to protect them you may not decompile, reverse engineer, disassemble, or otherwise reduce the Software to human-perceivable form. You may not modify, adapt, translate, rent, sublicense, assign, lease, loan, resell for profit, distribute, or network the Software, disk, or related materials or create derivative works based upon the Software or any part thereof.
Trademark	_____, _____, _____ and _____ are registered trademarks of XYZ, Inc. ("XYZ"). Other brands or products are trademarks or registered trademarks of their respective holders and should be treated as such.
Disk Warranty	The sole warranty regarding the Software and related materials is that the original disk is free from physical defects in material and workmanship, assuming proper use, for a period of ninety (90) days from date of purchase. If such defect occurs during this period, you may return your faulty disk to Licensor, along with a dated proof of purchase; Licensor will replace it free of charge. After 90 days, you may obtain a replacement by sending your defective disk and a check for $_____ (add sales tax of residents of AR, AZ, CA, CT, FL, IL, MA, MI, MN, NJ, NM, NV, PA, TX, UT, VA WA) to Licensor.
	Your sole and exclusive remedy for any breach of representation or warranty is that Licensor, at its option, either (a) will refund your payment for the Software upon your return of the Software and related materials, with a copy of your receipt, or (b) will replace it on an exchange basis without charge (except as provided above).
	EXCEPT FOR THE EXPRESS WARRANTY OF THE ORIGINAL DISKS SET FORTH ABOVE, THIS SOFTWARE IS PROVIDED "AS-IS," AND TO THE MAXIMUM EXTENT PERMITTED BY APPLICABLE LAW, LICENSOR DISCLAIMS ALL OTHER WARRANTIES, EXPRESS OR IMPLIED, BY STATUTE OR OTHERWISE, REGARDING THE SOFTWARE, DISK, AND RELATED MATERIALS, INCLUDING THEIR

(continued)

Form 11-1: Software License Agreement.

FITNESS FOR A PARTICULAR PURPOSE, THEIR QUALITY, THEIR MERCHANTABILITY, OR THEIR NONINFRINGEMENT. THE LIABILITY OF LICENSOR UNDER THE WARRANTY SET FORTH ABOVE SHALL BE LIMITED TO THE AMOUNT PAID BY THE CUSTOMER FOR THE PRODUCT. SOME STATES DO NOT ALLOW THE EXCLUSION OF IMPLIED WARRANTIES, SO THE ABOVE EXCLUSIONS MAY NOT APPLY TO YOU. IN THAT EVENT, ANY IMPLIED WARRANTIES ARE LIMITED IN DURATION TO 90 DAYS FROM THE DATE OF PURCHASE OF THE SOFTWARE. THIS WARRANTY GIVES YOU SPECIFIC LEGAL RIGHTS. YOU MAY HAVE OTHER RIGHTS, WHICH VARY FROM STATE TO STATE.

Certain Limitations

Licensor has no control over your use of the Software. Licensor does not and cannot warrant the performance or results that may be obtained by its use. Licensor does not represent, warrant, or guarantee the accuracy and timeliness of the data contained in the Software and Licensor shall have no liability of any kind whatsoever to you, or to any other party, on account of any inaccuracies in or untimeliness of the data, or for any delay in reporting such data contained in the Software. Various information in the Software constantly changes, and the information in the Software is only as of a particular date. Licensor does not warrant that the operation of the Software will be uninterrupted or error free. Licensor is not responsible for problems caused by accident, abuse, mishandling, alteration, or improper use. Licensor does not warrant or guarantee the suitability of the Software or that it will meet your requirements.

Limitation of Damages

TO THE MAXIMUM EXTENT PERMITTED BY APPLICABLE LAW, LICENSOR AND ITS SUPPLIERS WILL NOT BE LIABLE FOR ANY INDIRECT, SPECIAL, INCIDENTAL, OR CONSEQUENTIAL DAMAGES (INCLUDING DAMAGES FOR LOSS OF BUSINESS, LOSS OF PROFITS, OR THE LIKE), WHETHER BASED ON BREACH OF CONTRACT, TORT (INCLUDING NEGLIGENCE), PRODUCT LIABILITY OR OTHERWISE, EVEN IF LICENSOR OR ITS REPRESENTATIVES HAVE BEEN ADVISED OF THE POSSIBILITY OF SUCH DAMAGES AND EVEN IF A REMEDY SET FORTH HEREIN IS FOUND TO HAVE FAILED OF ITS ESSENTIAL PURPOSE. LICENSOR'S TOTAL LIABILITY TO YOU FOR ACTUAL DAMAGES FOR ANY CAUSE WHATSOEVER WILL BE LIMITED TO THE AMOUNT PAID BY YOU FOR THIS PRODUCT. SOME STATES DO NOT ALLOW THE LIMITATION OF EXCLUSION OF LIABILITY FOR INCIDENTAL OR CONSEQUENTIAL DAMAGES, SO THE ABOVE LIMITATION OR EXCLUSION MAY NOT APPLY TO YOU.

The limitations of damages set forth above fundamental elements of the bases of the bargain between Licensor and you. Licensor would not be able to provide this product on an economic basis without such limitations.

Miscellaneous

You acknowledge that, in providing you with the Software, Licensor has relied upon your agreement to be bound by the terms of this Agreement. You further acknowledge that you have read, understood, and agreed to be bound by the terms of this Agreement, and hereby reaffirm your acceptance of those terms. You further acknowledge that this Agreement constitutes the complete statement of the agreement between you and Licensor, and that the Agreement does not include any other prior or contemporaneous promises, representations, or descriptions regarding the Software. This Agreement is not, however to limit any rights that Licensor may have under trade secret, copyright, patent, or other laws that may be available to it. The agents, employees, distributors, and dealers of Licensor are not authorized to make modifications to this Agreement, or to make any additional representations, commitments, or warranties binding on Licensor. Accordingly, additional statements such as dealer or other advertising or presentations, whether oral or written, do not constitute representations or warranties by Licensor and should not be relied upon. This Agreement may be modified only in writing. If any provision of this Agreement is invalid or unenforceable under applicable law, it is to that extent, deemed omitted and the remaining provisions will continue in full force and effect. The validity and performance of this Agreement shall be governed by _____ law (without reference to choice of law principles), except as to copyright and trademark matters, which are covered by Federal laws. This Agreement is deemed entered into at _____, _____, and jurisdiction for resolution of any disputes shall reside solely in _____, _____. This Agreement shall be construed as to its fair meaning and not strictly for or against either party.

If you license some software that costs a significant amount of money (such as Oracle database software), you have the chance to negotiate the License Agreement to make sure it suits the needs of your business.

When negotiating significant software licenses, remember these seven things:

- ✔ Make sure that the license is broad enough for the intended use of the business.

- ✔ Make sure that the license contains clear representations and warranties concerning the expected functionality of the software.

- ✔ Make sure that the appropriate customer support exists, with prompt responses from the licensor to problems that arise.

- ✔ Make sure that the licensor indemnifies you for any claims of infringement by third parties.

- ✔ Make sure that the licensor clearly spells out the pricing for the software, and that the price is favorable.

- ✔ Make sure that the licensor promptly makes available upgrades and error corrections.

- ✔ Make sure the term of the license is appropriately long.

Form 11-2, which is also on the CD, is a Checklist of Issues in Drafting and Negotiating Software License Agreements.

**Checklist Of Issues In Drafting And Negotiating
Software License Agreements**

I.   Rights Granted under the License[1]
    A.   Exclusive vs. non-exclusive — primarily an issue for custom-made software
    B.   Revocable vs. irrevocable — more a breach issue
    C.   Right to use the user manual and related documentation

II.   Term of License
    A.   Perpetual or defined time period?
    B.   Renewal rights and terms

III.   Scope of License[2]
    A.   Licensee internal operations only?
    B.   Number of users — named users/concurrent users and variations
    C.   Number of sites/number of computers ("boxes")
    D.   Copying rights/backup — copyright rights
    E.   Use by subsidiaries and affiliates
    F.   Right to modify and combine with other products/who owns modifications?/Copyright issues
    G.   Prohibited uses

IV.   Transferability and Sublicensing Restrictions
    A.   Typically, license may not be assigned, transferred, sublicensed, or pledged
    B.   Typically, licensee may not use the software for third-party training, commercial time sharing, rental, or service bureau use
    C.   Restrictions on use at a particular location?

V.   Right to Source Code

---

[1] Sample pro-Licensor language:

"License. Subject to the terms and conditions herein, Licensor hereby grants to Licensee a limited, revocable, non-exclusive, non-transferable license to use the software listed on the first page hereof (the "Software") for Licensee's own internal business uses at the localities identified on the first page hereof, together with the associated manual and other related printed material ("Documentation") provided with this package for the term indicated on the first page hereof. The fees for the license hereunder are set forth on the first page hereof."

[2] Sample pre-Licensor language:

"Prohibited Uses. Licensee may not (a) make copies of the Software, Documentation or program disks, except for back-up proposes, which back-up copies are subject to the terms of this Agreement; (b) re-sell, loan, rent, pledge, assign, sub-license or otherwise transfer the Software, Documentation, or any related data, except as provided above; (c) alter, modify or adapt the Software or Documentation, including, but not limited to, translating, reverse engineering, decompiling, disassembling or creating derivative works; (d) utilize the Software in conjunction with any automated valuation software system, or (e) use the Software for commercial time-sharing, rental, or service bureau use."

Form 11-2: Checklist of Issues in Drafting and Negotiating Software License Agreements.

       A.   Does licensee need to obtain or have access to source code? How practical even if obtained?
       B.   Stability of licensor
       C.   Source code escrow and alternatives
       D.   Limitations on when source code could be accessed or used
       E.   Updating the source code available to the licensee

VI.   Ownership of the Software
       A.   Express statement that licensor owns and retains all title, copyright, and other proprietary rights in the software and documentation
       B.   Trade secret acknowledgement
       C.   Limiting access of employees, consultants, or third party
       D.   Representation of licensor as to ownership of the software
       E.   Ownership issues with respect to licensee modifications
       F.   Ownership of user-created copies

VII.   Payment Provisions[3]
       A.   Schedule of payments
       B.   Discounts
       C.   Payments linked to licensee accepting test of the software
       D.   Late fees
       E.   Shipping charges
       F.   Sales, use, property, value-added or other taxes to be paid by licensee, other than tax based on licensor income

VIII. Acceptance Procedures
       A.   Right to test for some designated period of time
       B.   Right to reject software and results of rejection

IX.   Training
       A.   Scope of training to be provided by licensor
       B.   Cost
       C.   Location of training sessions
       D.   Number of trainees
       E.   Training of new employees after initial training

X.   Warranties[4]

---

[3] Sample pro-Licensor provision:

"Payment and Taxes. All fees and other charges stated herein are due and payable within fifteen (15) days after the date of invoice. A charge of no more than one and one-half percent (1-1/2%) per month will be assessed on the late payments until paid in full. Amounts payable to Licensor as specified are payable in full to Licensor without deduction and are net of taxes; in addition to such amount, Licensee shall pay sums equal to all taxes (including, without limitation, sales, use privilege, ad valorem or excise taxes) however designated, levied or based on amounts payable to Licensor under this Agreement or on Licensee's use or possession of the Software and/or Documentation under this Agreement, but exclusive of United States federal, state and local taxes based on Licensor's net income."

(continued)

A. Licensor will want to give very limited warranties, e.g., the software media is free from physical defects in material and workmanship for a 90 day period
B. Licensee may demand a warranty that at least the software performs the functions described in the related documentation
C. Length of warranty
D. Procedure for notifying licensor of defects
E. Procedure and response time for licensor correction of problems
F. Modification of software terminates warranty?
G. Explicit disclaimers by licensor as to:
   1. Merchantability
   2. Fitness for particular purpose
   3. Error-free operation
   4. Any other warranties, express or implied, except as explicitly set forth in agreement

XI. <u>Limitations on Licensor Liability</u>
A. No liability for indirect, special, incidental, consequential damages, whether in tort, contract, or product liability
B. No liability for loss of profits, revenue, data or use or cost of substitute software, whether in tort, contract, or product liability
C. Limitation on the total amount of damages, e.g., all or a portion of the license fee paid
D. Shortened statute of limitations to commence action from when damage occurred (e.g., six months or one year)
E. Enforceability issue

XII. <u>Inspection Rights of Licensor to Monitor Licensee's Compliance with Agreement</u>

XIII. <u>Support and Maintenance Services</u>
A. Scope of support and maintenance
B. Response times by licensor to cure problems
C. Payment
D. Price increases allowed
E. May be subject to separate agreement or support policy

XIV. <u>Nondisclosure of Confidential Information</u>[5]

---

[4] Sample pro-Licensor provision:

"<u>Limited Warranty</u>. The sole warranty regarding the Software and Documentation is that the original disks (or CD-ROMs) are free from physical defects in material and workmanship, assuming proper use, for a period of thirty (30) days after delivery, and provided Licensee returns the item within thirty (30) days of delivery. Licensor will either, at its discretion, (i) replace the defective media or Documentation or (ii) refund the license fee paid for the defective disks. These are the Licensee's sole remedies for any breach of any representation or warranty."

[5] Sample pre-Licensor provision:

"<u>Nondisclosure</u>. The Software and the Documentation are agreed to be Licensor's proprietary information,

A.   Agreement to hold various information confidential
B.   Period of confidentiality
C.   Scope of protected information - terms of agreement, pricing, other information identified or marked confidential
D.   Exclusions:
  1.   Information that is or becomes part of the public domain through no act or omission of the other party
  2.   Information that was in the other party's lawful possession prior to the disclosure
  3.   Information that is lawfully obtained from a third party without restriction on disclosure
  4.   Information that is independently developed
E.   Covenant to use reasonable steps to make employees comply with confidentiality restrictions

XV.   Indemnity for Infringement
A.   Scope of indemnity
B.   Notification to licensor of claim of non-infringement
C.   Control of action and settlement by licensor
D.   Option of licensor to replace or repair software

XVI.   Termination[6]
A.   Right of licensor to terminate
B.   Right of licensee to terminate
C.   Failure to pay and disputes concerning whether payment required
D.   Effect of termination - survival of rights and payment obligations
E.   Return of software, documentation, and copies to licensor on termination
F.   Obligation of licensee to cease using software after termination
G.   Certification by licensee regarding the cessation of use of software after termination and the return of the software, copies and documentation

XVII.   Other Special Issues
A.   Most favored nation clause

---

intellectual property and trade secrets, whether or not any portion thereof is or may be validly copyrighted or patented. Licensee shall take all reasonable steps necessary to ensure that the Software and Documentation, and any portion thereof, are not made available or disclosed by Licensee or by any of its employees to any other person, firm or corporation. Licensee agrees that all those individuals having access to the Software under this Agreement shall observe and perform this nondisclosure covenant, and that, upon Licensor's reasonable request, it will advise Licensor of the procedures employed for this propose."

[6] Sample pro-Licensor provisions:

"Termination. This license and Licensee's right to use the Software and Documentation automatically terminates if it fails to comply with any provision of this Agreement. Upon termination, Licensee shall immediately return all Documentation and the Software."

"Survival. Termination of this Agreement shall not affect any of Licensor's right, remedies, and protections hereunder."

(continued)

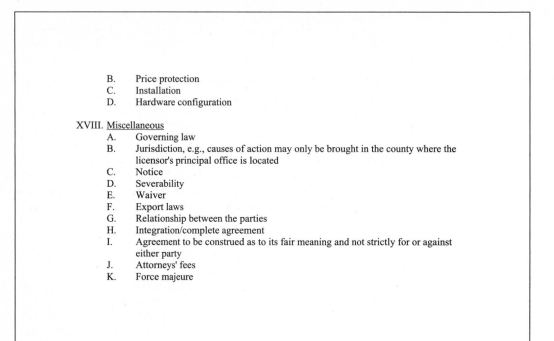

B. Price protection
C. Installation
D. Hardware configuration

XVIII. Miscellaneous
    A. Governing law
    B. Jurisdiction, e.g., causes of action may only be brought in the county where the licensor's principal office is located
    C. Notice
    D. Severability
    E. Waiver
    F. Export laws
    G. Relationship between the parties
    H. Integration/complete agreement
    I. Agreement to be construed as to its fair meaning and not strictly for or against either party
    J. Attorneys' fees
    K. Force majeure

Patent License Agreements

Patent Licenses typically grant a licensee the right to use, modify, and commercially exploit a particular patent. For example, ABC, Inc., may hold a patent to a new type of picture frame. This agreement can give the licensee the right to make the picture frames, the right to sell them, the right to make modifications to the frame, and more.

The key issues involved in patent licenses include the following:

✔ **Nature of the license:** Is the patent license exclusive or nonexclusive? An exclusive license means that no one else may use the patent during the term of the license. (If you want total exclusivity, make sure to spell out that the license exclusivity also includes the fact that the licensor may not use the patent.)

✔ **Term:** The length of the license is important. The licensee typically wants the term to be as long as possible. However, remember that patents don't last forever, and you can't get more rights in a patent than the patent holder actually has.

✔ **Uses:** You need to clearly spell out the uses of the license. Ideally, the licensee wants to be able to exploit the license for any purpose whatsoever, but the licensor may want to limit the use to certain applications, geographical territories, or markets.

✔ **Royalties:** How do you pay the licensor for the license? You can structure royalty payments in many ways: an up-front, one-time payment; periodic payments based on sales of the patented product; yearly payments; or formula payments based on aggregate products developed over time.

✔ **Infringement:** The licensee is very interested in making sure that the patent does not infringe on the rights of a third party, and expects some protection from claims of infringement against the licensee. The licensee typically does this by insisting upon an indemnity from the licensor in case of such infringement claims.

✔ **Termination:** The License Agreement also addresses the situation of when one side can terminate the license. Ideally, the licensee wants the license to be irrevocable. (At the very least, however, the licensor wants the right to terminate the license if the licensee does not make the required payments.) The licensor may want to build in several termination rights to retain flexibility if she doesn't think the licensee is exploiting the patent enough or maximizing revenues sufficiently to be licensor.

✔ **Licensee obligations:** The licensor may insist upon certain obligations of the licensee — for example, that the licensee spends a certain amount of money to develop and market the product, that the product remains of a certain quality, and that the licensee does not do anything to adversely affect the value of the patent.

✔ **Sublicense:** Typically, the licensee wants broad rights to be able to sublicense the patent, and the licensor may want limitations on that right.

✔ **Derivative products:** The License Agreement needs to address who owns any derivative products or technology developed by the licensee. Ideally, the licensee wants the licensor to deem him the owner, but most licensors resist that.

Patent licenses can be tricky, so you need to hire a good business lawyer to help you sort through the maze of issues.

Trade Name License Agreements

Sometimes, using another company's trade name for your particular business makes sense. Examples include Burger King, McDonald's, and Subway. Many of these situations involve franchises.

A *Trade Name License Agreement* spells out the terms allowing the use of the trade name. The typical Trade Name License Agreement covers the following points:

✔ The name being licensed

✔ The uses allowed for the name

✔ The territory where the name can be used

✔ Whether the license is exclusive or nonexclusive

✔ The term of the license plus any renewal rights

✔ The fees to be paid

Form 11-3 on the CD-ROM accompanying this book gives a sample Trade Name License Agreement.

Copyright License Agreements

Copyrights cover original works of authorship, such as articles, books, compilations of data, and photographs. A copyright gives the owner of the work the exclusive right to make copies of the work and to prepare derivative works (such as revisions) based on the copyrighted work.

A *Copyright License Agreement* sets forth the terms for the copyright holder (the licensor) to grant the right to use, publish, or reprint some or all of the copyrighted work to someone (the licensee).

The key terms of Copyright License Agreements include the following:

✔ **Rights granted:** The agreement needs to spell out the specific rights granted. What portion of the copyrighted work can you use? For what purpose? In what medium (for example, books, online, CD-ROMs)? Is the right exclusive or nonexclusive?

✔ **Term and termination:** How long is the license? Under what circumstances can the licensor or licensee terminate the license early?

✔ **Payments:** What payments, if any, does the licensee make to the licensor? Is the payment a flat rate or is it based on volume of sales that incorporate the copyrighted work? When are the payments due? What type of royalty statements accompany the payment?

✔ **Representations and warranties of licensor:** Does the licensor represent and warrant that the copyrighted work is owned solely by him and that it does not infringe on the rights of any third party? Does the licensor represent that she has the power and authority to grant the license? What other representations and warranties does the licensee need?

> ✔ **Obligations of licensee:** What obligations does the licensee have? The licensor, at the minimum, wants to have an acknowledgement in the new work that the licensed material is the copyrighted work of the licensor. The licensor may also insist on quality standards or a right to review and approve the new work incorporating the licensed material.

 The CD-ROM includes, as Form 11-5, a simple Copyright Permission Form for use in a book. The CD-ROM also contains Form 11-4, a Web Site Content License Agreement form.

Forms on the CD-ROM

Form 11-1	**Software License Agreement**	A sample shrink-wrap Software License Agreement
Form 11-2	**Checklist of Issues in Drafting and Negotiating Software License Agreements**	A checklist of issues to consider when drafting and negotiating Software License Agreements
Form 11-3	**Trade Name License Agreement**	A license granting the right to use a trade name
Form 11-4	**Web Site Content License Agreement**	A license to post content on a Web site
Form 11-5	**Copyright Permission Form for Use in Book**	A simple form for obtaining permission to use copyrighted information in a book
Form 11-6	**Notice of Infringement of Copyrighted Work**	A sample letter notifying a party of an infringement of a copyrighted work with a demand for an explanation

Chapter 12

Promissory Notes and Loan Agreements

"*N*either a borrower nor a lender be," said Polonius to his son, Laertes, in *Hamlet,* as Laertes embarked on a voyage. Although that may have been good advice in 1602 when William Shakespeare wrote *Hamlet,* a person starting and maintaining a business today cannot easily follow such sage words. (What Polonius actually said to Laertes in full is, "Neither a borrower nor a lender be for loan oft loses both itself and friend and borrowing dulls the edge of husbandry.")

You can obtain money for your business in many ways, and this chapter discusses some of the agreements used with loan financing. In this chapter, I guide you through several of the basic agreements you run across when borrowing money.

Promissory Notes

A *promissory note* is an unconditional written promise to pay a specified sum of money on demand or at a specified date. Quite simply, a promissory note documents a loan in such lending transactions as borrowing $2,000 from your parents or borrowing $15,000 from a bank to purchase inventory for your business.

Producing proper promissory notes

Unless the lender is a bank with its own form of loan agreement, a good promissory note is often sufficient evidence of a loan. Promissory notes do not require notarization to be legally valid in most states.

Promissory notes usually contain the following key points:

- ✔ The date of the note
- ✔ The borrower's name
- ✔ The lender's name
- ✔ The address where payments are to be sent
- ✔ The amount of the debt
- ✔ Whether the note is payable on demand or at a definite time
- ✔ Description of the collateral
- ✔ The interest rate
- ✔ The due dates for payment of interest and principal
- ✔ Whether the borrower can prepay the note
- ✔ Any late charges
- ✔ An attorneys' fees clause
- ✔ The borrower's proper signature

Forms 12-1 and 12-2 on the CD-ROM show sample promissory notes. Form 12-1 is a demand note, which grants the lender the power to call for payment of the note at any time. Form 12-2 shows a note providing that payment will be due on an agreed upon date in the future. These promissory notes are drafted to be protective of the lender.

PROMISSORY NOTE -
PAYABLE ON A DESIGNATED DATE

$_____   [City], [State]

For value received, the undersigned (Maker) promises to pay to _____ (Payee), or order, at its offices at [address], the principal sum of _____ Dollars ($_____), together with interest at the rate hereinafter provided for on the unpaid principal balance of this note from time to time outstanding until paid in full.

Interest shall accrue on the unpaid and outstanding principal balance of this note commencing on the date hereof and continuing until repayment of this note in full at a rate per annum equal to ___%. Interest only payments shall be made by Maker to Payee on or before the [1st] day of each [month]. The principal shall be due and payable in full on _____, ____.

Maker shall make all payments hereunder to Payee in lawful money of the United States and in immediately available funds.

The maturity of this note may be accelerated by Payee in the event Maker is in breach or default of any of the terms, conditions or covenants of any other agreement with Payee or its affiliates. Should default be made in payment of any installment when due hereunder the whole sum of principal and interest shall become immediately due and payable at the option of the holder of this note.

In the event any installment provided for herein is not paid on or before two (2) days following its due date, Maker promises to pay to the holder of this promissory note an amount equal to five percent (5%) of the amount of such installment. In addition, Maker promises to pay interest on any such unpaid installment from the date due until such installment is paid in full at a per annum rate equal to the lesser of eighteen percent (18%) or the highest rate permitted by law. Time is of the essence.

Maker waives presentment, demand, notice of demand, protest, notice of protest or notice of nonpayment in connection with the delivery, acceptance, performance, default or enforcement of this note or of any document or instrument evidencing any security for payment of this note.

Failure at any time to exercise any of the rights of Payee hereunder shall not constitute a waiver of such rights and shall not be a bar to exercise of any of such rights at a later date. In the event of commencement of suit to enforce payment of this note, the prevailing party shall be entitled to receive the costs of collection including reasonable attorneys' fees and court costs.

Nothing contained in this note shall be deemed to require the payment of interest or other charges by Maker or any other person in excess of the amount which the Payee may lawfully charge under the applicable usury laws. In the event that Payee shall collect moneys which are deemed to constitute interest which would increase the effective interest rate to a rate in excess of that permitted to be charged by applicable law, all such sums deemed to constitute interest in excess of the legal rate shall be credited against the principal balance of this note then outstanding, and any excess shall be returned to Maker.

IN WITNESS WHEREOF, the undersigned has caused this promissory note to be duly executed as of the date first written below.

Dated: _____   [Maker]_____

                                  By: _____

                                  Title: _____

Form 12-2: Promissory Note Payable on a Designated Date.

Loan Agreements

Loans are a well-known method of raising money for a business. A major disadvantage to a loan is that the bank (or other lender) requires you to pay back the loan whether or not your business is successful. One advantage of a typical loan is that if your business does well, the lender is only entitled to an interest return on its loan rather than a percentage of the business profits, or a share in the company, which is what an equity investor would expect.

A loan agreement covers many of the same points as a promissory note, but is a lengthier and more complicated document to cover a more complicated transaction.

Negotiating good loan terms

Whether you obtain your loan from a bank, individual, or other lender, a number of variables that go into the loan document can affect how good or bad a loan is for your business. You can negotiate virtually all the terms in a loan agreement; a "standard loan" does not exist. The key issues to negotiate when contemplating getting a loan for your business include the following:

✔ **Due date:** You need to set a date when you must repay the loan's principal. You can formulate this date as a lump sum payment at the end of the term of the loan, or as a periodic payment of principal with a final payment. For example, you can agree to borrow $50,000 with the entire principal due in two years. On the other hand, you can repay the principal in 20 equal monthly installments of $2,500. In any event, make sure that the payment schedule (interest and principal) is reasonable given your anticipated cash flow.

✔ **Interest payments:** The lender establishes the interest rate, which should be in compliance with the applicable state *usury* laws — laws that govern how much interest can be charged on a loan. See the section "Usury" later in this chapter for a more detailed discussion of usury. The loan payment dates should be clearly set forth (the most common method requires monthly payments by the first day of each month). If your cash flow situation is such that a great deal of cash comes in after the first day of the month, then try to adjust the timing of the required loan payments.

✔ **Loan fees:** The lender may charge up-front loan or processing fees. Be careful on the amount, and get an estimate as soon as possible so you can evaluate how attractive the loan is as a package.

✓**Prepayment:** Ideally, you want to be free to pay off the loan at any time, even earlier than its due date. Make sure that your loan agreement or promissory note (see the section "Promissory Notes," earlier in this chapter) gives you this flexibility. Try to avoid a prepayment penalty for paying off the loan early.

✓**Defaults:** The lender will likely insist that a variety of events can cause a default under the loan, including failure to make payment on time, bankruptcy, and breaches of any obligations in the loan documents. Negotiate for advance written notice of any alleged default, with a reasonable amount of time to cure the default.

✓ **Grace period:** Try to get a grace period for any payments. For example, the monthly payments may come due on the first day of the month but aren't deemed late until the fifth day of the month.

✓ **Late charge:** If the loan includes a fee for late payment, make sure that the charge is reasonable.

✓ **Collateral:** The lender may insist on a pledge or mortgage of some asset as security to protect the loan. Under a mortgage (for real property) or a security agreement (for personal property — see the section "Security Agreements," later in this chapter), if you default on the loan, the lender can foreclose upon the asset and sell it to repay the money owed to the lender. If the lender requires you to provide security, try to limit the amount you have to give to secure the loan. Make sure that when you repay the loan, the lender has to release its mortgage or security interest and make any governmental filings to acknowledge this release.

✓ **Co-signors and guarantors:** A lender may ask for a co-signer or guarantor as a way to further ensure that the loan will be repaid. A co-signer or guarantor runs the risk that his or her personal assets will be liable for repayment of the loan. See the section "Guaranty," later in this chapter, for more information.

✓ **Attorneys' fees:** The lender will likely insist on a clause saying that if you fail to make payments, you have to reimburse the lender's fees and costs in enforcing or collecting on the loan. Try to insert a qualifier that the reimbursement only covers "reasonable" attorneys' fees.

Form 12-3 gives a complete checklist of issues in negotiating a loan.

<u>Checklist of Issues in Negotiating a Loan</u>

Many banks and lending institutions have their own form of complex loan agreements when they make loans. There is no "standard" loan agreement, and there are many issues to consider when determining whether to accept a loan and in negotiating the loan terms. This is a checklist of some of these issues.

1. <u>Interest</u>

   (a) What is the interest payable?
   (b) How is the interest rate calculated? (Calculations based on a 360-day year are more unfavorable for the borrower than those based on a 365-day year.)
   (c) What is the default rate of interest and is it competitive?
   (d) Is the interest rate coupled with all fees, competitive with other available loans?
   (e) Is the interest rate fixed or variable?

2. <u>Payment Terms</u>

   (a) What are the monthly or other periodic payment obligations?
   (b) When is the final principal payment due?
   (c) Is there a right to extend the due date of the loan?

3. <u>Fees</u>

   (a) Are there any loan fees, commitment fees, placement fees, points payable upfront?
   (b) Are there any ongoing fees or charges during the life of the loan?

4. <u>Use of Loan Proceeds</u>

   (a) Are the loan proceeds restricted for certain uses? Are the uses broad enough?

5. <u>Representations and Warranties of the Borrower</u>

   (a) Due organization of the borrower
   (b) Duly qualified to do business
   (c) Authorization to do the loan
   (d) Enforceability of the loan agreement
   (e) Accuracy of the borrower's financial statements
   (f) No litigation
   (g) Compliance with laws
   (h) Payment of all taxes and filing of all tax returns
   (i) No adverse change in the business

Form 12-3: Checklist of Issues in Negotiating a Loan.

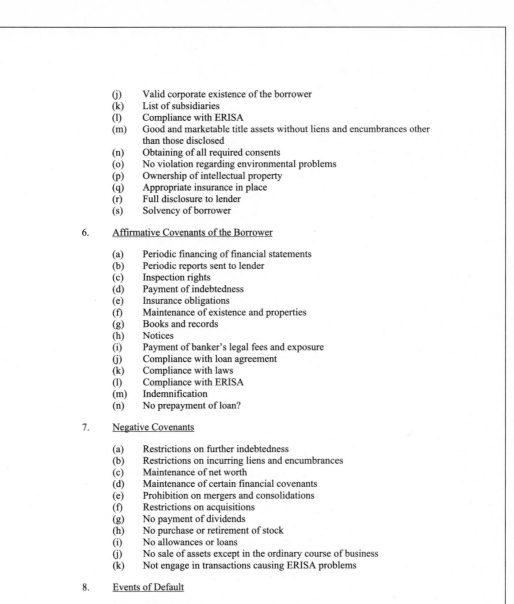

(j)   Valid corporate existence of the borrower
(k)   List of subsidiaries
(l)   Compliance with ERISA
(m)   Good and marketable title assets without liens and encumbrances other than those disclosed
(n)   Obtaining of all required consents
(o)   No violation regarding environmental problems
(p)   Ownership of intellectual property
(q)   Appropriate insurance in place
(r)   Full disclosure to lender
(s)   Solvency of borrower

6.   <u>Affirmative Covenants of the Borrower</u>

(a)   Periodic financing of financial statements
(b)   Periodic reports sent to lender
(c)   Inspection rights
(d)   Payment of indebtedness
(e)   Insurance obligations
(f)   Maintenance of existence and properties
(g)   Books and records
(h)   Notices
(i)   Payment of banker's legal fees and exposure
(j)   Compliance with loan agreement
(k)   Compliance with laws
(l)   Compliance with ERISA
(m)   Indemnification
(n)   No prepayment of loan?

7.   <u>Negative Covenants</u>

(a)   Restrictions on further indebtedness
(b)   Restrictions on incurring liens and encumbrances
(c)   Maintenance of net worth
(d)   Maintenance of certain financial covenants
(e)   Prohibition on mergers and consolidations
(f)   Restrictions on acquisitions
(g)   No payment of dividends
(h)   No purchase or retirement of stock
(i)   No allowances or loans
(j)   No sale of assets except in the ordinary course of business
(k)   Not engage in transactions causing ERISA problems

8.   <u>Events of Default</u>

(a)   Failure to pay
(b)   Breach of representation or warranty of borrower

(continued)

    (c)   Breach of covenants
    (d)   Bankruptcy or insolvency of borrower
    (e)   Various judgments against the borrower

9.   <u>Conditions to Closing</u>

    (a)   Execution of all required documents
    (b)   Certified copy of Board resolutions approving the loan
    (c)   Appropriate Officer's Certificate
    (d)   Opinion of legal counsel for borrower
    (e)   Good standing certificate
    (f)   Representations and warranties of the borrower are true and accurate
    (g)   Borrower has complied with all of its covenants
    (h)   No adverse change in the business of the borrower
    (i)   Completion of all due diligence by the lender

10.   <u>Miscellaneous</u>

    (a)   No assignment
    (b)   Amendments and waivers required to be in writing
    (c)   Entire agreement
    (d)   Survival of representations, warranties and covenants
    (e)   Notices
    (f)   Governing law
    (g)   Counterparts
    (h)   Right of setoff
    (i)   Severability
    (j)   No Third Parties Benefited
    (k)   Jurisdiction

* * *

Guaranty

A *guaranty* is a promise to answer for the payment, debt, or performance of an obligation if the person liable in the first instance fails to make payment or perform that obligation.

A number of lenders or other creditors may insist on a personal guaranty from a business's founders or major owners before extending credit or signing a contract. A *personal guaranty* requires that the person giving the guaranty (the *guarantor*) be responsible for paying the creditor's claim in case the company does not pay.

I have one precise legal word for guaranties: Yucch!

A personal guaranty exposes the guarantor's personal assets (savings, home, and so forth) for repayment of the obligation. Moreover, the lender can call up the personal guaranty even (or especially) if the business goes into bankruptcy. So, obviously, if you can, avoid giving any personal guaranties.

If the lender still insists on a personal guaranty, see if you can negotiate some of the following:

- ✔ **Security deposit:** Ask if the creditor will forego a personal guaranty if you put up a security deposit. Try also to get interest on any security deposit.

- ✔ **Limited term of guaranty:** Ask for the personal guaranty to go away after a certain period of time, so long as the company has complied with its obligations. For example, the personal guaranty could automatically terminate one year after a lease is signed with a landlord, so long as the business has been current on its rent obligations in that year.

- ✔ **Limited guaranty:** Instead of having the guaranty cover all of the borrower's obligations, consider negotiating a maximum amount of liability — such as $25,000.

If you happen to be the one requesting a guaranty, then make sure that the guaranty is broad and enforceable.

Form 12-4 on the CD-ROM contains a broad guaranty, and Form 12-5 on the CD-ROM contains a Demand to Guarantor for Payment.

Security Agreements

Any agreement that provides for or creates a security interest is a *Security Agreement*. A *security interest* is an interest in personal property, fixtures, or accounts (also referred to as *collateral*) that secures the payment or performance of an obligation. Security interest gives the person in whose favor the security interest is created the right to repossess and retain or dispose of the collateral if the person who owes the obligation fails to perform.

A security interest protects the secured party in the event that the debtor fails to pay or perform the obligation under the agreement — she can then look to some asset for repayment of the loan or obligation.

The *secured party* is the person in whose favor the security interest is created, usually the lender or seller of the collateral. The *debtor* is the person who owes the payment or other performance under the Security Agreement.

Key provisions for a Security Agreement

Although no specific language or terminology has to be included in a Security Agreement, consider the following list of key provisions:

- Identity of parties — debtor and secured party, including full names and addresses
- Description of collateral
- Priority of security interest — first lien? second lien?
- Identity of owner of collateral
- Value to be given by secured party to debtor
- Provisions regarding preservation of collateral, including these:
  - secured party's right to inspect collateral
  - debtor's obligation to make collateral available for inspection by secured party
  - debtor's duty to protect, maintain, and repair collateral
  - debtor's right to sell, exchange, or dispose of collateral, and so forth
- Limitations on secured party's right to assign security interest and debtor's right to receive notice of assignment
- Default provisions
- Lender's right to foreclose
- Provision for expiration of agreement on debtor's satisfaction of debts and provision that expiration of agreement terminates secured party's security interest
- Signatures of debtor (required) and secured party (if desired)

Perfecting by possession or filing a financing statement

If the debtor defaults on his or her obligation under the Security Agreement, the secured party can look to the collateral to satisfy the obligation. To obtain the maximum protection against the claims of third parties with possibly conflicting interests in the collateral, the secured party must *perfect* his or her security interest in the collateral.

Perfection generally protects the secured party against creditors and transferees of the debtor. In general, to perfect a security interest, the secured party must either file a financing statement at the proper public office or take possession of the collateral.

Financing statement

Filing a UCC Financing Statement is the preferred method of perfecting a security interest. Filing this statement provides the necessary notice to third parties and creditors. You can typically obtain the UCC Financing Statement from the office of your Secretary of State. After you fill it out, the statement is filed in the appropriate public office, such as the Secretary of State or county recorder (depending on your state's requirements). Your business lawyer can also provide you with the relevant forms.

Contents of the financing statement include the following:

- ✔ Debtor's name and address
- ✔ Secured party's name and address
- ✔ Numerical identification of the parties (for example, the party's federal taxpayer identification number or Social Security number)
- ✔ Description of collateral
- ✔ Signatures

After you file the original UCC Financing Statement, the relationship of the parties may change for a number of reasons. You can state many of these changes on a Financing Statement Change Form. The following types of changes are included on the UCC-2:

- ✔ Continuation
- ✔ Partial release of collateral
- ✔ Termination
- ✔ Amendment
- ✔ Assignment by secured creditor

Because Financing Statements are a matter of public record, you may obtain a certificate from the Secretary of State or county recorder showing whether any financing statement naming a particular debtor is on file, along with the time and date of the filing of any related financing statement. There's a charge for the certificate, and you can also obtain a copy of the actual financing statement for an additional fee.

Usury

A couple of words about *usury,* which is the lending of money at unusually high or unlawful interest: Don't do it! You can charge or be charged interest up to the legal interest rate of the moment, but not one penny more.

One definition of usury is the conscious and voluntary taking of more than the legal rate of interest. Usury laws exist to protect the public from those who would take advantage of those in need of borrowing money. In California, a person who willfully makes or negotiates a loan at a usurious interest rate is guilty of loan-sharking — a felony — unless the person is licensed to make or negotiate the loan or is expressly exempted from the licensing or usury laws.

Each state determines the legal interest rate, and it can vary significantly from state to state. Often, state usury laws don't apply to banks, and state laws often allow a higher interest rate for business purposes than for personal reasons. This is why you may find certain credit card companies located in one particular state — that state allows them to charge a higher interest rate.

If you are lending money, make sure you know what is the maximum you can charge.

Forms on the CD-ROM

Check out these forms on the CD-ROM relating to borrowing and lending money:

Form 12-1	**Promissory Note Payable on Demand**	A form of note where the holder of the note can demand payment at any time
Form 12-2	**Promissory Note Payable on a Designated Date**	A form of note where the principal is payable on a certain date
Form 12-3	**Checklist of Issues in Negotiating a Loan**	A comprehensive checklist of issues to address in loan agreements
Form 12-4	**Guaranty**	A pro-creditor-oriented form that guaranties performance and payment of obligations of the guarantor
Form 12-5	**Demand to Guarantor for Payment**	A notice to a guarantor of an obligation that the debtor is in default and payment is now being demanded from the guarantor

Chapter 13

Sales and Service Contracts and Forms

* *

In This Chapter

▶ Service Contracts

▶ Sales Contracts

▶ Distribution Agreements

▶ Extending credit

▶ Collecting past due amounts

* *

Sales or service contracts are essential to most businesses. A sales contract can be used for the sale of major products or goods, whereas a service contract is used when providing service of some kind.

When you decide to extend credit to a customer for a sale, you also need to take certain precautions. And if the customer doesn't pay, you then need to take various steps to collect.

In this chapter, I guide you in preparing good sales and service contracts, distribution agreements, and steps to extend credit and collect past due amounts.

Service Contracts

If your company is providing professional services as opposed to selling a product, you may find that you need a good *Agreement for Professional Services*. This type of agreement lays out the terms and conditions under which your business provides certain services. Examples of such services include accounting, engineering, consulting, software development, and property inspections.

Here are the key points to keep in mind when drafting or negotiating an Agreement for Professional Services:

- **Services to be rendered:** Clearly set forth the precise services to be rendered in the contract. Avoid broad or ambiguous language, such as "Company will provide all services necessary to make the Client's computer operations work quickly and efficiently." This type of language only leads to problems or litigation. Rather, consider language that specifically and narrowly describes what you can actually do, such as "Company will provide up to 50 hours of consulting time to assist Client in modifying its computer network to operate more quickly."

- **Fees:** Spell out the compensation that you expect to receive and when you expect to receive it. Do you expect an up-front retainer? Do you charge a lump sum for the project or by the hour? When are payments due?

- **Reimbursable costs:** If you expect the client to reimburse your out-of-pocket expenses or other costs, make sure that your contract specifically states this expectation.

- **Nonsolicitation of employees:** Consider adding a clause that prohibits your customer from soliciting or hiring away your employees who are working on the project. This clause is especially important if you have valuable, high-tech employees.

- **Late charges:** Use the contract to ensure that if the client doesn't pay your bill on time, interest begins to accrue. Typical late charges accrue at 1 percent to 1½ percent per month on unpaid sums.

- **Liability limitations:** Ideally, you want your contract to limit your liability in a number of ways. One typical provision is to say that the maximum amount of liability exposure you have is the amount of your fees. (After all, if your risk is greater than your fees, the job may not be worth taking.) Also consider a clause that states that you are not liable for consequential, punitive, or speculative damages or lost profits. Of course, various laws may limit the enforceability of such provisions, but you generally have little downside in including them in your contract.

- **Period for bringing claims:** Another way to potentially limit your liability is to limit the time period when a dissatisfied customer can bring a claim against you. For example, your contract may state that if the customer becomes aware of any problem with the services provided, then the customer has to notify you and bring a legal proceeding within one year of discovering the problem or waive the right to complain. The intention of this clause is to keep someone from bringing a claim against you after your memories about the work have faded.

- **Time to perform services:** Be wary of an absolute deadline by which you must complete the services. If you don't complete the work by the deadline, what rights does the customer have? You may be in a disastrous position if you find out that the customer can terminate the contract or withhold paying fees just because you're late finishing a project.

- **Suspension of services:** You typically want your contract to say that if you are not being paid on time, then you have the right to immediately terminate or suspend performing further services.

- **Force majeure:** This legalese clause says that if you are prevented from doing or completing your work by an act of God or unforeseen events (power failure, labor strike, earthquake, and so on), then your inability to perform the work will be excused — at least for a reasonable time.

Form 13-1 on the CD-ROM is a sample Agreement for Professional Services.

Sales Contracts

Many small businesses sell a product and therefore need a good *Sales Contract*. The Sales Contract lays out the price, terms, and conditions for the sale of goods, equipment, or other products. The actual Sales Contract can take the form of fine print on the other side of an order form or an invoice, or it can be tailor-made for a particular sale. The Sales Contract I discuss here can be the Purchase Order that I discuss in the following section, except the focus here is on you as the seller as opposed to the buyer.

From your company's perspective, you always want to start with your own form. Having your form preprinted helps it to look "standard" and nonnegotiable. (*Note:* No "standard" form of Sales Contract actually exists.) As the drafter of the Sales Contract, you can make the contract more favorable to you as the seller.

Here are some important terms to address in your Sales Contract:

- **Price:** Make sure that the Sales Contract correctly states the price (often by filling in a blank space provided on the form). The Sales Contract also needs to spell out any discounts, installation charges, and delivery charges.

- **Price adjustments:** Consider how you may increase the prices from time to time if you are entering into a long-term contract.

- **Taxes:** Try to ensure that the purchaser is responsible for all sales taxes.

- **Payment and credit terms:** Make sure to state when payment is due. If you don't require immediate payment, consider a small discount to the purchaser if payment is made within 10 days and a finance charge if payment is late (such as 30 days past due).

- ✔ **Warranties:** Decide what warranties you want to give. Ideally, you want to have limited warranties, but the competitive marketplace may require you to grant extensive warranties. Indeed, one advantage you may have over more established competitors is to offer a better warranty (one year, for example) than the current industry standard (which may be 90 days). Typical warranties state that for a designated period, the goods sold will be free from defects of workmanship and will conform to designated specifications. A form of Limited Warranty for a software product is included as Form 13-2 on the CD-ROM.

- ✔ **Disclaimers:** State clearly in your Sales Contract (after you have set forth what your warranties are) that no other warranties exist, express or implied, including merchantability or fitness for a particular purpose. This disclaimer is usually in all capital letters or boldfaced to stand out and comply with certain provisions of the Uniform Commercial Code.

- ✔ **Liability limitations:** Use the Sales Contract to attempt to limit your liability under the contract. A typical clause for liability states that the seller's maximum amount of liability is equal to the purchase price. Make sure, too, to include a sentence that says you are not responsible for consequential, punitive, and speculative damages or lost profits (although some laws may limit successful enforcement of this clause).

For a sample form of Equipment Sales Contract, see Form 13-3 on the CD-ROM. A sample amendment to an existing Sales Contract is included on Form 13-4.

Purchase Orders

If you are buying products from another company, you can often accomplish this purchase with a simple Purchase Order. A Purchase Order itself can be a contract. Whether the Purchase Order is your form or the seller's form, consider the following points:

- ✔ **Complete description of goods:** Does the Purchase Order contain a complete description of the goods that you think you're buying? (This information helps you avoid misunderstandings.) Does the description include all needed parts and related items? Are you getting the latest or most updated version or model of the goods being purchased?

- ✔ **Price:** Is the price clearly set forth? Does the purchase order include a statement that says the price sets forth the entire payment required? Be wary of hidden charges, handling fees, and delivery fees.

- ✔ **Delivery:** How are the goods provided — does the seller deliver them or do you pick them up? Are the goods guaranteed to be ready by a certain date? Is a penalty imposed if the goods aren't ready by the designated date?

✔ **Terms:** When is payment due? Is a partial payment required in advance? Net 30 days? Payable over time?

✔ **Refund and return policy:** What refund and return rights do you have, if any? The seller may want to limit your rights. At the very least, you should get a refund or return right if the goods prove defective, do not conform to your specifications, or are not reasonably satisfactory to you.

✔ **Tax:** How much tax must be paid? Who pays the tax?

✔ **Representations:** Are you buying the goods based on representations or statements from the seller or the seller's salespeople or agents? If so, make sure that the Purchase Order states that you are buying the goods based on those statements.

✔ **Warranties:** Do any warranties cover the goods? What do the warranties cover? How long are the warranties?

If the seller provides the Purchase Order form for you to sign, the document will undoubtedly be very one-sided (in the seller's favor). Look over the Purchase Order carefully and don't be afraid to make changes even if the document is a preprinted form.

Form 13-5 on the CD-ROM is a sample Purchase Order to buy goods.

Distribution Agreements

In many small businesses, the key to success depends on how well you can distribute your product. For example, if your company's products are retail items (such as food items, apparel, or kitchen appliances), you probably want to find an experienced distributor with a great sales force and contacts. The distributor may then contract with dealers or large chains to sell your product.

Customer payment policy

From the beginning, you need to implement clear-cut payment policies with your customers. A clear-cut policy prevents misunderstanding and lets the customer know when you expect payment. If you aren't getting cash up front, all your contracts and invoices need to clearly state something like the following:

Customer Payment Policy. All payments must be received by ABC, Inc., within 30 days of the date of an invoice. Any payments received after said date will be subject to a late interest fee of one-and-one-half percent (1½ %) per month. The customer shall also be responsible for all attorneys' fees, court costs, and related expenses incurred in the event that payment is not timely made and proceedings are brought by ABC, Inc., to collect sums owed.

Early payment discount

You can improve your cash flow and cut down on delinquent payments by offering a discount for early payment. Consider adding the following clause (or one similar to it) to your invoices and contracts.

Early Payment Discount. The Customer shall be entitled to receive a discount on the bill of two percent (2%) of the face amount of the bill. In order to receive this discount, ABC, Inc., must receive full payment within ten (10) days of the date of this invoice.

The key to your relationship with the distributor is the Distribution Agreement. Although the distributor may prefer to use its own form of Distribution Agreement (which of course will be one-sided in the distributor's favor), consider the following key terms in the negotiations:

✔ **Territory and markets:** The contract must clearly describe the distributor's territory or business area. The contract needs to define the market or customer category. For example, you may want your company to handle certain major customers (like national accounts) directly and the distributor to handle other outlets. Is the distributor's territory broad (such as the entire U.S.) or narrow (such as Hackensack, New Jersey)?

✔ **Exclusive versus nonexclusive:** The contract needs to specify whether the distributor is to have exclusive or nonexclusive rights to the company's products in a particular territory. But be careful here — you don't want to give exclusivity for one territory or market if you face significant risk of lousy performance by the distributor. If you plan to give exclusive rights, consider setting sales goals that the distributor has to meet in order to maintain exclusivity.

✔ **Obligations of the distributor:** The distributor's obligations need to be spelled out. Ideally, you want a clause that says the distributor must use its "best efforts to market your products," although the distributor may resist this phrase. So, consider setting forth in the contract the specific steps that the distributor must take (contacting all the major potential customers, appointing dealers, preparing marketing material and promotional activities, and so on).

✔ **Trademarks and logos:** The Distribution Agreement needs to prohibit the distributor from using the company's name, trademark, and logos in advertising, point-of-sale activities, and marketing materials except as provided in the Distribution Agreement or with the company's prior written consent. This restriction is important to ensure that your company's goodwill, reputation, and brand name are not hurt by the distributor's activities.

✔ **Product issues:** The contract needs to clearly identify the product or products that the Distribution Agreement covers. The agreement may also cover the issue of product availability and allocation of product among other distributors. The Distribution Agreement also needs to cover how the distributor handles product inventory and what rights of return are available.

✔ **Service:** Decide the terms for servicing the product. Does the distributor handle product servicing or warranty claims? Does the distributor have the expertise to do so? How can you compensate the distributor for servicing the product?

✔ **Price:** The contract needs to provide a pricing section. Generally, the price follows a schedule or the seller announces the price from time to time. The seller then typically provides an agreed discount to the distributor. You need to maintain flexibility on the price you can charge for your products.

✔ **Payment terms:** Industry practices often dictate payment terms. Ideally, you want to get an up-front deposit on a distributor's order with full payment due either 30 or 60 days after shipment. Make sure that you are comfortable with the distributor's creditworthiness.

✔ **Contract term and termination:** The distributor's term of the appointment and how such a term can be terminated or reviewed are very important issues in a Distribution Agreement. Negotiate for the right to terminate the contract for any reason, as long as you give at least 60–90 days' notice. Such a termination right gives you maximum flexibility to get out of a relationship that isn't working. Also, add a provision that allows you to immediately terminate the contract if the distributor breaches its obligations or becomes bankrupt or insolvent. You must also address the potentially complicated issue of what happens after termination with respect to products, sums owed, and servicing obligations.

Distribution Agreements can be complicated. You need to find out industry practice and see sample contracts from different distributors. Ask the distributors for their form of contracts.

Giving Credit Where Credit's Due

In many lines of business, making it as easy as possible for your customers to purchase your product or service can make the difference between a company that's holding on and a company that's prospering. But you don't have to give away the farm. This section tells you about forms that give you the best chance of getting your money after extending credit.

Preparing to extend credit

If you are going to extend any significant credit to a customer (other than accepting a credit card, in which case the credit card company takes care of this stuff), consider taking some or all of the following steps:

- ✔ **Credit Application:** Require the customer to fill out a Credit Application. This document solicits important information about the customer's background, style of operation (corporation, partnership, or sole proprietorship), trade, references (from other companies that extend credit to the customer), and bank references.

  Form 13-6 shows a sample Credit Application.

- ✔ **References:** Check the customer's references to make sure that the customer has paid other creditors on time.

- ✔ **Credit reports:** Consider obtaining a credit report from a credit rating agency, such as TRW, Dun & Bradstreet, or Equifax. To get information on individuals, you need their consent to do a search (the consent can be contained in the Credit Application). You typically need the individual's name, city, Social Security number, and, if the name is common, date of birth. After you get the credit report, review it carefully to determine the customer's payment history.

- ✔ **Guarantee:** If the customer is a company with minimal assets, request that the owners personally guarantee the company's obligations. Then make sure that the person giving the guarantee has some assets to back up the guarantee.

- ✔ **Security:** Take a *security interest* in the goods if you're selling them on credit and if they're expensive. A security interest provides you with the benefit that, if the customer doesn't pay, you can sell or take back the goods (as opposed to being simply one of the customer's unsecured creditors). In order to do this, you need the customer to sign a Security Agreement and UCC Financing Statement covering the goods. The UCC Financing Statement typically can be obtained from the office of your Secretary of State. The statement is then filed in the appropriate public office, such as the Secretary of State or county recorder (depending on your state's requirements). Also, your business lawyer can provide you with the relevant forms.

CREDIT APPLICATION

The undersigned is applying for credit with _____ (the "Company") and agrees to abide by the terms and conditions of the Company's standard contract.

1. Company Name
   and Address   _____

                      _____

                      _____

2. Phone (   ) _____ Fax (   ) _____

3. Federal Tax ID or Social Security No. _____

4. Type of Business _____ No. of Employees _____

5. Date Business Established _____

6. Types of Products You Will Purchase _____

7. Amount of Credit Requested $ _____

8. Check which is applicable to you:

   __ Corporation   __ General Partnership   __ Limited Partnership

   __ LLC   __ Sole Proprietorship   __ Other : _____

9. State where your company was organized : _____

10. Have you or any of your affiliates ever had credit with us before or purchased from us before? Yes ___ No ___

    If yes, under what name? _____

11. Name or title of persons authorized to act on your behalf : _____

12. Trade References

    Reference #1 Name and Address : _____

                                    _____

                                    _____

                      Phone (   ) _____

    Reference #2 Name and Address : _____

                                    _____

                                    _____

                      Phone (   ) _____

    Reference #3 Name and Address : _____

                                    _____

                                    _____

                      Phone (   ) _____

13. Bank References

    Bank #1 Account # _____ Phone (   ) _____

               Contact Person _____

Form 13-6: Credit Application.

(continued)

Name of Bank _____

Address _____

Bank #2 Account # _____ Phone ( ) _____

Contact Person _____

Name of Bank _____

Address _____

14. Financial Information about your Company :

    Assets: $ _____

    Liabilities: $ _____

    Approximate Annual
    Net Income: $ _____

15. Have you or your officers or affiliates ever filed a petition in bankruptcy? _____

16. Are you subject to any litigation? _____ If so, describe here : _____

_____

_____

17. Are you current in meeting your other financial obligations? _____

We declare that the above information is true, correct and complete and is given to induce the Company to extend credit. We authorize the Company to make such credit investigation as the Company sees fit, including contacting the above trade references and banks and obtaining credit reports. We authorize all trade references, banks and credit reporting agencies to disclose to the Company any and all information concerning the financial and credit history of my company and myself:

I have read the terms and conditions stated below and agree to all of those terms and conditions

Name of Company: _____

Authorized Signature: _____

Printed Name: _____

Title: _____ Date: _____

GENERAL TERMS AND CONDITIONS

1. All bills become payable in full ___ days after receipt. If not paid by such time, bills are considered past due.

2. A service charge of 5% per month will be added to all amounts billed if not paid by the end of the month, together with interest at the rate of 1½% per month.

Reducing the risk of nonpayment

Unless your customer pays you in cash at the time of the sale, you are likely to encounter a number of situations where the risk of nonpayment is significant. And for a small business, nonpayment can seriously impact profits and cash flow!

So here are some tips to reduce the risk of nonpayment:

- ✔ Send out bills as promptly as possible.

- ✔ Make sure that your bills clearly identify the goods or services rendered, the dates purchased, and any other relevant information.

- ✔ Send follow-up reminders of past due notices immediately, with a big "Past Due" stamped on the cover of the notice.

- ✔ Make sure that you monitor payments that are due daily. Forms 13-7 (Accounts Receivable Aging) and 13-8 (Accounts Receivable Monthly Customer Statement) on the CD-ROM can help you keep track of overdue payments.

- ✔ Telephone the customer or accounts payable department and ask what you can do to speed up payment.

- ✔ Have a set of demand letters ready to send when payment is overdue (see the section "Getting Your Money the Hard Way," later in this chapter).

- ✔ Consider compromising the amount owed or extending the time for payment if the customer has financial problems. If you do agree to extend time, insist on a periodic payment plan.

- ✔ Respond promptly, in writing, if the customer disputes the amount owed. Otherwise, you can lose some rights under various credit laws. If you decide to settle over a disputed amount, consider using Form 13-9 on the CD-ROM (Settlement of Disputed Amount).

- ✔ Consider stopping any future sales to the customer unless the bill is paid or a compromise reached. Also, consider cash payment on delivery as a condition to any new sale.

No matter what steps you choose to take, remember to be courteous and professional. Just make sure to keep on top of the problem before it escalates.

Getting Your Money the Hard Way

Sometimes you have to resort to tougher measures to get payment from your customer. This section provides you with some tools to wrench your just payment from deadbeat customers.

Collection letters

As part of your form arsenal, have several form letters ready to send out when a customer's account is past due. The letters can be increasingly firm. Forms 13-10, 13-11, and 13-12 on the CD-ROM are samples of increasingly firm letters.

Attorney letters

If your calls and letters have not worked, consider having your attorney send a letter demanding payment. The customer may view the request more seriously when it comes from an attorney and, consequently, may be more inclined to pay.

Form 13-13 is a sample attorney letter demanding payment. You can revise this form to fit your circumstances and have your attorney put it on his or her letterhead to send. By doing so, you may save yourself some legal fees because the attorney doesn't have to prepare this form.

Collection agencies

Collection agencies specialize in tracking down and extracting payment from overdue debtors. Collection agencies are typically used as a last resort (other than suing the customer in court) because they keep a large percentage of what they collect for themselves. Remember, too, that using a collection agency may alienate the customer (but then again, who wants customers who don't pay their debts?).

Attorney Letter Demanding Payment

[Law Firm or Attorney Letterhead]

[Date]

Mr. Joe Smith
President
Deadbeat, Inc.
777 Reno Ave.
San Francisco, CA

Re: <u>Legal Action Against Your Company</u>

We are legal counsel for ABC Suppliers, Inc., a California corporation ("ABC"). As you may know, ABC entered into a contract on April 15, ____ (the "Contract") providing for the delivery to you of various equipment. All of that equipment has been timely delivered to you under the terms of the Contract and ABC has otherwise fully performed under the terms of the Contract.

However, certain amounts due by you under the Contract have not been paid. Indeed, this amount has been overdue for over 120 days. Under the terms of the Contract, the amount owed incurs late interest at the rate of 1½% per month and a late fee of 5% of the principal amount owed if not paid within 30 days of the date owed. So as of September 15, ____, your overdue amount is equal to $15,000.

As you may also remember from the Contract, there is an attorneys' fees clause, such that if ABC were to bring legal action against you, it would be entitled to the overdue amount <u>plus</u> its legal fees and expenses.

ABC is fully prepared to bring legal action against your company unless payment is not made within 7 days of the date of this letter. If you have any questions, please feel free to call the undersigned at (415) 777-7000.

Very truly yours,

Richard Van Horn
Attorney-at-Law

Form 13-13: Attorney Letter Demanding Payment.

Forms on the CD-ROM

On the CD-ROM check out the following forms dealing with sales and customers:

Form 13-1	**Agreement for Professional Services**	A sample agreement for the rendering of professional services
Form 13-2	**Limited Warranty**	A form of Limited Warranty for a software product, with various disclaimers and limitations of liability
Form 13-3	**Equipment Sales Agreement**	A sample agreement for the sale of new equipment
Form 13-4	**Amendment to Sales Contract**	A sample form of amendment to an existing Sales Contract
Form 13-5	**Purchase Order**	A sample purchase order to buy goods
Form 13-6	**Credit Application**	An application to be filled out by a prospective customer prior to granting the customer credit
Form 13-7	**Accounts Receivable Aging**	A sample accounting report to keep track of accounts receivable status by customer
Form 13-8	**Accounts Receivable Monthly Customer Statement**	A sample report to keep track of accounts receivable status by customer
Form 13-9	**Settlement of Disputed Account**	An agreement to compromise on disputed amounts owed
Form 13-10	**Courtesy Reminder of Late Payment**	A sample letter courteously reminding the customer that payment is overdue
Form 13-11	**Demand for Payment**	A letter demanding payment on an overdue account
Form 13-12	**Final Demand for Payment**	A letter more forcefully demanding payment and labeled a "final demand"

Form 13-13	**Attorney Letter Demanding Payment**	A form of letter from an attorney demanding over-due payment
Form 13-14	**Delinquent Account Collection History**	A log to keep track of efforts to collect overdue accounts
Form 13-15	**Notice of Dishonored Check**	A notice to a customer that the customer's check has bounced
Form 13-16	**Bill of Sale and Assignment**	A sample form of Bill of Sale

Chapter 14

Confidentiality and Non-Disclosure Agreements

....

In This Chapter

▶ Using Confidentiality Agreements

▶ Using Mutual Confidentiality Agreements

▶ Including key provisions of Confidentiality Agreements

▶ Protecting yourself fully in Confidentiality Agreements

▶ Distinguishing between Employee and Consultant Confidentiality Agreements

....

*T*here are numerous instances where you may want to share confidential information with another party. But the key to doing so safely is making sure that the other party has already been bound to respect the confidential information you provide them and not use the information to your detriment.

One common way to protect the secrecy of confidential information given to another party is through the use of a Confidentiality Agreement, which is sometimes also referred to as a Non-Disclosure Agreement.

In this chapter, I guide you as to when it makes sense to have a Confidentiality Agreement and what the key terms of this agreement need to include.

When Does a Confidentiality Agreement Make Sense?

When does it make sense to require another party to sign a Confidentiality Agreement? Well, there are probably many instances where it may be appropriate. But the principal situations are those where you wish to convey something valuable about your business or idea, but you want to ensure that the other side doesn't steal the information or use it without your approval.

Here are some typical situations where you may want to use a Confidentiality Agreement:

- ✔ Presenting an invention or business idea to a potential partner, investor, or distributor

- ✔ Sharing financial, marketing, and other information with a prospective buyer of your business

- ✔ Showing a new product or technology to a prospective buyer or licensee

- ✔ Receiving services from a company or individual who may have access to some sensitive information in providing those services

- ✔ Allowing employees access to confidential and proprietary information of your business in the course of their job

To Be or Not to Be . . . Mutual

Confidentiality Agreements come in two basic formats — a mutual agreement, or a one-sided agreement. Use the one-sided agreement when you are contemplating that only one side will be sharing confidential information with the other side. The mutual form is for situations where each side may potentially share confidential information.

Although there's always some appeal to using a mutual form of Confidentiality Agreement, I really shy away from the mutual form if I'm not planning to receive confidential information from the other side. One way to decide this early on is to let the other side know that you don't want to receive any of their confidential information, so you don't see the need for a mutual form if they ask for one.

A sample one-sided form of Confidentiality Agreement is presented as Form 14-1 on the CD-ROM. A mutual Confidentiality Agreement is presented here as Form 14-2 and also appears on the CD-ROM.

Mutual Non-Disclosure Agreement

Each undersigned party (the "Receiving Party") understands that the other party (the "Disclosing Party") has disclosed or may disclose information relating to (i) [specific business information to be disclosed] in conjunction or (ii) the Disclosing Party's business (including, without limitation, computer programs, names and expertise of employees and consultants, know-how, formulas, processes, ideas, inventions (whether patentable or not) schematics and other technical, business, financial, customer and product development plans, forecasts, strategies and information), which to the extent previously, presently, or subsequently disclosed to the Receiving Party is hereinafter referred to as "Proprietary Information" of the Disclosing Party.

Notwithstanding the foregoing, nothing will be considered "Proprietary Information" of the Disclosing Party unless either (1) it is first disclosed in tangible form and is conspicuously marked "Confidential," "Proprietary" or the like or (2) it is first disclosed in nontangible form and orally identified as confidential at the time of disclosure and is summarized in tangible form conspicuously marked "Confidential" within 30 days of the original disclosure.

In consideration of the parties' discussions and any access the Receiving Party may have to Proprietary Information of the Disclosing Party, the Receiving Party hereby agrees as follows:

1. <u>Use of Proprietary Information</u>. The Receiving Party agrees:

   (a.) to hold the Disclosing Party's Proprietary Information in confidence and to take reasonable precautions to protect such Proprietary Information (including, without limitation, all precautions the Receiving Party employs with respect to its confidential materials),

   (b.) to not divulge any such Proprietary Information or any information derived therefrom to any third person (except consultants, subject to the conditions stated below),

   (c.) not to make any use whatsoever at any time of such Proprietary Information except to evaluate internally whether to enter into the currently contemplated agreement with the Disclosing Party; and

   (d.) not to copy or reverse engineer any such Proprietary Information.

   Any employee or consultant given access to any such Proprietary Information must have a legitimate "need to know" and shall be similarly bound in writing. Without granting any right or license, the Disclosing Party agrees that the foregoing clauses (a), (b), (c) and (d)shall not apply to any information that the Receiving Party can document (1) is (or through no improper action or inaction by the Receiving Party or any affiliate, agent, consultant or employee) generally available to the public, or (2) was in its possession or known by it prior to

Form 14-2: Mutual Non-Disclosure Agreement.

(continued)

receipt from the Disclosing Party, or (3) was rightfully disclosed to it by a third party without restriction, provided the Receiving Party complies with any restrictions imposed by the third party, or (4) was independently developed without use of any Proprietary Information of the Disclosing Party by employees of the Receiving Party who have had no access to such information. The Receiving Party may make disclosures required by court order, provided the Receiving Party uses reasonable efforts to limit disclosure and to obtain confidential treatment or a protective order and has allowed the Disclosing Party to participate in the proceeding.

      2.   <u>Return of Proprietary Information</u>. Immediately upon (i) the decision by either party not to enter into the agreement contemplated by paragraph 1, or (ii) a request by the Disclosing Party at any time (which will be effective if actually received or three days after mailed first class postage prepaid to the Receiving Party), the Receiving Party will turn over to the Disclosing Party all Proprietary Information of the Disclosing Party and all documents or media containing any such Proprietary Information and any and all copies or extracts thereof.

      3.   <u>Disclosure</u>. Except to the extent required by law, neither party shall disclose the existence or subject matter of the negotiations or business relationship contemplated between the parties.

      4.   <u>Miscellaneous</u>. The Receiving Party acknowledges and agrees that due to the unique nature of the Disclosing Party's Proprietary Information, there can be no adequate remedy at law for any breach of its obligations hereunder, that any such breach may allow the Receiving Party or third parties to unfairly compete with the Disclosing Party resulting in irreparable harm to the Disclosing Party, and therefore, that upon any such breach or any threat thereof, the Disclosing Party shall be entitled to appropriate equitable relief in addition to whatever remedies it might have at law and to be indemnified by the Receiving Party from any loss or harm, including, without limitation, attorneys' fees, in connection with any breach or enforcement of the Receiving Party's obligations hereunder or the unauthorized use or release of any such Proprietary Information. The Receiving Party will notify the Disclosing Party in writing immediately upon the occurrence of any such unauthorized release or other breach of which it is aware. In the event that any of the provisions of this Agreement shall be held by a court or other tribunal of competent jurisdiction to be illegal, invalid or unenforceable, such provisions shall be limited or eliminated to the minimum extent necessary so that this Agreement shall otherwise remain in full force and effect. This Agreement shall be governed by the law of the State of [State] without regard to the conflicts of law provisions thereof. This Agreement supersedes all prior discussions and writing and constitutes the entire agreement between the parties with respect to the subject matter hereof. The prevailing party in any action to enforce this Agreement shall be entitled to costs and attorneys' fees. No waiver or modification of this Agreement will be binding upon either party unless made in writing and signed by a duly authorized representative of such party and no failure or delay in enforcing any right will be deemed a waiver. This Agreement shall be construed as to its fair meaning and not strictly for or against either party.

In witness whereof, the parties have executed this Agreement as of the
_____ day of _____, 20__.

_____   _____

By: _____   By: _____
Title: _____   Title: _____

The Key Elements of Confidentiality Agreements

Confidentiality Agreements don't have to be long and complicated. In fact, the good ones usually don't run more than a few pages long.

The key elements of Confidentiality Agreements:

- Identification of the parties
- Definition of what is defined to be confidential
- The scope of the confidentiality obligation by the receiving party
- The exclusions from confidential treatment
- The term of the agreement

The parties to the agreement

The *parties to the agreement* is usually a straightforward description set forth at the beginning of the contract. If it's an agreement where only one side is providing confidential information, then the disclosing party can be referred to as the *disclosing party* and the recipient of the information can simply be referred to as the *recipient*.

The one tricky part here is to think about whether any other people or companies may also be a party to the agreement. Does the recipient expect to show the confidential information to a related or affiliated company? To a partner? To an agent? If so, then consider asking those other parties to also sign a Confidentiality Agreement or become parties to the one being signed by the main company.

What the heck is deemed confidential?

This section of the agreement deals with defining what confidential information means. Is it any information? Is it information that is only marked in writing as "confidential"? Can oral information conveyed be deemed confidential?

On the one hand, you the disclosing party want this definition to be as broad as possible to make sure that the other side doesn't find a loophole and start using your valuable secrets.

On the other hand, if you are the recipient of the information, you have a legitimate desire to make sure that the information that you are supposed to keep secret is clearly identified so that you know what you can and can't do.

Oral information in particular can be tricky to deal with. Many recipients of information may insist that only information conveyed in writing need be kept confidential. And, of course, the party giving oral information may say that that is too narrow. The usual compromise is that oral information can be deemed confidential information, but that the disclosing party has to confirm to the other side in writing sometime shortly after it's disclosed so that the receiving party is now on notice as to what oral statements are deemed confidential. Check out Form 14-3, Letter Confirming Disclosure of Confidential Information, on the CD-ROM.

Scope of the confidentiality obligation

The core of the Confidentiality Agreement is a two-part obligation on the receiver of the information: to keep the confidential information in fact confidential and not use the confidential information itself.

So the first part is that the receiver of the confidential information has to keep it secret. And this usually means that the receiver has to take reasonable steps not to let others have access to it. For example, reasonable steps could include that only a few people within the receiver's company have access to the information and they are all informed of the nature of the confidentiality restrictions.

The second part is also crucial — that recipients can't use the information themselves. After all, the last thing you want is for them to take your great idea or mailing list and make a bizillion dollars from it.

If the scope of the Confidentiality Agreement is broad enough, then you can sue for damages or to stop the recipients if they breach either their confidentiality obligations or their non-use agreement.

Exclusions from confidentiality treatment

Every Confidentiality Agreement has certain exclusions from the obligations of the receiving party. These exclusions are intended to address situations where it would be unfair or too burdensome for the other side to keep the information confidential.

The common exclusions include information that is

- ✔ Already known to the recipient.
- ✔ Already publicly known (as long as the recipient didn't wrongfully release it to the public).
- ✔ Independently developed by the recipient without reference to or use of the confidential information of the disclosing party.
- ✔ Disclosed to the recipient by some other party who has no duty of confidentiality to the disclosing party.

The Confidentiality Agreement can also deal with the situation where the recipient of the information is forced to disclose the information through a legal process. The recipient should be allowed to do that if forced by court order without breaching the Confidentiality Agreement as long as the recipient has warned the disclosing party in advance of the legal proceeding.

Term of the agreement

How long should the Confidentiality Agreement last? Some attorneys may argue that the Confidentiality Agreement should last forever. Why should someone have the right to use your confidential information at any time?

But if you are the recipient of the confidential information, you probably want to insist on a definite term where the agreement ends. After all, most information after a certain number of years becomes useless anyway, and the cost of policing confidentiality obligations can become expensive if it's a "forever" obligation.

So if you agree to a term, what is reasonable? Well, it really depends on the industry you're in and the type of information conveyed. In some businesses, a few years may be acceptable because the technology may change so fast as to render the information pretty much worthless.

Most agreements that I see (if they have a term) have a time limit of three to ten years. But your Confidentiality Agreement also needs to say that, even if the term is ended, the disclosing party isn't giving up any other rights that it may have under copyright, patent, or other intellectual property laws.

More stuff that may make sense for your Confidentiality Agreement

You may also want to add some other bells and whistles to your Confidentiality Agreement to protect your company from further infringement issues, depending on your situation. Here are some ideas:

- ✔ **Employee solicitation.** If the recipient has significant access to your employees, you may want to insert a clause that prevents the recipient from soliciting or hiring your employees for 12 months. The other side may sometimes agree to that, with some carve-outs. For example, the recipients may want the limitation to apply only to those employees that they have come into contact with during their review of information or interviews.

- ✔ **Jurisdiction in case of a dispute.** If you are the disclosing party, you want to make sure that if there is any dispute as to whether the other side has lived up to its obligations, then the dispute will be handled exclusively in your city. You don't want to have to travel far away and incur additional costs to enforce your Confidentiality Agreement.

- ✔ **Injunction.** Make sure that you have a clause that gives you the right to injunctive relief to stop the other side from breaching the agreement. This clause simply says that you can get a court order stopping the other party from doing the breaching act (as opposed to just getting money damages after it's too late).

- ✔ **No rights in the receiving party.** It's sometimes helpful to have a clause that says that because you are going to share confidential information with them, the other side doesn't get diddlysquat rights to your ideas or even a right to enter into a deal with you (the so-called "diddlysquat" clause).

Confidentiality and Invention Assignment Agreements with Employees

Employees, especially if the business is high-tech–oriented, often have access to lots of the company's confidential information. Companies also expect their employees to come up with ideas, work product, and inventions that are useful to the business.

To make sure that employees keep the company's proprietary information confidential, require them to sign a Confidentiality and Invention Assignment Agreement. This agreement deals with the confidentiality issue, but it can also provide that the ideas, work product, and inventions that the employee creates relating to the company business belong to the company — not to the employee.

This seems fair, doesn't it? Because the company is paying the employee to produce such stuff, you want to make sure that the company has the legal right to these developments.

A good Employee Confidentiality and Invention Assignment Agreement covers the following key points:

- ✔ The employee may not use any of the company's confidential information for his or her own benefit or use.

- ✔ The employee must promptly disclose to the company any inventions, ideas, discoveries, and work product related to the company's business that he or she makes during the period of employment.

- ✔ The company is the owner of such inventions, ideas, discoveries, and work product.

- ✔ The employee's employment with the company does not and will not breach any agreement or duty that the employee has with anyone else, nor may the employee disclose to the company or use on its behalf any confidential information belonging to others.

- ✔ The employee's confidentiality obligations under the agreement will continue after termination of employment.

- ✔ The agreement does not by itself represent any guarantee of continued employment.

Form 14-4 on the CD-ROM shows a sample form Employee Confidentiality and Invention Assignment Agreement.

Confidentiality and Invention Assignment Agreements with Consultants

Your consultants may have access to lots of the company's confidential information. And you may expect the consultants to come up with ideas, work product, and inventions useful to your business.

In areas where you are particularly sensitive about confidentiality and the company's ownership of the product developed, require consultants to sign a Confidentiality and Invention Assignment Agreement. This agreement deals with the confidentiality issue, but can also provide that the ideas, work product, and inventions that the consultant creates in connection with services performed for your business belong to the company (not the consultant).

A good Consultant Confidentiality and Invention Assignment Agreement covers the following key points:

✔ The consultant may not use any of the company's confidential information for his or her own benefit or use.

✔ The consultant must promptly disclose to the company any inventions, ideas, discoveries, and work product related to the company's business that he or she makes during the period of work.

✔ The company owns such inventions, ideas, discoveries, and work product.

✔ The consultant's work with the company does not and will not breach any agreement or duty that the consultant has with anyone else, nor may the consultant disclose to the company or use on its behalf any confidential information belonging to others.

✔ The consultant's confidentiality obligations under the agreement will continue after termination of the relationship.

Form 14-5 shows a sample Consultant Confidentiality and Invention Assignment Agreement. This form is very extensive and pro-company–oriented.

Forms on the CD-ROM

Form 14-1	**Confidentiality Agreement (Not Mutual)**	An agreement where the recipient agrees to keep confidential an idea, product, or other confidential information presented
Form 14-2	**Mutual Non-Disclosure Agreement**	An agreement allowing two companies to exchange confidential information with mutual protection obligations
Form 14-3	**Letter Confirming Disclosure of Confidential Information**	A letter confirming in writing the disclosure of confidential information given to another party
Form 14-4	**Employee Confidentiality and Invention Assignment Agreement**	An agreement in which the employee agrees to keep company information confidential and to assign to the company business-related inventions developed by the employee
Form 14-5	**Consultant Confidentiality and Invention Assignment Agreement**	An agreement that requires the consultant to keep company information confidential and to assign to the company ownership of inventions and materials developed as part of the work for the company

Part IV
The Brave New World of the Web

In this part . . .

Doing business on the Internet presents all kinds of challenges. Truth is, many legal questions haven't been answered yet when it comes to things like copyrights, fair use, and linking. Heaven knows you don't want your business on the wrong end of a lawsuit that helps decide what the laws are going to be, so your best bet is to cover your butt. The forms in this part can help.

Chapter 15

Contracts Related to Web Site Creation

*B*usinesses of every size are embracing the World Wide Web. The Web is fundamentally changing how almost every business is conducted, and a growing company has to have a Web strategy if it intends to become large and successful. Even large companies that are already successful have to implement a great Web strategy in order to stay successful.

When creating a business Web site, you face numerous legal, business, intellectual property, and contractual issues. In this chapter, I navigate you through some of the trap doors so that you can properly set up your Web site.

(Chicken Chow) Domain Name

In order to establish your business Web site, you need to get a *domain name* that hasn't already been taken. The domain name is your address on the Web.

The domain name has two parts. The second part, indicated in the extension, is the top-level domain (such as .com, .org, .edu, .gov, .mil, or .us). The first part identifies the site's name (IBM, Intel, and so on). So, for example, Microsoft's domain name is: microsoft.com.

Businesses (commercial enterprises) end with `.com`, educational institutions end with `.edu`, government offices with `.gov`, military sites end in `.mil`, networking organizations end in `.net`, and miscellaneous organizations end in `.org`. Sites in countries other than the United States typically have a two-letter zone such as `.fr` for France or `.au` for Australia.

Because each domain name has to be unique, check to make sure that the name you want hasn't already been taken. This experience can be frustrating because many domain names have already been registered. Following are just a few of the names that are already taken:

- `favoritesites.com`
- `e-visionary.com`
- `ibm.com`
- `money.com`
- `software.com`
- `pokerchampion.com`

Running a check on a domain name

Say that you have come up with a catchy domain name for your business — how about `catchyname.com`?

To check the domain name availability, you can go to the Network Solutions' Web site (at `www.networksolutions.com`) or other commercial sites (such as `www.register.com`).

Registering a domain name

You can register a name quickly online. The charge for covering two years of ownership is $70 to register a domain name. After the two years, maintaining the name costs $35 a year. Some registrars have started to charge less.

Of Domains and Trademarks

Registering a domain name doesn't give you any trademark rights to that name, but domain names and trademark rights can overlap. Trademarks aim to prevent confusion between familiar words, symbols, and distinctive combinations used in a commercial manner. A company may choose not to register every name associated with its products as a domain name. However, that name may still qualify as a trademark because it is associated with that company. Consequently, the ownership and use of domain names has caused some disputes.

In your registration application, you certify that using the proposed domain name doesn't interfere with or infringe the right of any third party in any jurisdiction with respect to trademark or any other intellectual property right. Furthermore, you have to agree to give up a domain name if a competing claimant presents evidence that the granted domain name is identical to a valid and subsisting trademark or service mark owned by someone else.

Before you spend a lot of time creating your Web site, consider hiring an experienced search organization to perform a domain name and related trademark search. Several companies, such as Thomson & Thomson, routinely perform these searches for less than $500. These searches reveal whether the desired domain name and its variants are still unregistered. They also determine whether other entities or people — who may later make a proprietary claim on the desired domain name — are already using the name, or variants of it, on the Web.

You can find the official Trademark Registration form on Form 15-1 on the CD-ROM. This form lets you register with the Patent and Trademark Office (PTO). Form 15-2 on the CD-ROM shows a sample cover letter for the PTO. You can also register online through www.uspto.gov.

Domain Name Purchase Agreements

Because many domain names are already taken, you may find that you have to purchase your desired domain name for your Web site from an existing registered holder. If so, you want to cover some key points in a Domain Name Purchase Agreement.

✔ **Transfer.** The agreement needs to provide that the domain name holder transfers all right, title, and interest to the name, and will execute all necessary paperwork with Network Solutions Inc. (the main registrar of domain names) to effect the transfer.

> ✔ **Representations and warranties.** The purchaser of the domain name may want to get various representations and warranties, such as that the seller is the rightful owner of the name and that there are no liens and encumbrances on the name.
>
> ✔ **Payment.** The payment terms need to specify how much and when the amount will be paid. Think about payments in installments, with one installment paid after all necessary paperwork to effect the name transfer has been accepted by Network Solutions Inc. Good domain names can get very expensive to buy — `WallStreet.com` sold for $1 million and `business.com` for $7.5 million!

See Form 15-3 for a sample Domain Name Purchase Agreement.

Web Site Development Contracts

Unless you happen to be a techie-type person or have nothing better to do with your time than try to understand Web design, HTML, and Web graphics, consider contracting with a Web site developer to develop your site. Finding the right developer is not always easy, but, when you do, make sure that the developer signs a well-prepared contract (and not the developer's standard form). These contracts can cover many issues, which I discuss in the following section, "Ownership and intellectual property issues."

A sample form of a pro-customer–oriented Web Site Development Agreement is included as Form 15-4 on the CD-ROM.

Being master of your domain name

Thinking of an unused domain name can be a frustrating process. Here are a few tips to keep in mind before you expend a great deal of money promoting a name:

✔ The name cannot contain any spaces nor any of the following characters: @, #, $, %, &, or *.

✔ Avoid common names — they are most likely to be taken already.

✔ Keep your name simple so users can easily remember it.

✔ Do a trademark search on the name.

DOMAIN NAME PURCHASE AGREEMENT

This is an agreement between _____ ("Purchaser") and _____ ("Seller").

WHEREAS, Seller is the legal owner of the World Wide Web domain name "_____" (the "Domain Name"); and

WHEREAS, Purchaser wishes to purchase the Domain Name and all related rights thereto;

THEREFORE, the parties agree as follows:

1.   Purchase. Seller hereby transfers and assigns to Purchaser:

    (a)   all right, title and interest in and to the Domain Name;

    (b)   any registered or unregistered trademarks, service marks, copyrights or other intellectual property or proprietary rights based on a related to the Domain Name; and

    (c)   all goodwill associated with the Domain Name.

2.   Payment. As consideration for the matters set forth in Section 1, Purchaser agrees to pay the sum of (a) $_____ on the date hereof, and (b) $_____ when the Domain Name has been fully transferred on the books and records of Network Solutions, Inc. pursuant to Section 3 hereof.

3.   Registration of Transfer. Seller is simultaneously executing and notarizing the attached Domain Name Transfer Agreement to be filed with Network Solutions, Inc. Seller shall cooperate as reasonably requested by Purchaser to ensure that the Domain Name is validly transferred to Purchaser.

4.   Representations and Warranties of Seller. Seller hereby represents and warrants to Purchaser as follows:

    (a)   Seller is the sole owner of all right, title and interest to the Domain Name.

    (b)   The Domain Name is being transferred to Purchaser free of any liens, encumbrances, restrictions, licenses, or security interests.

    (c)   Seller has the right, power and authority to enter into this Agreement.

    (d)   To Seller's best knowledge, the Domain Name and use of the Domain Name by Purchaser does not and will not violate or infringe any trademark, service mark or other right of any third party.

    (e)   The Domain Name has not been, and is not currently, the subject of any litigation, claims, arbitration or other legal proceeding nor has the Seller received any notice of any such pending items.

Form 15-3: Domain Name Purchase Agreement.   *(continued)*

5.   MISCELLANEOUS

(a)   Choice of Law. This Agreement, and any dispute arising from the relationship between the parties to this Agreement, shall be governed by [e.g., California] law, excluding any laws that direct the application of another jurisdictions laws.

(b)   Attorney Fees Provision. In any litigation, arbitration, or other proceeding by which one party either seeks to enforce its rights under this Agreement (whether in contract, tort, or both) or seeks a declaration of any rights or obligations under this Agreement, the prevailing party shall be awarded its reasonable attorney fees, and costs and expenses incurred.

(c)   Modification of Agreement. This Agreement may be supplemented, amended, or modified only by the mutual agreement of the parties. No supplement, amendment, or modification of this Agreement shall be binding unless it is in writing and signed by all parties.

(d)   Entire Agreement. This Agreement and all other agreements, exhibits, and schedules referred to in this Agreement constitutes the final, complete, and exclusive statement of the terms of the agreement between the parties pertaining to the subject matter of this Agreement and supersedes all prior and contemporaneous understandings or agreements of the parties. This Agreement may not be contradicted by evidence of any prior or contemporaneous statements or agreements. No party has been induced to enter into this Agreement by, nor is any party relying on, any representation, understanding, agreement, commitment or warranty outside those expressly set forth in this Agreement.

(e)   Ambiguities. Each party and its counsel have participated fully in the review and revision of this Agreement. Any rule of construction to the effect that ambiguities are to be resolved against the drafting party shall not apply in interpreting this Agreement. The language in this Agreement shall be interpreted as to its fair meaning and not strictly for or against any party.

(f)   Necessary Acts, Further Assurances. The parties shall at their own cost and expense execute and deliver such further documents and instruments and shall take such other actions as may be reasonably required or appropriate to evidence or carry out the intent and purposes of this Agreement.

(g)   Specific Performance. The parties acknowledge that it will be impossible to measure in money the damage to them caused by any failure to comply with the covenants set forth herein, that each such covenant is material, and that in the event of any such failure, the injured party will not have an adequate remedy at law or in damages. Therefore, the parties consent to the issuance of an injunction or the enforcement of other equitable remedies against them at the suit of the other, without bond or other security, to compel performance of all of the terms of this Agreement, and waive the defense of the availability of relief in damages.

(h)   Notice. Any notices required or permitted to be given hereunder shall be given in writing and shall be delivered (a)°in person, (b)°by certified mail, postage prepaid, return receipt requested, (c)°by facsimile, or (d)°by a commercial overnight courier that guarantees next day delivery and provides a receipt, and such notices shall be addressed as follows:

If to _____: _____
                             _____
                             _____
                             Attention:
                             Fax:

If to _____: _____
                             _____
                             _____
                             Attention:
                             Fax:

or to such other address as either party may from time to time specify in writing to the other party. Any notice shall be effective only upon delivery, which for any notice given by facsimile shall mean notice which has been received by the party to whom it is sent as evidenced by confirmation slip.

    (i)   <u>Representation on Authority of Parties/Signatories</u>. Each person signing this Agreement represents and warrants that he or she is duly authorized and has legal capacity to execute and deliver this Agreement. Each party represents and warrants to the other that the execution and delivery of the Agreement and the performance of such partys obligations hereunder have been duly authorized and that the Agreement is a valid and legal agreement binding on such party and enforceable in accordance with its terms.

Date: _____   _____
                                    Purchaser

                                    _____
                                    Seller

(continued)

EXHIBIT 1

DOMAIN NAME TRANSFER AGREEMENT
WITH NETWORK SOLUTIONS, INC.

Ownership and intellectual property issues

The Web Site Development Agreement needs to clearly address the issue of ownership and intellectual property issues related to the content, screens, software, and information developed. The agreement can address the following points:

- ✔ The Web site developer is an independent contractor performing a "work for hire" service under the Copyright Act.

- ✔ All screens, graphics, domain names, content, and the look-and-feel of the site developed will be owned solely by the site owner, together with all underlying software, object code, digital programming, source code, and the like.

- ✔ All intellectual property developed in connection with the site will be owned solely by the site owner.

- ✔ The developer will not infringe or violate the copyright and other intellectual property rights of third parties in developing the site.

- ✔ The site owner will receive a perpetual, irrevocable, worldwide, royalty-free transferable license to any prior intellectual property that the developer owns that it is bundling or using in the site.

Hiring someone to develop your Web site

Unless computers are your stock and trade, you may prefer to have someone else develop your Web site. Web site development companies have sprung up like mushrooms in the last few years. They all promise to get your Web site up and running, but their prices vary from $1,000 to $100,000, depending on the bells and whistles you want (e-commerce capabilities, for instance, cost more). Also, some companies (such as www.bigstep.com) now even offer free basic Web sites. Here are some places to start looking for a developer for your Web site:

✔ Review a number of commercial Web sites. Sites often list the developer and include a link to the developer's Web site.

✔ Ask your business associates whom they have used and what experience they had.

✔ Check newspaper and magazine listings — many Web site developers now advertise their services.

The development process

The development agreement can address various issues associated with the development of the site, progress payments, and acceptance procedures. Such provisions may include the following:

✔ A timetable for completion of the site, including specific milestones as progress is made on site development

✔ Payment mechanisms, whether by the hour or the project, plus a maximum on the amount to be incurred

✔ A mechanism allowing the company to change specifications for the site, without the change orders resulting in exorbitant extra costs or delays

✔ The developer's timely provision of documentation and source codes for all software associated with the site

✔ Assumption of responsibility by the developer for transferring the site — including all software — to the company's server and (if applicable) overseeing the site's installation on that server

✔ Alternative Web pages (with graphics) provided by the developer for the company to review and decide upon

✔ A commitment by the developer to a period of joint beta testing of the site and a subsequent acceptance testing period during which the company may evaluate the site on its premises to make sure that the site functions as anticipated and in accordance with the agreement

✔ The company's right to reject the site if it doesn't meet designated specifications and the company's options regarding corrections at the time of a rejection

Functionality of the site

The Web Site Development Agreement should (but doesn't absolutely have to) clearly specify the anticipated functionality and technological requirements of the site, including provisions that address the following:

- Use by the developer of the most current standards of technology in development of the site

- Maximum download time for any Web page

- Compatibility of the site with the latest versions of Internet browser software, especially the Microsoft, Netscape, and AOL browsers

- Functionality of the site 24 hours a day, seven days a week, except for scheduled maintenance/downtime

- The number of users who can simultaneously access the site, as well as response time for user requests

- The site owner's ability to make additions, corrections, or modifications to the site without interference with site operations

- Security safeguards, procedures, and firewalls that the site must contain

- Expected functionality of online credit verification and acceptance procedures

- Scope and procedure for the company to easily access, record, and compile information about the site's users and customers

Problems and corrective measures

The Web Site Development Agreement should (but doesn't have to) address the problems that may arise and the developer's duty to promptly correct such problems, including the following:

- The developer's duty to fix any bugs and failed links, including the maximum time for correction

- The revision of the site to comply with the functionality specifications

- Any particular warranties or disclaimers by the developer

- The developer's assurance that the software for the site is free of any viruses or disabling devices

Covenants of the developer

The development agreement may impose a variety of additional duties on the developer, such as:

- ✔ The developer must comply with all applicable laws in connection with its activities.

- ✔ The developer must maintain satisfactory insurance and provide proof of its policies.

- ✔ The services must be completed in a professional, high-quality manner by experienced individuals.

- ✔ No subcontracting of services can occur without the approval of the site owner.

Confidentiality

The site owner usually wants to obligate the developer to keep all confidential or proprietary information that the developer learns about the company or the company's customers strictly confidential. The site owner also wants to make sure that the developer may not use such information other than in connection with the developer's obligations under the agreement. The agreement may also require that the developer's employees and consultants working on the site-development project execute a Confidentiality and Invention Assignment Agreement (check out the discussion in Chapter 14).

Web Site Content License Agreements

In creating a Web site, you may want to include lots of information or advice on the site. Although you can create all of this information on your own (or hire writers to do it for you), sometimes the most efficient way is to find information, articles, or other advice already written somewhere else and acquire the right to post them to your site.

The agreement that can accomplish this is a Web Site Content License Agreement. Basically, this agreement gives you (the "Licensee") the right to use (a "License") content owned by a third party (the "Licensor") for placement on your site.

Of course, most people who own valuable content aren't just going to hand it over to you for free and give you the right to do anything with it willy-nilly. So the Web Site Content License Agreement lays out the scope of the license, the payment terms, the length of the license, and other key provisions. Here are some of the more important ones:

- ✔ **Scope of the license.** The Licensor generally wants the agreement to have a clear statement as to where and how you can use his materials. You need to clearly spell out what it is that you are licensing and the different places you plan to use the materials. The Licensor wants the licensed materials posted only on your Web site and not elsewhere.

- ✔ **Exclusive versus nonexclusive.** In most instances, the Licensor grants only a nonexclusive right to the content. In some circumstances, you can limit who the Licensor licenses the content to (for example, no other license to your competitors for some period of time).

- ✔ **Term of the license.** The agreement must spell out how long the license will be good for. The best term from the Licensee's perspective is to get a perpetual (forever) license, but many times the Licensor agrees only to a set time period. If you are the Licensee, think about renewal rights.

- ✔ **Payment.** The agreement has a payment clause, which spells out how much the Licensor pays for the license, and by when.

- ✔ **Representations and warranties of Licensor.** The Licensee may request some important statements from the Licensor, such as that the Licensor owns the licensed content, that it isn't libelous or in breach of someone else's rights, and that the Licensor has the right to grant the license.

- ✔ **Indemnification.** The Licensee asks the Licensor to indemnify the Licensee in the event the Licensor breaches its representations and warranties.

- ✔ **Covenants of the Licensee.** The Licensor typically expects some promises from the Licensee, such as that the site will be operated in a professional legal manner and that the licensed content placed on the site will have a proper acknowledgement that the content is the copyrighted work of the Licensor.

- ✔ **Termination.** The agreement usually deals with termination issues, such as when the Licensor or Licensee has the right to terminate the agreement and the consequences of termination.

You can review a sample Web Site Content License Agreement in this chapter and Form 15-6 on the CD-ROM accompanying this book. This form is pro-Licensee–oriented.

WEB SITE CONTENT
LICENSE AGREEMENT

This is an agreement between _____, a _____ corporation ("Licensee") and _____, a _____ ("Licensor").

WHEREAS, Licensee has established a World Wide Web site and affiliated sites with the Web addresses of _____, _____, and _____ (the "Site"), and Licensor has various information or content that Licensee wishes to license;

NOW, THEREFORE, the parties hereby agree as follows:

1. <u>License.</u>

(a) Licensor hereby grants to Licensee a nonexclusive worldwide license (the "License") for the use, publication and posting on the Site of the information and content itemized in Exhibit A (the "Licensed Content").

(b) Licensor shall provide the Licensed Content within thirty (30) days in a format that will allow Licensee to easily upload or post the Licensed Content onto the Site.

2. <u>Payment.</u>

In connection with the License, Licensee shall pay to the Licensor the following fees: _____. Such payment(s) shall be due on: _____.

3. <u>Term.</u>

(a) The term of this Agreement shall be for _____ (_) years and will be automatically renewed for successive one (1) year periods unless either party elects to terminate this Agreement effective as of the end of the initial term or renewal term(s) as appropriate.

(b) Notice of termination shall be made no later than 60 days prior to the end of the initial term or renewal term(s), as appropriate.

4. <u>Representations and Warranties Regarding Licensed Content.</u>

(a) Licensor hereby represents and warrants that: (1) the Licensed Content is owned or licensed by Licensor and does not breach or infringe any copyright, common law right, or other right of any third party; (2) the Licensed Content does not contain any matter which is scandalous, libelous, obscene, an invasion of privacy, or otherwise unlawful; and (3) Licensor has the right, power and authority to enter into and perform this Agreement.

(b) Licensor shall defend, indemnify, and hold harmless Licensee from any claims, demands, liabilities, losses, damages, judgments, and the like (including but not limited to attorneys' fees incurred) directly or indirectly relating to any claim by a third party of infringement of any copyright or other right with respect to the Licensed Content and from the breach of the other representations and warranties contained in this Section 4.

Form 15-6: Web Site Content License Agreement.   *(continued)*

(c) During the term of this agreement, Licensor shall not license or assign the Licensed Content to the following competitors of Licensee: _____, _____, and _____.

5. Licensee Covenants.

(a) Licensee covenants that the Site will be operated in a professional manner in compliance with all laws in all material respects.

(b) Licensee covenants to properly acknowledge on the Site that the Licensed Content is the copyrighted work of Licensor.

6. Miscellaneous.

This Agreement shall be governed by and construed in accordance with the laws of the State of __[State]__ without regard to conflict of law principles. If Licensee changes the Site Web address, this License shall be deemed to apply to such changed sites at Licensee's discretion. This Agreement contains the entire agreement and understanding between the parties hereto with respect to its subject matter and supersedes any prior or contemporaneous written or oral agreements, representations, discussions, proposals, understandings, and the like respecting the subject matter hereof. The headings and captions of this Agreement are provided for convenience only and are intended to have no effect in construing or interpreting this Agreement. The language in all parts of this Agreement shall be in all cases construed according to its fair meaning and not strictly for or against either party. The prevailing party in any dispute shall be awarded its attorneys' fees and expenses incurred. The parties will cooperate with each other as reasonably requested to effectuate the purposes and provisions of this Agreement. This Agreement may be amended only by a writing signed by the parties.

Dated: _____

By: _____ ("Licensee")

Title: _____

By: _____ ("Licensor")

Title: _____

Forms on the CD-ROM

Form 15-1	**Trademark Registration Form**	An official document for registering a trademark with the Patent and Trademark Office
Form 15-2	**Cover Letter to USPTO**	Cover Letter for the Trademark Registration
Form 15-3	**Domain Name Purchase Agreement**	A sample agreement for the purchase of an Internet domain name owned by a third party
Form 15-4	**Checklist of Issues for Web Site Development Contracts**	A checklist of issues to review when negotiatng and drafting a Web Site Development Agreement
Form 15-5	**Web Site Development Agreement**	A sample pro-customer–orinted agreement for development of a business-oriented Web site a by third party developer
Form 15-6	**Web Site Content License Agreement**	A sample agreement granting a Web site owner the right to post content owned by a third party on the site

Chapter 16

Contracts and Policies Related to Web Site Operation

● ●

In This Chapter

▶ Understanding Web Site Hosting Agreements

▶ Reviewing common notices and disclaimers on Web sites

▶ Making the most of a Terms of Use Agreement

▶ Providing for online sales

▶ Exploring a Privacy Policy

▶ Looking over E-Commerce Agreements

▶ Using Affiliate Agreements

● ●

A Web site helps you tap into a whole new channel of business opportunity, but you also need to contend with some legal issues: How do you handle user privacy? Do you need special provisions for online sales? This chapter shows you the notices, agreements, and other policies you need on your site.

Web Site Hosting Agreements

After you develop the Web site and ready it for viewing by the outside world, you need to transfer it to a server connected to the Internet. Most Web site owners decide to have a third-party hosting service make the site available, and a Web Site Hosting Agreement usually embodies the terms and conditions of such services. And yes, you want to look for the "Host with the Most!"

The key provisions for Web Site Hosting Agreements include the following:

▸ **Scope of Services.** The document needs to precisely identify the specific services provided by the hosting service.

▸ **Updates and Modifications.** The agreement needs to spell out the mechanism and obligations of the hosting service for updates and modifications to the site.

✔ **Performance.** The agreement needs to address various performance issues, including minimum performance criteria, uptime, server response time, problem response time, technical assistance, and remedies for system failure.

✔ **Termination and Transfer.** The Web site owner should have relative flexibility to terminate the agreement for any reason. Upon termination, the hosting service should be obligated to use reasonable efforts to transfer the site to a successor hosting service.

✔ **Warranties.** The Web site owner will want a number of warranties from the host provider, primarily dealing with performance and the technology provided by the hosting service.

✔ **Liability.** The agreement needs to address the liability for breach by the hosting service, although many providers attempt to limit their liability to the amount of fees paid to the provider under the agreement.

Web Site Notices and Disclaimers

The Web site owner may want to consider adding various notices and disclaimers on the site. Review the common notices in the following sections. Sometimes the owner puts several of these in one place under a "Legal Notices" or "Terms of Use" section.

Copyright notice

The United States Copyright Act protects information, logos, and graphics on a Web site. Copyright status can prevent others from copying and using tangible works of authorship, such as information contained on a Web page.

You should place a copyright notice on your site. A typical copyright notice is:

Copyright© 2002 by ABC, Inc. All Rights Reserved.

The CD-ROM contains another sample copyright notice as Form 16-1.

Disclosure of terms of use or online contract

The site needs to contain continuing prominent references to the Terms of Use Agreement or other online contract for purposes of users of the site or buyers of goods or services from the site. A disclosure can read — with a hyperlink to the full text of the contract — as follows:

The use of this site, and the terms and conditions for the sale of any goods and services, is governed by a <u>Terms of Use Agreement</u>. By using this site you acknowledge that you have read the <u>Terms of Use Agreement</u> and the disclaimers and caveats contained in this site, and that you accept and will be bound by the terms thereof.

The CD-ROM contains this disclaimer as Form 16-2.

General disclaimers of liability

The site can contain a limitation of liability of the Web site owner — including the typical uppercased and bold-faced disclaimers about goods, services, or information being provided "as-is" with no representations or warranties — and disclaimers of any implied warranties of merchantability and fitness for a particular purpose. For example:

THE SERVICE AND CONTENT FROM OR THROUGH THIS SITE ARE PROVIDED "AS-IS," "AS AVAILABLE," AND ALL WARRANTIES, EXPRESS OR IMPLIED, ARE DISCLAIMED (INCLUDING BUT NOT LIMITED TO THE DISCLAIMER OF ANY IMPLIED WARRANTIES OF MERCHANTABILITY AND FITNESS FOR A PARTICULAR PURPOSE). THE INFORMATION HEREIN MAY CONTAIN BUGS, ERRORS, PROBLEMS OR OTHER LIMITATIONS. THE OWNER OF THIS SITE ASSUMES NO LIABILITY OR RESPONSIBILITY FOR ANY ERRORS OR OMISSIONS ON THIS SITE.

Form 16-3 on the CD-ROM provides a broader form of disclaimer, whereas Form 16-4 provides a short reference to the disclaimer that you can place on the site.

Hyperlink disclaimers

A Web site often contains hyperlinks to other sites. Your company may want to consider including a *link disclaimer* that alerts the users of the site that the site owner does not endorse or approve the linked sites. Consider adding a paragraph similar to the following:

This site contains links to other Internet sites. Such links are not endorsements of any products or services in such sites, and no information in such site has been endorsed or approved by us.

The CD-ROM includes an alternative sample hyperlink as Form 16-5.

Limitation on access by minors

Any company doing business prohibited to minors needs to prominently display a disclaimer alerting users to this fact. Posting this message as a gateway to the Web site's homepage is wise, so that it can warn excluded or easily offendable users that they should not proceed onto the site. For example:

> **WARNING. This site contains sexually oriented adult material intended for individuals 18 years of age or older. If you are not yet 18, if adult material offends you, or if you are accessing this site from any country or locale where adult material is prohibited by law, PLEASE LEAVE NOW! If you understand and accept these terms, you may ENTER.**

Trademarks

Many sites refer to registered trademarks. You may want to include a disclosure as to the specifics of trademark status, such as the following one from the Microsoft site at www.microsoft.com:

> **TRADEMARKS: Microsoft, Windows, Windows NT, MSN, The Microsoft Network and/or other Microsoft products referenced herein are either trademarks or registered trademarks of Microsoft. Other product and company names mentioned herein may be trademarks of their respective owners.**

Privacy policy

The site may need to refer to the Company's "Privacy Policy" concerning how information from a user or registrant of the site will be used. See the section later in this chapter on "Privacy Policy."

Terms of Use Agreements

Just like in real-world stores, libraries, parking lots, and amusement parks, you need to post on your Internet site notices and policies that you expect to govern the use of materials, services, and goods that you provide.

Web sites should typically include a "Terms of Use Agreement" that is intended to act as a "contract" between the Web site owner and the viewers/customers of the site. Word the contract carefully to protect the company from liability and address the key terms and conditions for the provision of information, goods, or services. Make the contract available and display it conspicuously. Ideally, each page of the site or key portions of the site should contain a statement that use of the site or the purchase of goods and services through the site is governed by the contract with a hyperlink to the full contract.

See Form 16-2 on the CD-ROM for a sample reference to a Terms of Use Agreement.

The general expectation is that a Web site owner can enforce such online agreements. No assurances in this regard exist, however, and a number of cases addressing this issue will probably be litigated in the coming years.

Key provisions of Terms of Use Agreements

Important provisions in Terms of Use Agreements include the following:

- **Limited Right to Use.** The agreement needs to identify any limitations on the permitted use of any information made available, together with notices regarding the restrictions on copying, reuse, and distribution of information provided.

- **Indemnification.** The agreement can require the user to indemnify, defend, and hold you and your affiliates harmless from any liability, loss, claim, and expense, including attorneys' fees and expenses, related to a user's violation of the agreement or use of the Web site.

- **Disclaimers.** You generally want to make disclaimers, with notice that you are providing the information "as-is" with no representations and warranties. Check out the section "Web Site Notices and Disclaimers," earlier in this chapter.

- **Forum Selection.** In this provision, the company states that any person with a dispute or claim must bring the claim in the city that is the company's principal place of business. This forum selection may help you avoid being sued in foreign states or territories.

- **Remedies.** You need to feature the limitation of the remedies available to a disgruntled party (for example, a waiver of any indirect, consequential, or speculative damages or lost profits) prominently in the agreement.

- **Statute of Limitations.** The agreement can include a shortened Statute of Limitations in the event of any claim brought by an unhappy customer. For example: "Any cause of action by the customer must be instituted within one (1) year after the claim arises or be forever waived and barred."

- **Acceptance of the Agreement.** Unlike traditional agreements, no opportunity to collect the customer's signature before use exists. Most Web sites provide that a Terms of Use Agreement governs the use of the site, with a hyperlink to the agreement (see sample language under "Web Site Notices and Disclaimers," earlier in this chapter).

Form 16-6 on the CD-ROM provides a sample Terms of Use Agreement.

Additional provisions for the sales of services or goods

If the site sells services or goods, the following additional provisions may be appropriate:

✔ **Services or Goods.** The contract should include a clearly worded description of the goods or services provided by the company.

✔ **Payment for Goods and Payment of Applicable Taxes.** The agreement should state that the customer must pay any charges and any sales or use tax. Be careful what you say about shipping costs — customers have sued companies for misleading customers about their shipping charge.

✔ **Limitation of Liability.** A provision stating that the company is not liable for anything other than the price of the product or service purchased is usually desirable.

✔ **Refund and Return Policies.** You need to state your refund and return policy because certain states require this by law. The policy should include arrangements to either mail a full refund or ship substitute goods if more than a certain number of days elapses from the time you receive payment.

You can state all of these provisions as part of the Terms of Use Agreement, or as a separate online contract where users use their mouse to click on phrases such as "accept"/"agree" or "decline"/"don't agree" to the agreement. These clicks become the user's acceptance of the terms.

The CD-ROM includes a sample of an Online Contract as Form 16-7.

Privacy Policy

Each site that asks the user to submit any personal information needs to establish a Privacy Policy. You can make this policy part of your Terms of Use Agreement, or list it separately. If you require a large amount of personal information from users, listing this policy separately is best.

The Privacy Policy addresses the company's rights to the use of any personal information from the user and whether the company keeps this information strictly confidential or uses it for other purposes or provides it to other parties. Providing a clear explanation is important for legal reasons, but you may also find that being up front with your users about your intentions may enhance your relationship with them. Make sure that your Privacy Policy doesn't restrict you from disclosing information if legally compelled to do so.

The CD-ROM contains a sample Privacy Policy as Form 16-8. You can also see one right here.

Privacy Policy

Our Commitment to Privacy
Our Privacy Policy was developed as an extension of our commitment to combine the highest-quality products and services with the highest level of integrity in dealing with our clients and partners. The Policy is designed to assist you in understanding how we collect, use and safeguard the personal information you provide to us and to assist you in making informed decisions when using our site and our products and services. This statement will be continuously assessed against new technologies, business practices and our customers' needs.

What Information Do We Collect?
When you visit our Web site you may provide us with two types of information: personal information you knowingly choose to disclose that is collected on an individual basis and Web site use information collected on an aggregate basis as you and others browse our Web site.

1.   Personal Information You Choose to Provide

Credit Card Information
If you choose to purchase products or services from us or our partners, you may need to give personal information and authorization to obtain information from various credit services. For example, you may need to provide the following information:

> Name
> Mailing address
> Email address
> Credit card number
> Home and business phone number
> Other personal information (i.e. mother's maiden name)

Email Information
In addition to providing the foregoing information to our partners, if you choose to correspond further with us through email, we may retain the content of your email messages together with your email address and our responses. We provide the same protections for these electronic communications that we employ in the maintenance of information received by mail and telephone.

2.   Web Site Use Information

Similar to other commercial Web sites, our Web site utilizes a standard technology called "cookies" (see explanation below, "What Are Cookies?") and Web server logs to collect information about how our Web site is used. Information gathered through cookies and Web server logs may include the date and time of visits, the pages viewed, time spent at our Web site, and the Web sites visited just before and just after our Web site. This information is collected on an aggregate basis. None of this information is associated with you as an individual.

(continued)

Form 16-8: Privacy Policy.

How Do We Use the Information That You Provide to Us?

Broadly speaking, we use personal information for purposes of administering our business activities, providing customer service and making available other products and services to our customers and prospective customers. Occasionally, we may also use the information we collect to notify you about important changes to our Web site, new services and special offers we think you will find valuable. The lists used to send you product and service offers are developed and managed under our traditional corporate standards designed to safeguard the security and privacy of our customers' personal information. As a customer, you will be given the opportunity, at least once annually, to notify us of your desire not to receive these offers.

What Are Cookies? Cookies are a feature of Web browser software that allows Web servers to recognize the computer used to access a Web site. Cookies are small pieces of data that are stored by a user's Web browser on the user's hard drive. Cookies can remember what information a user accesses on one Web page to simplify subsequent interactions with that Web site by the same user or to use the information to streamline the user's transactions on related Web pages. This makes it easier for a user to move from Web page to Web page and to complete commercial transactions over the Internet. Cookies should make your online experience easier and more personalized.

How Do We Use Information We Collect from Cookies?

We use Web site browser software tools such as cookies and Web server logs to gather information about our Web site users' browsing activities, in order to constantly improve our Web site and better serve our customers. This information assists us to design and arrange our Web pages in the most user-friendly manner and to continually improve our Web site to better meet the needs of our customers and prospective customers.

Cookies help us collect important business and technical statistics. The information in the cookies lets us trace the paths followed by users to our Web site as they move from one page to another. Web server logs allow us to count how many people visit our Web site and evaluate our Web site's visitor capacity. We do not use these technologies to capture your individual email address or any personally identifying information about you although they do permit us to send focused online banner advertisements or other such responses to you.

Sharing Information with Affiliates

From time to time you may notice offers from outside companies advertised on our Web site. We take measures to select product or service providers that are responsible and afford privacy protections to their customers. However, we cannot make any representations about the practices and policies of these companies.

Sharing Information with Strategic Partners

We may enter into strategic marketing alliances or partnerships with third parties who may be given access to personal information including your name, address, telephone number and email for the purpose of providing you information regarding products and services that we think will be of interest to you. In connection with strategic marketing alliances or partnerships, we will retain all ownership rights to the information, and we will not share information regarding your social security number or other personal financial data.

Notice of New Services and Changes

Occasionally, we may also use the information we collect to notify you about important changes to our Web site, new services and special offers we think you will find valuable. As our client, you will be given the opportunity to notify us of your desire not to receive these offers by clicking on a response box when you receive such an offer or by sending us an email request at _____.

How Do We Secure Information Transmissions?

When you send confidential personal credit card information to us on our Web site, a secure server software which we have licensed encrypts all information you input before it is sent to us. The information is scrambled en route and decoded once it reaches our Web site.

Other email that you may send to us may not be secure unless we advise you that security measures will be in place prior to your transmitting the information. For that reason, we ask that you do not send confidential information such as Social Security or account numbers to us through an unsecured email.

How Do We Protect Your Information?

Information Security. We utilize encryption/security software to safeguard the confidentiality of personal information we collect from unauthorized access or disclosure and accidental loss, alteration or destruction.

Evaluation of Information Protection Practices. Periodically, our operations and business practices are reviewed for compliance with corporate policies and procedures governing the security, confidentiality and quality of our information.

Employee Access, Training and Expectations. Our corporate values, ethical standards, policies and practices are committed to the protection of customer information. In general, our business practices limit employee access to confidential information, and limit the use and disclosure of such information to authorized persons, processes and transactions.

How Can You Access and Correct Your Information?

You may request access to all your personally identifiable information that we collect online and maintain in our database by emailing _____.

Do We Disclose Information to Outside Parties?

We may provide aggregate information about our customers, sales, Web site traffic patterns and related Web site information to our affiliates or reputable third parties, but this information will not include personally identifying data, except as otherwise provided in this Privacy Policy.

What About Legally Compelled Disclosure of Information?

We may disclose information when legally compelled to do so, in other words, when we, in good faith, believe that the law requires it or for the protection of our legal rights.

(continued)

What About Other Web Sites Linked to Our Web Site?
We are not responsible for the practices employed by Web sites linked to or from our Web site nor the information or content contained therein. Often links to other Web sites are provided solely as pointers to information on topics that may be useful to the users of our Web site.

Please remember that when you use a link to go from our Web site to another Web site, our Privacy Policy is no longer in effect. Your browsing and interaction on any other Web site, including Web sites which have a link on our Web site, is subject to that Web site's own rules and policies. Please read over those rules and policies before proceeding.

Your Consent
By using our Web site you consent to our collection and use of your personal information as described in this Privacy Policy. If we change our privacy policies and procedures, we will post those changes on our Web site to keep you aware of what information we collect, how we use it and under what circumstances we may disclose it.

E-Commerce Agreements

Commercial Web sites often sell products or services provided by a third party. For example, your Web site may sell specialized equipment or Internet-related services provided by another company.

An E-Commerce Agreement can be the document that sets forth the contractual relationship between the Web site owner and the third party. The E-Commerce Agreement can cover the following matters:

- **Product or Service.** What is the product or service to be marketed on the Web site? Is it a whole category of products or services or only specific items?

- **Fees.** What fee or commission does the Web site owner get if he sells the products or services through the site?

- **Customer Payment.** How do customers pay for the purchases? Does the mechanism run through the Web site owner's site or through the third party? Who handles credit card–related issues?

- **Customer Information.** Who "owns" the customer and the information provided by the customer? Ideally, the Web site owner "owns" the customer because his efforts obtained the customer. The third party, however, often insists upon ownership rights. A compromise that is sometimes employed is that the parties "co-own" the customer or that each party has certain rights to use the customer information. Of course, all this needs to be consistent with the site's Privacy Policy and applicable law.

- ✔ **Trademarks and Logos.** The Web site owner typically wants to use the trademarks and logos of the third party on the site, and in that case the agreement needs to grant the Web site owner a limited right to use such trademarks and logos.

- ✔ **Term.** What is the term of agreement? Often, simple agreements are on a year-to-year basis. Occasionally, one party gains the right to terminate early on 30 or 60 days' advance written notice. Make sure that the length of the term justifies the time and resources spent on marketing the products and services.

- ✔ **Marketing.** Will you undertake any specific marketing to highlight the third party's products or services? The third party may insist upon certain prominence or placement on the site and/or a minimum level of ads or sales.

The following Form 16-9 (also on the CD-ROM) is a sample E-Commerce Agreement. This form is drafted more for the benefit of the Web site owner.

Affiliate Agreements

A number of e-commerce sites are establishing *affiliate* or *associate* programs, as a way to encourage other Web sites to send viewers and potential customers to the e-commerce site, by paying commissions or referral fees. You can think of it as "send me money if I send you business."

By way of example, Amazon.com, the leading online bookseller (which has expanded into music, videos, and other items) has an "Associate Program." This program allows its associates to offer books and other products on their site, through special links to Amazon. When a customer comes to your site, follows the link to Amazon's site, and purchases something, Amazon commits to pay you a referral fee (5 to 15 percent of the product sold, depending on the product.)

From Amazon's perspective, this program drives more traffic to its site and increases sales. From the associate's perspective, the program provides more products on its site to viewers and the associate potentially receives fees.

E-COMMERCE AGREEMENT

This E-Commerce Agreement (the "Agreement") is entered into between _____, a _____ corporation (the "Company") and _____, a _____ corporation (the "Strategic Partner").

RECITALS

I.   The Company has a Web site that is focused on:

_____
_____
_____ (the "Site").

II. Strategic Partner is interested in working with the Company in marketing and e-commerce arrangements.

III. Certain initially capitalized terms are defined in Exhibit 1.

Therefore, the parties agree as follows:

1.   **Promotion of Strategic Partner's Products.**

(a) Strategic Partner grants to the Company a non-exclusive right to promote Strategic Partner's Products during the term of this Agreement.

(b) The Company shall promote the Products in the manner determined appropriate by the Company, which may include links to Strategic Partner's web sites, framing over various pages of Strategic Partner's web sites, or through mutual development of co-branded web pages. All sales of Products will be effected through Strategic Partner's billing, server and computer systems, unless otherwise provided for in Exhibit 1. At some future point, billing may be done through the Company in an arrangement to be mutually agreed upon by the Company and the Strategic Partner.

(c) Strategic Partner agrees to provide all customer service and support for the Products with reasonable responsiveness and turn-around times.

(d) Strategic Partner will reasonably cooperate with the Company to effect the items contemplated above.

2.   **Term.**

The initial term of this Agreement shall be one (1) year from the date hereof. Thereafter this Agreement will renew automatically for additional terms of one (1) year unless either party shall given written notice at least 30 days prior to any such renewal that the Agreement shall not so renew.

3.   **Compensation.**

(a) Strategic Partner will pay the Company a commission on Products sold to Company Customers, in the amount set forth in Exhibit 2.

(b) Payments for the commission owed for all Products sold to Company Customers shall be made within 30 days after the close of the month in which purchases are made. If the payment due hereunder is less than $100, the payment shall be held until aggregate amounts owed exceed $100 and then the full payment shall be made to the Company.

(c) Any late payments of commissions shall accrue interest at the rate of 1% per month, or the maximum permitted by law, whichever is less.

(d) Strategic Partner shall provide to the Company a written commission report within 30 days after the close of each month setting forth (1) the names, addresses, phone numbers and email addresses (when provided) of Company Customers; (2) the Products purchased by Company Customers with sales prices, (3) the commission owed to the Company, and (4) such additional information as may be reasonably requested by Company.

4.   **Strategic Partner Content.**

(a) Strategic Partner shall provide to the Company articles, advice, tips, or FAQ's useful for the Company in connection with promoting the Products (the "Strategic Partner Content") and as set forth in Exhibit 2. The Strategic Partner Content shall be provided in formats and electronic files as reasonably requested by the Company.

(b) Strategic Partner shall assist the Company in connection with any revisions to the Strategic Partner Content for posting on the Site.

(c) Strategic Partner represents that it has all the rights to the Strategic Partner Content, that it does not infringe or violate any third party's rights, that it is accurate, complete and up-to-date, and that it does not violate any law or regulation.

(d) Strategic Partner grants to the Company during the term of this Agreement a worldwide, non-exclusive,

Form 16-9: E-Commerce Agreement.

royalty free license to produce, publicly publish and distribute, in both print and electronic form, the Strategic Partner Content. Company may also create derivative works or modifications to the Strategic Partner Content for editorial or stylistic reasons. Strategic Partner grants the Company the right to permit viewers or customers to copy, print and use the Strategic Partner Content for their personal or internal purposes.

5.   Intellectual Property Rights.

Neither party will acquire any ownership interest in each other's intellectual property. All names and other information concerning a Company Customer shall be deemed jointly owned by the Company and Strategic Partner with each side free to use such names and information as they see fit in compliance with applicable law. With the approval of the Strategic Partner (which approval shall not be unreasonably withheld or delayed), Company shall have the right to place the Strategic Partner's logo, tradename and trademark on the Site as a means to identify the Strategic Partner and to otherwise use such items in connection with the purposes of this Agreement. The Company shall follow all reasonable directions from the Strategic Partner concerning the protection under applicable laws of such logo, tradename and trademark.

6.   Confidential Information.

(a)   Each party acknowledges and agrees that any Confidential Information received from the other party will be the sole and exclusive property of the other party and may not be used or disclosed except as necessary to perform the obligations required under this Agreement.

(b)   Upon termination of this Agreement, each party shall promptly return all information, documents, manuals and other materials belonging to the other party except as otherwise provided in this Agreement.

7.   Promotional Materials/Press Releases.

Each party shall submit to the other for approval (which approval shall not be unreasonably withheld or delayed), marketing, advertising, press releases, and other promotional materials related to this Agreement, provided, however, that each party shall be permitted to disclose the existence of this Agreement and the nature of the relationship without the consent of the other.

8.   Limitation of Liability.

(a)   UNDER NO CIRCUMSTANCES SHALL EITHER PARTY BE LIABLE TO THE OTHER PARTY OR ANY THIRD PARTY FOR INDIRECT, INCIDENTAL, CONSEQUENTIAL, SPECIAL OR EXEMPLARY DAMAGES (EVEN IF THAT PARTY HAS BEEN ADVISED OF THE POSSIBILITY OF SUCH DAMAGES), ARISING FROM THE PRODUCTS OR ANY OTHER PROVISION OF THIS AGREEMENT, SUCH AS, BUT NOT LIMITED TO, LOSS OF REVENUE OR ANTICIPATED PROFITS OR LOST BUSINESS, COSTS OF DELAY, OR LIABILITIES TO THIRD PARTIES ARISING FROM ANY SOURCE.

(b)   The Strategic Partner shall bear (i) all collection risk (including, without limitation, credit card fraud and any other type of credit fraud) with respect to sales of the Products and (ii) all responsibility and liability for the proper payment of all taxes which may be levied or assessed (including, without limitation, sales taxes) which may be levied in respect of sales of the Products.

(c)   Company has no obligation to attempt to monitor or regulate the quality, suitability or content of the Products and Strategic Partner agrees to hold the Company harmless in the event of any claims by customers with respect to problems with the Products. The Strategic Partner hereby represents and warrants to the Company that the Products will not infringe on or violate the Intellectual Property Rights or other rights of any third party and will not contain any content which violates any applicable law, regulation or third party right.

9.   Relationship of Parties.

The parties shall perform all of their duties under this Agreement as independent contractors. Nothing in this Agreement shall be construed to give either party the power to direct or control the daily activities of the other party, or to constitute the parties as principal and agent, employer and employee, franchisor and franchisee, partners, joint venturers, co-owners, or otherwise as participants in a joint undertaking.

10.   Miscellaneous.

(a)   This agreement constitutes and contains the entire agreement between the parties with respect to the subject matter hereof and supersedes any prior or contemporaneous oral or written agreements. Each party acknowledges and agrees that the other has not

(continued)

made any representations, warranties or agreements of any kind, except as expressly set forth herein.

(b)   This Agreement may not be modified or amended, except by an instrument in writing signed by duly authorized officers of both of the parties hereto.

(c)   This Agreement may be executed in counterparts each of which shall be deemed an original and all such counterparts shall constitute one and the same agreement.

(d)   This Agreement will be deemed entered into in California and will be governed by and interpreted in accordance with the laws of the State of California, excluding that body of law known as conflicts of law. The parties agree that any dispute arising under this Agreement will be resolved solely in the state or federal courts in San Francisco, California, and the parties hereby expressly consent to jurisdiction therein. In the event of any dispute, the prevailing party shall be entitled to recover its reasonable attorneys' costs from the non-prevailing party.

(e)   The provisions of this Agreement relating to payment of any fees or other amounts owed, payment of any interest on unpaid fees, confidentiality and warranties and intellectual property shall survive any termination or expiration of this Agreement.

(f)   The language in this Agreement shall be construed as to its fair meaning and not strictly for or against either party.

11.   **Additional Terms**.

Exhibit 1 contains certain additional terms.

IN WITNESS WHEREOF, the parties have executed this Agreement as of _____ of _____, _____.

[COMPANY]

_____
_____
_____
Phone: (   ) _____
Fax: (   ) _____

By: _____
Title: _____

STRATEGIC PARTNER

_____
_____
_____
Phone: (   ) _____
Fax: (   ) _____

By: _____
Title: _____

<u>EXHIBIT 1</u>

<u>Certain Definitions</u>.

The following definitions shall apply to this Agreement.

"Site" is defined in Recital A of the Agreement.

"Company Customers" means persons who purchase any Products from Strategic Partner and who are referred to Strategic Partner or its Web site(s) by the Company, or customers who originated from the Site and were transported to Strategic Partner's Web site through a hyperlink from the Site.

"Confidential Information" means any data or information, oral or written, treated as confidential that relates to either party's (or, if either party is bound to protect the confidentiality of any third party's information, such third party's) past, present, or future research, development or business activities, including any unannounced product(s) and service(s), any information relating to services, developments, inventions, processes, plans, financial information, forecasts, and projections and the financial terms of this Agreement. Notwithstanding the foregoing, Confidential Information shall not be deemed to include information if: (i) it was already known to the receiving party prior to the date of this Agreement as established by documentary evidence; (ii) it is in or has entered the public domain through no breach of this Agreement or other wrongful act of the receiving party; (iii) it has been rightfully received by the receiving party from a third party and without breach of any obligation of confidentiality of such third party to the owner of the Confidential Information; or (iv) it is required to be disclosed pursuant to final binding order of a governmental agency or court of competent jurisdiction, provided that the owner of the Confidential Information has been given reasonable notice of the pendency of such an order.

"Products" means those products and/or services of the Strategic Partners which are promoted or sold as a result of the Company's efforts. The initial products and/or services contemplated hereunder are set forth in Exhibit 2.

"Strategic Partner Content" is defined in Section 4(a) of the Agreement.

(continued)

EXHIBIT 2

1.	Products or Services of Strategic Partner:	_____ _____ _____ _____

2.   Strategic Partner Content to be Provided:

In addition to the items set forth in Section 2(a) of the Agreement, the Strategic Partner Content shall include

_____
_____
_____
_____

3.   Commission:

(a)   ___% of the gross sales price of the Products sold, excluding taxes and any shipping charges, increasing to __% once at least $_____ of Products have been sold as a result of the relationship between the Company and Strategic Partner.

(b)   The parties will discuss sharing of ad revenues generated from customer traffic on Strategic Partner's web sites as a result of the promotional efforts of the Company.

4.   Any Additional Terms:

_____
_____
_____
_____
_____

Key provisions of Affiliate Agreements

If you set up an affiliate program, you need an *Affiliate Agreement*. Typically, you post your form of agreement online on your Web site and the potential affiliate partner needs to agree to your Affiliate Agreement to enroll in your program. The key provisions to address in your Affiliate Agreement are

✔ **Enrollment.** The prospective affiliate should submit an application to become an affiliate with your site, which retains the right to accept or reject the application. After all, you may not want affiliates that promote violence or whose sites contain sexually explicit materials.

✔ **Links.** The agreement should spell out what types of links you provide to the affiliate — a product link, a search box link, or some general link.

✔ **Tracking.** The agreement should spell out how you track and report the referred customers.

✔ **Referral Fees.** The agreement should define the precise referral fees. How much do you pay for which customer purchases?

✔ **Payment Terms.** How often do you pay the referral fees? (Quarterly payments are typical.) Also, consider a provision that you don't have to send a check until the associate accrues at least $100 in referral fees.

✔ **Customers.** Most agreements provide that the e-commerce site selling the product or service "owns" the customer. This means that all information about the customer belongs solely to the e-commerce site.

✔ **License.** Most agreements provide for a nonexclusive revocable right to use certain graphic images and text of the e-commerce site. The affiliate may not modify the images in any way and must follow the provided trademark guidelines.

✔ **Terms of Agreement.** How long does the agreement last? Most Affiliate Agreements provide that either party may terminate the agreement at any time.

✔ **Modification.** How can the agreement be modified? Most Affiliate Agreements allow the e-commerce owner to change the terms of the agreement at any time, and if the affiliate doesn't like the change, the affiliate's only right is to terminate the agreement.

✔ **Limitations and Disclaimers.** What limitations of liability should exist? Most agreements state that the e-commerce owner is not liable for indirect, special, or consequential damages. In any event, the well-drafted agreement typically limits the liability to the amount of referral fees paid or payable under the agreement.

What else to post on the affiliate section of your site

Setting up information about your affiliate program on your site is often helpful. This information can include a general description of the program, step-by-step instructions, and a listing of current affiliates.

Adding an FAQ (Frequently Asked Questions) section can also be helpful. Make sure that what you say in the FAQ is consistent with your Affiliate Agreement.

Great affiliate programs

When thinking about setting up an affiliate program for your Web site, seeing what other sites have done is useful. Check out some of the following sites, which have well-thought-out programs:

✔ **Amazon.com:** Associate Program for sale of books, videos, music, and more.

✔ **BarnesandNoble.com:** Affiliate Program for sale of books, magazines, or software.

✔ **Egghead.com:** Affiliate Program for online software sales.

✔ **BigStar.com:** Affiliate Program for filmed entertainment, including videos and DVDs.

Forms on the CD-ROM

Form 16-1	**Sample Online Copyright and Trademark Protection Notice**	A notice for placement on a Web site regarding copyright and trademarks
Form 16-2	**Online Disclosure Regarding Terms of Use**	A notice for placement on a Web site regarding the user being subject to a Terms of Use Agreement
Form 16-3	**Online Disclaimer Regarding Information**	A disclaimer for placement on a Web site regarding information provided on the site
Form 16-4	**Online Disclaimer Reference**	A general disclaimer reference for a Web site
Form 16-5	**Online Disclaimer Re: Hyperlinks**	A disclaimer for placement on a Web site regarding non-endorsement of hyperlinked sites
Form 16-6	**Terms of Use Agreement**	A sample Web site Terms of Use Agreement
Form 16-7	**Online Contract**	A sample online contract or sale of goods or services
Form 16-8	**Privacy Policy**	A sample online Privacy Policy regarding use of viewer and registrant information

Form 16-9	**E-Commerce Agreement**	An agreement regarding the offering and selling of a third party's products or services on a commercial Web site
Form 16-10	**Web Linking License Agreement**	A sample agreement allowing the linking of one site to another

Part V
The Part of Tens

The 5th Wave   By Rich Tennant

"They've been that way for over 10 minutes. Larry's either having a staring contest with the customer, or he's afraid to ask for the sale again."

In this part . . .

Every *For Dummies* book ends with top-ten lists, and this one is no exception. Here, you can find ten mistakes to avoid, ten great resources for forms, and ten key contracts for small businesses.

Chapter 17

Top Ten Agreement Drafting Mistakes

In This Chapter

▶ Identifying key drafting mistakes

▶ Recognizing these mistakes

▶ Avoiding these mistakes

Numerous ways exist to make mistakes when negotiating and drafting an agreement.

In this chapter, I give you the top ten agreement drafting mistakes — although the chapter could have been a great deal longer. Think about how to avoid the mistakes I list in this chapter.

Not Drafting the First Draft

You always want to volunteer to draw up the first draft of a contract (or have your lawyer volunteer). Doing so can give you a tremendous advantage in the negotiations; it allows you to structure the initial deal by using your own wish list and with terms most beneficial to you.

Moreover, from a legal cost perspective, having your lawyer draft the first draft is often more cost-effective than having him or her responding to another lawyer's one-sided draft.

Check out Chapter 2 for more reasons as to why you want to take charge of the draft.

Not Including Explicit Payment Terms

Almost everyone understands that payment terms are an essential part of an agreement. Don't omit them or leave them to be decided until after you sign the agreement.

Clearly lay out the payment terms in your agreement. Avoid ambiguity as to the amount owed or provide a clear formula for determining the amount owed. Include terms that explicitly state how much is owed and when, and what happens if the other party doesn't pay or pays late. Furthermore, make sure to allocate who pays any taxes involved.

Not Including All Deal Terms in the Agreement

Include all "deal terms" in your agreement. This means that you need to include not only all the legal mumbo-jumbo, but also the things upon which you relied when you entered the agreement.

Deal terms to consider include the following:

- ✔ What is your reason for entering into the agreement with the other party?
- ✔ Did the party state that he or she has been in business a long time or has a particular type of expertise in a particular field?
- ✔ What did the other person agree that he or she would do for you and what did you agree to do in return?
- ✔ When did you agree this would happen?
- ✔ Did you discuss special circumstances in negotiating the agreement that led you to an agreement with this particular company?
- ✔ Did you tell the other person that you have a critical deadline for receiving goods or services?
- ✔ Was there some key event or condition that was to happen before you became fully obligated?

You can include the answers to all of these questions within the agreement so that if at any point the deal falls apart, you can show that you relied on specific answers to these questions.

Making Assumptions

Don't make any assumptions when drafting the agreement. Discuss any assumptions you find yourself in danger of making. You need to spell out all the obligations and assumptions under the agreement within the agreement itself. For example:

- ✔ If you are purchasing produce, do not assume that the other party knows to deliver the products before they spoil. Spell out the procedure explicitly.

- ✔ Don't assume that the other party will know that if you receive the goods you purchased late, then your company will lose thousands of dollars. Put a "time is of the essence" clause in your agreement if this is true.

- ✔ If you and the other party agree that the agreement begins on a Tuesday, make sure that you both mean the same Tuesday.

- ✔ If you agree to have goods shipped and delivered to a certain location, make sure you both agree on the same ship, the same city, and who pays for shipping costs.

If you only think you understand something in the negotiation phase, ask. If you are unclear on any portion of the agreement, get an explanation — don't make the mistake of assuming that the other party understands what you mean. Conversely, if the other party seems unclear on a point, explain it and spell it out in the agreement.

Not Paying Attention to Boilerplate Terms

Boilerplate terms are an essential part of any agreement and affect your rights under the agreement as much as any other terms. You can negotiate these terms in the same manner as all other terms in your agreement. If you are not clear on this concept, please review Chapter 3 for a detailed discussion of boilerplate terms.

Key boilerplate terms include the following:

- ✔ The prevailing party in any dispute receives its attorney's fees.
- ✔ Amendments to the agreement can only be made in writing.
- ✔ Neither party may assign the contract.
- ✔ The contract includes all representations, warranties, and agreements of the parties.

Not Negotiating All Important Points

Everything is negotiable. Everything. Even the things the other party tells you are not negotiable are negotiable. You can even negotiate preprinted forms and boilerplate terms.

Some portions of your agreement are more important to you than others, but everything can be important in case of a problem. You will need to give and take in negotiating your agreement — decide in advance which things you can't live without and which things you can live with. Negotiating everything means that you discuss, argue, deliberate, and ultimately agree upon all terms of the agreement. The other party to a deal expects you to negotiate.

Not Knowing When Enough Is Enough

In much the same way as negotiating all material terms is important (see the preceding section), knowing when to stop negotiating and sign the agreement is also significant. If you go one inch beyond *enough,* your negotiations may fall apart and leave you with no agreement.

Leverage is the key in many negotiations. Do you or the other side have more leverage? Knowing who has the advantage can help you decide when enough is enough.

Not Including a Termination Clause

A termination clause can be important in many agreements. The termination clause states how you can escape your agreement if the agreement isn't working. No one likes to plan for the ending of a relationship, but you need to include a termination clause to protect yourself in the event that you aren't satisfied with the relationship.

In the termination clause, you set up the terms under which you can exit the agreement. Planning this clause in advance is better than not having it if things turn sour. Think of the termination clause as a *divorce clause* or *prenuptial agreement.*

Not Stating the Jurisdiction Governing the Agreement

Don't neglect to negotiate where any disputes relating to the agreement will take place. This information is critical, particularly when parties to an agreement reside in or do business in two different states, different countries, or, in the case of large states (such as Texas or California), two different counties.

The typical choices for hearing disputes are where you reside or do business, or where the other party resides or does business. Try to have the other party agree to come to you — if a dispute arises, you don't want to travel to a court or an arbitrator's office 3,000 or even 300 miles away. This clause is particularly important if you deal with companies in foreign countries.

Not Having a Lawyer Review Important Contracts

Lawyers cost money. Consequently, some companies try to avoid using lawyers even in important contracts. This is a BIG mistake. A good business lawyer may end up saving you thousands of dollars and make your contract more bulletproof. A really good lawyer may even point out business or deal points that you didn't think about.

So, find an experienced contracts or corporate lawyer and treat him or her nicely! Send your lawyer gifts and continually lavish praise on him or her.

Chapter 18

Ten Great Resources for Contracts and Forms

*E*verybody's talking about the World Wide Web and how it helps people obtain information that was formerly available only to larger competitors. If you're not sure where you're surfing, however, cyberspace quickly deteriorates into a time sinkhole. This chapter provides you with a map and a compass to get you started in the right direction. I list ten Web sites that may come in handy for finding forms or agreements and useful explanations of contracts, contract negotiations, and legal issues. Check out each one and then bookmark them all for frequent, easy access. I've done the searching; all you have to do is surf the Net.

AllBusiness.com

www.allbusiness.com

AllBusiness.com is one of the premier sites on the Web dedicated to helping small and growing businesses. The site provides a comprehensive mixture of services, tools, information, and products. It includes special sections dedicated to entrepreneurs, financing, legal, Internet, sales and marketing, and more.

Especially useful are the over 300 sample forms, agreements, and checklists — free for merely registering with the site. The forms and agreements cover employment, financing, venture capital, contracts, the Web, start-up businesses, shareholder documents, corporate formation, letters of intent, and more. Definitely check out www.allbusiness.com.

LegalAgreements.com

www.legalagreements.com

Legal Agreements.com is a great resource for sample forms, contracts, and checklists. It has links to many quality forms and necessary agreements, which are downloadable directly from the Web for a small charge.

The key areas covered by LegalAgreements.com include the following:

- Start-Up Companies
- Intellectual Property
- Mergers & Acquisitions
- Computers & Software
- Partnerships, Joint Ventures, & LLCs
- Real Estate
- Commercial Transactions
- Employment & Consulting
- The Web
- Corporate
- Securities

Reviewing this site is essential if you want to find some high-quality sample agreements.

Law.com

www.law.com

Law.com bills itself as your portal to the law. It contains comprehensive sections devoted to the public, lawyers, students, and professionals. It has free help for many legal questions and contains law guides, dictionaries, lawyer locators, legal news, guides for starting and running a business, checklists, and more.

The site also has articles, forms and sample contracts dealing with starting a business, employment/HR issues, Internet issues, tax, stock options, stock issuances, and more. Most of the material is free and very good. You can even find some articles and forms that I posted on the site, at the request of Law.com!

Securities & Exchange Commission

www.sec.gov

The Securities and Exchange Commission Web site is full of useful forms and agreements relating to securities matters.

You can use the Edgar database contained as part of the site to access the securities law filings of publicly held corporations. In those filings, you find thousands of real-life prospectuses, business contracts, employment contracts, stock purchase agreements, merger agreements, and more. And it's all free. This site can be an extremely valuable resource.

Copyright Office

www.loc.gov/copyright

The Web site for the U.S. Copyright Office is full of application forms, letters, reports, fact sheets, and advice relating to copyrighting your work. The site also contains links to many other helpful sites containing copyright information.

Particularly helpful are the frequently asked questions and answers, including:

- What does copyright protect?
- When is my work protected?
- Do I have to register my work with the Copyright Office to be protected?
- How do I register my copyright?

The Small Business Administration

www.sba.gov

The Small Business Administration Web site is huge. The site map alone lists 25 areas — each with several pages, forms, and services. Definitely plan to check out Financing Your Business, which describes all the different ways that the SBA can help you secure business funding. You can also find on this site references to various small business laws and regulations.

The SBA goes out of its way to connect small businesses with a wide range of services, including links and descriptions of various non-SBA resources — both federal and state. The site boasts a 28-page list of shareware, which you can download from the site. This site also provides information on the Electronic Federal Tax Payment System (EFTPS) and includes a searchable database of business cards submitted by small companies across the country. For once, the government is actually helpful.

The Internal Revenue Service

www.irs.ustreas.gov

Granted, you don't want to contact the IRS unless you absolutely have to. But on those occasions when you do, the Web offers you a way to get in touch with the IRS without leaving home — or being put on hold. This site is a great repository for IRS forms and publications. It also provides access to advice concerning taxpayer rights, electronic payment services, and the addresses of all the IRS service centers and offices. You can even join an e-mail list for updates on various IRS regulations and changes to forms.

You may also want to check out the Tax Info for Business section. This page contains the Business Tax Kit — which provides the IRS forms applicable to small businesses — as well as answers to questions, links to other non-tax Web sites, tax calendars, and other services.

You can use the IRS Web site to find the site for your state's taxation agency. Just link to the Federation of Tax Administrators home page (or find it yourself at www.taxadmin.org/fta), find your state, and use that link to go to the site.

U.S. Patent and Trademark Office

www.uspto.gov

The U.S. Patent and Trademark Office Web site contains comprehensive information, advice, and forms related to patents, trademarks, and service marks.

Particularly useful on the Web site are the following:

- Basic Facts About Trademarks
- Basic Facts About Patents
- Trademark Examination of Domain Names
- Frequently Asked Questions
- Functions of the Patent and Trademark Office

Start-Up & Emerging Companies: Planning, Financing and Operating the Successful Business

This two-volume book is an extensive resource, containing over 1,600 pages of useful legal and business advice for start-up and emerging companies. The book is full of advice for entrepreneurs and growing businesses.

The topics covered include the following:

- Organizing a corporation
- Selling stock and the securities laws
- Key contracts
- Partnerships
- Preparing the company for an IPO
- Legal issues associated with Web sites
- Venture capital
- Private placements
- Employment agreements

> ✔ Licensing agreements
>
> ✔ Strategic alliances
>
> ✔ Tax considerations

The book comes with a diskette that contains over 75 useful forms for start-up and emerging companies.

R. Harroch, Law Journal Seminars-Press, 1998, rev. ed., 1,600 pages; phone 800-888-8300

Small Business Kit For Dummies

Small Business Kit For Dummies is part of the award-winning *For Dummies* line of books. This book is so popular, it even made the *Wall Street Journal* Best Selling Business Books List.

The book provides business solutions for small and growing businesses, with over 250 sample forms, agreements, documents, and checklists. The areas covered include business plans, funding the business, employer issues, book-keeping and accounting, protecting your ideas and inventions, creating a business Web site, dealing with customers, and negotiating cost-effective leases.

R. Harroch, IDG Books, 1998, 372 pages.

Chapter 19

Ten Key Contracts for Small and Growing Businesses

. . . .

In This Chapter

▶ Employee Offer Letters

▶ Confidentiality and Invention Assignment Agreements

▶ Service Contracts

▶ Sales Contracts

▶ Confidentiality Agreements

▶ Web Site Terms of Use Agreements

▶ Letters of Intent

▶ Stock Purchase Agreements

▶ Leases

▶ Loan Agreements

. . . .

*I*n this chapter, I summarize ten key contracts for small and growing businesses. These contracts need to be well thought out and well drafted and can be crucial to the success of a business.

I also refer you to the discussion and sample forms in this book where I discuss these contracts in detail.

Employment Offer Letters

One of the best ways to protect your business from legal liability and misunderstandings with employees is to have an employment offer letter issued and sent to the prospective employee. The employee should then be required to sign it, evidencing the valid employment relationship between the parties.

A good employment offer letter covers the following points:

- The particular job offered
- The responsibilities of the job
- The salary and benefits
- That the employment is "at will," meaning the employee can quit or the employer can fire him or her at any time
- That the employee is required to sign a Confidentiality and Invention Assignment Agreement (discussed below)
- That the letter constitutes the entire agreement of the parties, and can only be amended in the future in writing, signed by the employer and the employee

Businesses should have their own form of standard offer letter. The CD-ROM accompanying this book contains a good sample as Form 7-7.

Confidentiality and Invention Assignment Agreements

Employees have access to a company's confidential information. Moreover, many businesses expect their employees to come up with ideas, work product, business strategies, and inventions.

To make sure the employees keep the proprietary information of the company confidential, you should require them to sign a Confidentiality and Invention Assignment Agreement. This agreement deals with the confidentiality issue, but it can also provide that the ideas, business strategies and other work product developed by the employee belong to the company, and not to the employee.

If you expect to have venture capital or other professional investors invest in your company, they will expect that you have these agreements in place for all of your employees. So, make sure to get them from every employee.

Check out a sample Employee Confidentiality and Invention Assignment Agreement on the CD-ROM accompanying this book (Form 7-10).

Service Contracts

If your company provides professional services as opposed to selling a product, it needs to have its own good, standard form Services Contract (which can be labeled many things, including an *Agreement for Professional Services*). This type of agreement lays out the terms and conditions under which you provide services and tries to lay out specifically your responsibilities and liability.

Having a good contract here is important. You want to avoid misunderstandings and undue liability. Ideally, this agreement gives you flexibility in completing the services, spells out the fees for the job (and additional fees if you encounter unforeseen circumstances), and spells out the situations for your maximum exposure. Check out Chapter 13 for more information.

The CD-ROM contains a sample form Agreement for Professional Services as Form 13-1.

Sales Contracts

Many businesses sell products, and therefore need a good Sales Contract. The Sales Contract lays out the price, terms, and conditions for the sale of goods, equipment, or other products. Of course, some businesses (like the corner grocery store) don't need Sales Contracts, but if your products sell for significant dollars, then you likely need a Sales Contract.

The actual Sales Contract can take the form of fine print on an order form or an invoice, or it can be tailor-made for a particular sale. You always want to start with your own form of contract. The key terms in Sales Contracts include: price, price adjustments in certain events, responsibility for taxes, payment and credit terms, warranties to be given, disclaimers of various warranties, and liability limitations. Check out Chapter 13 for a detailed discussion of Sales Contracts.

Form 13-3 on the CD-ROM contains a sample Equipment Sales Agreement.

Confidentiality Agreement

Numerous instances arise in which you want to share confidential or proprietary information with another party. You may want to show the information to get them interested in doing a deal with you, investing in your company, or working together on some strategic arrangement. Producing an agreement to prevent the other side from stealing or using your ideas is very important in these situations.

The Confidentiality Agreement provides that the recipient of information holds the information in strict confidence and only uses the information for purposes of evaluating whether to enter into a business relationship with you. The key to this agreement is that you should enter into the agreement before any disclosure.

A good Confidentiality Agreement lays out the recipients' confidentiality obligations, the exclusions from confidentiality (such as information already in the public domain), how long the confidentiality obligation lasts, limitations on the use of the information, and the right of the disclosing party to seek injunctive relief to stop the other side from disclosing the information.

Check out Form 14-1 on the CD-ROM for a sample Confidentiality Agreement. This is a one-sided form, where only one side provides confidential information. Form 14-2 on the CD-ROM is a Mutual Confidentiality Agreement.

Web Site Terms of Use Agreement

Most growing businesses have established (or should establish) a Web site marketing their company and their products. Essential to these Web sites is a Terms of Use Agreement, which is intended to be a contract between the Web site owner and the users of the site and any purchasers of goods or services from the site.

A good Terms of Use Agreement is essential for avoiding legal liability to the site owner. The well-drafted agreement includes: limitations on how the site can be used, copyright protection warnings, disclaimers, liability limitations, disclosure on the site's privacy policy in dealing with customer information, jurisdiction where any disputes must be brought (ideally, the home town of the site owner), and much more. Check out the full discussion in Chapter 16.

The CD-ROM provides a sample Terms of Use Agreement as Form 16-6.

Letters of Intent

A Letter of Intent can be a very advantageous and quick way to get momentum for a deal. The idea for a Letter of Intent is for the parties to get a "handshake" deal on the major points, and then move to creating definitive legal agreements.

You need to be very careful about what you want to be binding or nonbinding in the letter. Most Letters of Intent are nonbinding and merely are expressions of the parties that they have a particular deal in mind and want to further negotiate to get there. Letters of Intent can also be binding contracts, however, so be careful what you say in these letters.

Form 6-4 on the CD-ROM gives you a sample Letter of Intent for acquiring a business.

Stock Purchase Agreements

Start-up and emerging businesses often need to raise capital to fund their business. They often do this by selling stock in the company.

Stock Purchase Agreements are the vehicle where stock sales can be effected. Such agreements can run from a few pages to 50 or more, depending on the investors and the complexity of the deal.

In most agreements, you need to carefully lay out: the type of stock sold, the price and number of shares, the representations and warranties of the investors, the representations and warranties of the company, the conditions to closing, the rights of the investors, and potentially much, much more. This is an agreement on which you typically need advice from an experienced corporate counsel. Check out Chapter 5 for more information.

Form 5-1 on the CD-ROM provides you with a Checklist for Issuing Stock.

Leases

A business lease for office or retail space is often one of the most significant contracts for a business. The starting place for most lease negotiations is the landlord's allegedly "standard" lease — which tends to be incredibly one-sided in favor of the landlord.

Because the lease can constitute a major commitment of the business, you have to watch out for all the "gotchas." (I discuss "gotchas" in Chapter 10.) Most importantly, you have to ensure that:

- ✓ The space suits your needs
- ✓ The uses the landlord permits are broad enough for your business
- ✓ The lease term is sufficient, with a right to extend if possible

✔ The economic terms are competitive

✔ The lease clearly spells out the landlord's obligations

✔ You have some flexibility in assigning or subletting the lease

Form 10-1 on the CD-ROM shows you the "Checklist for Office Leases." Additionally, Chapter 10 presents information and forms on leases.

Loan Agreements

Many businesses enter Loan Agreements with banks or financial institutions and simply sign the lender's "standard" form. The standard form tends to be very one-sided in favor of the lender, with various restrictions on the borrower.

The borrower under a Loan Agreement needs to fully understand (and negotiate better terms than those contained in the standard form) a number of key issues, including the following:

✔ The total cost of the loan

✔ The payment schedule

✔ The right to prepay the loan without penalty

✔ The flexibility on use of the loan proceeds

✔ The right to cure defaults

✔ The appropriate representations and warranties of the borrower

Check out the full discussion of loan agreements in Chapter 12 and Form 12-3 on the CD-ROM ("Checklist of Issues in Negotiating a Loan").

Appendix

About the CD

- -

*H*ere's some of what you can find on the *Business Contracts Kit For Dummies* CD-ROM:

- ✔ Over 200 business forms and contracts
- ✔ Adobe Acrobat Reader for Mac and Windows, a freeware version that allows you to read the forms on this CD

System Requirements

Make sure that your computer meets the minimum system requirements listed below. If your computer doesn't match up to most of these requirements, you may have problems using the contents of the CD.

- ✔ A PC with a 486 or faster processor, or a Mac OS computer with a 68040 or faster processor.
- ✔ Microsoft Windows 95 or later, or Mac OS system software 7.55 or later.
- ✔ At least 16MB of total RAM installed on your computer. For best performance, we recommend at least 32MB of RAM installed.
- ✔ At least 30MB of hard drive space available to install all the software from this CD. (You'll need less space if you don't install every program.)
- ✔ A CD-ROM drive — double-speed (2x) or faster.
- ✔ A sound card for PCs. (Mac OS computers have built-in sound support.)
- ✔ A monitor capable of displaying at least 256 colors or grayscale.
- ✔ A modem with a speed of at least 14,400 bps.

If you need more information on the basics, check out *PCs For Dummies,* 7th Edition, by Dan Gookin; *Macs For Dummies,*6th Edition, by David Pogue; *iMac For Dummies,* by David Pogue; *Windows 95 For Dummies,* 2nd Edition, or *Windows 98 For Dummies,* both by Andy Rathbone (all published by IDG Books Worldwide, Inc.).

Using the CD with Microsoft Windows

1. **Insert the CD into your computer's CD-ROM drive.**

    Give your computer a moment to take a look at the CD.

2. **Open your browser.**

    If you do not have a browser, follow the easy steps as described in the "Using the CD" section to install one: For your convenience, I have included Microsoft Internet Explorer.

3. **Click File⇨Open (Internet Explorer) or on File⇨Open Page (Netscape).**

4. **Double-click the file called License.txt.**

    This file contains the end-user license that you agree to by using the CD. When you are done reading the license, close the program (most likely NotePad) that displayed the file.

5. **Double-click the file called Readme.txt.**

    This file contains instructions about installing the software from this CD. It might be helpful to leave this text file open while you are using the CD.

6. **In the dialog box that appears, type D:\START.HTM and click OK.**

7. **Replace the letter D with the correct letter for your CD-ROM drive, if it is not D.**

    This action displays the file that walks you through the content of the CD.

8. **To navigate within the interface, simply click any topic of interest to take you to an explanation of the files on the CD and how to use or install them.**

9. **To install the software from the CD, simply click the software name.**

    You see two options — the option to run or open the file from the current location and the option to save the file to your hard drive. Choose to run or open the file from its current location and the installation procedure will continue. After you are done with the interface, simply close your browser as usual.

To run some of the programs, you may need to keep the CD inside your CD-ROM drive. This is a Good Thing. Otherwise, the installed program would have required you to install a very large chunk of the program to your hard drive space, which would have kept you from installing other software.

Using the CD with Mac OS

To install the items from the CD to your hard drive, follow these steps.

1. **Insert the CD into your computer's CD-ROM drive.**

   In a moment, an icon representing the CD you just inserted appears on your Mac desktop. Chances are, the icon looks like a CD-ROM.

2. **Double-click the CD icon to show the CD's contents.**

3. **Double-click the Read Me First icon.**

   This text file contains information about the CD's programs and any last-minute instructions you need to know about installing the programs on the CD that I don't cover in this appendix.

4. **Open your browser.**

   If you don't have a browser, I have included Microsoft Internet Explorer. You'll find separate folders containing all of the PDF and RTF files on the CD.

5. **Click File⇨Open and select the CD entitled Business Contracts Kit. Double-click the Links.htm file to see an explanation of all files and folders included on the CD.**

6. **Some programs come with installer programs — with those you simply open the program's folder on the CD and double-click the icon with the words "Install" or "Installer."**

   Once you have installed the programs that you want, you can eject the CD. Carefully place it back in the plastic jacket of the book for safekeeping.

What You'll Find on the CD

What follows is a list of all the forms on the CD, organized by chapter. Each form is available to you as a PDF file, and almost every form is available to you as an RTF file as well. You need to use Adobe Acrobat Reader, which is included on this CD, to view and print PDF files. You can use your favorite word processor to view, print, *and* edit the RTF files.

Acrobat Reader 4.0 from Adobe Systems

For Mac and Windows. Evaluation version.

This program lets you view and print Portable Document Format (PDF) files.

To learn more about using Acrobat Reader, choose the Reader Online Guide from the Help menu, or view the Acrobat.pdf file installed in the same folder as the program. You can also get more information by visiting the Adobe Systems Web site, at www.adobe.com.

Internet Explorer from Microsoft

Version 5.0 for Windows and Version 4.5 for Mac. Commercial product.

Microsoft Internet Explorer provides the best support to date for Dynamic HTML and CSS. This browser from Microsoft enables you to view Web pages and perform a host of other Internet functions, including e-mail, newsgroups, and word processing. Keep an eye on the Microsoft Web site at www.microsoft.com. This program is updated frequently!

Chapter 2

Form 2-1	Contract Checklist
Form 2-2	Sample Representations and Warranties
Form 2-3	Sample Payment Terms
Form 2-4	Sample Limitations of Liability
Form 2-5	Sample Indemnification Provisions

Chapter 3

Form 3-1	Boilerplate

Chapter 4

Note: Forms ending in a C or D are the same form for use in California or Delaware, respectively.

Form 4-1	Checklist for Formation of a California Corporation
Form 4-2	Guide to Operation of Newly Formed California Corporation
Form 4-3C	Articles of Incorporation (California corp.)
Form 4-3D	Certificate of Incorporation (Delaware corp.)
Form 4-4C	Transmittal Letter Enclosing Articles of Incorporation to the California Secretary of State
Form 4-4D	Transmittal Letter Enclosing Certificate of Incorporation to the Delaware Secretary of State
Form 4-5C	Action of Incorporator (California corp.)
Form 4-5D	Action of Incorporator (Delaware corp.)
Form 4-6C	Bylaws (California corp.)
Form 4-6D	Bylaws (Delaware corp.)
Form 4-7C	Action by Unanimous Written Consent of Board of Directors in Lieu of Organizational Meeting (California corp.)
Form 4-7D	Action by Unanimous Consent of the Board of Directors in Lieu of Organizational Meeting (Delaware corp.)
Form 4-8	Notice of Meeting of Board of Directors
Form 4-9	Declaration of Mailing Notice of Board Meeting
Form 4-10	Waiver of Notice and Consent to Holding Meeting of Board of Directors
Form 4-11	Action by Unanimous Written Consent of Board of Directors
Form 4-12	Minutes of Meeting of the Board of Directors
Form 4-13	Board Resolution Approving Agreement
Form 4-14	Board Resolution Approving Borrowing
Form 4-15	Board Resolution Approving Sale of Common Stock
Form 4-16	Board Resolution Approving a Stock Option Plan
Form 4-17	Board Resolution Approving Amendment of Bylaws
Form 4-18	Board Resolution Approving Articles of Incorporation

(continued)

Chapter 4 (continued)

Chapter 5

(continued)

Chapter 5 (continued)

Chapter 6

Chapter 7

Chapter 8

(continued)

Chapter 8 (continued)

Chapter 9

Chapter 10

Chapter 11

Chapter 12

Chapter 13

Chapter 14

Chapter 15

√ Chapter 16

If You've Got Problems (Of the CD Kind)

I tried my best to compile programs that work on most computers with the minimum system requirements. Alas, your computer may differ, and some programs may not work properly for some reason.

The two likeliest problems are that you don't have enough memory (RAM) for the programs you want to use, or you have other programs running that are affecting installation or running of a program. If you get error messages like Not enough memory or Setup cannot continue, try one or more of these methods and then try using the software again:

- Turn off any anti-virus software that you have on your computer. Installers sometimes mimic virus activity and may make your computer incorrectly believe that it is being infected by a virus.

- Close all running programs. The more programs you're running, the less memory is available to other programs. Installers also typically update files and programs. So if you keep other programs running, installation may not work properly.

- Have your local computer store add more RAM to your computer. This is, admittedly, a drastic and somewhat expensive step. However, if you have a Windows 95 PC or a Mac OS computer with a PowerPC chip, adding more memory can really help the speed of your computer and allow more programs to run at the same time.

If you still have trouble with installing the items from the CD, please call the Hungry Minds Customer Care phone number: 800-762-2974 (outside the U.S.: 317-572-3342).

Index

• C •

• F •

Notes

Wiley Publishing, Inc.
End-User License Agreement

READ THIS. You should carefully read these terms and conditions before opening the software packet(s) included with this book "Book". This is a license agreement "Agreement" between you and Wiley Publishing, Inc. "WPI". By opening the accompanying software packet(s), you acknowledge that you have read and accept the following terms and conditions. If you do not agree and do not want to be bound by such terms and conditions, promptly return the Book and the unopened software packet(s) to the place you obtained them for a full refund.

1. **License Grant.** WPI grants to you (either an individual or entity) a nonexclusive license to use one copy of the enclosed software program(s) (collectively, the "Software" solely for your own personal or business purposes on a single computer (whether a standard computer or a workstation component of a multi-user network). The Software is in use on a computer when it is loaded into temporary memory (RAM) or installed into permanent memory (hard disk, CD-ROM, or other storage device). WPI reserves all rights not expressly granted herein.

2. **Ownership.** WPI is the owner of all right, title, and interest, including copyright, in and to the compilation of the Software recorded on the disk(s) or CD-ROM "Software Media". Copyright to the individual programs recorded on the Software Media is owned by the author or other authorized copyright owner of each program. Ownership of the Software and all proprietary rights relating thereto remain with WPI and its licensers.

3. **Restrictions On Use and Transfer.**

   (a) You may only (i) make one copy of the Software for backup or archival purposes, or (ii) transfer the Software to a single hard disk, provided that you keep the original for backup or archival purposes. You may not (i) rent or lease the Software, (ii) copy or reproduce the Software through a LAN or other network system or through any computer subscriber system or bulletin- board system, or (iii) modify, adapt, or create derivative works based on the Software.

   (b) You may not reverse engineer, decompile, or disassemble the Software. You may transfer the Software and user documentation on a permanent basis, provided that the transferee agrees to accept the terms and conditions of this Agreement and you retain no copies. If the Software is an update or has been updated, any transfer must include the most recent update and all prior versions.

4. **Restrictions on Use of Individual Programs.** You must follow the individual requirements and restrictions detailed for each individual program in the "About the CD" appendix of this Book. These limitations are also contained in the individual license agreements recorded on the Software Media. These limitations may include a requirement that after using the program for a specified period of time, the user must pay a registration fee or discontinue use. By opening the Software packet(s), you will be agreeing to abide by the licenses and restrictions for these individual programs that are detailed in the "About the CD" appendix and on the Software Media. None of the material on this Software Media or listed in this Book may ever be redistributed, in original or modified form, for commercial purposes.

5. **Limited Warranty.**

   (a) WPI warrants that the Software and Software Media are free from defects in materials and workmanship under normal use for a period of sixty (60) days from the date of purchase of this Book. If WPI receives notification within the warranty period of defects in materials or workmanship, WPI will replace the defective Software Media.

   (b) WPI AND THE AUTHOR OF THE BOOK DISCLAIM ALL OTHER WARRANTIES, EXPRESS OR IMPLIED, INCLUDING WITHOUT LIMITATION IMPLIED WARRANTIES OF MERCHANTABILITY AND FITNESS FOR A PARTICULAR PURPOSE, WITH RESPECT TO THE SOFTWARE, THE PROGRAMS, THE SOURCE CODE CONTAINED THEREIN, AND/OR THE TECHNIQUES DESCRIBED IN THIS BOOK. WPI DOES NOT WARRANT THAT THE FUNCTIONS CONTAINED IN THE SOFTWARE WILL MEET YOUR REQUIREMENTS OR THAT THE OPERATION OF THE SOFTWARE WILL BE ERROR FREE.

   (c) This limited warranty gives you specific legal rights, and you may have other rights that vary from jurisdiction to jurisdiction.

6. **Remedies.**

   (a) WPI's entire liability and your exclusive remedy for defects in materials and workmanship shall be limited to replacement of the Software Media, which may be returned to WPI with a copy of your receipt at the following address: Software Media Fulfillment Department, Attn.: *Business Contracts Kit For Dummies,* Wiley Publishing, Inc., 10475 Crosspoint Blvd., Indianapolis, IN 46256, or call 1-800-762-2974. Please allow four to six weeks for delivery. This Limited Warranty is void if failure of the Software Media has resulted from accident, abuse, or misapplication. Any replacement Software Media will be warranted for the remainder of the original warranty period or thirty (30) days, whichever is longer.

   (b) In no event shall WPI or the author be liable for any damages whatsoever (including without limitation damages for loss of business profits, business interruption, loss of business information, or any other pecuniary loss) arising from the use of or inability to use the Book or the Software, even if WPI has been advised of the possibility of such damages.

   (c) Because some jurisdictions do not allow the exclusion or limitation of liability for consequential or incidental damages, the above limitation or exclusion may not apply to you.

7. **U.S. Government Restricted Rights.** Use, duplication, or disclosure of the Software for or on behalf of the United States of America, its agencies and/or instrumentalities "U.S. Government" is subject to restrictions as stated in paragraph (c)(1)(ii) of the Rights in Technical Data and Computer Software clause of DFARS 252.227-7013, or subparagraphs (c) (1) and (2) of the Commercial Computer Software - Restricted Rights clause at FAR 52.227-19, and in similar clauses in the NASA FAR supplement, as applicable.

8. **General.** This Agreement constitutes the entire understanding of the parties and revokes and supersedes all prior agreements, oral or written, between them and may not be modified or amended except in a writing signed by both parties hereto that specifically refers to this Agreement. This Agreement shall take precedence over any other documents that may be in conflict herewith. If any one or more provisions contained in this Agreement are held by any court or tribunal to be invalid, illegal, or otherwise unenforceable, each and every other provision shall remain in full force and effect.

Installation Instructions

The *Business Contracts Kit For Dummies* CD offers valuable information that you won't want to miss. To install the items from the CD to your hard drive, follow these steps (which are for computers using Windows):

1. **Insert the CD into your computer's CD-ROM drive.**

   Give your computer a moment to take a look at the CD.

2. **Open your browser.** Click on File⇨Open (Internet Explorer) or on File⇨Open Page (Netscape).

3. **Double-click the file called License.txt.**

   This file contains the end-user license that you agree to by using the CD. When you are done reading the license, close the program, most likely NotePad, that displayed the file.

4. **Double-click the file called Readme.txt.**

   This file contains instructions about installing the software from this CD. It might be helpful to leave this text file open while you are using the CD.

5. **In the dialog box that appears, type** D:\START.HTM **and click on OK.**

6. **Replace the letter D: with the correct letter for your CD-ROM drive, if it is not "D".**

   This action will display the file that will walk you through the content of the CD.

7. **To navigate within the interface, simply click on any topic of interest to take you to an explanation of the files on the CD and how to use or install them.** You will see Install buttons that will install the software for you. When you select that option, instead of installing directly from the CD, select Open this file when the Download File dialog box pops up. After you are done with the interface, simply close your browser as usual.

If you use a Macintosh computer, you can also use the documents on this CD. Simply insert the CD into your computer's CD-ROM drive, double-click the CD icon when it appears on the desktop, read the Read Me file, and then look in the RTFs and PDFs folders to see the documents on the CD.

For more information, please see the "About the CD" appendix in this book.

Notes

Notes